RECORDING CULTURE

Refiguring American Music

A series edited by Ronald Radano and Josh Kun

Charles McGovern, contributing editor

CHRISTOPHER A. SCALES

RECORDING CULTURE

POWWOW MUSIC AND THE

ABORIGINAL RECORDING INDUSTRY

ON THE NORTHERN PLAINS

Duke University Press :: *Durham and London* :: 2012

Printed in the United States of
America on acid-free paper ⊗
Designed by Amy Ruth Buchanan
Typeset in Chaparral Pro and Scala Sans
by Tseng Information Systems, Inc.
Library of Congress Cataloging-in-
Publication Data appear on the last
printed page of this book.

*Duke University Press gratefully
acknowledges the support of Michigan
State University, which provided funds
toward the publication of this book.*

The songs on the accompanying CD were
compiled from the following albums:

Campfire (Arbor Records AR-11572):
    "Rita's Way (Honor Song)"
Dance With Us (Arbor Records AR-11392):
    "Attacking," "Bells," and "They're Coming In"
Ikwe-Nagamonan: Jingle Dress Songs
(Arbor Records AR-11282):
    "Zig-Zag"
November Winds (Arbor Records AR-13032):
    "November Winds"
21st Century (Arbor Records AR-11122):
    "Dancin' 2000," "KFC," "My Better Half,"
    "Shake, Rattle & Roll," and "Side Windin'
    (Dianne's Song)"

All songs © Arbor Records LTD

FOR JOANNA AND FOR ELLERY

CONTENTS

Acknowledgments ix

Introduction 1

PART I :: NORTHERN PLAINS POWWOW CULTURE

1. Powwow Practices: Competition and the Discourse of Tradition 27
2. Powwow Songs: Aesthetics and Performance Practice 63
3. Drum Groups and Singers 112

PART II :: THE MEDIATION OF POWWOWS

4. The Powwow Recording Industry in Western Canada: Race, Culture, and Commerce 143
5. Powwow Music in the Studio: Mediation and Musical Fields 187
6. Producing Powwow Music: The Aesthetics of Liveness 212
7. Powwows "Live" and "Mediated" 241

Coda :: Recording Culture in the Twenty-First Century 268

Appendix :: Notes on the CD Tracks 282

Notes 289

References 311

Index 323

A photo gallery appears after page 140.

....

ACKNOWLEDGMENTS

....

It has often been said that there are no (or at least precious few) truly new or original ideas, only an ignorance of sources. Anything "new" that might, through design or accident, be revealed within these pages is most certainly due to the extraordinary guidance, inspiration, and instruction of a great many people. With apologies to those sources that have already been forgotten, I wish to acknowledge and celebrate those who remain at the center of this work. First and foremost I wish to thank my principal teachers, whose breadth of expertise and generosity in sharing their time and knowledge made this research so enjoyable. Much of what I know about Ojibwa lifeways, powwows, and powwow singing is due to Michael Esquash and his family (his father and mother, Gerald and Linda; brother, Kevin; sister, Jerilynn; wife, Terri; and children, Dempsey, Daylen, and Mike Jr.), all of whom welcomed me into their homes and into their lives. Without Mike's friendship, patience, wisdom, and kindness, this research would certainly have not been possible. It has also been an extraordinary privilege to work with the multitalented Gabriel Desrosiers. Our continued dialogue and our creative and scholarly partnership over the last decade have provided some of the most rich and rewarding moments of my career. Brandon Friesen, my recording studio guru, is a force of nature, a man of boundless energy, ambition, vision, and musical and technological talent. He has forgotten more about the music business and record production than I could ever hope to know. All are dear and valued friends.

I also owe an enormous debt of gratitude to all of my academic teachers, who have broadened and transformed my intellectual horizons. Bruno Nettl was my dissertation advisor at the University of Illinois, where the first draft of this book, in the form of my dissertation, was written. Bruno provided for me — as for countless students before me — a model of how to be a productive scholar in the fullest and most generous sense of the word: as an intellectual, humanist, teacher, trickster. Tom Turino was another guiding light at Illinois. His ideas about music and social life have become so fundamental to my own ethnomusicological tool kit that I can scarcely imagine what kind of scholar I'd be without his guidance. Various iterations of this research have been shared and discussed with many friends and colleagues, including Michael Largey, Donna Buchanan, Fred Hoxie, Anne Rasmussen, Tara Browner, Celia Cain, Anna Hoefnagels, Klisala Harrison, Vicky Levine, and Tom Vennum, and I thank them all for their input and insights. Special thanks to Beverley Diamond, who has been both a beacon of inspiration and a steadfast supporter of my work and my career, and Karl Neuenfeldt, a kindred spirit living on the other side of the globe.

It has been a great pleasure and honor to meet, talk to, and work with so many talented drums: Bear Creek, The Boyz, Little Otter, Northern Wind, Red Tail, White Lodge, Whitefish Bay, and a host of others. Special thanks to the Northern Wind Singers for supplying the music for the CD that accompanies this book, and to the boys of the Spirit Sands Singers for giving the white guy a chance to sing. The staffs at Studio 11, Studio 441, and Arbor Records were incredibly patient with me and made my time there immensely enjoyable: Paul Scinocca, Jaimie Friesen, John Marlow, Justin "Dutch" Hartlooper, Rob Shallcross, Waylon Wityshyn, Stewart Astleford, Shawn Schibler, and Arthur Pearson. Thank you all.

I owe a particular debt of gratitude to Stephen Esquith, Dean of the Residential College in the Arts and Humanities at Michigan State University, who not only hired me but immediately gave me a semester's teaching leave, which allowed me to finish writing this book. The two anonymous readers contracted by the press to review this manuscript provided incredibly detailed, insightful, and critically helpful comments. Thanks to Charlie McGovern for recommending Duke University Press to me; to Ronald Radano and Josh Kun, the editors for the Refiguring American Music series; and to Ken Wissoker and Christine Dahlin, who helped shepherd this project through to completion at the press. My professorial assistant at Michigan State University, Elena Dunckel, helped with countless bits of editorial work and manuscript preparation.

Most importantly, I thank my family. My wife, Joanna Bosse, has been at my side from the earliest stages of this research. Not only steadfast in her love and support, she is also a wise and valued colleague who patiently discusses and reads through all of my work with an uncompromising editorial eye and a remarkable knack for dragging out of me some of my best thinking. Finally, I thank my parents, James and Marlene Scales. My father toiled for over forty years at a steel mill while my mother worked at home raising her three children, both laboring to provide for me the gift of freedom in choosing my own educational and career path. This book is as much the result of their hard work as it is mine.

This research was partially funded by a doctoral fellowship from the Social Science and Humanities Research Council of Canada, a College of William and Mary Summer Research Grant, a Reeves Center International Travel Grant, and a Rusack Coastal Studies Fellowship from Bowdoin College. I gratefully acknowledge their support.

In the summer of 1914 Frances Densmore was having trouble recording and collecting songs among the Uinta and White River bands of Northern Utes at Fort Duquesne, Utah. Densmore, one of the most prolific and important Native Americanist ethnologists of the first half of the century, had worked successfully in many Native communities securing the cooperation of singers who were swayed by the promise of payment and the idea that the wax cylinder recordings they were creating would preserve their music for future generations.[1] The Utes, however, were unimpressed by these incentives, and her work was openly ridiculed. In desperation Densmore arranged a meeting with their chief, Red Cap, and through an interpreter she complained about her treatment in the community and forcefully explained the importance of her work. Red Cap responded by offering the cooperation of one of the communities' best singers, but in return he had a request of his own. Red Cap was not a singer, but he *also* wanted to make a recording. He proposed: "I will talk and I want you to play the record for the Indian Commissioner in Washington. I want to tell him that we do not like this [Bureau of Indian Affairs] Agent. We want him sent someplace else. We don't like the things he does. What we tell him does not get to the Commissioner but I want the Commissioner to hear my voice. I want you to play this so he will hear my words, and I want you to give him a good translation of my speech. We want to get rid of this Agent" (Densmore [1917] 1968, 39–43). Densmore agreed to the bargain, recorded the chief's words, and, six months later, played them for Cato Sells, the commissioner of Indian Affairs at the time, but, alas, without a proper translator or transcript of the speech.[2]

This story is a reminder that almost a century ago recording technology was already playing an important part in mediating intercultural exchange. Native musicians have been recording their music from almost the very beginnings of sound recording technology. When Jesse Walter

Fewkes first used an Edison phonograph to record Passamaquoddy singers in Maine on March 18, 1890, so began a century-long entanglement with recording technologies and practices on the part of North American indigenous musicians and nonindigenous recordists. Here, with Densmore and Red Cap, we see two people cleverly maneuvering to obtain very different social and political objectives. Both had very specific ideas about how recording technology could be used, under what conditions the recording process could take place, what exactly could and should be recorded, and the social and political efficacy of the subsequent recorded products. The story also, significantly, points to how the recording process is laced through with politics and filled with moments of social and technological mediations. The products of these mediations—the recordings themselves—subsequently enter larger discursive and social worlds where outcomes are not guaranteed and there are multiple strategies for deployment and multiple possibilities for articulation. The "meaning" of recordings, their articulation in the flux of social life, can sometimes exist quite apart from the conditions of their production.

Of course, early ethnologists like Densmore and Fewkes were using recording technology as part of a larger project to make ethnological records of Native American cultural and musical practices widely believed to be "disappearing," casualties of the relentless march of American "modernity." Flash forward a century and I am standing over the Ojibwa powwow drum group Bear Creek as they perform for a Men's Traditional competition dance at the 2007 Schemitzun Annual Green Corn Festival and Powwow. Like Densmore and Fewkes before me, I am making an audio recording of the performance. In place of the phonograph I am holding a small, hand-held solid-state digital audio recorder high over my head. I am not alone. Literally dozens of other people—singers, dancers, and fans of Bear Creek's music—are also standing around the drum and making recordings, and my device is part of a sea of technology: cellphones, video cameras, iPods with microphones attached, and tape recorders, all capturing the same performance. If my recording device breaks down, no worries; I can wander out to the vendors area that surrounds the outside of the dance arena and buy one of the several commercially produced CDs by the group from any one of the number of vendors that sell powwow recordings. Or I can save my money. A quick Google search with the keywords "Bear Creek" and "Schemitzun" will yield a number of hits on YouTube, where I can watch and listen to their performances. In fact, the more you start looking, the more evidence you will find of two rather indisputable facts: first, contrary to the prognostications of early twentieth-century ethnologists, Native North Americans did not, in fact, disappear in the modern world, but rather embraced the cultural and social upheavals of American modernity and transformed them (Deloria 2004). Second, Native Americans are still making recordings. Lots of them.

This book is an ethnographically grounded examination of contemporary powwow culture. More specifically, this work focuses on the transformative effects on powwow music aesthetics and social practice as musicians move from performing on reservations and on powwow grounds to working at urban recording studios and record labels. Recording technologies and mass media are enmeshed in a network of discourses about ethics, power, the relationship between "modernity" and "tradition," and racial and ethnic identity. In working through and within these discourses, the social world of contemporary powwows has been fundamentally shaped through what I have termed "recording culture." In one sense, this phrase refers to the process of recording cultural phenomena like powwow music performances through sound reproduction technologies (phonographs, tape recorders, digital recorders), an act that transforms unique cultural *practices* into reified, mass-produced, and commercially available cultural *products*. But recording culture may also be understood as the "culture of recording," the ideas and behaviors of particular social groups who engage in the practice of recording music. This book explores the intersection of these two meanings, arguing that the culture of recording developed in and through the powwow recording industry has been deeply affected by an understanding of Native American "culture" as something that can be "owned" by Native musicians, and a belief that elements of this culture (like powwow music) can and should be "captured" through the recording process by audio engineers and record producers and disseminated through the unique distribution networks of the Aboriginal recording industry to other indigenous and nonindigenous peoples throughout North America and around the world. Linked to the twin discourses of tradition and modernity, these mass-distributed objects of "Native culture," in turn, provide a material base for new imaginings of intertribal Native identity.

In exploring these ideas, this book shifts between micro- and macroscopic analyses, constructing a large-scale narrative about the development of the Aboriginal recording industry and the vast amount of cultural work that it does, while also examining specific musical and social gestures and moving outward from lived, productive moments of musical creativity on the part of indigenous musicians and the people who record them, both in recording studios and on the powwow grounds. As such, it is a synchronic study of the powwow recording industry as it coexists and intersects with a complex network of social affiliations and aesthetic allegiances generated through Native American participation on the northern Plains powwow circuit. It is a temporally and geographically bounded snapshot of the Aboriginal music industry and the powwow social world that supports it at the turn of the twenty-first century.

Powwows as Popular Culture

Powwows are large intertribal gatherings of Native American singers, dancers, and spectators that have become a ubiquitous part of musical and social life for many Native Americans living on reserves and in urban areas.[3] Given the centrality of powwow music in contemporary Native American musical life, it is surprising that rigorous and sustained scholarship addressing contemporary powwow music performance practices has only recently begun to emerge. This literature has typically either focused on the delineation of important aspects of regional (e.g., Northern versus Southern) or tribal styles, or has treated powwow events more generally as fluid sites for the negotiation of tribal, intertribal, pan-tribal, or "Pan-Indian" identity.[4] However, without exception, the existing body of scholarship deals with powwow singing as a live and unmediated performative act. While recording has become a regular part of the musical life of contemporary powwow singers, the aesthetic practices of these musicians have been virtually ignored in the study of Native American expressive cultures. In the late twentieth and early twenty-first centuries, powwow music became increasingly mediated through technologies of print, audio, and video recording, and several new corporate entities emerged on the Canadian Plains that together created a media infrastructure dedicated to serving Aboriginal peoples in Canada and the United States.

This book has emerged from a series of basic questions about powwow recording culture. How have indigenous musicians, specifically powwow drum groups, utilized recording technology in the late twentieth and early twenty-first centuries? What are the unique aesthetic principles of recorded powwow music, and how do these practices and ideologies differ from performances on the powwow grounds? What is the nature of the re-lationship between drum groups and the Native music labels and record-ing studios that record them, and how does this relationship affect prac-tice? And finally, how has the rise of specifically "competition" powwows (events organized around a series of weekend-long singing and dancing competitions) shaped the repertoire and aesthetics of drum groups in and out of the studio? Underlying all of these questions is a central prem-ise: the development of competition (as opposed to traditional) powwows has been critical to the rise and development of the powwow recording industry.

As powwows have become an increasingly mediated musical activity, drum groups who regularly participate on the competition powwow cir-cuit seek out record labels and recording contracts in the hopes of having new CDs to sell on the powwow trail with each new powwow season. Recordings have become a central and essential part of the social and cultural landscape of powwow practices around the continent, and one would be hard-pressed indeed to find a regularly participating powwow person who did not own a single commercial or bootleg powwow record-ing. In focusing on recording practices of indigenous musicians, cast in re-lief against traditional contexts for powwow performances (the powwow grounds), this book sheds light on how cultural heritage, social hierarchies within an institutional structure, and economic considerations combine to produce a complex hybrid of musical, social, and aesthetic values that incorporates a multiplicity of sociocultural subject positions.

The Aboriginal Recording Industry in North America

While the venerable Canyon Records has been producing and distribut-ing Native American music since the 1950s, the 1990s, in particular, were an important decade that saw the establishment of several new media institutions dedicated to the promotion of Native American music and culture. During this period there was a proliferation of reservation (and some urban) radio stations that featured significant Native music pro-gramming, as well as the creation, in Canada, of APTN (the Aboriginal Public Television Network), both of which provided invaluable media ex-posure for Native musicians. At the same time, powwow musicians, and Native musicians more generally, also began to be more officially recog-nized by the larger institutions of the North American recording indus-try. In 1994 CARAS (the Canadian Academy of Recording Arts and Science) established a Juno award category for "Best Music of Aboriginal Canada Recording" (changed in 2002 to "Aboriginal Recording of the Year"). In 1999 NARAS (the National Academy of Recording Arts and Sciences) followed suit by creating a Grammy award category for "Best Native American Music Album." While these awards have been dominated by "Contemporary Native" (i.e., pop music) artists, powwow drum groups are very often nominees, and, significantly, a powwow compilation CD won the inaugural Native American Music Grammy.[5] Several other industry "indigenous only" award institutions were formed at this time as well, including the Native American Music Awards (the "Nammies") and Canadian Aboriginal Music Awards (the "Cammies"), and more recently, the Aboriginal Peoples Choice Music Awards. All of these organizations feature multiple award categories for powwow recordings and drum groups.

The growth of all of these media and industry institutions was predicated upon the rise of several new independent record labels created specifically for the promotion and distribution of North American indigenous music, joining a small handful of already established music-related corporate entities. Independent labels in North America that produce and distribute powwow music can be productively grouped into one of three general categories based on the size of their catalogue, the generic variety within the catalogue, marketing strategies, and the size, stability, and corporate organization of the label. The first group includes what I will term "major independents," labels distinguished by large, generically diverse catalogues, national and sometimes international distribution and marketing, and a relatively stable corporate infrastructure. Labels fitting this description include Canyon Records and Sound of America Records (SOAR) in the United States and, in Canada, Arbor Records and Sunshine Records, both located in Winnipeg, Manitoba. While these labels produce and market a wide variety of Aboriginal artists and musical genres, powwow music takes up a significant portion of their catalogues. The second group comprises small-scale or "boutique independents," which are, by comparison, smaller labels with fewer staff whose catalogues exhibit a narrower set of generic interests, and which feature marketing strategies and distribution networks commensurate with a more generically focused catalogue. Labels such as Indian House Records, Silver Wave Records, and Makoché Records are all exemplars. Of these labels, Indian House is the oldest (it has been in business since 1966) and the most important distributor of powwow music and related tribal and intertribal genres.

Finally, there are a number of labels dedicated *specifically* to powwow recordings (and related intertribal genres, such as Round Dance songs). These labels are characterized by their generically homogeneous catalogues and unique methods of distribution. Powwow labels, because of their small size and the small niche market they fill, are notoriously unstable corporate entities, and labels are constantly emerging, producing a few dozen recordings over a four- or five-year period, and then closing down. Some of the larger and relatively more stable labels include Sweet Grass Records in Regina, Saskatchewan, and Drumhop Productions in Bismarck, North Dakota, while some of the more intermittently active or (now) completely defunct labels include Turtle Island Music, Wacipi Records, Rez Cue Records, and War Pony Records, among a variety of others. Add to these labels a host of DIY (do-it-yourself) labels, record companies started by individual powwow musicians as a form of "self-publication" and promotion. These labels, of which there are dozens, typically produce and distribute only a handful of recordings and feature a catalogue typically constituted of only one or possibly two musicians or musical groups.

While some have been in business for decades (most notably Canyon Records, Indian House Records, and Sunshine Records), the vast majority of smaller powwow labels came into (and sometimes out of) existence between 1995 and 2005, a time that also featured a rapid expansion in both the size and number of competition powwows on the northern Plains. Powwow culture at the turn of the century was deeply intertwined with both the rise of competition and the expansion of the Aboriginal recording industry, the two key conjunctural forces shaping that particular historical moment.[6]

Indigenous Modernities and Articulation

In examining the rise of recording culture in the powwow social world, I am attempting to map a particular, historically specific kind of "indigenous modernity," generated, in part, through the commingling of powwow culture and recording practices. In the broadest of brushstrokes, I would suggest that some of the more salient and important aspects of this social formation include historically unprecedented levels of intertribal interconnectivity, a deep engagement with media technologies, and increasingly complex, sophisticated, and creative engagements with tradition and modernity both as sets of practices and as mutually constitutive discursive universes.

David Samuels, in his excellent monograph about San Carlos Apache rock and country bands, threw down the gauntlet to all students and scholars of Native American expressive culture in posing the question: "How do things cohere? How can we begin to make sense of the fact that the expressive lives of people in the reservation's communities involve more than the maintenance or disappearance of traditional cultural forms? One of the major tasks in a materialist anthropology of modernity, I believe, is to consider what the ethnography of negotiation might look like" (2004, 15). On the powwow grounds and in the academy, powwows (and often Native music in general) are topics often connected to arguments either about "preserving or maintaining culture" or "the disappearance of culture." However, powwows, if nothing else, are thoroughly modern phenomena. The story of powwows is a story that follows the arc and trajectory of twentieth-century (and twenty-first-century) modernity. To be sure, some of the musical and dance styles currently performed have long and complex histories that predate the rise of American and Canadian modernity, and one could certainly choose to narrate a history of powwows in the cast of "cultural survival," of the maintenance and proliferation of Indian social and aesthetic practices *against* or *in spite of* the often violent and virulent social and political domination of Euroamericans in North America. One could also choose to frame this story as one of cultural destruction and defeat (Howard 1983; Whidden 2007), as part of a losing battle with the forces of modernity. But I would like instead to call for a little caution in speaking about indigenous lives using the discourses of modernity and tradition simply because contemporary indigenous realities often escape such a simple binary opposition.

In working through the complexities of indigenous modernity in this book, I frequently turn to Stuart Hall's concept of "articulation." Hall's (1986) use of the term plays on the double meaning of the verb *articulate*, which means both "to speak" or "to express" *and* "to connect." Understood in the first sense of the term, we articulate our ideas in talking (or using other kinds of nonlinguistic codes) with other people. As such, articulation is a process that involves speakers and listeners; it is always "directed," so that "an artist is always articulating, via various intermediaries, to audiences who are always part of the process of 'articulating' cultural meaning" (Negus 1996, 134). The second meaning of the term refers generally to the linking together of two separate elements (an articulated lorry in Hall's well-known example). Articulation theory suggests that the connections between practices, ideologies, structures, and discourses are the *expression* of a particular meaning at a certain moment in history. Some of these articulations are quite durable, others fleeting, but none are *guaranteed* through time; they can at any moment be disarticulated and rearticulated in the flux of social life. A particular connection or articulation *becomes* the meaning of a particular event (the performance of a powwow song or dance) or object (a commercial recording of a powwow song) because the expression of meaning happens through a particular connection between different elements (e.g., the connection of a recorded powwow song with a particular audience, ideology, or discourse). Thus, articulation theory locates culture as a process that exists within an ideological field of struggle—the struggle to create common-sense meanings, a taken-for-granted or tacit understanding of the world. Articulation theory politicizes culture and forces us to pay attention to how power is implicated in cultural processes.

The importance of articulation theory for a discussion of powwow music in live and mediated settings lies in questioning the oft-heard assertion that powwow music is somehow an "expression" of Native identity. This kind of generic statement about the meaning of powwow music is one that I heard constantly on the powwow trail. And it is also a conclusion that has been reached by several scholars who have written about this music. I am not interested in challenging the truth value of the claim, but rather in examining exactly how this expression is accomplished. There are certainly many instances in which I think, for both performers and audiences, this music does indeed express "Native identity" (whatever that may mean to someone). But this expression or meaning or *articulation* is never guaranteed and must be actively produced by all involved in the social production and consumption of powwow music. Particular *elements* of Native identity must be articulated to particular elements of powwow musical or choreographic or social style. Certain ideas about the nature, definition, and content of Native tradition must be articulated to particular social and musical values. I am not claiming in this book that powwow music is always an expression of any particular aspect of indigenous modernity or that powwow music's meanings are generally limited to (or exhausted in) expressions of modern indigenous identity. What I am willing to argue, however, is that within the current historical conjuncture, the lives of indigenous peoples in North America are, to a certain degree, structured through or in relation to a modern indigenous social formation and that powwow music, live and mediated, has a somewhat unique propensity to articulate with elements of this formation in specific ways.[7]

Keith Negus has cast this approach to understanding identity and culture as part of a larger "shift from *essentialist* ideas about cultural identity—the notion that individuals of a particular social type possess certain essential characteristics and that these are found *expressed* in particular cultural practices—towards the idea that cultural identities are not fixed in any essential way but are actually created through particular communication processes, social practices and 'articulations' within specific circumstances" (1996, 100). Articulation theory helps us to head off discussions about "authentic" Native identity before they begin. Or at least it helps to put theoretically sticky ideas like "authenticity" and "tradition" in their place: as discourses that are strategically deployed and creatively articulated to cultural or ideological projects and political interests. In focusing on articulations—how they are formed, and what effects, or structures of effects result from particular linkages—we focus on the dynamic process of cultural production and meaning making rather than structurally guaranteed "cultural meanings." Ultimately, articulation theory suggests that we take a step back from telling stories of resistance and accommodation in order to observe how particular people and particular practices come to be articulated to discourses of resistance or discourses of accommodation at particular times. In taking such an analytic posture, I am attempting to give a little cultural and historical space for Native Americans to operate, taking seriously and giving respect to indigenous individuals and their own "personal histories of modernity" (Deloria 2004, 240).

Finding Powwow Music

Research for this book took place from 1998 to 2010. During that time I attended powwows from Denver, Colorado, to Charles City, Virginia, and from Pleasant Point, Maine, to Saddle Lake, Alberta, a geographical breadth indicative of the widespread diffusion of powwow practices across North America. This kind of cross-country travel is not unusual for many powwow participants, particularly drum groups and singers interested in competing in contests, who spend the year seeking out high dollar competition powwows that are held across Canada and the United States at various times throughout the year. Indeed the diffuse nature of the "powwow music scene" is one of the central challenges in undertaking significant research within this social space. The unique nature of powwow culture is that it is both very locally grounded and very widely dispersed at the same time. This dialectic plays out in real time and space through the emergence of several geographically defined and often overlapping powwow "circuits," the sum total of which make up what powwow participants generally refer to as the "powwow trail." These circuits are constituted through the preferences and travel habits of singers and dancers who live in particular regions of the continent, and they are generally established by simple pragmatic concerns: how far is one willing or able to drive for a weekend powwow? For many powwow participants living in the central Plains of Canada and the northern Plains of the United States it is very easy to fill one's summer calendar with powwows every weekend without having to travel more than five or six hours from one's home (although often some more distant powwows may lure powwow participants much farther afield with the promise of extravagant cash prizes for song and dance competitions).

The center of my "home" powwow circuit for the majority of my research was Winnipeg, Manitoba. Winnipeg is an important location for powwow musical culture for several reasons. First, the city is at the center of a powwow circuit that stretches from southern Manitoba to northern South Dakota and from western Saskatchewan to northwestern Ontario, a region that is home to a great many champion dancers and singers who travel the Northern powwow trail.[8] Further, the city is home to the largest per capita population of Natives of any urban center in Canada. As such, it is a nexus of Native American musical activity and the home to the two largest Aboriginal music labels in Canada: Sunshine Records and Arbor Records.

After a one-month exploratory visit to Winnipeg in the summer of 1998, I moved there the following summer for a fifteen-month extended stay from June 1999 until the end of August 2000, allowing me two full summers to travel the Northern powwow trail. I returned there in the summers of 2001 and 2006 for shorter four- to six-week stays. Because of the geographically defined nature of this circuit I saw many of the same dancers and many of the same drum groups at powwow after powwow, each of them guided by a similar calculus that involved weighing driving distance with their desire to attend specific kinds of powwows (competition, traditional, reservation-based, urban, hosted by particular Cree, Ojibwa, Dakota, or Assiniboine communities, etc.). During July and August, the peak powwow season, I often had my choice of powwows to attend as there might be two or three different celebrations within a four- or five-hour drive from Winnipeg.

In 1999, during my second summer of research, I had the privilege and good fortune to meet the Ojibwa singer and songmaker Michael Esquash from the Swan Lake First Nation (*Gaabiskiigamug*), an Anishinabe community in south-central Manitoba. Born in 1973 to parents of Plains Ojibwa and Plains Cree heritage, Mike has been singing since he was ten years old. His grandfather was a ceremonial singer in the Swan Lake community, and as a young boy Mike tagged along when he performed at sundances in the area, the place where Mike first learned about singing. He began powwow singing as a teenager, joining the well-known intertribal group Elk's Whistle. Since 1996 Mike has been the leader, lead singer, songmaker, and driving force for the Spirit Sands Singers, a group originally composed of singers mainly from his home community, although over the years the membership has turned over several times. Mike and the Spirit Sands Singers perform a somewhat unique style of Northern powwow singing that he regularly describes as "Northern style with a Southern blast," a catchphrase that refers to the group's propensity for singing in a distinctly lower register more commonly associated with Southern-style powwow singing, while maintaining all of the other typical stylistic and formal markers that characterize the Northern style. This unique style has made the Spirit Sands Singers well known on the powwow circuit throughout the central Plains of Canada. Since 2005 Mike has worked as a cultural interpreter, programming and coordinating cultural events and providing counseling for Native American inmates at the Stony Mountain Correctional facility in North Winnipeg. I first met Mike in the late summer of 1999 at the Heartbeat of Nations Powwow in Winnipeg. Over the course of the following winter Mike and his family invited me to their home on numerous occasions—for drum group rehearsals, sweat lodges, and other ceremonial events—or simply for a visit. The following summer Mike invited me to join his group and since that time I have sung and traveled with the Spirit Sands Singers whenever I have visited the area. Mike, more than any other individual, has made this research possible. He took me under his wing, took me to powwows, taught me how to sing and sit at a powwow drum, and consistently humbled me with his extraordinary patience and generosity as a teacher and loyalty as a friend.

But the powwow trail was only one of two qualitatively different but interconnected social worlds that I inhabited during the course of my research. Set against this world of constant travel was the comparatively sedentary world of the recording studio. When I first visited Winnipeg in 1998 I immediately sought out Brandon Friesen who was, at the time, a producer and chief engineer for Sunshine Records and was responsible for recording the vast majority of Sunshine's powwow catalogue, as well as a long list of Aboriginal pop music recordings. Later that fall Brandon left Sunshine to open his own recording studio, Studio 11. In January 1999, he also formed Arbor Records, a company that quickly gained a reputation on the powwow trail as the new powerhouse of the powwow music industry, due mostly to Brandon's reputation as a producer of Aboriginal music.[9]

Brandon Friesen has worked in various positions within the Canadian music industry since he was a teenager. At various points in his career he has been a professional guitarist, record producer, recording and mix engineer, A&R representative, salesman, artistic promoter, artistic manager, graphic artist, and record-label owner. He graduated high school in 1992 and almost immediately landed a job working part-time for Sunshine Records, filling and shipping orders during the day and using downtime at night to work in the Sunshine studios, engineering his own music projects and recording and producing for local Winnipeg rock bands. A self-taught mix engineer and producer, he learned his craft by building and then working in his own home studio. In 1998, after working for Sunshine for over six years, he left the company to open Studio 11 with his friend and fellow record producer Paul Scinocca. Within a year he started Arbor Records. In 2005 Brandon and Paul sold Studio 11 and opened 441 Studios in downtown Winnipeg. At this same time Brandon also created two new record labels dedicated to hard rock acts, C12 Records and C4 Records, as well as Race Day Promotions, a music promotion company. Since 2009 Brandon has spent a good deal of his time in Los Angeles, where he is a highly sought-after producer and engineer; his work has earned him several Canadian Juno awards and American Grammy nominations. Working with Brandon can be a disorienting and breathless experience. A perpetual motion machine, his modus operandi is to work on six things at once while planning a dozen more. He has seemingly endless energy and interest in all things related to the commercial music industry, and he possesses the rare ability to be completely dedicated and focused equally on both the business-oriented and creative aspects of commercial music production.

The timing of my arrival in Winnipeg in 1999 for my extended fieldwork research was quite fortuitous. Both Studio 11 and Arbor Records had been in operation for less than a year. They were running with a skeleton crew of employees, and the administrative structures of the companies were still quite fluid. This opened up several opportunities for me to make myself useful and be a working and contributing member of those companies rather than an academic bystander/interloper. By the end of my first summer in Winnipeg I began to work closely with Brandon and Arbor Records, first informally and later as a regular employee, from September 1999 until I left Winnipeg the following summer. My role at the label and at Studio 11 expanded with each passing month. I began writing press release sheets and copyediting CD inserts. Then I helped to compile powwow compilation CDs from a catalogue of hundreds of songs that Arbor Records had archived.[10] I also became the first or second engineer on studio powwow recordings that went on during that winter. By the spring I was regularly heading out to reservations to do remote recordings either live at powwows or in community centers on reservations. In the summer of 2000, weekends not spent singing with the Spirit Sands Singers were spent at powwows recording for Arbor Records. I eventually became Arbor's primary powwow specialist and was involved in the engineering, production, and post-production of almost every powwow recording project. I mastered all the CDs, did a good deal of field (powwow), remote (on-location), and studio recording of powwow groups, and compiled anthology CDs.[11]

My role at Arbor and Studio 11 became much larger than I had originally intended and presented a number of methodological problems in research. First, because of my own social history and biography, formal and even informal interviews were difficult to conduct. I was a (relatively) young, white, rock guitar player just like many of the other studio employees. We shared similar biographies, or at least it was assumed that we did. I knew something about audio production and recording from previous work I had done during my undergraduate years mixing sound "live" for bands in bars and then later working at a small recording studio at the University of British Columbia, producing books on tape using a modest—and by modern standards primitive—hard-drive digital recording system. In terms of familiarity with studio gear and sound reinforcement technology, to a certain degree, we "spoke the same language." Thus, it became difficult for me to ask basic ethnographic questions like "how does a compressor work and how is it used?" because they already assumed that I knew. As such, I rarely got straight answers to what were perceived by them to be "simple" and thus ridiculous questions. As a result, most of my research at the studio was of the nature of participant observation. Most of the formal interviews I arranged were conducted very early in my tenure there because, after a while, they just considered me "one of them," and thus formal interviews were awkward at best.

Second, my deep involvement in the recording of powwow music contradicted and interfered with one of my central research goals: to record and analyze the recording process, which meant tracking the mix of social, political, and cultural relationships between record producers, recording engineers, and the powwow groups they recorded. When I became the primary recording engineer, this interaction became something else entirely. I took on one of the social roles I was hoping to study. Painfully aware of this methodological conundrum, I nonetheless felt that it was a role I could not refuse. To put it plainly, it was how I earned my keep, and it became one of the main reasons why Arbor employees tolerated my initially ubiquitous and nosy presence at their workplace. And while this role posed ethnographic problems, it also opened up certain opportunities. I became someone who was, to a certain degree, "in training" and thus was afforded more opportunity and tolerance in asking questions. My job at Arbor also allowed me to understand the social role of a recording engineer and a white producer of powwow music, and the relationship between producer and powwow performers, in a deep and forceful way.

Of course, aligning myself with Arbor Records made it much more difficult to present myself to other record companies as an impartial researcher. Interviews with the owners and employees of competing companies were often more guarded and awkward than I would have liked. In the end, however, what was sacrificed in terms of breadth was more than adequately compensated for by the depth of my experience at Arbor. My association with Arbor also altered my relationships with powwow singers and groups. Certain drum groups wanted nothing to do with me, either because they were currently signed and loyal to a competing label, or because they had previously been signed to Arbor and had since moved on. Other performers were anxious to talk to me, not as a researcher but as a record producer and representative of the label; I was seen as something of a "talent scout," and those who were interested in making a recording with Arbor often approached me to discuss contract terms (something I never handled).

This became a mixed blessing. On the one hand, I was able to meet and speak with more drum groups and singers than I might otherwise have if I had presented myself simply as a curious white academic (as I routinely did during the first summer of my research). As a representative of a record label, I had something to offer to them. On the other hand, the quality of my interactions with singers was dictated by my perceived standing as an industry insider. It changed the power relationship of the interaction. As a researcher, I made it clear to people with whom I spoke that I was there to learn from them. They were the teachers and I was the eager student of Native American music and culture. When I became recognized as a record producer, I was perceived to wield more power. As a result I was also treated with more suspicion, as many powwow singers believed that record producers—especially white record producers—were not to be trusted.

It was through my work with Arbor Records that I came to know Gabe Desrosiers, leader of the Ojibwa drum group the Northern Wind Singers, and a veteran singer, songmaker, and champion grass dancer who has been active on the powwow circuit for most of his life. Born January 25, 1963, he is an enrolled member of the Northwest Angle First Nation located in the Lake of the Woods area in western Ontario. Singing since the age of six, he became well known on the powwow trail, making songs and performing throughout the 1970s and 1980s with the champion powwow group the Whitefish Bay Singers from the Whitefish Bay Reserve. Gabe left that group in 1991 to lead his own group Northern Wind, one of the most requested and respected drum groups on the North American powwow circuit. Gabe also has an international reputation as a dancer and has performed all over North America, Eastern and Western Europe, and the Mideast as a Grass Dancer and Eagle Dancer, in addition to winning many powwow competitions across North America. When I first met Gabe in 1999 he was employed as a school bus driver on the Sisseton-Wahpeton Oyate in North Dakota (his wife's home community). Since that time he has returned to school, earning a bachelor's and then a master's in Native Studies (the latter degree included a specialization in Native Language retention and revitalization). Since graduating, Gabe has worked as a teacher, first for the Tiospa Zina tribal school, teaching classes on music and Native American history, and more recently as an Ojibwa language instructor and co-coordinator of multiethnic cultural outreach for a satellite campus of the University of Minnesota. I first worked with Gabe in the early spring of 2000 when I served as an engineer and producer for the Northern Wind CD *Ikwe Nagamonan: Women's Songs*. Since that time I have invited Gabe to several of the schools where I have taught to give various lectures, performances, and demonstrations. Each time we get together we continue our ongoing conversation about the current state of powwow singing and dancing and the ever-changing nature of Northern powwow culture. The voices of Gabe Desrosiers, Brandon Friesen, and Mike Esquash are laced throughout the chapters that follow, and these musicians became my principal teachers in the complexities of powwow singing and Ojibwa culture, as well as the labyrinthine technicalities of studio recording and the North American music industry.

Ways of Knowing

Many times in conversation with Native consultants, direct questions about a particular song or dance style or an aspect of tribal history were met with answers that began "well, when I was a boy . . ." or "you know, I was told by my grandfather. . . ." This kind of deep contextualization of personal knowledge reveals, I think, an understanding of knowledge and knowing that is common in many Native American communities.[12] Following the example of the many friends, informants, coworkers, and fellow musicians and singers I spoke with, I feel it necessary to begin this particular story by saying that this book represents my *own* understanding about powwows and the recording industry, and how these larger social worlds articulate a unique and important kind of indigenous modernity. There are certainly many well-qualified and articulate singers, dancers, and elders who have a far greater knowledge of powwow culture than I could ever hope to achieve. There are also many music industry personnel who have far more extensive technical training and a practical breadth and depth of experience in the recording industry. What I believe I bring to the discussion is the unique perspective of someone who has studied the complex and intricate nature of powwow singing as well as someone who has worked and studied within the Aboriginal music industry. My hope is to make sense of these two social institutions and their continuing dialectical interaction and interdependence. I say this not to try to somehow establish my authority on the topic (the reader can come to his or her own conclusions regarding that issue) but simply to make clear my own social and cultural position vis-à-vis this work, to contextualize my own knowledge of powwows and the recording industry. I make note of this to be perfectly clear about the very real *limits* of my authority. Like James Clifford's (perhaps apocryphal) Cree hunter providing court testimony about the fate of his ancestral hunting lands, I can't promise to tell the truth, I can only tell you what I know (Clifford 1986, 8).

Authorial voice has become a preoccupation of ethnographers in the wake of the broad and sweeping critique of the ethnographic research and writing processes of anthropology initiated in the mid-1980s (see Clifford 1988; Clifford and Marcus 1986; Marcus and Fisher 1986). Throughout this work there are numerous and often lengthy direct quotations from many different friends, informants, coworkers, and fellow musicians. A good deal of ink has been spilled in postmodern ruminations upon the values and problems inherent in such an approach, questions that I took very seriously in dealing with the issues of representation and authorial voice within this book. Quotations found within the regular flow of the text are used to indicate *indirect* quotes from people, part of my own telling of particular events. Many of these events are distilled versions of field notes and few quotations attributed to others in these sections are "word for word," but rather were recalled and written down by myself afterward. Thus, these sections represent *my* stories and experiences, not those with whom I have worked (although I have tried to be as honest and accurate as possible in representing them). Quotes taken directly from transcribed tapes (of either interviews or simply contexts within which my tape recorder or video recorder was running) are indented, set apart from the general flow of the text, and always assigned to specific people.[13] The true identities and full names of people have been revealed only with their express permission. In cases where I have not obtained permission, names have been withheld.

I have included lengthy interview excerpts in order to foreground some of the processes involved in the production of ethnographic knowledge. Many of the aesthetic and ethical issues surrounding singing and dancing are constantly being developed and argued on the powwow trail. Often the opinions of individuals are not reducible to generalized ethnographic truths. These excerpts represent some of the many differing opinions of powwow participants, opinions developed within the objective sociocultural conditions of my consultants. I make no pretense about attempts at strategic dialogism. I made specific decisions about what and whom to include, and interpretations of other people's words and actions are my own (although different consultants have seen various drafts of this work and have provided invaluable critical feedback). While often employed as supporting evidence in my own arguments, these interview excerpts also stand on their own as a way of foregrounding the context within which the information has been received. The ethnographic interview is not a context for revealing knowledge ("the Native's point of view") but a process of *producing* knowledge (Negus 1999, 10–11). In this way it is a convenient metaphor, or even microcosm, of how ethnographic knowledge, more generally, is produced—in similar contexts of back-and-forth exchange: Geertz's hermeneutic method.[14]

This book is organized into two large sections. "Part I: Northern Plains Powwow Culture" consists of three chapters that focus almost exclusively on the values and aesthetics of competition powwows, as the styles of singing, codes of behavior, and ideologies developed within the competition context are those most relevant in understanding the practices of the powwow recording industry. In chapter 1, I argue that powwows are unique cultural performances assembled in a modular way from a bounded set of practices and ideologies that become formalized through the dichotomy between competition and tradition. The heart of this chapter includes detailed ethnographic descriptions of a small traditional powwow and a large competition powwow. Both of these events follow the general form of a Northern-style powwow, feature the same styles of singing and dancing, and engage similar protocols and ritual behaviors (Grand Entry, feather pickups, scheduled dance events, feasts); yet in each case certain structural features are highlighted or suppressed as different practices, ideologies, and discourses are articulated and disarticulated and particular meanings and interpretations are celebrated, reinforced, or contested.

In chapter 2, I argue that the aesthetic ideologies developed in and through singing competitions articulate a unique ethic of professionalization and commercialization. The ethical dimensions of singing are negotiated through contested ideas about the traditional value of powwow songs and the celebration of innovation, which has become a central component of success in singing contests. Participation in singing competitions has not only served to develop a more standardized set of aesthetic preferences for singers and dancers, aesthetic values that become a shared element of intertribal ideology as expressed on the powwow grounds, but has also served to delineate a stylistic universe for powwow recordings. Competition singing styles, repertoire, compositional styles, and performance practices all play important roles in the kinds of songs and performances that become recorded and distributed by the recording industry. Perhaps most importantly, drum groups who regularly participate in singing contests are those most likely to enter the recording studio, as creating and selling recordings have become a regular part of the process of professionalization demanded by competition powwows. In laying out this argument, this chapter provides a musicological description of the various powwow song and dance style categories, discussed in terms of musical form, melody, rhythm, beat patterns, cadence patterns, and performance practice.

In chapter 3, I juxtapose the concepts of "traveling culture" (how "rooted" musical practices travel through space and time) and "the culture of travel" (specific cultural practices, ideologies, and discourses that emerge and develop through traveling as a general mode of life) in order to demonstrate that travel is an essential and deeply embedded aspect of powwows that informs and structures social practice on multiple levels. The constant travel required for participation on the competition powwow circuit creates opportunities for participants to forge more, and more varied, kinds of intertribal relationships. Travel is also a key component in expanding a drum group's fan base, creating an increasingly intertribal market demographic for their commercial CDs. Following and comparing the travel habits of two different drum groups, the Northern Wind Singers and the Spirit Sands Singers, in this chapter I examine how exchange between drum groups (exchange of people, ideas, songs) is shaped by the transitory nature of the competition circuit; the terms and nature of this interaction are forged on and between the powwow grounds as social categories of age, tribal affiliation, and gender are constructed and contested. New ideas about Native American identity are forged and existing ideas are reworked in and through these intertribal social relationships every weekend at powwow celebrations.

"Part II: The Mediation of Powwows" consists of a series of chapters that grapple with the social and political practices of the powwow recording industry using the core metaphor of "mediation," a concept invoked in each chapter in order to highlight a different social, cultural, or technological process. Collectively, these chapters focus on the social, economic, and cultural organization of the Aboriginal recording industry and how it relates to and interacts with the social dynamics and aesthetic conventions of competition powwows.

Chapter 4 deals with how the concepts of race and culture were deployed discursively by both Natives and non-Natives in negotiating through the power structure of record labels as corporate entities. Focusing particularly on the white-owned Arbor Records, I examine how the shared ideas, behaviors, and expectations of powwow performers recording at the label were often misunderstood and misconstrued by non-Native music industry personnel. These negotiations were often framed within the shared discourse of race; that is, the tacit assumption that "racial" difference (meaning phenotypic traits) equals "cultural" difference (meaning ideology and behavior). I suggest, however, that, in reality, the differences that separate singers and record producers are composed of a number of socially structured cleavages that cut across issues of race, class, gender, and age. I characterize powwow music labels as intercultural "contact zones" (Pratt 1991; Sahlins 1994) where competing commonsense notions about music, musical performance, musical ownership and authorship, and "normal" rules of social conduct and social relations continually rub up against one another. This dialectic produces a hybrid corporate culture with concessions negotiated and established by both parties.

I directly compare a powwow recording session (*Honouring Our Elders* by the Lake of the Woods Singers) and a "Contemporary Native" music recording session (*The Spirit Within* by Mishi Donovan) in chapter 5 in order to show that the act of making a powwow recording is distinguished from other kinds of commercial recording processes by a unique distribution of social power. In the interactions between powwow singers and recording engineers and record producers, powwow singers claim a "cultural authority" and ownership over the music that allows them to exert a greater degree of control over the recording process than would typically occur in other studio recording contexts. In an attempt to explain social interaction in somewhat structuralist terms, I describe these two different recording contexts through an application of Bourdieu's theory of "social fields" (Bourdieu 1993). Highlighting the meaning of mediation as "social interaction and negotiation," I describe musical creation in the studio in terms of the negotiations between different agents who occupy different structural positions within a social space. Each recording situation is described as a specific "musical field" characterized by a particular set of accompanying behaviors and discourses.

Chapter 6 provides a fine-grained examination of the technological mediations that are a regular feature of powwow recording practices. Through a detailed analysis of the production and "post-production" processes of two different Arbor Records powwow CDs (21st Century by the Northern Wind Singers and Red Tail, Volume 1 by the Red Tail Singers), I identify "liveness" as a key component of powwow recordings. In comparing "live" versus "studio" recording processes, I focus specifically on the creative use of reverb, timbral manipulation ("equalization"), and the digital manipulation of dynamics ("compression") in order to show how liveness, through a series of semiotic and technological mediations, is encoded as a musical style. Liveness, as both an aesthetic discourse and a technological practice, is linked both to the perceived "cultural authenticity" of the recording (for both musical producers and consumers) and to a singing group's connection to a more generalized imagining of Native American tradition.

In chapter 7, I examine the unique "social life" (Appadurai 1986) of recordings in terms of how they are valued and evaluated and how they differ from live performances. In particular, the "aesthetics of liveness" functions to link recordings to the powwow grounds and an authentic Native American identity that is constituted through the liveness discourse. The aesthetics of liveness cultivated in and through powwow "recording culture" is a creative cultural response to the hegemony of the twin discourses of modernity and tradition, discursive formations operating within both the academy and in many Native communities in North America. The practices of "recording culture" (creating and consuming commercial powwow CDs) express a unique kind of indigenous modernity that allows Native Americans to be simultaneously modern and traditional. I conclude this chapter by expanding upon the various levels of meaning in the phrase "recording culture" and offer a mild critique of ethnomusicological recording practices, calling for a more theoretically engaged focus on the status of recording practices and recorded products in ethnomusicology.

In the coda, I briefly describe how both northern Plains powwow culture and the Aboriginal recording industry have developed and changed since my first long-term fieldwork in 1999–2000 and detail the rise of several new indigenous-owned record labels that could potentially change the social and economic organization of powwow recording.

PART I

NORTHERN

PLAINS

POWWOW

CULTURE

Powwow Practices

Competition and the

Discourse of Tradition

For Native Americans and Canadians themselves, each pow wow reflects the cultural specificity of a tribal nation, a unique community, a particular ceremony. But for the different Native people who experience them, pow wows express certain cultural similarities and a deeply felt and shared sense of "being Indian" that threads through the dichotomies used to analyze power and identity—belonging and exclusion, knowledge and ignorance, control and resistance—all signified by the rhythm of the drum and the collective singing of seemingly wordless songs. In this site of cultural struggle over conflicting identities and competing ideologies, Natives, newcomers, performers, and spectators negotiate the meaning of Indianness.

—GAIL VALASKAKIS (2005, 152)

Tradition . . . is less about preservation than about transformative practice and the selective symbolization of continuity.

—JAMES CLIFFORD (2000, 100)

Powwows as events in time and space emerge out of the complex social interactions of a myriad of social actors: dancers, singers, drummers, performers and spectators, "hosts" and "guests," Native Americans and non-Natives, those who are "working" and those who are "recreating." Clifford Geertz's well-known metaphor for culture—"webs of significance"— provocatively describes the process of meaning making for these various social agents, and these webs are spun by all who participate in a powwow on any given weekend. In the Geertzian tradition, my understanding of powwow performances, and the emergent ethics and aesthetics engendered in and through these events, is guided by an attempt to trace out some of the strands of these webs, noting intersections and divergences and moments of coherence and conflict. Powwows, as events, are filled with countless productive moments when various participants make claims about the interpretation of particular behaviors and cultural practices, based on the social position and habitus of the social agents (Bourdieu 1977). Powwow participants are all hermeneutic scholars reading and interpreting the social text of a powwow, and creating their own interpretive narratives that add to, combine, or compete with other narratives. But not all these narratives have equal weight or equal resonance or equal power to persuade, and each narrator generates his or her meanings from a particular social position. In this way the experience of powwows is soaked through with power and politics.

Tara Browner has asserted that "*all* pow-wows have a larger, underlying tribal or regional framework, and by either merging with or deviating from it participants reinforce personal tribal affiliation" (2002, 4). As such, her monograph describing Northern powwow practices is structured to highlight similarities and differences in behaviors and meanings for Lakota and Anishinaabeg (Ojibwa) powwow celebrations. She is certainly correct in pointing out that tribally and regionally defined cultural differences have a significant impact on the form, structure, and meaning of powwows for participants. However, tribal differences are only one aspect among many that may be examined. It is true enough that Lakotas and Ojibwas have different powwows and different understandings of powwows; but what about a teenaged Ojibwa who has lived her entire life in an urban center, or a Lakota elder for whom English is a second language and who still has vivid and bitter memories of boarding school? How do these individuals participate in and interpret powwow performances and experiences? Age, gender, living arrangements (urban or reservation), personal politics, class, and education all contribute to the habitus of powwow performers and participants. It is not that tribal affiliation is unimportant; however, it may be the case that other social factors are equally or in some cases more important. At the same time, ethnographic work is rarely about the study of individuals but rather the study of collectives. I am not suggesting that individuals are so varied and complex that generalities cannot be ascribed to tribal practices and meanings, simply that tribal affiliation is only one of the many vectors of identity that generate differences in powwow practices and interpretations.

In this chapter I examine some of the practical and ideological differences between what are known as *competition* (sometimes called *contemporary*) powwows and *traditional* powwows. In the central Plains of Canada and the northern Plains of the United States, powwow participants use the terms *competition* and *traditional* almost exclusively to describe and categorize powwow events. In some sense, these terms may be understood as regionally specific genre categories with locally ascribed meanings. For example, southern Plains powwow culture, centered in Oklahoma, does not share the same binary categorization and features a much wider variety of events in structure, organization, and cultural meaning (see Ellis 2003; Lassiter 1998). Further, as powwow events spread to new geographic areas (the east and west coasts for instance) and become popular with different tribal groups, new practices are created and understood outside of, or in between, the basic genre bifurcation of "traditional" and "competition." However, the northern Plains area is one of the centers of powwow culture today and strongly influences practices as they are adopted across the continent. As such, the structural division of powwows into these two basic categories (with some variation in nomenclature) has become increasingly common outside of this region (although certainly not universal).

The competition powwow circuit began to form in the 1950s as a loosely related aggregate of song-and-dance events that offered modest cash prizes to participants. This circuit became larger and more structurally coherent by the 1970s as more and more reservations began holding annual celebrations open to intertribal participation. The 1980s and '90s saw the emergence of "mega-powwows" with such events as the Gathering of Nations in Albuquerque, the Denver March Powwow, the Mashantucket Pequot's "Schemitzun" Green Corn Powwow, and Coeur d'Alene's Julyamsh. Drawing thousands of participants from across North America and fueled in part by the large injection of capital generated through the proliferation of reservation-based casinos, these powwows began offering cash prizes on the order of thousands of dollars for dance events and tens of thousands for singing contests. More and more powwows are now explicitly stating in their advertising whether they are competition or traditional powwows. In doing so, powwow committees are actively strategizing about the kind of event they are going to host. Explicitly marketing a powwow as a competition event will inevitably bring more dancers, attract more—and probably more professional—drum groups, and require a different kind of monetary investment.

In order to explore some of the important practical and ideological differences between these two types of events, two ethnographic case studies will be presented and analyzed, the first an Assiniboine, reservation-based competition powwow, and the second a reservation-based, Ojibwa traditional powwow. In presenting these two cases I wish to construct a general model of powwow events as cultural performances assembled in a modular way from a bounded set of practices and ideologies. Each of these events follows the general form of a Northern-style powwow, features the same kinds of singing and dancing, and engages similar protocols and standardized behaviors (Grand Entry, feather pickups, scheduled dance events, feasts, etc.); yet in each case certain structural features are highlighted or suppressed, and different practices, ideologies, and discourses are articulated and disarticulated as particular meanings and interpretations are celebrated, reinforced, or contested. In this way, powwow performances, and the meanings and interpretations of these performances, have a unique "emergent" quality (Bauman 1977).

Competition and Traditional Powwows

Since first meeting and working with Gabe Desrosiers in 1999, I have arranged a number of guest lecture/performances for him at the various universities where I have worked. During his visits, I make very few demands about the content of his presentations, suggesting only that he speak in some way about his life as a singer, songmaker, and dancer. When he came to speak in my classes in the spring of 2002, his lectures became more and more thematically structured with each presentation. A central theme that emerged in his talks was the important distinction between what he called "traditional" and "competition" powwows. What struck me about his presentations was not simply the distinction he was drawing, but his use of space in metaphorically demonstrating the point. In speaking about traditional powwows he would point to his right, offering comments about typical practices found at these kinds of events; then, pointing or gesturing to his left, he would speak about what occurred at a competition powwow. Traditional powwows were to the right, competition powwows to the left, and he was in between. Gabe's careful spatial separation of traditional and competition powwows was a forceful expression of how these two worlds are understood by many powwow participants. Their overlapping nature is suggested by Gabe's position in the middle of these two poles, an indication of his ability to travel from one to the other as one of the many powwow participants who take part in both worlds. The complex interrelationship of these two kinds of events is indicated by his struggling comments to explain to undergraduate music students the significant differences between these worlds, saying things like "We have these things [activities and events] over here [at traditional powwows], too, but at competition powwows it's . . . [struggling for words] it's different." Gabe's difficulty in verbalizing these differences stems from the fact that often what distinguishes traditional powwows from competition powwows is not necessarily the different kinds of behaviors or practices that take place but the way those behaviors are interpreted—what and how they mean and are felt.[1]

At the most basic level, the central element distinguishing competition and traditional powwow events is that competition powwows feature formal singing and dancing competitions with cash prizes for participants, while traditional powwows do not. Competition powwows are also generally much larger events and feature a much greater degree of intertribal participation. These events are highly structured proceedings with fairly strict adherence to a schedule of events. They also place a greater emphasis on the strict division of contest singing and dancing categories and do not regularly emphasize community or tribal concerns or local dance traditions. Because these powwows are generally well funded by tribal councils, and increasingly through capital generated by tribal casinos, drum groups hired to host these events are typically well paid, and cash prizes for the competition events can range from $500 to $2,000 or more for dancers and between $5,000 and $25,000 for singing groups. Conversely, traditional powwows are very often smaller gatherings that operate on a relatively modest budget and emphasize community friendship over formal competition. Instead of holding competitions, each participating dancer or singer receives a modest sum of money from the powwow committee to help offset the expenses of travel, food, and lodging. Dancing and singing activities are undertaken informally, and the proceedings will often feature a number of "giveaways," "Honor songs," and other events that highlight or emphasize local community concerns.

However, while there are real, practical differences between traditional and competition powwows, perhaps more important are the ideologically constructed *meanings* associated with particular practices found at these events. Interpretive meaning for participants within these different contexts is generated within and through tribal and pan-tribal discourses about "tradition" and "culture," and these terms are key "discursive tropes" (Stokes 1994, 7) employed by powwow (and powwow music industry) participants to capture a wide range of practices and link them to ideologies of historical continuity, authenticity, and difference. Broadly speaking, traditional powwows are articulated to (and experienced and interpreted as embodying) "local," tribally specific, and more culturally "authentic" values and practices, while competition powwows articulate (inter)national, pan-tribal, and variably inauthentic kinds of activities. Authenticity is defined in both cases in terms of actions and ideologies culturally specific to Native American groups as distinguished from non-Natives, and legitimated through the rhetorical force of history.

Powwow people invoke "tradition" for multiple purposes, with multiple objectives, and in multiple social domains. Singing styles are identified either as traditional (sometimes also called "original") and contemporary, and drum groups become known for their expertise in one or the other of these styles (see chapter 2). At larger competition powwows, singing contests are similarly divided into these two basic style categories. Since the mid-1990s it has become increasingly common to find dance contests split into old-style and contemporary-style dance categories.[2] In each case the stylistic markers and practices that distinguish tradition from its categorical opposite vary but the ideological features remain somewhat consistent. The discourse of tradition often plays itself out in the intercommunity negotiation of the "continuity of tradition," which attempts to mediate the ideologically conflicting discourses of modernity and tradition. The terms "traditional" and "contemporary" stand in for discursive universes that articulate "authentic" Native identity to song and dance practices and tribal pasts to pan-tribal and intertribal futures.[3]

A Northern Competition Powwow

The Carry the Kettle Assiniboine Nation Indian reservation is located approximately one hundred miles east of Regina along the Trans Canada Highway, just outside the small prairie farming town of Sintaluta, Saskatchewan, on the central Canadian Plains.[4] Measuring approximately fourteen square kilometers, the band boasts a population of just under two thousand four hundred members, approximately eight hundred and fifty of whom reside on the reserve. Every year, often on one of the last weekends of July, Carry the Kettle (CTK) hosts its annual powwow celebration.[5] The CTK powwow is large and well established, and many singers, dancers, and other participants mark their calendars and annually travel to Saskatchewan for this popular event. Like many powwow grounds on the Canadian Plains, the CTK reservation has set aside a large tract of land dedicated to this annual event, found at the end of a dirt road near the heart of the reservation.

....

Saturday, July 24, 1999, at 10:30 AM. The sun is already high in the sky, hot and unrelenting. Campers have been driven from their sleep at dawn as the morning sun quickly heats their tents to unbearable temperatures. Very little shade exists on the grounds save for those areas carefully constructed by campers using blue and orange tarpaulins held aloft by tent poles or scavenged tree branches. Those who spend their summers traveling the powwow trail know the value of shade on the Canadian prairies. Cars and trailers display license plates from near and far: Saskatchewan, Alberta, Manitoba, Ontario, Montana, North Dakota, Minnesota. People are sleepily, leisurely beginning their day. The dancing of the previous night continued until after 1 AM. At the time of the first Grand Entry, Friday at 8 PM, sixteen different drum groups and more than 250 dancers crowded the arena. The Grand Entry was large and impressive and the dance arena was packed with dancers all night long. But Friday night was just a warm-up. Saturday is when the powwow really begins. By Saturday's first Grand Entry at 1 PM, all the dancers and singers will have arrived and registered for the appropriate competitions. Spectator crowds will be at their peak on Saturday night.

But on this morning, a gentle calm still pervades the powwow grounds as people relax in the shade, prepare breakfast on an open fire or camp stove, sleep late, wash their hair using water obtained from the water truck that recently made its rounds, braid hair for the coming Grand Entry, and visit with relatives and friends whom they see every so often on the powwow trail. Typical of reservation powwows such as this, children are everywhere, generally unsupervised by their parents but safe from harm or trouble under the watchful eyes of friends, relatives, or other adults who understand that, on the powwow grounds, everyone is responsible for and to each other.

Both the physical organization of people and the temporal organization of events have become somewhat standardized for competition events across the northern Plains. Powwow grounds are typically structured as a series of increasingly larger concentric circles (Browner 2002). At the center of the CTK grounds stands the dance arena, often called the dance "arbor," which is surrounded immediately by singing groups who set up their drums on blankets and specially designed drum stands (a drum must never be placed directly on the ground), with folding metal or plastic chairs encircling each drum. Behind the drum groups are seven or eight rows of lawn chairs where elders, dancers, and relatives of dancers and singers sit and watch the weekend's events unfold. Encircling these rows of chairs are several stadium-style wooden benches, an informal seating area for the overflow of dancers and singers and for the many spectators. At one end of the dance arena sits a permanent, simply designed, wood-framed building, the booth where members of the powwow committee and the emcees for the event sit and oversee the proceedings.

A myriad of craft booths, vendors' booths, and fast food stands surround the dance arena and seating area on all sides. These businesses travel the Northern powwow circuit all summer, setting up makeshift structures from which to conduct business.[6] The craft booths sell a wide assortment of handmade jewelry, clothing, and powwow supplies: beads, feathers, finished hides, belts, fans, roaches (men's headdresses made from porcupine hairs), moccasins, and various sundries needed to make or add to a dancer's regalia (dance outfit). The vendors' booths sell commercial items: name-brand clothing and hats, children's toys and games, and quick-pick lottery tickets. The food vendors sell coffee, homemade frybread, soups, hamburgers, hot dogs, "Indian tacos" (frybread with chili), candy, and soda. Tents, trailers, campers, vans, cars, and lean-tos, the weekend shelter for participants and audience members, fill the rest of the powwow grounds. Portable toilets dot the area and a semipermanent building serves as a crude shower stall for the dancers. Expecting to find a similar organization at reserve powwows across North America, powwow singers and dancers quickly learn to negotiate the social and geographical space of the powwow grounds. The consistency of this structure makes powwow participants feel "at home" at the powwow no matter where they are in North America.

The order of events at competition powwows has also become some-what standardized. Similar to Carry the Kettle, a typical powwow begins Friday evening and lasts until Sunday evening. That time is divided into five different dance sessions, each session beginning with a Grand Entry followed by a series of intertribal dances, and then rounds of competition dancing. Each of these sessions generally lasts between four and six hours. The first Grand Entry begins between 7:00 and 9:00 PM Friday night. Saturday's and Sunday's Grand Entries begin at 1:00 PM and 7:00 PM with a two-hour supper break between afternoon and evening sessions.

As Saturday afternoon's Grand Entry time approaches, the emcee Robert Fourstar, a veteran of the powwow trail and a popular emcee on the Northern powwow circuit, begins casually speaking through the public address system, his voice echoing through the grounds. At a large competition powwow such as this there are often two or three emcees who will take turns over the course of the weekend, constantly announcing the order of events. Events are also kept moving by one or sometimes two "arena directors" who work in the dance arena and make sure dancers are ready to dance and drum groups are ready to sing. The arena director, the head judges, and the emcee all work in close contact to make sure events run as smoothly as possible. This morning Mr. Fourstar speaks about the importance of powwows as places where Indian people come together to share music and stories and build community ties. "A 'giveaway' can make relatives," he says. "We should be able to carry on this relative making. It's important for our children to know these traditions. These are the ways of our Indian Nations." And a little later, "Come on all you dancers, Grand Entry is in fifteen minutes! Grand Entry is at 1:00 sharp. No 'Indian time' at this powwow. Grand Entry starts at 1:00 sharp!"[7]

Drum groups begin assembling and setting up their drums on the edges of the dance arena. There are two host drums at the CTK powwow: Eya-Hey Nakoda, an Assiniboine drum group from Morley, Alberta, and Elk's Whistle, an intertribal group from Regina, Saskatchewan. As Grand Entry approaches, Eya-Hey Nakoda begins to set up their circle. They place tobacco on the drum in five small piles, one in each of the four directions (N, S, E, W) and one in the center. A singer beats the drum four times and then all the singers touch the drum with their hands and then touch their chests and throats, an action thought to enable singers to gain strength from the drum. The group includes men between the ages of thirty and fifty, noticeably older than many other drum groups in attendance, which consist of younger children, teenagers, and men in their early twenties. Eya-Hey Nakoda is a well-respected and experienced drum group that takes the job of host drum very seriously. After blessing the drum the group begins to set up several microphones and plug them into a portable sound system with speakers pointed into the center of the dance area. At most competition powwows drum groups are amplified by a central PA system with a cordless traveling microphone (or two) carried from drum to drum and held over each group as they perform. However, at CTK, only the emcees and committee use the central PA system, whereas drum groups are responsible for providing their own amplification. Groups who are fairly well established own and travel with a small PA system and have come to expect this kind of arrangement at many reservation-based competition and traditional powwows. At CTK, drums without their own PA share with neighboring drums, with microphones quickly being transported from one drum to the next between performances.

Nineteen drum groups in total circle the dance arena. Just before Grand Entry the emcee announces a drum roll call, calling out each drum group's name, with each group responding with a stroke on the drum: Red Dog, Iron Swing, Cree Spirit, White Shield, Wood River Cree, Red Bull, Grey Buffalo, Eagle Hill, Crooked Lake, and a host of others. Roll call is important at competition powwows for two reasons. First, for drum groups that are participating in the singing contest, points are awarded for those that are prompt and ready to sing at the beginning of every session (or conversely, points are deducted for those competing drum groups who are absent from the roll call). Second, it establishes a drum order for the dance session.

Just before Grand Entry the emcee begins speaking about the flags and the "Eagle Staffs" (decorated staffs that serve as the "national" tribal emblems of the reserve or that represent particular families from a reserve) that will be brought into the dance arena, noting how the present-day practice of the "color procession" is a continuation and elaboration of a time-honored Indian tradition:

> The camp would stand as they [the warriors] would come into the camp circle. There would be people standing and singing. They would come in riding their horses, whatever they brought back. And we would welcome them home. And that's what we're doing here this afternoon. These staffs, these flags represent the warriors of old who defended our peoples through-

out time. For if it wasn't for our warriors, we wouldn't be a nation today. And so as we bring these colors in; and these veterans so graciously give up their time to help us, we should respect that. We should stand up, if we're able to. Let's not let our pride get in our way. [Don't say]: "I'm a European, I'm not going to stand up for this." Our peoples, many of them, gave their lives for these colors. So with that—so with that we're going to go down here to Elk's Whistle for Grand Entry. Then back to Eya-Hey Nakoda. *Wana*, let's bring them in, boys. You're on the air.

Saturday afternoon's Grand Entry begins with Elk's Whistle breaking into a Grand Entry song. Audience members all rise to their feet and remove their hats. A procession enters from the eastern side of the dance circle led by Native American military veterans, known as the "Color Guard," carrying Canadian and U.S. flags and three Eagle Staffs. Honored guests of the event—visiting tribal leaders and other political figures— follow the flag bearers. Next are the "head dancers," a male and a female, each a well-respected dancer hired by the local powwow organizing committee to lead and inspire dancers for the weekend, and then the "visiting royalty" (various Powwow Princesses attending the event). Dancing into the arena behind this group of political figures are all the dancers, entering the dance arena in an order determined by sex, dance style, and age. Senior men's dancers are followed by senior women, in turn followed by men then women, boys then girls, and finally the young children ("tiny tots"). The line slowly enters the dance arena and circles the dance area in a clockwise direction. The Grand Entry is a procession into the dance arena by all the dancers present at the powwow, by this time more than three hundred. The bright colors, beadwork, and feathers of the dancers present a stark contrast to the drum groups, many of whom are dressed casually in jeans, button-down shirts, and baseball caps or cowboy hats. Elk's Whistle and Eya-Hey Nakoda each sing four push-ups (verses) and then yield to the other, trading songs back and forth until all the dancers have entered the arena. When all the dancers have entered the arena, the singing stops and the emcee addresses the crowd:

There you have it ladies and gentlemen, your Grand Entry for 1:00. Let's give them a big round of applause [*applause follows*]. Hey, we have people here that are listening! OK, as we gather, they told us that when you gather, at least two of you, when you're gonna talk about something, when you're gonna do something, you always ask somebody to talk to the Creator for whatever it is you're gonna do. And this afternoon, our Grand Entry here, we want everybody to have a good time. People that have planned things for this afternoon, we want them to go the way they want them to go. We want everybody to be healthy, to enjoy yourselves while you're here with us at Carry the Kettle. So we have asked one of our elders here from Carry the Kettle to talk to the Creator on our behalf. So with that, ladies and gentlemen, I'm going to turn the microphone over to Mr. John Heywahe for a word to the Creator on our behalf.

[*Mr. Heywahe approaches the microphone and begins to speak:*] OK, ladies and gentlemen, I'd like to say a few words before we start the affair. Now we all know, every weekend there's a powwow somewhere. And we're heading there. Pack up the old wagon and take off. Today, you're on the grounds here. This area was dedicated to the Assiniboine people. And we all have . . . a place to enjoy ourselves. We have a place to go for the weekend and have a good holiday. This was sacred ground for the Assiniboine people a long time ago. . . . But today it's powwow. It's good to see a lot of people out there enjoying themselves. . . . So I'd like to say a prayer . . . [*begins a prayer in the Nakota language*].

It is common for invocations to mix languages like this. Sometimes those giving invocations will begin in their Aboriginal tongue and then provide an English translation. When Mr. Heywahe is finished, Eya-Hey Nakoda begins the "Flag song" while all in attendance, including all the dancers in the dance arena, remain standing in place. This is followed immediately by Elk's Whistle's rendering of the "Victory song" (sometimes called a "Veteran's dance"), a song that honors all the military veterans in attendance. All the dancers in the arena begin to dance slowly in place. When this is over the flag carriers are announced and the flags are posted.[8] Then visiting royalty (Powwow Princesses and Braves) and political figures are introduced by name to the audience. James O'Watch, the chief of Carry the Kettle, and Mr. Morely Watson, vice-chief of the intertribal political organization called the Federation of Saskatchewan Indian Nations, both address the crowd, thanking them and the powwow committee and welcoming people to the CTK community. The emcee takes over again: "OK, with that we're gonna go with two intertribals! Eya-Hey Nakoda, you are live, you're on the air."

Eya-Hey Nakoda breaks into a Shake song, after which a Crow Hop song is performed by Elk's Whistle. After that, the drum order is followed and intertribal "Straight" songs are sung exclusively. The afternoon's dance session begins in earnest.

Rounds of "intertribal dancing" directly succeed most Grand Entries. These dances are open to participation by dancers of all ages and styles and may even include spectators, singers, and others present who wish to join the proceedings. During this round of dancing a drum order is followed as the various drum groups each perform a song in the order set by the drum roll call. This system allows singers in these groups to predict when they will be expected to be at their drum to sing, thus affording them time to leave their drum to visit with friends, eat a meal, and wander the powwow grounds. Often, the round of intertribals ends when every drum group attending has had an opportunity to sing at least one song, after which the competition dancing may begin.

Saturday's Grand Entry was completed without incident. Friday night's Grand Entry had been marred by the fact that during the Victory song an eagle feather fan had been dropped on the ground by one of the dancers. When the Grand Entry was complete the emcee announced that the dance floor should be cleared so that the fan could be picked up. Four veteran dancers were called to the dance arena. Three were in dance outfits while the fourth was in street clothes. The four elder men circled the fallen feathers, each man facing one of the four directions. The emcee asked Elk's Whistle to render an "Eagle Feather Pickup" song. The song was rendered with four push-ups while the veterans surrounding the fan danced on the spot. With the beginning of each new push-up they moved in a clockwise direction to face another of the four directions (E, S, W, N). Each of the dancers gestured toward the fallen fan with their hands or with their own feather fans, their hands outstretched at the time of the honor beats in the song. After the four verses of the song were complete the veterans made a tobacco offering to the fallen fan and then one of the men picked it up and they walked out of the arena toward the dancer who had dropped it. The emcee began speaking over the PA system, saying, "This is a very sad time for Indian people. It is believed that when an eagle feather drops a relative goes to the spirit world." As the fan was returned to the young Traditional dancer who had lost it, he continued, "It is important to pass on the rules and traditions of feather pickup to the younger people and to explain the significance of why it is a special ceremony."

As is typical, the singing competition did not begin until Saturday. Drum groups and singers generally arrive at powwows throughout the night on Friday, and thus there may be members missing from the group. By Saturday, all drum groups are expected to have the full complement of singers for that weekend's competition with all singers properly registered. For instance, Roseau River Ramblers, a drum group from the Roseau River Reserve in southern Manitoba, was announced on Friday as a participating drum group, but by Saturday, because so few of the regular singers of that group were present (there were only half a dozen—generally too small a group to win a singing competition, simply because the group will not sound loud or powerful enough), they joined up with Iron Swing and the two groups sang in the competition under the name Iron Swing. For the singing competition on Saturday, all of the competing drum groups were being judged on the singing of one intertribal song and one dance contest song. Participation in the contest requires participation in all of the contest songs and intertribals and immediate responses to song requests. The judges for this round of competition were culled from members of the two host drum groups, whose duties as hosts precluded them from competing.

During the first round of intertribals, the four judges traveled from drum to drum with clipboards containing a number of rating sheets. They filled out the sheets after each performance and handed them to one of the arena directors or another designated "runner" who delivers the sheets to the judging committee for tabulation.[9] While the singing competition started with the judging of intertribals, there were a large number of "specials" scheduled for the day of dancing. Specials typically refer to any number of dance events that are held apart from either intertribals or regularly scheduled contest dancing and may feature "memorial" dance competitions or exhibitions of any of the six major dance categories (where the memory of a particular dancer is celebrated through the sponsoring of a special competition dance, often accompanied by a giveaway). More "presentational" dance styles (such as Hoop dancing), or other tribally specific dance traditions (e.g., Chicken dancing or Crow dancing), as well as more "participatory" dances (in which members of the audience may be involved), such as couples dances (e.g., the Rabbit dance), Round dances (group-oriented circle dances), or line dances (e.g., the Snake dance) are also common. Specials may also feature non-Indian dance exhibitions such as Aztec dancing (Browner 2002, 62–63; Goertzen 2001, 85) or even Australian Aboriginal dancing styles (see below).

Today, in order to make time for all the different specials, after only three intertribals the tiny tots danced to a song (after which they were each "paid" with a few dollars and a box of juice) and then the adult men and adult women were "danced out" (men first, then women), each dancing to one song.[10] A special sponsored by James O'Watch followed immediately after these dances. The event began with Chief O'Watch reciting his family history beginning from 1890. Eya-Hey Nakoda then performed a "welcome song" for certain members of the family returning to the reserve for the occasion of the powwow. O'Watch then gave a blanket to his sister, who was one of the returning family members, and to her (non-Native) foster parents. While Eya-Hey Nakoda sang, the family danced once around the arbor, and when they finished they invited everyone in attendance to come and feast with them at the Elder's Lodge. After Eya-Hey Nakoda finished singing, they were invited to receive a monetary gift for helping with the special and singing the song.

When the special was finished the contest dancing began in earnest, starting with the junior categories: two songs for each contest category. The emcee announced that the songs were going to be "drummer's choice" (meaning the singers could choose the type of song they would perform for the dancers), but more often than not, the emcee would specify the song types the committee and dance judges wanted for each dance category. Dance competitions are typically organized according to age group, sex, and dance style category: Tiny Tots (ages 6 and younger, mixed dance categories and gender), Junior Boys and Junior Girls (ages 7–17), Adult Men and Adult Women (ages 18–55), Senior Men and Senior Women (ages 55 and older). At larger competition events adult categories are often further separated into two age categories: 18–35 and 36–55. Northern competition powwows feature six standard competition dance styles, distinguished by gender, choreography, and regalia, with each style constituting a separate contest category. There are three men's styles, Men's Traditional dance, Men's Grass dance, and Men's Fancy dance; and three women's styles, Women's Traditional dance, Women's Jingle Dress dance, and Women's Fancy Shawl dance.[11] Afternoon sessions of competition dancing typically start with Tiny Tots (all dance styles), each of whom are awarded a small cash prize or other modest token of participation, followed by the Senior categories. Then the Junior Boys and the Junior Girls compete, each category (style) of dance being performed for one song, with the song type chosen by the powwow committee or head judges and announced by the emcee at the beginning of each competition dance. At powwows such as CTK, where afternoon sessions are devoted to specials and junior and teen dancing, these competitions may sometimes be preceded by "exhibition dances" for adult categories, a time when men and women dancers are featured. These exhibitions occur because it is often the last time that adult dancers will have a chance to dance until that evening's session.

The drum groups drew large crowds on Saturday afternoon and the emcee repeatedly requested that "tapers" (those holding hand-held recording devices to record the performances) and audience members crowding around the drums make room for the singing judges so that they could make their way to the drum groups. During most performances a sea of hand-held tape recorders could be seen over the drummers as they performed, as singers, dancers, or other powwow music fans tried to catch the latest songs of their favorite groups. The emcee also announced a curfew for young children because the powwow grounds were chaotic and noisy all Friday night into the early dawn as kids ran and played throughout the night. Saturday, the curfew was set at one hour after the powwow ended (which turned out to be just before two in the morning).

After the contest rounds were complete, five more intertribals were performed, in part to give the dancers who had not danced all afternoon an opportunity to stretch their legs, and in part to get through the judging of more intertribal songs for the singing contest. The retiring of the flags followed. The two arena directors loosened the Eagle Staffs and flags from the stands in the center of the arena and handed them to the veterans. Elk's Whistle sang a Flag song and the veterans stood in front of the emcee's booth holding the flags. By this point the stands had almost emptied, with most of the crowd and the drum groups heading back to their campsites for the supper break. After the Flag song the veterans went into the circle and led a procession in a circle around the arbor, with the veterans following the flags. Some other dancers and audience members in street clothes followed behind them. In all, five flags and three Eagle Staffs were retired; two flags, Canadian Royal Union and United States, flew outside the arbor, while Canadian, U.S., and CTK flags, along with three Eagle Staffs, were posted in the dance arena. After going around the arena once, all the veterans and dancers exited by the emcee's booth and handed the flags to the arena directors.

Saturday evening's dance session was notable (and unusual) for the large number of dance specials featured. The first, which took place shortly after the Grand Entry was completed, featured a professional Australian Aboriginal dance troupe.[12] After three intervening intertribals, a second special began immediately, this one again sponsored by James O'Watch and his family. This was a giveaway intended to honor two of his sons who were returning from Europe, one of whom had worked as a trick horse rider for Euro Disney in France. A giveaway is a public and formalized session of gift giving. Giveaways are typically organized and sponsored by individuals, families, or other social or political groups. Families generally must plan these public spectacles months in advance, slowly accumulating the various blankets, shawls, articles of clothing, housewares, tobacco, and other homemade and commercially produced products to be given away. At the behest of the family organizing the event, gifts are given to particular individuals or particular groups (e.g., all the male traditional dancers at the powwow).[13]

The O'Watch giveaway began with a speech introducing the boys and explaining their accomplishments. This was followed by an Honor song, rendered by Elk's Whistle, while the family walked slowly around the arbor. As they proceeded, a large number of dancers, singers, and audience members entered the dance arena, shook hands with members of the family, and then fell in behind them in the procession, a sign of respect to those being honored. After the Honor song, Chief O'Watch began the proceedings by giving away a horse, a gesture considered by many in attendance to be extremely generous. Then a number of family members and friends of the family were called upon to make their way to the front of the emcee's booth to receive gifts. After this, the family began calling other groups of people, such as "three elder dancers," "three Grass dancers," or "three Traditional dancers." When all the gifts were given, Elk's Whistle was called upon to sing an Appreciation song (also sometimes called a Thank-you song). The group rendered a Round dance song and all those who received gifts danced in a large circle within the arbor, performing the typical side step associated with these songs. When the honor beats of the song were performed, participants lifted their gifts above their heads in a fashion similar to that of Traditional dancers and Jingle Dress dancers, who choreograph these beats by raising their fans.

Following a few more intertribals (which were judged for the singing contest), a third special began, this one a competition contest dance special for Women's Fancy Shawl dancers. As with the previous specials, the event began with an Honor song. Following this, all of the Women's Fancy

Shawl dancers were called into the arbor for a three-song dance competition, the first a straight song performed by Eya-Hey Nakoda, the second a "Trick song" rendered by Elk's Whistle, and the third an Oklahoma style Fancy dance song, again provided by Eya-Hey Nakoda. The members of the family sponsoring the event chose first- through fifth-place winners. The fourth-place winner took the microphone and announced that she was giving her money to Elk's Whistle because she was "dancing with a heavy heart," as one of her relatives was recently deceased. The emcee responded to this gesture, commenting, "That's very Indian of you—very First Nations."

Yet another contest special followed, this time a Men's Fancy dance competition, sponsored by a local Fancy dancer. High Noon, another drum group in attendance, performed an Honor song as the sponsoring Fancy dancer danced around the circle followed by his family and all the dancers who were to participate in the competition. Two competition songs were then sung: a Shake song and an Oklahoma-style (Southern-style Fancy dance) contest song. Five dancers were chosen by the family to continue dancing and they danced to two more songs: a Crow Hop and another Shake song. Three winners were picked and a Victory song followed. The crowd was extremely enthusiastic in their response to the Fancy dancers, whose dancing always proves to be a crowd favorite. Two intertribals followed, and by then it was almost midnight. The committee called on veterans to retire the colors. Once the flags had been danced out of the arena the adult competition dances finally began.

The Sunday afternoon and evening sessions proceeded in the same way as the previous day's schedule. Competition dances were interspersed among a number of specials. The singing and dancing contests continued with new judges. Sunday's dinner break was filled with activity as people all over the grounds began to break up camp. Many would leave after the final evening dance session and drive through the night. At the end of the evening session winners were announced in all categories, first through fifth place for each dance category. The order of the announcements was the reverse of that in the Grand Entry procession. Junior categories were announced first, followed by teen categories, senior categories, and finally adult categories. As each dancer's number and name was announced he or she approached the emcee's booth and received an envelope containing a prize. Singing contest winners were then announced, again in reverse order: fifth through first place. By the time the last contest winners had been announced it was close to 1:00 in the morning and very few people were left in the stands. The singers and dancers said their final farewells and began their journeys home.

A Northern Traditional Powwow

On July 29, 1999, the Brokenhead Ojibway Nation Indian Reserve held its first annual traditional powwow. Brokenhead is located north of Winnipeg, just over an hour's drive from the city's downtown. Because it was the first year of the powwow, the powwow grounds were new, situated in a small natural clearing approximately a hundred yards in from a gravel road. A new path through the bush to the grounds had to be cleared, and by 1:00 on Saturday, the advertised time of the first Grand Entry, heavy construction trucks were still busy clearing out trees and flattening the ground, creating a crude dirt road into the powwow grounds. The arbor was a very recent creation, and a circle of birch poles had been erected with the leafed branches of the trees placed over the top of a rough frame to provide shade for dancers, singers, and audience members. The dancing area remained uncovered. On the western edge of the powwow grounds a footpath led through the woods to another clearing where several large tipis were standing. In 1999 Brokenhead Reserve ran a tourist business where visitors — mostly Europeans — would spend several nights sleeping in tipis, cooking over open fires, and attending Indian "cultural events" like powwows, accompanied by local residents, who were hired by the reserve and functioned as cultural interpreters.

By 1:00 there was only a handful of people on the grounds, with no sign that the event was even going to start at all. A few cars and vans dotted the edge of the clearing where tents were set up, and dancers leisurely began unpacking their outfits. There was one booth that sold food and drinks, a small makeshift stand set up by the "local arrangements" committee. The only other commercial booth was a table set up by the reservation band council that sold Brokenhead Reserve t-shirts and sweatshirts. Because this was a new powwow, it is reasonable to assume that very few vendors knew of its existence, and those that did might still have chosen to go to a more established venue. Traditional powwows rarely feature the same size and number of commercial enterprises that are found at competition events; the latter promise much larger consumer bases. Late July is the height of the powwow season and craft and vendors' booths can choose from any number of powwows, both traditional and competition.

Grand Entry finally began at 2:30 PM after the emcee for the afternoon explained over the PA system that traditional powwows may start only once there are four or more male Traditional dancers who are ready to dance. As Grand Entry began, a ceremonial fire was started outside of the dance arena. This fire was tended for the duration of the powwow and was used by the drum groups to warm and tighten the skins of their drums. There were four drum groups set up at the time of Grand Entry. It is more accurate to say, however, that there were four drums (instruments) set up and perhaps enough singers to make up two full drum groups. At the beginning of each Grand Entry the arena director gave each dancer a bit of tobacco. After Grand Entry was over, the emcee told the dancers to use the tobacco in any way they wanted. Some put it in the ceremonial fire, others dropped it on the ground where they were standing, and some walked to the center of the dance arena where they offered it to the Eagle Staff posted there. When the Victory song was rendered, dancers were encouraged by the emcee to dance one full circle around the arbor (as opposed to standing in place and dancing). Some responded to this request while others simply danced in place, as is more typical.

Because there were so few people in attendance I was somewhat conspicuous in the crowd. My car sported Illinois license plates and was the only vehicle on the grounds with out-of-province plates. And apart from a few European tourists who wandered into the powwow grounds during the evening session, I was also the only non-Native in attendance. Several people approached me and expressed amazement that I had driven so far and that I, a white person, was interested in powwow music. My attendance was also remarked upon several times by the emcee of the event, and he made a special point during the comments that followed the Grand Entry to welcome me to the powwow. He later also announced that I was welcome to join in and dance during the intertribal dancing. Near the close of the afternoon dance session, he also let me know that I was welcome to partake of the feast that was being provided by the powwow committee and members of the Brokenhead community during the supper break.

There was no formal schedule of dance events or specials, and almost all of the dancing was intertribal. Interspersed among these dances were occasional exhibition dances that featured particular dance categories (e.g., all the male Traditional dancers). Preparations for the feast began soon after the dancing stopped. Tables were set out on the grass and homemade food began to arrive in a number of vehicles. The feast consisted of mashed potatoes, wild rice, roast beef, potato salad, soup, bannock, juice, water, and iced tea. The order of feasting was announced by the emcee: elders, dancers (oldest to youngest), singers, and finally the rest of the audience members. After dinner during the break a few members of one of the drum groups began to toss a small Nerf football around. Soon an impromptu game of touch football began, involving myself and a number of singers from the drum groups.

At 7:30 PM the evening dance session began. By this time two more drum groups had arrived, bringing the total to six, and the number of dancers increased to just over fifty, an increase from the thirty-eight dancers who had participated in the afternoon session. Of these, approximately one-third were tiny tot, junior, and teen dancers. There were no Fancy dancers (male or female) in attendance and almost all of the adult males were Traditional dancers. This session lasted until 10:00 PM, at which time, because there were no electric lights installed on the grounds, the dance session ended and we all retired to our camps and campfires.

It is difficult to make broad generalizations about northern Plains traditional powwows because they are community-based and reflect unique community concerns and practices. Indeed, the variability of traditional powwows—compared to the relatively standardized form of competition powwows—is an important feature that marks the two events as categorically different. It is possible, however, to speak about a few broad similarities, although my experience with traditional powwows is rather limited; I attended perhaps a little more than a dozen during the course of my fieldwork, almost all of them hosted by Ojibwa communities. Differences between competition powwows and traditional powwows include the following observations.

Traditional powwows place a much greater emphasis on intertribal dancing. While occasional dance exhibitions for certain categories may take place, the majority of dancing that takes place is intertribal. This has an effect on the kinds of songs that drum groups can perform, as intertribal dancing generally requires "straight beat" dance songs (see chapter 2).

There are no contests at traditional powwows, and as such, no cash prizes. Instead, both dancers and singers are paid through what are known as "drum splits" and "dance splits." Powwow organizing committees will set aside a certain amount of money to pay the singers and dancers in attendance. This money is usually a modest sum and is intended only to help offset the travel costs. In order to be eligible for the dance and drum splits, each participant must register as a participating singer or dancer (or both). Competition powwows also feature drum (and sometimes dance) splits, but this is only one of many sources of possible income for competition participants (see chapter 3). Drum and dance splits serve to foster a "host-guest" relationship at powwows. When inviting others to one's home, there is an obligation to make sure that the guests are comfortable and do not suffer any hardship as a result of their visit. Drum and dance splits, as well as feasts, are mechanisms by which local communities welcome visitors and reflect the host-guest obligations that occur more generally in everyday reservation life.

There is a much higher degree of "drum hopping" at traditional powwows. Singers will jump from one drum to the next and sing with several different drum groups. In many Ojibwa communities certain individuals are drumkeepers for "traditional drums," which are drums that belong to a particular individual or a particular family and are passed down from one generation to the next. Traditional drums are used only for traditional powwows and are never used for singing competitions. These drums are named, are "fed" at the changing of the seasons (four times a year), and have certain songs attached to them that are owned by the drumkeeper.[14] Unlike competition powwow songs, which are usually freely exchanged between singers, many of the songs sung around a traditional drum stay with the drum and are only performed using that particular instrument. A pipe (and often other ritual paraphernalia) is also associated with these drums and is smoked before the drum is used at a powwow.[15]

Drumkeepers who care for the drums often do not have a functioning drum group or a regular group of singers with whom they perform. Instead they may simply show up at a traditional powwow and rely on other singers from the community (or sometimes from outside of the community) to come together around the drum and sing when called upon. Drum hopping is also common because there are many "family drums" present, small drum groups that consist of only family members. As these groups consist of only four or five people, other singers will often join them to strengthen the sound of the drum. Traditional powwows will also feature a larger number of songs that belong to a particular community, and thus many singers from the community will know them. This shared community repertoire allows for even infrequently performing singers to join in and sing with a number of drums. This is markedly different from the arrangement of competition powwows, where drum hopping is often expressly forbidden for drums competing in a singing contest.

Andy White is an Ojibwa from Whitefish Bay Reserve in the Lake of the Woods area in northwestern Ontario. He is a singer and drumkeeper for a traditional drum as well as the leader of the competition drum group the Whitefish Bay Singers. In a formal interview he described the role of traditional drums in this way:

> So we kind of formed a group where I had my grandfather—who passed away a long time ago. He was a very traditional medicine man; he was a medicine man. And he gave me this drum, for me to carry. And he instructed me [in] a lot of the ways that I should carry the drum. How I should act around the drum, you know, respect the drum and how—these ways, these old, traditional ways. And that's what we did. And that's when he gave me another drum. Because I had a traditional drum, which we call in a very traditional way—where we use these drums in a very ceremonial way. Where they have an Indian traditional ceremonial gathering, these are the drums that will be used. Those drums that you see here, at this powwow, where they have a big gathering like this one here, like the one we have here in Winnipeg [Heartbeat of Nations Competition Powwow, September 3–6, 1999], you don't see any *traditional* drums here. They're more like "contemporary drums" is what they call them, you know. But the traditional drums are the ones that have a lot of respect, and they do a lot of traditional feasts for the drum, you know. You treat it like as—well, in our way, it's our grandfather. You know, we call it our grandfather and we treat it as one of our grandfathers that . . . you know, real human, kind of. That's the way we have to respect our drum. Because they say the history of the drum is—because we [my family] have been around elders for a long time. Like my uncle, my oldest uncle is ninety years old. And then we have another uncle, my wife's uncle who was here yesterday, he's in a wheelchair, he can't walk, he's ninety-three years old. But these are our teachers that are, you know, kinda working for all these years. They'll teach us a lot of traditional songs, a lot of old songs that have been passed on from generation to generation, you know. And these are the songs that

are passing on to us. And one of my brothers back home, it's he and I [who] are the ones these [people]—our uncles, our grandfathers—look for to pass these songs to us.

But we don't use them at this kind of [competition] powwow. We use them for ceremonial purposes. At times, you know, when there is what you would call a "traditional powwow," these songs will come out every once and a while to sing in a traditional way. [We only use them at traditional powwows] because of the respect [for the drum]! And because these songs are not the ones that they use today, like you just start humming something and then you make a song [newly composed songs performed at competition powwows]. You know, back in the old days, when a song was given to an elder, a lot of these songs would come through dreams. You know, they're all through a dream. And then he'll sing it and then he'll start talking about it. Every song, back in the old days, had some sort of history and background story. The old traditional songs. And this is the way that's been . . . that's what has been taught to us. (Andy White interview, September 1999)

Generally speaking, there is a far greater frequency of "drum whistling" at traditional powwows. Eagle whistles (or eagle-bone whistles) are typically carried by male Traditional dancers who may spontaneously blow the whistle over a drum either during a song (to encourage the drum to continue singing) or to request that a drum group begin singing. Once the whistle has been blown, the drum is obliged to render four more verses ("push-ups") of a song. When this occurs, one of the arena directors will make his way over to the whistled drum in order to clear a path between the drum group and the dancer who has whistled the push-ups. The whistle blower will dance in an area directly in front of the drum, and as each verse draws to a close he will once again approach the drum and blow the whistle a number of times.[16] At larger competition powwows drum whistling is sometimes expressly prohibited or strongly discouraged; at other times the frequency and number of whistles that are allowed to occur is limited (for instance, it may be announced that a drum cannot be whistled by two dancers consecutively, expressing an attempt to limit the length of performances). While these restrictions are implemented in order to keep dance schedules running on time, traditional powwows have no such concerns. Andy White suggested to me that while eagle whistling is considered both "traditional" and "sacred," it can also be subject to misuse through a lack of knowledge of history and tradition.

AW: I've got an eagle whistle, but I hardly ever use it. I've only used it once at the powwow.

CS: So singers carry eagle whistles?

AW: Yeah, some of them, yeah. That's another thing, especially back home [Whitefish Bay Reserve] where it's just getting out of hand, you know. Too many eagle whistles. It's the same thing as when something is handed down to you. The whistle will be given to you by the Creator to use, to make people happy. I remember — 'cause like I said, I've been kind of raised around the drum and around the powwow for a long time — my grandfather was the old eagle whistler back in the old days at Whitefish Bay. And the thing that's really changed. Maybe it's [because of the] different ways of different tribes. But our ways — my old grandfather on my dad's side, [who] passed away a long time ago, was the eagle whistler. He used to blow his whistle when people were just having a good time and everybody was just dancing hard. He wouldn't do it by the drum, though [as is typically done at pow-wows today]. He would just sit by the doorway — like at a roundhouse, like an old powwow roundhouse — he would just sit by the door and that's where he'd blow his whistle. And he wouldn't do it four times [as is the current standard practice]. He would just blow his whistle. As long as people were having a good time, you know. Nowadays, you see everybody blowing whistles for four — four times.

CS: You don't know where that came from?

AW: I don't know where that came from. I don't know where that came from. A different tribe maybe does it [that way]. But *our* ways, our ways are like my grandfather. He was about ninety years old when he passed away. That was a long time ago. He passed away back in . . . probably about [the nineteen] fifties — in the middle fifties he passed away. That's when I start to wonder sometimes, you know. Things change, [like] about the ways of the whistles. About the ways of . . . how they use the whistles. Some guys back home they're just over-doing it. Like, you know, it's pretty hard for my drum group just to go to a regular traditional powwow back home. Because this is, like I said, this [an eagle whistle carrier] is one of the most respected kinds of people back home. And they'll blow that whistle, [and] maybe you have to sing for maybe six sometimes eight whistles [*laughs*]. Holy mackerel it's . . . it just wears you down, you know. You just have to lose your voice. Eight [whistles], that's about thirty-two push-ups you have to [sing]—and you've already done about four or five push-ups, eh! And all of a sudden you have to . . . you have to finish all the— [*laughs*]. Sometimes I think it's just out of hand back home, eh. Nobody tries to understand what the whistle's all about. (Andy White interview, September 1999)

Finally, traditional powwows rarely attract non-Native spectators. This is because they are smaller, community-based, and much more "participatory" rather than "presentational" in orientation (Turino 2008). My presence at the Brokenhead powwow was frequently remarked upon because it was an oddity to see a non-Native at a traditional powwow. While I was often the only non-Native to camp on the powwow grounds at reservation-based competition powwows, I was not usually the only non-Native in attendance. Quite often, competition powwows attract non-Native locals, especially on Saturday night when competition singing and dancing is at its most intense. While non-Natives are certainly a small minority at competition powwows, their presence is nonetheless acknowledged and in fact encouraged. Dance competitions are thought to offer some of the "best" Native American dancing in the country and so non-Native spectatorship is welcomed. At traditional powwows, where there are no competitions, dancing is very informal and there is no element of showmanship or concern for entertaining an audience. Almost all in attendance are participants in some way, either as singers and dancers or as family members who are actively visiting with other family and friends; there is no element of spectacle. The Grand Entry is not as formal and dance schedules are provisional at best. Traditional powwow dancing is meant to be experienced and enjoyed; it is not meant to be watched. As such, my presence at the Brokenhead powwow as a mere spectator and a stranger and outsider to the reserve was considered quite a novelty. Traditional and competition powwows are thus also often marked by the degree to which they are open, public events.

Culture, Tradition, and the "Problem" of Competition

My friend Carolyne Longclaws—a Jingle Dress dancer—and I were sitting in the stands at the 2000 Annual Waywayseecappo First Nation competition powwow, picking our favorite dancers for each category and then trying to guess who the judges would pick.[17] Still unclear as to what specific criteria were important for competition dancing, I asked Carolyne what it was exactly that separated a good dancer from an average one. She responded offhandedly, "You know, footwork, timing [dancing in time and in steady synchronization with the drumbeat], gracefulness . . ." She paused, began laughing, and playfully added "last name." Her only half-joking comment speaks to a common complaint at competitions: favoritism and judging based on reputation and the family connections and friendships of dancers and singers rather than individual performances. There is, of course, no way to substantiate these claims, but the insinuation that singing and dancing competitions can be—and often are—unfair is the source of a good deal of intertribal tension. Other dancers have told me that they do not like to "play the game" of competition dancing, a process involving social networking and ingratiating yourself to other dancers. This is done because judging is always performed by one's peers, and the hope is that judges will base their decisions on whom they know and whom they like. This kind of conjecture about the motivations of judges is rampant.

The widespread growth and development of competition powwows over the last number of decades and the degree to which these events promote or obfuscate "traditional" Indian ceremonial singing and dancing practices are almost constant topics of conversation among powwow people. Competition is celebrated at the same time that it is viewed with suspicion because it is thought to be the root of potential riffs and disagreements between individuals and groups. Verbal discourse surrounding competition powwows is often located between the poles of critical suspicion and celebration of competition. These two viewpoints are captured in the following "Reflections" articles that appeared in the national American Indian newspaper *Indian Country Today*. I include these short editorials in their entirety because they encapsulate many of the conflicting ideologies surrounding competition, deploying the discourses of culture and tradition to validate their claims:

Reflections from the Pow wow Trail

When I was a young girl in the 1960s, I remember going to social pow wows on the Crow Reservation. I don't remember there being any dance contests, grand entries, or point systems.

After my family moved back to the Flathead Reservation, we went to the 4th of July pow wow every summer. By the early 1970s, dance contests had become routine. The groups of dancers would be called out by gender and age, and the judges would select the winners from the groups. Most of the time, everyone could enjoy intertribal dancing and round dancing and sometimes there was hoop dancing. Tony Brown (Lakota/Salish), as a five-year old, was a very accomplished hoop dancer.

By the late 1970s, dance contests had become the core of the war dancing. Dancers were judged on how much they participated in the entire pow wow, in addition to their exhibition of dancing in their category. Point systems were developed that included grand entries, exhibitions and "spotchecks." This caused dancers to participate whether they wanted to or not. I have seen many dancers who walk around with only part of their regalia and they only dance when it's grand entry, exhibition or contest.

By the 1980s, dance contest "specials" came about. These were dance contests sponsored by individuals or families such as men's traditional, women's fancy, etc., that were held in addition to the regular sponsored contests. "Special" is an accurate term for these contests because often it appears that dancers are chosen not necessarily for their dancing ability. The "special" was a way to honor dancers who might not ordinarily be selected as winners.

By the late 1980s, the "mega pow wow" was emerging. The Gathering of Nations in Albuquerque, the Denver March Pow wow, the Mashantucket Pequot's Schemitzun and the Coeur d'Alene's Julyamsh are the forerunners of today's mega pow wow. Cash prizes for adult dance contests were four figures. Drum contests emerged with five figure prizes. The mega pow wows broke a long-standing tradition: Everyone, even dancers and drummers, has to pay to get into the pow wow.

Having been both a participant and an organizer of various pow wows for the last twenty years, I'm a little disillusioned by all the changes. Our pow wows long ago were sponsored entirely by individuals and everyone came because of the social aspects. Being together with family and friends was the emphasis. In today's times, attendance at pow wows is based on "Who's the host drum?" "Who's the MC?" "How much is the prize money?" "Is there a special contest for this or that category?" Pow wows are rated on how many drum groups attended, how many dancers registered, and so on. Quantity takes precedence over quality.

Now I'll admit that things can't always stay the same, and some changes are for the better. But there has to be a medium between tradition and outright greed. For example, I've seen dance contestants cheating. They do this by having other people wear their outfit and contestant number, lying to the pow wow committee about why they were late for grand entry or missed a contest round, and lying about their age and registering in categories for which they weren't eligible. This dishonest behavior is all the more outrageous when it is children doing it with the knowledge of their parents.

Is winning the money so important that a person has to cheat? Is taking part in the pow wow a chore and not a joy?

My children have been dancing since they were infants. They usually compete in contests, and sometimes they place. I always remind them that they need to be thankful that they can dance, that they are well enough to be attending the pow wow, and that they should be proud to be carrying on a part of their culture and traditions. All of this is more important than winning any contest for any amount of money.

At some of the mega pow wows, people have to show a Tribal ID and a Social Security card to register in the contests. This sounds extreme, but it's an attempt to curtail the improprieties described above. Unfortunately, it just bears out how far from tradition the pow wow may have come.

As a child, my parents taught me that an Indian's word was truthful and as an Indian person, I needed to live up to that standard. Ask yourself if you value honesty and truthfulness in the tradition of your ancestors, and if you have taught this to your children. (Quequesah 2002)

....

More Reflections from the Pow wow Trail

I breathe in the fresh smell of grass and dirt as I drive into the pow wow grounds. Ah! It feels good to be here! I look at the sunset and see the same colors of the setting sun in the grand entry as I watch the dancers enter the dance arena. I look around and see them dancing. I see them singing at the drum. I see them in the audience. Who do I see? Pow wow bums! Then I smell food in the air. Realizing I haven't eaten yet, I wonder [sic] over to a nearby stand.

Women are standing there in their aprons smelling like frybread and their hands covered in dough. Of course, a real pow wow bum doesn't always get the pleasure of frybread and Pepsi or mutton stew or bannock burger. We usually get stuck with bologna sandwiches and water. Our mouths water when we hear the announcer mention that a family is putting on a feed during supper break! All the pow wow bums run over and get some pow wow stew, bread, potatoes, and watermelon. You don't need Slim Fast to lose weight. You just need to go on the pow wow trail and get on the pow wow diet! You will surely lose more than enough weight!

After finishing some stew and frybread, I walk back to my car to set up my tent. While walking back, I look around and see all the pow wow vans and rez rides. Many of which got to the pow wow just somehow . . . on luck. Going from one pow wow to the next saying "I hope it makes it!" On several rides I see a tarp on top of them, carrying Indian suitcases—garbage bags! We also may find pow wow bums with those old faithful suitcases from years and years of pow wow trails. It looks like it came from Salvation Army or something. It's something Salvation Army wouldn't even accept as a donation!

It's all duct-taped up! Somehow you just can't get yourself to buy a new suitcase, that trusty old thing has brought you many memories. It held all those snagging clothes and black socks that were once white!

I set up my tent. I wish I could have placed at the last pow wow so I could be like one of those rich pow wow bums and get a hotel room. They've got the luxury of not having to go to the bathroom in a portable. Or not having to wait in line for over an hour to take a shower. They don't have to hear teenagers all hours of the night. Yep, those rich pow wow bums don't have to wake up to the hot sun and hear babies crying.

But sleeping on the hard ground, hearing the sounds of laughter and babies crying all hours of the night is not so bad . . . if you're a tipi creeper! You love whispering into the ear of your snag, "come stay at my tipi tonight." Especially them singers. They don't whisper it. They sing it. Make it into a round dance song. Them tipi creepers sometimes wake up the next morning, take off to the shower and get back just in time to braid their hair and slap on their outfit and run off to grand entry. Usually, they wake up just in time to slap on their outfits and go through grand entry with bushy braids and hickies!

The afternoon grand entry is always hot and sweaty. But it's worth it. It's more than earning points. After hearing those pow wow jams I always just let go and start to get that feeling. I can't explain it. It's a feeling of true happiness. Perhaps something more. When I'm out dancing, I dance not only for myself. I dance for the elders. The ones wrapped in blankets when it starts to get dark. The ones that sit in the front row wishing their legs had strength to dance.

The sun is rising. The air is getting warm. I breathe in the fresh air as I drive out of the pow wow ground. Another pow wow come and gone . . . (Smith 2002)

The first article clearly critiques competition and competition pow-wows through an appeal to tradition, as expressed through the author's own experience of history, beginning with the story of her childhood, a time when there were no competition powwows. Competition is thus explicitly marked as nontraditional. With competition came the formalized aspects of powwow procedures: Grand Entry, the "points system," exhibitions, and "spot checks."[18] These formalized aspects led to other "nontraditional" behaviors such as cheating, lying, greed, and the harmful corruption of children. The author also asserts that the emphasis on competition has led to the devaluation of important social aspects of powwow, "being together with family and friends." Further, "value and tradition" are claimed as inherently "Indian" as expressed through the "tradition of . . . ancestors." The rhetorical force of this argument is generated through a discourse of tradition that links authentic (often pan-tribal) Indian values (like honesty and concern for the moral fiber of children) to historical truths ("in my youth it was not done this way").[19]

The author of the second reflection article eschews a diachronic description of powwows for a synchronic account. In this romantic celebration of modern competition powwow culture, many of the troubling hardships of traveling the powwow trail are glorified, including "rez rides" (beat-up, old cars), "Indian suitcases" (garbage bags or old cases held together with duct tape), and poverty (the inability to buy food or stay in a hotel), as well as portable toilets, the hot sun, and sleep deprivation. However, this author frames competitions and competition powwows as "more than just earning points" and, thus, more than just about earning money. Here the competition powwow is a context within which other, more worthwhile activities can be pursued, such as "snagging" (courtship) and the euphoria of dancing for oneself and one's elders. In both articles, powwows are a site within which different ideas about what it is to be (and behave) like an "Indian" are worked out; each one constructs a "practical essentialism" (Herzfeld 1997) about Indian identity as expressed through behavior on the powwow grounds.[20] In designating powwows as either competition (and thus contemporary) or traditional, and associating particular traditional and contemporary behaviors and ideologies with each of the two events, powwow participants negotiate and work through some of the complications and contradictions of modern Native American life, shaping images of authentic Native "self" and non-Native "other."

Because of the ambivalence surrounding the place of competition in the larger powwow community and the worry that participation in competition powwows can potentially lead one to "un-Indian" behaviors, participation in *traditional* powwows is thought to be an essential part of singing and dancing. For example, when drum groups participate *only* in competition events at the expense of traditional powwows, their behavior is often regarded as problematic, as the following interview excerpts indicate:

> In our schedule I always try to put in some traditional powwows. Because, you know, out there [on the powwow trail], there's a couple of years we hardly went to traditional powwows. And we heard back. People used to say, "Why isn't Northern Wind coming to our powwows? Are we too small for them now or do they think they're too good for us now?" We always heard stuff like that. It always kind of bothered me because we don't even *think* like that. So you know, we try and always fit in traditional powwows in our schedule. (Gabe Desrosiers interview, May 2000)

> John Menenick (Yakama, mentor for the Red Tail Singers, champion Traditional dancer, and father of D. J. Menenick): What I feel, too, is that you go to the bigger powwows but you also have to go back to the smaller powwows.
>
> D. J. Menenick (leader and lead singer for the Red Tail Singers): One week we'll be at Gathering [of Nations] and the next week we'll skip a big powwow and go to a one-night powwow in Spokane [and] sing for fun.
>
> JM: We like to keep our heads down . . . small . . .
>
> DJM: Try not to get a big head . . .
>
> JM: And I try to bring them [the group] back [down to earth]. Because powwows we go to that's just [for] fun times, we have a lot of fun there. At the big competition powwows, everyone's staring daggers at you. And it's not [*pauses*] too fun anymore. But we go to a small powwow, everybody's laughing and having a good time and that's what the boys like . . . (Red Tail Singers interview, March 2000)

The history of Native people, the history of it [powwow] is for everybody to feel good around the drum, you know. And there's a lot of culture that's not—maybe not disappearing, but not wanting to be used, in a way. . . . That's why they had drums in the middle a long time ago [the middle of the dance arena, which is still a common practice at traditional powwows in the Lake of the Woods area where Mr. White is from]. You'll dance around the drum—dance around. Nowadays [at competition powwows] you see them in the side corner. I don't know what it means—that the respect's not there, I don't know. You know, it's just the way it is. I know back home though, all the powwows, they have all the drums are in the middle, drums in the center. That's traditionally the way it is. Maybe it's, today, so people can see, because more or less it's like a show now. You know, so people come. I mean it's enjoyable, everybody's kind of healed and happy. And that's why they talk about no creation of animosity when you have powwows. Because [at competition powwows] there's one champion coming out—one category. And there's about forty of them [competing dancers], so what do you do? Same thing with the singing contest, you know, there's forty of them [drum groups competing] and there's only—one coming out [winning]. So that's why they try to preach a lot of this respect—not to have animosity. You don't try to think, "I'm competing with the other guy." I'm *not* competing with the other guy. I'm only trying to sing the way I can sing, the way we can do our best. You know, just try to make people happy. (Andy White interview, September 1999)

Here, both Gabe and the members of the Red Tail Singers point to a kind of ethical self-policing that goes on within the powwow circuit. Singing groups that participate only in competitions may be accused of being conceited, self-important, and greedy. John and D. J. insist that singers need to "keep their heads down." Singing at traditional powwows is a way to ensure that one stays modest. By singing at smaller, traditional powwows one does not become too ensnared in the world of competition, where "people are staring daggers at you." Thus, participation in competition powwows brings with it the danger of conceit and the possibility of tribal or intertribal division and animosity. I have often heard these comments echoed in discussions about the importance of being "humble," dancing and singing not for oneself but for others: one's children, elders, and community. These excerpts also speak to the suspicion that groups that sing only at competitions sing only for financial gain, something considered to be a serious breach of moral conduct. At traditional powwows you sing for "fun" and not for the money that can be earned through competition. Many singers have commented to me about the ethical duty of singing. As a singer, one's traditional social role is to sing for the people and be of service to the community. Andy White's comments go further, suggesting that traditional powwows are repositories of local (often tribally defined) culture and tradition, both of which are framed as "resources" that are not used at competition powwows. For example, at traditional powwows, drums are treated as sacred objects, and thus given a place of honor at the center of the dance arena. At many competition powwows on the northern Plains, this traditional practice is abandoned.

Sacred and Secular Spaces

Mike Esquash once described the various ceremonies in which he and his family (and I) took part as existing on a continuum of sacred to secular practices. Rituals like Yuwipi and Shaking Tent gatherings were described by Mike as very "high" ceremonies and were thus located toward the more sacred (and thus more "powerful") end of the spectrum. Sweat lodge ceremonies were described as "not quite as high," meaning not quite as sacred. Powwows were positioned toward the "secular" end of the continuum with traditional powwows considered to be "more sacred" than competition events. Understanding ceremonies, and ritual actions within ceremonies, on such a continuum helps us to understand the various differences in structure, behaviors, and meaning of these powwows. For Mike, ideologies of the sacred and secular were constituted in the discourses of tradition, culture, and essentialized ideas of Native and non-Native difference. Sacredness is, in some ways, an indexical *expression* of authentic, traditional, Native identity. The relative sacredness of traditional powwows (compared to competition events) is not necessarily determined by the presence or absence of specifically designated "sacred" events. As we saw in our ethnographic examples, one is likely to find sacred practices like feather pickup ceremonies, the blessing of drums with tobacco, and the blowing of eagle-bone whistles at both traditional and competition powwows. Just as singers and dancers understand their participation in traditional powwows to be an ethical duty, so, too, is it necessary for *all* powwows to adhere to some traditional, ceremonial, and uniquely Indian practices. The legitimacy of competition powwows as an authentically Native practice is determined in part by the inclusion of these sacred elements. The "modernity" of competition powwows must be tempered through adherence to more traditional Indian practices and beliefs, even if these practices and beliefs are known to have been significantly altered by intertribal interaction (Andy White's story about the use of eagle whistles) or, in some cases, are practices unique to intertribal powwows (feather pickups).

One overt way in which sacred and secular spaces and moments are marked is through the level of public access. In the general flow of Native life, sacred events like sun dances or Yuwipi ceremonies are typically less open to public access and public interpretation (by non-Natives or even, in some cases, noncommunity members). Traditional powwows are characterized by a high degree of locally defined behaviors (songs and dances) and interpretations. As such, at these events there is a greater delineation between locals and visitors (hosts and guests). Participation in traditional powwows by singers, dancers, and community members is thought to be an expression of local identity as well as an ethical imperative, as it symbolizes one's knowledge and commitment to traditional Indian values (locally or tribally defined). Competition powwows, in contrast, are more *intertribal* spaces where meanings are constructed and contested jointly through the multiple interpretations of various participants. The formalization of schedules, social roles, and appropriate social behaviors also define the parameters of competition and traditional powwows. Traditional powwows do not adhere to strict scheduling and are often characterized by a fluidity of social roles for participants. Singers jump from drum to drum and dancers are free to dance without obligation to judges or committees. Competition powwows feature more formalized schedules of events and require a particular code of conduct for singers and dancers.

Clyde Ellis rightly points out that "dance and song are bound up in the construction of social memory, and so, in relationships that mold and influence ritual, economic, and cultural power. Thus, dance occupies an important and sometimes bitterly contested place in many communities" (2001, 356). The construction of social memory also plays a key role in distinguishing these two powwow types. Traditional powwows are understood to be the repository of local, tribal, and thus more traditional practices and ideologies. Many of the practices of competition powwows are thought to lie outside of traditional ceremonial and belief systems, at best a "reinterpretation" or "modernization" of tradition. As such, competition powwows exist as a particularly fertile context within which pan-tribal and intertribal ideologies are ascribed to particular songs and dances. Competition powwows, by their very nature, encourage a greater degree of emphasis on pan-tribal and intertribal ideologies. These powwows feature a much greater degree of intertribal participation and as such have become fertile sites for the negotiation of standardized intertribally agreed upon behaviors and meanings—intertribally shared cultural norms that become widespread and shared among many tribal communities.

The comparison of these two powwows highlights how modern Indian identity is variably constructed in different powwow contexts. Central to the experience of powwows for participants is the discourse of tradition, deployed in various contexts to construct unique and specific understandings of Native American history, culture, and identity. The binary opposition of competition (contemporary) and traditional powwows structures not only the organization of powwow events into two paradigmatic types, but also structures the experience of powwows for participants. The twin discourses of modernity and tradition shape powwow experiences for participants in both more deeply structural (the division of powwows into contemporary and traditional) and contingent (invoking traditional practices at various points at both traditional and contemporary powwows) ways. These discourses have led to a wide-ranging discussion among Native American participants in powwow culture as to the value and potential dangers of competition powwows, events that stray further and further from what are considered to be the authentic Native American values and practices that are articulated to and through traditional powwows.

CHAPTER 2

Powwow Songs

Aesthetics and

Performance Practice

CS: What's the ideal sound of the drum?
Shonto Pete: One beat, one voice.
D. J. Menenick: One *people*, one voice.
—RED TAIL SINGERS interview (March 2000)

In this chapter I introduce some of the central elements of Northern-style singing as it exists in and through competition powwows. In doing so I investigate how aesthetic values are linked to social ethics, and how both the ethics and aesthetics of singing are constantly being developed within the context of competition. Competition powwows are linked to the development of the Aboriginal recording industry in many ways. Participation in singing competitions has not only served to develop a more standardized set of aesthetic preferences for singers and dancers—aesthetic values that become elements of a shared intertribal ideology as expressed on the powwow grounds—but has also served to delineate a stylistic universe for powwow recordings. Competition singing styles, repertoire, compositional styles, and performance practices all play important roles in the kinds of songs and the kinds of performances that become recorded and distributed by the recording industry. Perhaps most importantly, drum groups that regularly participate in singing contests are those most likely to enter the recording studio, since creating and selling recordings have become regular parts of the process of professionalization demanded by singing competitions at competition powwows.

Theory, Language, and Aesthetics

When I first began formally interviewing singers during the early stages of my research, I would often ask them directly: "What do you think makes a good singer?" or "What distinguishes a good singer from a bad singer?" While answers varied, they reflected a common theme:

> *Andy White* (Ojibwa, leader and drumkeeper for the Whitefish Bay Singers): Every singer that can take a drumstick and start singing is a good singer. He's a good, champion singer. It doesn't matter what you see at a singing contest. (Andy White interview, September 1999)

> *John Morris* (Ojibwa, leader of the Eyabay Singers): What makes a good singer? Everybody's a good singer as long as they're trying to sing, you know. Yeah, it's not—it's not that you're the biggest, loudest or the highest or anything like that. But as long as you're doing what you're supposed to be doing, and that's making them dance, then you're a good singer. Even the smallest drum group, you know, just a few guys sitting there, you know, as long as they're trying their best, they're good singers to us. (John Morris interview, October 1999)

> *Mike Esquash* (Ojibwa, leader and lead singer of the Spirit Sands Singers): Putting out, trying their best. And they—as long as you see people trying hard, and having a good time at it, you know. . . . You got to have some seriousness, but not totally. Too serious will kill it right away. It's gotta be fun, you know. (Mike Esquash interview, September 1999)

These kinds of comments are in keeping with what I came to characterize as the "party line" of powwow singers. At the time of these particular formal interviews I was a curiosity to these singers, an inquisitive white academic who had very little social standing on the powwow grounds or in the larger social world of powwows. But these comments also reflect a central aspect of the rhetoric found on the powwow grounds. Making public, critical comments about another group or individual singer is not generally accepted as part of the discursive practices of powwow participants. This refusal to make comments critical of others reflects the desire to keep powwows friendly and noncompetitive. It is also in keeping with how drum groups are created and maintained.

However, as singers came to know me (and thus became less suspicious of me), it became apparent that, despite the desire to minimize competitive and disparaging comments, critical evaluation of different drum groups and singers goes on all the time. This is especially true at competition powwows where singers are constantly circling the arena and standing around listening to other groups as they perform, often with recording device in hand. This activity is now a matter of routine for singers who dedicate themselves to success on the competition powwow circuit. The rise in popularity and the proliferation of competition powwows have combined to create a new form of verbal discourse among powwow participants, a more systematic attempt to express the technical and aesthetic principles of powwow musical style. Singing contests at competition powwows have had the effect of formalizing many aspects of Northern-style singing. This is not to say that all drums are starting to sound the same. Regional and personal stylistic variations continue to develop; indeed, competition has in some cases fostered a higher degree of stylistic experimentation, as drum groups experiment with novel approaches to form, drumbeat patterns, and melodic shape, all in an attempt to grab the ear of judges with something new (Desrosiers and Scales 2012). However, what has become more standardized is the *evaluation* of these stylistic developments.

The discussion of powwow performance aesthetics presented here is informed to a large degree by the aesthetic principles developed on the Northern competition powwow trail. The principles discussed represent an amalgam of these formalized aesthetic criteria based on formal and informal discussions with a number of singers regarding the business of singing. Many of the singers and drum groups I interviewed, recorded, or otherwise interacted with consisted of young men between the ages of eighteen and forty, who have grown up learning to sing in the context of competition powwows and who have thus absorbed those aesthetic values. Almost all of the singers I interviewed or interacted with were male, a reflection of the gendered nature of singing. Most powwow participants consider powwow singing to be a male domain, and while women may join a song at certain points and sing an octave above the main melody, as "harmonizers," it is rare indeed to find a woman sitting at the drum at a competition powwow (Hatton 1986). Since singers (and sometimes male dancers) almost always serve as judges for singing competitions, these aesthetic criteria are thus the result of exclusively male aesthetic preferences. This discussion also represents my own synthesis of aesthetic values learned through informal conversations with musicians as well as through my own experiences as a singer. These observations are mixed with numerous quotes and interview excerpts with a number of powwow musicians. The formal interview setting is not an accurate representation of how musicians typically talk to each other about singing and musical performance. However, these conversations did produce a higher degree of analytic specificity than I usually encountered during informal conversations, which I rarely recorded.

Musicians and participants, through a mixture of verbal and nonverbal practices, express aesthetic evaluations and principles of powwow performances. Tara Browner, in discussing the relative lack of technical terms for, or discussions of, powwow musical performance, has suggested that powwow musicians employ an "unconscious theory," a kind of internal, often nonverbalized aesthetic knowledge that informs their practices and musical decisions (2002, 10). And she is certainly correct in pointing out that there is a dearth of specialized technical language (in English) employed to talk about powwow music.[1] Time and again I was confounded in my attempts to get singers to talk about structural components of song form in technical terms. However, I think the idea of an unconscious theory serves, in the end, to muddy the waters.

The problem is twofold. First, "theory" is a unique kind of discourse that categorically implies symbolic mediation (i.e., language); it is a meta-discourse that attempts to mediate between musical experiences and linguistic representations of those experiences.[2] One is certainly able to "know" something musically without being able to articulate it linguistically, and distinguishing between these two different ways of knowing is important for any attempt at understanding the specificity of music as a semiotic system (see Feld 1984; Nettl 2005, 44–51; Seeger 1977; Turino 1999). If it is unspoken—that is, not linguistically mediated and not existing in the realm of symbolic discourse—then it is not a theory but something else, some other kind of semiotic system at work. Theoretical knowledge is categorically symbolic (i.e., linguistic) and thus unconscious theory strikes me as a contradiction in terms.[3] If you can't talk about it, you can't theorize about it. Second, the term "unconscious theory" implies that these musicians are somehow guided by aesthetic and musical principles of which they have no "conscious" awareness, a supposition that appears to be contradicted by the fact that musicians often do speak about aesthetic aspects of musical performance; they're just using a different kind of poetics. In categorizing and evaluating different aspects of performance practice, powwow musicians often rely on *analogy*.

In August 2001 I traveled to the Shakopee Mdewakanton Indian reservation in Shakopee, Minnesota, for the community's annual summer powwow. I had been asked by Arbor Records to engineer a recording of Bear Creek, an Ojibwa drum group from Sault Sainte Marie, Ontario, who were quickly earning a reputation on the powwow trail as a very good, young, up-and-coming group. This would be their first CD. Saturday was a bust, both for recording and for the powwow in general, since most of the afternoon's dancing was canceled due to rain. Late Saturday night we were all back in the hotel room after the powwow. Members of the group had flocked to the late-night buffet, then hung out in the casino. Nobody won. We were smoking, not really ready to sleep yet. There was a nondescript science fiction movie on the TV. One of the singers was pacing the room. He started singing the Side-step song the group had tried unsuccessfully to record a few hours earlier, after the powwow had ended. Because of the rain we hadn't gotten much recording done and we wanted to get one more song "in the can." It turned out to be a mistake. It was already well past midnight when we finally finished. Immediately after, members of the group chuckled to themselves and shook their heads. The performance was lifeless and uninspired. It had been a long and frustrating day.

Now in the hotel room a singer was pacing the room and singing, tapping the beat out on his leg. "Man, that Side-step . . . what's wrong with that song?! It's a hard song to lead [sing a lead]. I hear the lead in my head but when I start to sing it the beat gets turned around." He was referring to the reversing of the strong and weak beats of the triple meter. The weak beat should feel like a pick-up to the strong beat, which is ostensibly the downbeat of the measure. He began tapping again and started singing. "See what I mean," he continued. "We turn it around when we start singing. We shouldn't use that song on the CD. That's not a BC [Bear Creek] song. That sounds like Whitefish Bay or Northern Wind or somethin'. It ain't BC!"

This singer's brief analysis and evaluation of his group's (and his own) performance is fairly typical, and exemplifies how powwow singers talk about and evaluate musical style and musical performance. Through analogy to other individual and group singing styles, musicians mark the various stylistic subtleties of composition and performance. For example, in speaking about different types of vibrato, instead of having specific technical terms for them, singers will make comments such as, "We sing more like High Noon," or "They sing like Bear Creek," categorizing different vibrato types according to the singers and groups who use them.[4]

This singer's comments also direct our attention to the importance of individual and unique singing styles for powwow singers. Singers acknowledge differences in singing styles (for individuals and drum groups) at both tribal and regional levels. Several scholars of powwow music have noted large-scale regional differences in singing styles. For example, William Powers emphasized differences in Northern and Southern powwow circuits, stating, "The essential Southern Plains style, performed at intertribal functions, is divided into Fancy Dancing and Straight Dancing. These styles are regional in nature: Fancy Dancing is primarily associated with western Oklahoma and Straight Dancing with northern Oklahoma. On the Northern Plains are four regional styles: (1) North Dakota, (2) Blackfeet, (3) Crow, and (4) South Dakota. . . . Style is differentiated not on the basis of song or dance structure but on the interrelationships between music, dance, and, importantly, related material culture" (1990, 25).

Powers is unclear as to whether he or his informants had delineated these regional styles, but these categorizations resonate with my own observations and I think most powwow people would also agree with his assessment. Unfortunately, Powers fails to elaborate further on what *specific* style features are salient to Native singers and dancers in differentiating these various styles.

Tara Browner (2002) makes a similar argument for a regional understanding of powwow music and dance styles, and she structures her entire monograph by delineating differences in styles and meanings between Anishinaabeg (Ojibwa) and Lakota powwow practices. She also notes differences in vocal and drumming cadential patterns between Northern and Southern styles and details variants that exist between different northern Plains groups (e.g., Lakota vs. Cree vs. Ojibwa). These regional distinctions were also noted by many of the singers I spoke with:

CS: So different drum groups have different singing styles. Do they have different drumming styles too?

ME: I think some—some groups have different styles of drumming. There's more of a choppy slow beat. More of a bouncy tune. Then you have some groups that sing quick tempoed a lot of the time. The tempo is pretty quick. They start off quick and they end quick. Some are just slow and just choppy kinda . . . [*pause*] bounce along. Mellow songs. Yeah there are some groups that have different styles. Like Northern and Southern, big difference there. Drumming and singing. There are some groups, even up north [that have] . . . different styles. (Mike Esquash interview, September 1999)

A unique, recognizable style of singing and song making is highly valued among powwow musicians. Musicians identify, evaluate, and categorize drum groups not only through recognition of particular songs, but by general style features, some of which are regional, or tribal, and some of which are individual. Regional styles are distinguished by features such as tessitura (how high a group will sing), the amount and depth of vocal vibrato, the presence of particular native language texts, and specialization of song genres. For example, Cree drums are known for singing with an extremely high tessitura and for specializing in Round dance songs performed on hand drums and on the big drum. By comparison, Ojibwa groups often have a slightly lower tessitura and are known for particularly good renditions of Jingle Dress songs, especially Side-step songs. More generally, Canadian drums are known for excellent renditions of Chicken dance songs, while Oklahoma drums are the recognized champions of Fancy dance songs.

On an individual basis, drums may also be known for particular song categories. The Northern Wind Singers and Whitefish Bay Singers are both from the Lake of the Woods area in Northwestern Ontario, widely thought to be the home and birthplace of the Jingle Dress dance. As such, both groups are regarded as experts at singing Jingle Dress songs. The Bear Creek singer's lament regarding his own group's Jingle Dress song was an expression of both the association between Jingle Dress songs and Lake of the Woods drum groups, and the fact that some of the more subtle compositional and performative elements of the song (such as melodic shape and the relationship between the vocal rhythm and the drumbeat) were also too reminiscent of other singing groups. Again, these kinds of evaluations rarely make use of any special language but instead invoke the names of the groups to indicate a particular stylistic feature or constellation of features.

On the competition powwow trail, participants value recognizably unique singing styles, and it is generally understood that in order to be successful a drum group must develop its own sound. For instance, the Ojibwa drum group Eyabay from Red Lake, Minnesota, has consistently been one of the most popular on the Northern circuit, from the mid-1990s to the present. As a result many young singers and drum groups have been heavily influenced by their particular singing style, marked by a high, screaming, extremely aggressive vocal style and their interesting, technically difficult vocal melodies. However, I have heard some drum groups criticized for sounding "too much like Eyabay," and these groups are often judged as needing more time to develop their own unique style.

Singing Competitions

You know, we were told, so many times [by our elders] that, you know, singing contests are not proper. Because these songs—these songs, that gathering, is to make you feel good. It's to make you happy. To be healed, you know. And that's what these powwow songs are all about. And I think, I myself as an individual, I don't go for these contests. But my boys, the guys I sing with, the guys I'm talking to today, are the ones that wanted to compete. If I had my way, I would tell them, "We're not going to compete. We're just going to sing for the people." You know, and make them feel good. That's the way it should be. And the singing contest, it's something that this younger generation are getting into.
—ANDY WHITE interview (September 1999)

Here, Andy White is expressing a sentiment that is repeated often by pow-wow people. Like many older singers, he is expressing concern and skepticism for the practice of singing competitions at competition powwows. He also rightly points out that these competitions are the domain of the "younger generation."

Singing contests at competition powwows have had the effect of formalizing and concretizing many aspects of Northern-style singing. Stephen Blum (1972, 5) has suggested that musical style itself resides not in a set of musical practices, nor in a set of linguistic practices (a discourse) but at their intersection. The kinds of linguistic mediations that Feld (1984) has named "interpretive moves" attempt to symbolically locate a musical experience within a particular discourse of style. Musical experiences (listening or performing) may happen within the *context* of symbolic discourse, but are not themselves part of that discourse because of the status of language and music as different semiotic modes. But musical styles are forged in the dialectic of these two modes, with groups performing music and evaluating musical performances and musical experiences through language. This dialectic plays out endlessly at competition powwows.

The judging of singing competitions goes on all weekend long. At these powwows, singers are judged by their peers—other singers and dancers chosen by the head singing judge—although, as a rule, one is disqualified from judging if they are related to any of the competitors. Typically, groups are judged on the performance of at least one intertribal song and one dance competition song per day. Each day new judges are selected, and sometimes for each round of judging. For any one contest round, three to five judges participate. Thus, at the end of the weekend a group's final score will be the result of the evaluation of between ten and twenty different judges. For every round of competition, the group of judges will travel from drum to drum (generally following the drum order), clipboard in hand, and observe the performances. Scores are written down on a scoring sheet and submitted to the head judge. Judging standards and criteria vary from powwow to powwow and according to the dispositions of the head judges. There are typically a fixed number of general criteria, often organized into between four and six categories, each of which is graded on a numeric scale (e.g., 1 through 5 or 10 through 100 in increments of 10). These categories represent a fascinating mix of aesthetic preferences that address issues of musical ability, style, and appropriate behavior and decorum. It should also be noted that often the stylistic traits that are judged concern not large-scale aspects of compositional style and form, but subtleties of performance practice. Judging criteria instead evaluate significant elements of style that are difficult to notate but that become essential in establishing a drum group's unique and personal performance style.

Judging criteria for competition powwows may include any number of the following items. This list is not presented as comprehensive but simply presents a number of judging criteria that appeared regularly on judging sheets at competition powwows that I witnessed or participated in between the summers of 1998 and 2006.

Unity of drumbeat (all drummers beating the drum in clear unison).

ME: I think the goal of the singing group is to sound together. Everybody's voice matches.

CS: Oh yeah, so blending is good?

ME: Blending. And then the rhythm of the beat is good and the beat is on time. Everybody's beating the same. Yeah, everybody at exactly the same time. You got ten guys with ten sticks and they've got to all hit the drum at the same time. They go off beat, you can hear it, eh. It's like Mother Earth's heart, they say. That's what it represents. You know, it's like our own hearts. If it skips a beat, you're gonna feel that. So it's always in rhythm, in time. And that's what we try to do is keep in time. I notice when we go—like listen to a Southern drum, they have it. You stand close to them you can kind of feel that heart . . . that beat on your chest and stuff. And the power. I like that power, that blast. (Mike Esquash interview, September 1999)

Typically, judges like to see all members of the group drumming and all drummers striking the drum toward the center of the drum with equal force. Often, less experienced singers will strike the drum on the rim or closer to the rim (as I was often encouraged to do) because it is less audible. Judges, usually singers themselves, are aware of this practice and when judging they may look for it and deduct points if they see any member of the drum trying to "hide" his drumbeat on the rim. It is also common to see judges tapping along to the beat of the drum with their pen on their clipboard. This kinesthetic mimesis allows judges to measure the steadiness of the tempo (by experiencing the tempo physically through participation) and also expresses an attempt to find the "center of the beat." The aesthetic ideal is for all the drummers to sound "as one."

Equal participation by all members of the drum group. Often judges can be seen performing a "head count" when evaluating a drum group performance. When a drum group initially registers for a competition at the beginning of a powwow they must list all the performers who will be singing that weekend. The number of singers registered becomes the set number of drum members that *must* sing every time the group is being judged. Points are deducted if a group performs with any singers missing; similarly, having too many singers (more than they initially registered) may disqualify a drum from the competition or at least that round of judging. This criterion is set in place to limit the now common activity of "drum hopping" and is also an expression of the value placed on singers and drum groups who take the responsibility of singing seriously.

The number of members within a drum group who can "sing lead"—the ability to sing the opening phrase of a verse (see below)—is also a consideration. Groups with many lead singers are awarded more points than those who rely on only one or possibly two singers to perform all the leads. The degree to which a large number of lead singers are valued varies from powwow to powwow. In my experience, this often seems to be an important factor at large, urban competition powwows. At reserve competition powwows it appears less often as a judging category as groups are simply judged on how they sound in performance. The concern with the number of lead singers may also stem from the rather recent phenomenon of "stacking" a group for a particular competition event. Stacked drum groups are those that feature a number of lead singers who are not regular members of that drum but are singing with the group for a particular weekend, to give the group an added advantage in the competition.

Clarity, quality, power of singing voice, and blend of vocals.

CS: So, power is important?

ME: Yeah, very important. It wakes you up from . . . being bored, whatever. It gets you up there, kinda "Hey." It gets you excited, eh. Good songs are like that. A lot of Northern styles are like that too, eh. Like, I like Eyabay. They sing deadly, man. Those guys are pros.

CS: What's good about their singing?

ME: They got deadly songs. The power, the power. I see those guys, I watch them sing. Every song I see them pushing more. So they are *in* that song, they are *giving*. And that's good. There's nothing like that at all. It's *real* singing; they're real singers. That's what I like. A group, I think, has gotta sound . . . like one person. And that's one focus, that everyone should sound the same. Same level, same tune. (Mike Esquash interview, September 1999)

CS: So, when you're singing together what kind of sound do you try to get. Do you try to have all the voices blended or do you have . . . What's the sound of a good powwow group?

D. J. Menenick: A good powwow group? Drumbeat, singing, style, togetherness.

CS: So, singing together in unison so that all the voices are blending?

Shonto Pete: Combining all the bass and the highs and the medium and combining all of that.

DJM: That way people can hear our style and actually *feel* the songs.

SP: You try to make it sound like just one voice, one voice, everyone sounds—you can't pick all the singers. It's just one voice and one style too. That style's not going to match any other style. It's going to have its own style. Twelve guys all trying to sing one thing.

CS: So it's that particular blend of voices that makes a particular style for a drum group? What their blending sounds like when they sing together?

SP: Yeah, when you hit that blend, you can feel it . . .

DJM: I don't know if you've ever noticed or not, but if you ever think about it, the best drum groups are family groups.

CS: And you think that's because they just sing together all the time?

DJM: Cuz they're always around each other all the time.

CS: So they blend easier?

DJM: Yeah.

CS: So what do you think makes a good sounding voice?

DJM: Practicing!

CS: But what's the *sound* of a good voice?

DJM: What's the sound?

[*Choosing demonstration over analysis, Shonto Pete starts singing, playfully offering his own singing voice as an ideal type. Everyone laughs uproariously.*]

DJM: [*laughing*] High, clear, all the turns [melodic contours], all the accents, everything. (Red Tail Singers interview, March 2000)

Aesthetic preferences regarding ideal voice production vary widely among powwow musicians and frequently depend on a host of factors including age, tribal affiliation, geographic region, and personal taste. At competition powwows, however, there does seem to be some degree of agreement regarding some elements of vocal production. "High," "clear," and "powerful" were adjectives often employed when describing ideal vocal production. High, clear voices are a hallmark of the Northern style of singing and as such, the use of these terms is not surprising. If a singer's (especially a lead singer's) voice cracks or falters during a performance that is being judged, points are generally deducted. Sometimes however, less than smooth vocal performances can be overlooked if the group is singing with exceptional power (meaning both volume and intensity). These preferences are repeatedly demonstrated when singers list groups who are considered by them to be the top performing drum groups on the Northern circuit: Eyabay, Northern Cree, Blacklodge, Blackstone,

Bear Creek, and Midnite Express. All of these groups, who consistently win or place in singing competitions, are known for their high and powerful singing styles. Groups may also be known for either strong command of the upper range of their vocals (usually exhibited during the beginning phrases of a verse) or lower range (exhibited during the last phrases of a verse) of their vocals. Having control and power at both ends of the vocal spectrum is considered ideal.

Respect for the drum.

ME: You have to take care of a drum. A drum is very important. Not anyone can just, you know, have a drum. It takes a lot of work. You can't always be perfect, but you try to do the best you can.

CS: Is that why the cleanliness of the drum area is important?

ME: Yeah, it's very important. Respect for the drum, you know. You take care of the drum. It's alive. Everything we have is alive, you know. That drum—what I was taught is you take care of that drum, that drum will take care of you. And I believe that. It's really—again it goes back to the spiritual side. Everything, I think pretty much—a lot with singing is a very spiritual thing; as well as a social thing. It's a good time but it [*pause*] . . . it means a lot, eh. You know, the connection there. (Mike Esquash interview, September 1999)

This judging criterion appears with remarkable consistency, perhaps an indication that drum group professionalization must still incorporate what are deemed to be some of the "traditional" values associated with singing. Cleanliness of the drum area is something taken quite seriously by most singers. Singers generally agree that good vocal performances stem directly from the power of the drum. It is considered disrespectful to the drum to have refuse or clutter nearby, and while the drum area might become cluttered between performances with cigarette packages, drum sticks and drum stick bags, cans of coke, and bottles of water (as singers will often turn around the folding chairs to watch the powwow, eat supper, or sit and smoke and drink coffee), when their turn comes to sing, the drum area is quickly cleaned and tidied.

Dancer participation and reaction.

ME: One thing important is you have to watch the dancers, how they are reacting to your beat. If it's too slow of a beat and they're kind of just walking along or pacing, you know. And if you up your tempo a bit, you up your song, you know, you might be able to catch them and start, you know—"hey"—they'll start bouncing along and having a good time. It's just . . . you have to watch as a singer.

CS: Is that your job?

ME: Yeah I watch, I really watch how they're doing it. I try my best to see, to judge. I listen. When we sing a song, I'll listen to a couple of drums ahead of us [before their turn in the drum order]. One or two away from us. I'll see how they're singing, what kind of style they're singing, watch the dancers. And if it doesn't work for the dancers—how fast the tempo is, whatever—I'll switch. I'll go fast or I'll go slower or I'll try different things. It's for the dancers. That's what it's for. (Mike Esquash interview, September 1999)

The way in which dancers respond is often thought by judges to indicate the success of a singing performance. Thus when judging an intertribal song, regardless of what a particular judge may think of the style or song the group is performing, it is hard to argue with success (measured by dancer participation). Different singers I interviewed supported Mike's assertion that a good drum group leader will always gauge the response of the dancers. However, this stated goal is more of an ideal, and in reality, during most competition powwows, it can be difficult for drum group members to see the dance area. Often they're surrounded on all sides by "tapers" (those making personal recordings with hand-held recording devices) and other interested listeners. Thus, in a typical competition setting, singers can really only guess at the response of the dancers, although the size of the crowd around the group during a performance is often an equally good indicator of how well the song is being received.

Appropriateness of song to the dance category for which they are performing.

CS: So you're always gauging your songs towards the dancers?

ME: Yeah. You gotta. It's for them, that's what you're singing for. It's for them to enjoy. It's a connection, eh. We want them to connect with the music. Hopefully you can make your music sound good. You can have good music for them, so they can enjoy what they're doing. When they're competing, I think, like it's important to sing dancers real good songs. Suitable to them. Because they'll have a better time dancing to it. And they'll do all their moves or whatever. They perform better. You know—it's just important. Cuz that's who you're singing for—the dancers. Everybody works together. (Mike Esquash interview, September 1999)

Crosscutting the various dance styles are a number of song types, each of which may be played only for certain dance styles. At competition pow-wows in particular, the importance of making clear distinctions between the different types is underscored by the value placed on the "appropriateness" of the song type for the dance category for which the drum group is performing. Two components determine appropriateness in this performance context. First, a song is deemed appropriate if it is rendered at the right tempo and with the right meter and beat pattern. Powwow songs are dance music and the primary performance venue for all drum groups is powwows, performing as accompaniment to the dancers. Second, at many large competition powwows, committees or head dance judges will call for particular kinds of songs for particular dance categories. Once announced, the drum group is expected to perform what has been requested. If a drum group is being judged during a Jingle Dress competition dance, they will lose points for singing a song that is difficult for the dancers to dance to or if it is not the song type that the emcee requested of them. There are several possible reasons a drum group might not comply with the requests of the powwow committee; younger groups may not know the particular song type required, or they may not have been paying attention when a particular song was being announced.

....

These formalized criteria are interesting because there is an implicit tension within them between "presentational" and "participatory" values (Turino 2008). There is a clear articulation in these criteria that the best drum groups are those who display maximum participation by all members. But it is a particular kind of participation that is prescribed. Participation as a social ethic at singing competitions is valued as an expression of musical *ability*. All members must share a similar degree of drumming expertise. All must drum with a similar force and volume. The greater the number of singers who possess the ability to sing a lead, the more skilled a group is considered to be. This kind of evaluation of individual skill and virtuosity is somewhat at odds with the informal way in which drum groups form and the inclusivity that is encouraged in participation. The ethics expressed in the quotations found at the beginning of this chapter, that "everyone who wants to be a singer is a good singer," is absent from these evaluations. Competence and skill, values associated with presentational styles of music making, are valued over participation. This is also evident in the formation of many new drum groups or the stacking of existing groups for particular competition events. There exists a collection of singers who are informally recognized as top-level singers (current or former members of top level competition drum groups) who drum hop and sing with a number of different groups, both at powwows and on recordings. Sometimes these groups become regularly competing drums, while others simply feature a more fluid and rotating membership.

This tension between participatory and presentational ethics is perhaps a function of the difference in values between traditional and competition powwows. The judging categories listed above reflect these two competing powwow aesthetics: commitment to dancers and cleanliness of the drum area are values that carry over and become even more important at traditional powwows. On the other hand, judging categories that evaluate musicianship—such as singing and drumming as one, and valuing a high and equal level of talent among drum members—are the product of competition. At traditional powwows, participation is the goal and the focus of the event for both singers and dancers. Drum hopping is endemic and expected as a traditional drum carrier may simply show up with his drum. Singers from other groups will then gather around to sing the songs associated with that person and that drum. In this instance, drum hopping is not only encouraged but required. At competition powwows, drum hopping is most often formally disallowed as part of the rules for participation in a singing contest.

Much like the interplay between participatory and presentational ethics, there is a similar tension between regionally idiosyncratic and nationally standardized singing styles. The Spirit Sands Singers performed in the singing contest at the Onion Lake powwow in July 2000. The Onion Lake Cree Indian Reserve is located in central Saskatchewan, a drive of more than ten hours from the Swan Lake Ojibwa reserve, where Mike and many singers of the Spirit Sands drum were living at the time. It was an unusually long drive for the group. Mike wanted to sing there in part because Onion Lake was close to a small town in Alberta where his girlfriend at the time was living. It was a good excuse to visit her while singing with the group. The Spirit Sands Singers had performed well for all of their competition songs and group members were anticipating placing in the competition. "We sang well enough to place here, man," a group member observed. "We're not gonna place," said Buff (another singer) with a smile. "We don't have the word 'Cree' in our name."

The dynamic between standardization and regionalism is played out in numerous ways and at numerous sites. Reserve-based competition pow- wows mix individual, regional, and pan-tribal stylistic criteria in the judg- ing of singing competitions. Head singing judges, sometimes in consul- tation with the powwow committee, create judging sheets that list the categories and criteria to be judged. This list is dependent on the indi- vidual preference of the head judge and what he looks for in a perfor- mance, as well as on the opinion of the committee and what they would like to encourage in performance. Local singers who serve as head judges may thus design judging sheets that reflect local aesthetic preferences. However, increasingly, especially at urban competition powwows and other highly intertribal events where no single tribal group predominates, head judges are hired from across North America, and judging sheets are less reflective of tribal or regional bias. Thus, while regional styles still play a part in competition judging, there is an increasing uniformity in the judging criteria of many large competition powwows.

Northern Plains Singing Style

Northern-style powwow singing is so named because of a particular clus- ter of stylistic features that have historically been associated with a spe- cific geographic region (the northern Plains in the United States and the central Plains of Canada). This regional demarcation, however, is now be- ginning to break down as Native communities and musicians across the United States and Canada have adopted Northern-style singing, includ- ing singers in Oklahoma, stronghold of the Southern style (Ellis 2003, Lassiter 1998). Further, while Northern-style singing dominates today's Northern powwows, one will often see any number of Southern drums (drum groups who sing in the Southern style) also participating at many medium and large competition powwows on the northern Plains. Many Northern drums can similarly be seen performing in Oklahoma and at other Southern powwows. Indeed, the presence of both Northern and Southern host drum groups has become a regular feature at many large competition powwows.

Despite regional variation, several musical features typify the Northern style. These general features include the following:

1. *A musical texture featuring unison singing to the accompaniment of a steady drumbeat.* While the degree to which singers attempt or achieve perfect unison is a matter of both regional and personal choice, most Northern-style singers agree that perfect unison is a performance goal. As the members of the Red Tail Singers succinctly stated, a drum group should sound like "One voice, one beat. . . . One *people*, one beat!" If women join in the singing, they generally will sing an octave higher than the men at specifically designated sections of the song.

2. *A high, tense, loud vocal production is generally preferred, although again this differs by region and by singing group.* For example, Canadian Cree groups are renowned in the Northern powwow world for their ability to sing with a very high tessitura. A tense, pinched, vocal timbre is ideal, and singers go to great lengths to achieve this, including pinching their larynx (known as "throat grabbing") while singing. There are generational differences in aesthetic preferences for this musical feature. Older singers generally do not place as great a value on high tessitura or volume, while younger singers value these characteristics to a much greater degree. It has been explained to me that part of the reason for this is that present-day competition powwows, which feature between ten and sometimes thirty or more drum groups, may require each group to sing only three or four songs in the course of an entire day. As such, singers allow themselves to sing at a volume and tessitura that they would be unable to sustain if called upon to sing more regularly. Conversely, older singers learned to sing at a time when powwows generally featured far fewer drum groups and each group was responsible for singing dozens of songs every day. This increased singing load made singers very conscious of protecting their voices, so they developed a lower style of singing that would allow them to sing all day long.

3. *A terraced, descending melodic line is the typical melodic shape of a Northern song and there is a startling degree of consistency in this regard.* The opening phrase features the highest notes of the song, and each subsequent phrase generally employs collections of pitches lower than the previous phrase. In addition, powwow singing in practice does not feature fixed or stable tonal centers: the starting and ending pitches of a song in any given performance are relative, depending on who is singing and how

high particular singers are able to begin an opening phrase. Generally lead singers will start songs at the highest pitch level they can manage. It is not uncommon for subsequent renditions of each verse, if led by other singers in the group, to be microtonally altered slightly higher or lower, according to the individual ability and aesthetic preferences of each singer.[5]

4. *One of the most striking and unique features of this musical style is the "rhythmic displacement" of melody and drumbeat, the melody being sung slightly behind or slightly ahead of the beat of the drum.* This results in a performance that sounds as if the melody is "floating" above the steady rhythmic pulse of the drum. I refer to this technique as "displaced syncopation" because during performance it feels similar to the rhythmic energy associated with regular syncopation (the unexpected accent of beats). Singers and dancers alike recognize singing "off the beat" as an essential stylistic feature of powwow song performance and I have heard many singers critique younger drum groups for singing too "on the beat." Displaced syncopation creates a tension that provides much of the energy and dynamism in powwow songs; it is a large part of what inspires "good" and energetic dancing.

In trying to discover what made a song particularly "danceable" I asked a number of singers who were also active powwow dancers what they thought made a song or a performance good to dance to. The response I received more than any other was "the melody"; the melody inspired the dancing. Expecting that singers and dancers would answer by indicating some detail of rhythm or drumming technique, I was somewhat puzzled. Listening for particular melodic features in powwow songs that were particularly appreciated by dancers at powwows, I failed to find any particular structural features of the melodies to these songs that shared any obvious similarities. It was not until I began singing in a group myself that it became clear that the danceable, physical quality of a great song or performance was found not in the structure of the melody but in the relationship of the melody to the drumbeat. Songs that are considered to be really "fun" and "easy" to dance to are those that exhibit the right amount of displaced syncopation. The degree of rhythmic displacement varies according to the individual stylistic preferences of drum groups and tribal styles. For example, many singers have commented to me that Saskatchewan Cree groups in particular sing much more "off the beat" than their Ojibwa, Assiniboine, and Dakota neighbors.

Form and Structure

Early in my fieldwork I attempted numerous times to engage singers in discussions of song form and structure, convinced that some technical terminology must exist for the different formal elements of Northern powwow songs given their uncanny uniformity. Time and again, singers in both formal and informal interviews and in casual conversation made very few comments about the phrase structure of songs, even when asked directly about it. Nor would they speak of the consistent downward melodic motion of each phrase. It was clear they were aware of these structural and formal elements, but saw them as unimportant when discussing central elements of song style or describing how a song is composed or properly rendered.

However there are some emic terms that describe the formal and structural elements of songs.[6] A "push-up" is the general term for a verse of a song.[7] Performance practice dictates that the typical rendition of a song should consist of four repetitions of a single verse or push-up.[8] Each push-up is divided into two sections: the "lead" and the "seconds." The lead refers both to the opening phrase of the push-up and the singer who performs it. The seconds are the remaining phrases of each verse and all the singers who perform those phrases. Many non-Native scholars of this music have generally glossed these structural divisions through a discussion of phrase structure. While there have been some differences in opinion among various scholars as to the exact spelling of the formal structure, generally speaking the form of a powwow song is described as "incomplete repetition" and has a phrase structure represented as AA′BCBC or AA′BCDBCD (Browner 2000, 2002; Powers 1990; Vennum 1980). The initial A phrase is the lead and all ensuing phrases are the seconds. There is generally a high degree of motivic relationship between the different phrases: the A′ phrase is a repetition of the A phrase with an extended ending, while the B, C, and possibly D phrases all may share a large degree of melodic material with the A phrase and with each other. The BC and, when appropriate, the D phrases and their repetition are sometimes also collectively called the "body" of a song by powwow singers, as opposed to the "lead" phrase. It is a common practice for the seconds to overlap with the lead at two points within the push-up: first as the A′ phrase, sung by the seconds, begins just before the lead singer's phrase begins to trail, and again as the final C phrase of the push-up is being rendered, at which time the lead singer will often begin the A phrase of the new verse slightly before the C phrase has ended.

The repetition of the BC or BCD phrases, sometimes referred to by indigenous musicians as the second side of the verse, are structurally marked through the use of honor beats (also sometimes called check beats or hard beats) executed on the drum. Honor beats refer to a series of louder, accented beats that occur on alternate drum strokes that generally number between five and eight. These drum strokes are performed by specified members of a drum group who strike the drum closer to the center and with a marked increase in force while the other members of the group simultaneously reduce the force (and thus volume) of their drumming. Honor beats are said to honor the four directions and thus five beats are common (although far from universal): one hard beat to signal the beginning of the honor beats, followed by a grouping of four.[9]

The practice of check beating can also refer to other drumming techniques that alter the regular flow of the drumbeat. In practice, drum groups strive to vary the volume, tempo, and intensity of each push-up in order to give dynamic and dramatic shape to their performances. Thus the leader of the group may use check beats (hard beats) to signal to other members of the group either to increase the tempo, or to increase or decrease the force and volume of their drumming and singing. Each rendition of a push-up is also varied through the use of improvised shouts, cries or other vocal sound effects rendered by one or more members of a group. These shouts were originally completely improvised and performed spontaneously by group members who were feeling particularly moved by a performance. Nowadays, many professional drum groups designate certain singers within the group to perform these cries and shouts, often at important structural points in the song (e.g., during the first BC section of a push-up or during the honor beats) (see Vennum 2002). The seconds section can also be structurally demarcated in performance by women who, when present, enter at the first rendition of the B phrase, singing an octave higher than the men, and who continue until the end of each verse, often letting their voices trail much longer than the men (using an extended downward portamento) at the completion of the final C phrase.

Powwow songs may also be performed with a "tail," or coda, which consists of another repetition of the B and C phrases sung immediately after the end of the final push-up. Often a space of one beat is left silent before the drum begins again and sings the final BC phrases. Gabe Desrosiers of the Northern Wind Singers has stated that all traditional Ojibwa songs have a tail. Traditional Grass dance songs similarly are always performed with a tail. Today, on the powwow trail, drum groups will often add a tail to their songs spontaneously and, as such, the tail has become both a matter of compositional practice and performance practice.

Song Types

CS: And what are the different styles of drumbeats that you need to know for a powwow?

D. J. Menenick: Slow [*taps on the table, quarter note = 140 mm.*], fast [*taps approx. quarter note = 168 mm.*], ultrafast for Southern [*taps approx. quarter note = 240 mm.*], slow graceful Round dance for the women [*taps approx. dotted quarter note = 68 mm.*], fast type of Owl dance [*taps approx. dotted quarter note = 80 mm.*].

CS: Owl dance? Who does Owl dancing?

Shonto Pete: Couples. Kind of like a couples song. They'll call it an Owl dance.

CS: So like the Rabbit dance of the Sioux?

SP and DJM [*simultaneously*]: Yeah.

CS: Any other beats?

DJM: Slide [Side-step], like Ojibwas do for their Jingle Dress dancers [*taps approx. dotted quarter note = 108 mm.*]; Crow Hop [*taps approx. quarter note = 106 mm.*]; and then there's Sneak-up [*taps tremolo beat*]; Honor song; Flag song, a really slow beat [*taps approx. quarter note = 54 mm.*].

CS: Do you guys do Chicken dance too?

SP: Oh yeah, Chicken dance is another . . .

DJM: We [Yakima] got a round bustle too [a dance outfit and dance style similar to the Chicken dance]. It's a Chicken dance but it's a . . . we got more bustles. [Dancers] got them on their arms and legs.

CS: But is it the same kind of beat?

SP: Yeah, well [*starts tapping beat*] . . .

DJM: It first originated out of a . . .

SP: Fast songs.

DJM: . . . Fast songs like this [*taps fast beat*]. You had to keep on beat like that and there'd be like seven or eight verses, too. And they'd have heavy bells on, too.

CS: So just testing [the dancer's] stamina?

DJM: Yeah.

SP: But they do that Chicken style for Grass dancers too sometimes [*taps approx. quarter note = 145 mm.*]. But like they emphasize that soft and hard beat more.

CS: So the Chicken dance is just really emphasizing the hard and soft beats?

SP: Yeah basically. In the certain part of the song.

— RED TAIL SINGERS interview (March 2000)

Powwow musicians distinguish different song types (called song styles or song categories by indigenous musicians) according to both musical and extra-musical criteria. As all powwow songs exhibit the same general melodic and formal features listed above, musical criteria that powwow musicians use to distinguish song types include meter, tempo, and drumming patterns. Given powwow music's close association with dancing, it is not surprising that elements of rhythm should figure prominently in these distinctions. However, despite this association, the types of songs employed in the contemporary Northern competition powwow exist, to a certain degree, apart from six common competition dance categories. In the evolution of the contemporary contest powwow, drum groups have continually adopted and employed new song styles as accompaniment to various dance styles (Hautom 2002a, 2002b).

As the interview excerpt above indicates, song types currently performed at powwows are named for the dance style with which they are associated. Thus, a Chicken dance song is called as such because it is linked to Chicken dancing. But while Chicken dancing is seldom employed as a separate dance category at Northern powwows (although increasing in popularity with each passing season), Chicken dance songs are commonly used to accompany Grass dancing. Performing a Chicken dance song for Grass dancers then requires that these dancers must incorporate dance steps and movements imported from the Chicken dance style, a further challenge for dancers during competition. Thus, it is now commonly understood by both singers and dancers that each of the six competition dance categories may have a number of different types of songs associated with it; competition dancers are expected to know dance steps to any number of song types (or develop steps appropriate for the different song types). While this practice of incorporation is constantly evolving,

Table 1

Dance Category	Song Types
Men's Traditional	Straight-beat (medium), Sneak-up, Duck-and-dive songs
Grass dance	Straight-beat (slow), Crow Hop, Chicken dance, Duck-and-dive, Double Beat songs
Men's Fancy Bustle	Straight-beat (fast), Crow Hop, Southern Straight, Shake/Ruffle, Double Beat, Trick songs
Women's Traditional	Straight-beat (slow), Round dance songs
Jingle Dress	Straight-beat (medium), Side-step songs (occasionally Crow Hop and Double Beat songs)
Women's Fancy Shawl	Straight-beat (fast, although rarely as fast as Men's Fancy), Crow Hop, Double Beat songs

certain song types have become fixed and associated with certain dance categories. Table 1 lists the general practices at powwows that I have witnessed in the last ten years. It is by no means comprehensive or definitive, because different powwow committees and dance competition committees are endlessly creative in the ways they choose to link dance styles and song types.

Between 1998 and 2001 there were nine major song types commonly employed for the six competition dance categories found at Northern powwows: So-called War dance songs (Straight/Traditional and Contemporary/Word—really six different song types because each competition category has a War dance song rendered at a different tempo), Chicken dance songs, Crow Hops, Shake/Ruffle songs, Sneak-up songs, Side-step songs, Round dance songs, Fancy contest songs (Southern Straight), and Trick songs. By 2006 two other song types had emerged and were currently enjoying great popularity on the powwow trail: Double Beat songs and Duck-and-dive songs. The emergence of these two new song types speaks to the constantly developing trends in the powwow world. Just as particular styles of dress, particular decorations, and elaborations to dance regalia wax and wane in popularity among dancers, so, too, do particular song types enter the powwow circuit and capture the imagination of singers and dancers. This occurs through a somewhat regularized process. Tribally specific song types will often make appearances at specific powwows either as part of a special dance contest or exhibition, or integrated somehow into the regular course of events.[10] Often reservation powwows outside the central Plains of Canada and the northern Plains of the United States will incorporate local dance and song traditions into their weekend schedule. If a particular local song type becomes well liked by dancers, they will begin to request that song type at other powwows outside of that particular region. Drum groups will then feel obliged either to learn the original songs from a particular region, or to compose their own songs using the central stylistic and compositional features of that song type.

Powwow singers distinguish song types according to a complex of *stylistic features* (which may include tempo, drumbeat, meter, text, and melodic type) and *use* (such as Flag songs, Victory songs, Honor songs, Memorial songs, intertribal songs, competition dance songs, and so on).

War Dance Song Complex

> *John Menenick* (father to three of the members of Red Tail, mentor to the group, and also a champion Traditional dancer): There's Contemporary, Traditional, and there's also old-style Traditional. These guys [Red Tail] sing Contemporary Straight, and they sing regular Straight.
>
> *Shonto Pete*: Because there's just a Straight—Straight old-style they call it—and then I think there's a Contemporary Straight too. Because it sounds way different than the old-style Straight. They're just more jazzy, they got more than just the "wey ya's" in there instead of just the [*sings just using the vocable yaaahhh*]. They're just like singing, changing their pitch. But Contemporary is like [*sings using other vocables: wey ya wey ya wey ooo yo wey wey ha*] you know it's all jazzy compared to [*sings again on one vocable and using more vibrato in his voice and at a lower register*].
>
> JM: That's why I say that it's pretty hard to define . . .
>
> SP: There's even some word songs that sound not too Contemporary. I think Blacklodge, a lot of their word songs are like [*pause*] . . . they seem like they're not too Contemporary.
>
> CS: They seem pretty Straight?
>
> SP: Pretty mellow, yeah. Pretty Straight. They still got words in them . . .

CS: And they're considered Contemporary?

SP: Yeah, just cause they got words in them.

—RED TAIL SINGERS interview (March 2000)

William Powers writes, "War dance today is the most vital and popular of all Plains Indian music and dance . . . the nucleus of today's tribal and intertribal powwows both on reservations and in urban Indian communities" (1990, 29). In scholarly literature, the term "War dance song" has become the common designation for a powwow song, but its ubiquitous use in this literature, as the general name for songs used at powwows, has been the cause of some confusion. As Powers rightly points out, War dance songs are also known by many different names throughout Northern and Southern powwow circuits, such as "Omaha dance" by the Lakota, "Wolf dance" by the Shoshone, "Grass dance" by Standing Rock Lakota and a number of Canadian communities, and either as Fancy dance songs or Straight dance songs by southern Plains groups (1990, 30).[11] Remarkably, in the communities and reserves where I researched, visited, or sang I did *not once* hear a powwow musician refer to a powwow song as a "War dance song," or by any of the other names that Powers lists. There are two possible explanations for this. First, it may simply be that regional variation continues to play a large role in defining musical nomenclature and Powers and I have simply worked in different communities. Second, it may indicate a certain standardization of terms in the Northern powwow world in recent years, an effect of the widespread dispersion and popularity of competition powwows, which have formalized many aspects of practice.

Instead of "War dance song," the terms I encountered during the course of my research that served as general designations for powwow songs can be categorized into two basic subtypes: Straight (also called Traditional or Original) songs (e.g., CD, track 1) and Contemporary (also called Word) songs (e.g., CD, track 2). As the above interview excerpt with members of the Red Tail Singers demonstrates, these are perhaps the most polysemic terms in use on the powwow trail because they are used in so many ways, both general and specific. At the most basic level, Straight songs are those that use only vocables (syllables without any lexical meaning, e.g., he ya, ho, ye, ha). While these songs do not feature any linguistic text, the vocables are nevertheless recognized as the lyrics of the song, and particular vocables and vocable patterns are thought to be integral parts of a composition. While vocables have no lexical meaning, they have an essential musical meaning (Nettl 1989). Contemporary or Word songs feature lyrics in a Native language or in a mix of Native texts and vocables. When songs mix vocables and texts, the texts are often (although not always) set to the B and C phrases of the song form.

Further confusing the matter, the term "straight" is also commonly used to describe a particular drumming style: a duple meter beat at a medium-fast tempo, to be used as part of the basic repertoire of songs which can accompany any of the six competition dance categories, as well as intertribal songs, Honor songs, Victory songs, and Memorial songs. A straight *drumbeat* is one in which the beat is relatively even throughout. I emphasize *relatively* because straight beats are considered to have strong beats and weak beats, but the distinction between the two is barely perceptible. Despite the subtlety, all singers are very aware of where the strong and weak beats are and where the vocal melody falls within this strong-weak pattern (as it is the strong beat that is emphasized during the honor beats while the weak beat disappears completely).

Straight-beat songs are by far the most prominent at powwows because they are the staple song type performed for all dance categories and all intertribal songs. When the emcee of a powwow asks a drum group for a Straight song, he is not asking for a Traditional song (i.e., a song with vocables only), but for any song in duple meter rendered at an appropriate tempo for the particular dance category being performed. When an intertribal song is called for, it is assumed that a straight-beat song will be performed. The appropriateness of the straight-beat song for the different dance styles is determined by tempo. Straight-beat songs used to accompany Women's Traditional dancing employ the slowest tempos, followed by Men's Grass dancing, Men's Traditional dancing, Women's Jingle Dress dancing, and Women's and Men's Fancy dance songs, which feature the quickest tempos. Thus at a powwow, when asked for a straight song to accompany a dance, a group can perform a Contemporary (Word) song or a Traditional song (containing only vocables) as long as it is in duple meter, performed in the proper rhythm, and at an appropriate tempo.

At many larger competition powwows, the difference between Straight and Contemporary song types is marked through separate Traditional (or Original) and Contemporary song contests. Drum groups generally dedicate themselves to specializing in one of the two singing styles; at powwows large enough to have separate competitions, they will register for the appropriate contest at the beginning of the powwow. Like many other aspects of powwow practice, these two styles have waxed and waned in popularity over the years. In the 1990s Contemporary singing reigned supreme and most new, young drum groups began their careers as Contemporary-style singers. In fact several singers I spoke with made mention of the fact that in the 1990s it was hard to win competitions if your drum group sang in a Traditional style, and only "older singers" sang this way. The rise to prominence in the 1990s of Eyabay, the paradigmatic Contemporary-style drum group, represents the dominance of this style during this time. Beginning around 2005 Traditional-style singing started to make a comeback on the powwow circuit, fueled in part by the rise in popularity of the great Straight-style Minnesota Ojibwa drum groups Midnite Express and Battle River as well as the continued strong singing of Traditional-style stalwarts like Mandaree and High Noon. Many younger groups again took an interest in Straight-style singing and some Contemporary-style groups started composing and singing more Straight-style songs or switching completely to Traditional-style singing. Such are the cyclic trends of powwow culture.

As exemplified in the Red Tail interview excerpt above, "Traditional" and "Contemporary" are conventional terms and do not necessarily refer to the history of particular songs or song types. Thus both Word songs and Straight songs continue to be newly composed and performed today. Similarly, many older songs featuring Native-language texts and considered traditional in the general sense of the word (i.e., an old song transmitted through multiple generations) are still considered part of the larger general category of Word songs. Importantly, these two general song styles do not limit the other song types that can be rendered in these styles. Both Contemporary- and Traditional-style singing groups have repertoires that contain the full range of song types needed for competition powwow participation (e.g., Crow Hops, Flag songs, Chicken dance songs, etc.).

Red Tail's explanation of these terms further hints at their complexity when used to categorize songs or drum groups at the level of musical style. Old-style Traditional (old-style Straight) songs may be distinguished from contemporary (newly composed) Straight songs by the presence or absence of particular ("more jazzy") vocables, the variety of vocables used, and the way those vocables are rendered. Old-style Straight songs are also distinguished by other characteristic features of vocal production, such as a lower register, a quicker and more pronounced vibrato (than more modern-style singing), and a less undulating melodic line. Thus the terms contemporary and traditional are also used as stylistic descriptors that may not refer to the actual age of a song, the presence or absence of words, or the type of drumbeat used. For example, groups like the Mandaree Singers—a group of mostly elderly and very well-respected singers on the Northern powwow trail—are said to sing in a traditional Straight style not by virtue of the age of their songs but by their particular style of singing (although traditional Straight singing does connote an older style of powwow singing). Conversely, groups like High Noon (a group of singers originally from the Cree Thunderbird Reserve in Saskatchewan) or Midnite Express (a mixed group of Ojibwa and Dakota singers from Minneapolis) sing in a more contemporary Straight style, meaning the melodies of their songs are more undulating and complex, and they use a greater variety of vocables. The staggeringly popular group Eyabay (a group of Ojibwa singers) is known more for singing contemporary-style Word songs.

Sneak-up Songs and Shake Songs

Sneak-up songs possess what dancers call a mixed beat that features sections of a straight, duple meter beat and contrasting sections of a quick drum tremolo performed by all the members of a drum group, with one or two members of the group randomly performing hard beats during the tremolo sections (e.g., CD, track 3). The tremolo beat is employed throughout the A and A' phrases at the start of each push-up, followed directly by straight, duple drumming accompanying the B and C phrases. This alternation of tremolo and straight-style drumming is repeated with every push-up except for the fourth time through the verse, at which point the entire push-up employs the straight duple beat. Sneak-up songs are commonly performed to accompany Men's Traditional dancing only. When these songs are performed at a much quicker tempo (usually to accompany Men's Fancy dancing) they are called Shake songs, or Ruffle songs, because the choreography of the dancers changes during the tremolo section to feature quicker jerking and shaking movements. The other difference between the Sneak-up and the Shake/Ruffle song is that the Sneak-up songs often feature three hard beats at the end of each push-up. The verses of a Ruffle song simply end without any distinguishing drum cadence patterns (which, in some cases, can make them trickier to dance to).

Gabe Desrosiers has suggested to me that the Sneak-up song style originated with the Lakota and Dakota peoples in the northern Plains of the United States and began to be incorporated into competition pow-wows in the 1970s.

> CS: Now I've heard that that's how other songs got into powwows. Like I've heard that about Sneak-up songs. Nobody was singing Sneak-up songs in the early 1970s and then . . .
>
> GD: . . . up until the Dakotas and Lakotas brought that out. The Plains tribes. Like the old Porcupine Singers. Mandaree, . . . who else . . . Badlands. They started singing those Sneak-up songs. And those were like their [*pause*] . . . I don't know if they were really ceremonial songs, but they practiced them when they came back from a hunt or from a war with another tribe or whoever. And what they did was they would come home and their women would greet them, you know. And then they'd have a ceremony for that victory. And they had these songs. And these songs were the ones they practiced because the dancers, the warriors, would tell their stories through song. And then they would dance and they had a Sneak-up. They were sneaking up on their game or their enemy. So it was a story. So in later years, drums like Porcupine said, "We'll sing them." And they really became popular early. The '70s I think it was when you would hear those a lot. (Gabe Desrosiers interview, September 2007)

This assertion is corroborated by Rainer Hatoum's research (2002a, 2002b) into the evolution of song categories in Northern competition powwows. In his interview with Arlie Neskahai, this singer describes how in the mid-1970s only one Sneak-up song was sung at powwows in the Dakotas, and it was generally sung only for dance "specials." As this song type grew in popularity, drum groups began composing new songs using the Sneak-up rhythm and it became a regular part of competition dancing for Traditional dancers (Hautom 2002a, 2).

Round Dance Songs

Round dance songs are a generic term for songs that feature a triple meter with drumbeats occurring on the first and third beat of each three-beat grouping (e.g., CD, track 4). They are used to accompany a variety of dances at powwows including the Women's Traditional dance and myriad social and couples dances, many of which have tribally specific names (e.g., Rabbit dance or Owl dance).[12] Round dance songs may often feature a mix of vocables and English-language texts. These English lyrics usually are humorous and mildly erotic, often alluding to male-female relationships or the desire for a relationship. Similar to other Word songs, the texts usually are employed during the B and C phrases of the song form.

In the central Plains of Canada, Round dance songs are widely thought to be the special domain of the Cree, who have created a tradition of social round dancing to the accompaniment of a small group of singers who play single-headed, hand-held frame drums. The Cree style of hand drumming is unique in the northern Plains and features a significantly altered style of drumming than is typically performed on the "big drum." Cree Round dances performed on hand drums are rendered in a compound triple meter (6/8 time) that is subdivided into two three-beat groupings by "snaring" the fourth eighth note of each measure, a technique where the drummer uses the index or middle finger of the hand that is holding the drum and lightly touches his fingernail to the inside of the drumhead, causing a buzzing sound (essentially using one's fingernail as a snare). The performer also then lightly plays a pick-up beat on the sixth eighth note of the measure. This style of hand drumming has become popular on the powwow trail and many non-Crees (especially younger-generation singers) now use this drumming style when performing Round dance songs on hand drums. Hand drum contests, where one finds this beat is used exclusively, are also now quite common at medium- and large-scale competition powwows.

Crow Hop Songs

Crow Hop (sometimes called "Foot Slide") songs are generally attributed to the Crow nation of Montana. These songs are used to accompany Crow Hop dancing, a style of dance also associated with the Crow people (Browner 2002) (e.g., CD, track 5). This dance has been adapted for use at powwows as Grass dancers and Men's and Women's Fancy dancers (and less often Women's Jingle Dress dancers) are sometimes called upon to dance a "Crow Hop" (which means to dance to a Crow Hop song and dance in a way similar to the analogous Crow dance). These songs are distinguished by a unique drumming pattern referred to as a "one-half beat" or a "single beat" (Browner 2002, 85), referring to a drum pattern in which every other beat of a rather quick triple-meter Round dance drumming pattern is left out (the weaker, pick-up beat of the three-beat pattern).

The result is a drumming pattern that sounds as though it is proceeding at half the speed of the vocal line. Rising in popularity a little later than the Sneak-up songs, the Crow Hop had become a regularly performed song genre by the early 1980s.

Double Beat Songs

Related to the Crow Hop song type is the newly popular Double Beat song, which features a quick triple-meter, Round dance–style drumming pattern. According to Gabe Desrosiers, the Double Beat drum pattern is the traditional way of performing a Crow Hop beat. The Double Beat is so named because both drum strokes of the Crow Hop beat (the downbeat and the pick-up beat) are performed. Significantly, as with the related Crow Hop, dancers do not alter their footwork to match the fast triple-meter rhythm of the Double Beat. Instead they choreograph footwork similar to that of the Crow Hop, ignoring the pick-up beat and dancing to the song as if it were in a medium-slow duple meter, synchronizing their footwork to every downbeat of the measure. Double Beat songs are appropriate for all dance categories except the Women's Traditional.

GD: The Double Beat is supposed to be like the traditional way of singing Crow Hop. It's supposed to be a Crow Hop. But now they've added the double [*starts tapping a Double Beat rhythm, which sounds like a fast Round dance*]. Instead of just going like this [*keeps same tempo but takes away the soft beat*] . . .

CS: Oh they've added a beat in between—softer beats in between . . .

GD: Yeah, now they have a . . . [*continues with double beat*]

CS: . . . and it goes like that [*I start matching Gabe's beat*].

GD: Yeah, and then you're doing the Crow Hop.

CS: But this is more like a Round dance beat, right?

GD: Yeah.

CS: So they're doing a Round dance beat but they're singing a Crow Hop melody over top.

GD: Yeah, yeah. So that's supposed to be the original beat of the Crows [*starts tapping double beat again*]. Like this. And they'd Crow Hop. You don't follow the exact three beats. You just . . .

CS: So when it got changed to just this [*taps Crow Hop beat*] that was a new thing?

GD: That was a new thing. That's the concept that I understand. . . . Instead of doing this initially [taps *Double Beat*] like they should have done, they just went to [taps *Crow Hop beat*], just the one Crow Hop like that. So now this [taps *Double Beat*] is supposed to be the initial double-beat Crow Hop. (Gabe Desrosiers interview, September 2007)

Side-step Songs

Side-step songs (sometimes also called "slide step" or "slides") are associated specifically with the Jingle Dress dance and they are considered a specialty of Ojibwa singers and songmakers, due to the historical link between the tribe and the dance style (e.g., CD, track 6). These songs are some of the most rhythmically complex in the powwow repertoire, and there is some argument as to the proper way to describe the beat pattern as it is "felt" in performance by singers and dancers. Singers unfailingly refer to the Side-step as a "triple-beat" dance, described to me as a Round dance beat that is simply "sped up." In practice, however, the drumming pattern of these songs hovers dramatically between a duple and a triple meter. It has been my own experience that Ojibwa drum groups, in particular those whose members hail from the Lake of the Woods region of northwestern Ontario (widely believed to be the birthplace of the Jingle Dress dance and song style), are the most skilled at capturing the unique "in-between" rhythmic feel of these songs (Northern Wind Singers and Whitefish Bay Singers are both particularly adept). Many dancers and other powwow people on the Northern powwow trail share this opinion, and at larger competition powwows I have often seen Ojibwa drums called upon to sing outside of the regular drum rotation in order to furnish a Side-step song for a Jingle Dress dance competition.

I gained an invaluable insight into the particularities and subtleties of this song style while working with Gabe Desrosiers and the Northern Wind Singers on their 2000 recording *Ikwe Nagamonan: Women's Songs* (AR-11282), a CD that features a mix of Side-step and straight-beat songs specifically for Jingle Dress dancing.[13] The group came together the night before the recording session to learn all of the songs. During the session the next day, because the songs were still so new to the singers, Gabe sang each song through again, before the group would perform them, to remind the other singers of the melody. On occasion, Gabe and other members of the drum group would strike the drum quietly while singing and listening to the song, trying to catch the entire melody. During this rehearsal time, the group sometimes sang the song while playing only the strong beat of the triple pattern. This had the effect of making the songs sound like Crow Hop songs. It was only after the group was comfortable with the melody and with how the melody fit with the strong-beat drum accompaniment that the weaker beat was added. When the weaker beat was added, it served as a quasi-pick-up beat to the strong beat. Learning from this practice as well as from my subsequent experience in performing this style of song, I came to understand that for a singer, the strong beat is the important beat for feeling the melody in relation to the rhythmic pattern, that is, how to fit the melody to the pulse of the drum. But it is the placement of the weak beat—closer to the strong beat so that it sounds like a triple meter or farther away so that it sounds more like a duple meter subdivision of the larger measure—that gives this drumming pattern its uniqueness.

The variety of ways that different drum groups place that weak beat within the measure determines their unique rhythmic style in performing these songs. Thus it has been my experience that Cree drums render this rhythmic pattern as a sped-up version of a Round dance, a practice not surprising considering their specialization in the latter style of drumming. Conversely, a number of Lakota and Dakota drums I have heard tend to play these songs with a rhythmic articulation that is far more reminiscent of a straight duple-beat pattern. This is simply an informal observation and I make no claims to have systematically studied this tendency. However it does explain (to a certain degree) why dancers and powwow committees consistently prefer Ojibwa drums when a Side-step song is required, as these drums most effectively capture the "in between" feel of the rhythmic pattern.

According to Gabe Desrosiers, there are other characteristics that distinguish traditionally composed Side-step songs. These songs begin without drum accompaniment. The A phrase is sung a cappella and the drumming pattern begins with the entrance of the seconds at the A′ phrase. Further, traditional Side-step songs have a tail, a repetition of the BC phrases after the completion of the fourth push-up. After a short pause at the end of the fourth push-up, the tail begins with one hard beat. The drumbeat then slowly crescendos as the final melodic phrases are rendered. Gabe discussed with me the nature of traditional-style Side-step songs after the *Ikwe Nagamonan* recording session:

When I was a kid, I used to go to these traditional powwows, when I was young. And I can remember, you know, the old style. What I mean is, when the old singer started up the song they did it without the drum, in the beginning. And then when the second came in, that's when they started hitting the drum in unison. And I could always remember how beautiful that sounded. And there's a certain sound to these traditional songs that's—you can't describe, unless you are a part of that culture or that tradition. You recognize it through—through being a part of it, so to speak. If I was from a different tribe then I wouldn't get that feeling, cuz you wouldn't be a part of that culture and tradition. So to me, it's the sound of [*pause*] . . . it's a distinct sound that automatically you know [*snaps fingers*], it's an old style traditional song. But today there's songs that are composed contemporarily, by other drum groups, by other nations, and it's not the same. The ingredient is not there, that sound is not there . . . (Gabe Desrosiers interview, May 2000)

Chicken Dance Songs

Chicken dance songs are widely thought to have originated with the Blackfeet of Alberta and were originally used to accompany a warrior society dance (Wissler 1913).[14] The dance itself employs a choreography that mimics the movements of the prairie chicken. In 1999 and 2000 Chicken dancing experienced a revival on the northern Plains powwow circuit as one of the newest song types to be adapted to powwow performances. Many Chicken dance "specials" became a regular event at powwows and featured dancers performing strictly in a Chicken dance style (with unique Chicken dance regalia). Grass dancers are also called upon to perform to Chicken dance songs and many Grass dancers will incorporate choreography and footwork from the Blackfeet-style Chicken dance. Chicken dance songs are distinguished by a special drumming pattern, a steady duple rhythm with clearly articulated strong and weak beats (e.g., CD, track 7). Often this alternation of strong-weak is abandoned for a regular straight-beat after two push-ups (verses). Many Chicken dance songs may also begin with a tremolo drumbeat accompanying the first half of the verse, similar to the Sneak-up song.

Duck-and-Dive Songs

In 2006 the Duck-and-dive song was spreading like wildfire across powwows on the northern Plains, requested by dancers and powwow committees at almost every powwow I attended. At that time the dance and song were very recent additions to the powwow circuit, a trend that started only a year or two earlier. The origins of the song type remain somewhat obscure, and I have heard various stories from different singers and dancers who have claimed that it originated with one of the Nez Perce, the Crow, or the Blackfeet. Similar to how the Sneak-up song style was introduced, in 2006 there was still only *one* Duck-and-dive song that every drum group performed (sometimes with some minor variation). It was such a unique song, and so new to powwow singers, that it had yet to be adopted by songmakers as a category to be used as the basis for new compositions. Usually performed only for Men's Traditional dancers, the song is distinguished by a set of abrupt single hard beats performed during the c section (both the initial c and the repetition) of the standard powwow song form. These drumstrokes are said to be iconic representations of cannon fire or gunshots, and the dancers choreograph these parts of the song by ducking and diving to avoid being "shot." Gabe Desrosiers described the song in the following way:

> It's a ceremonial song that someone brought out into the open. And what the Duck-and-dive is supposed to mean is—the story behind that song is that when the cavalry or someone was fighting them, every time they would shoot at them, they'd dive. So that's why they go like [*starts tapping*] that one part of that song represents a gunshot. When they hit it down [*hits one hard beat*] then they hit it down again [*brief drum crescendo and then one hard beat*]. That's when they go down on each one. Yeah. [*starts singing the Duck-and-dive song*] and then kind of goes down [*one hard beat*] it goes down twice. On each side of the verse. The A and B. It does it twice here and twice over there. That's supposed to represent the gunshot. That's when they duck down. (Gabe Desrosiers interview, September 2007)

Flag Songs

Flag songs are not associated with any dance but instead are part of the Grand Entry ceremony. They are sung in honor of the Eagle Staff (often referred to as "the first flag of North America"), the United States and Canadian flags, and by extension, the veterans who carry these flags and fought under them in wartime. Each feather on the Eagle Staff represents a warrior, symbolic of a traditional practice among many Plains tribes in which warriors would take a feather into battle and bring it back to post on the staff. Flag songs feature a drumbeat rendered softly at a very slow tempo.

Most of these songs have words in an indigenous language. While many drum groups compose their own Flag songs to perform at powwows, it is equally common to find drum groups singing other popular Flag songs that were composed by other singers or drum groups. For example, while traveling the powwow trail in the summer of 2006, a Flag song composed by Mystic River (a tribally mixed drum group from the Pequot community in Connecticut) was a favorite performed at almost every powwow I attended.

Trick Songs

Trick songs include a wide variety of songs whose only commonality is that they all have a formal structure that has been altered in an unusual way, making it very difficult for dancers to know what to expect (e.g., CD, track 8). The point of a trick song is to trick the dancers into "overstepping" (continuing to dance after the drumbeat stops) or understepping (stopping one's dance before the song ends). Trick songs are most commonly employed for Men's Fancy dance contests. They are often mixed-beat songs that make use of any number of drumming styles (straight-beat, tremolo, Round dance style, Crow Hop, Chicken dance style). They may also feature sudden or abrupt starts and stops in drumming and singing, unexpected omissions of formal sections (the repetition of the BC phrases, for example), or out-of-the-ordinary drumming cadential patterns, all of which serve to trick the dancers in some way.

Southern Straight

Southern Straight songs are the southern equivalent to the Northern-style straight-beat songs and form a large part of a Southern-style pow-wow group's repertoire. Southern Straight songs are performed in both fast and slow tempos, the former used to accompany Fancy dancing while the latter is associated with the Southern Straight–style of dance commonly found at Southern powwows. I include this song style as a category of Northern powwow singing for two reasons. First, Southern-style songs are heard with ever increasing frequency at many Northern powwows, particularly larger competition powwows, because so many Southern drum groups are invited to perform at Northern events; when a Southern group is present, they will almost always be called upon to sing for Fancy dance competitions. Second, it is also becoming more common for Northern groups to have a few Southern songs in their repertoire. For example, the Spirit Sands Singers knew a couple of Southern Straight songs and even performed them occasionally as warm-up songs (songs sung to entertain the audience during the time leading up to the Grand Entry).[15]

Southern Straight songs have the same basic phrase structure as Northern songs (incomplete repetition: AA′BC[D]BC[D]). However a much lower vocal register, a more relaxed vocal production, and a different placement of the honor beats all differentiate the Southern style from its Northern counterpart. Honor beats, as in Northern songs, function to mark structurally important parts of the form. Three hard beats, performed by all members of the group, are played between the end of the first statement of the BC phrases and the repetition of these phrases, and serve as a clear structural marker for the dancers. Creative Fancy dancers will often choreograph specific moves or footwork patterns to accentuate these hard beats, since their placement within the song is entirely predictable. The dynamic and dramatic arc of the performance is also somewhat formalized. The first two push-ups are rendered at a slower tempo, with the speed and volume of the drumming picking up markedly during the repetition of the C phrase at the end of the second push-up. Following this, the A phrases (the lead phrases) of the third and fourth push-ups are truncated, including only the opening few notes of the regular A phrase, and are often rendered within a higher melodic compass. The rest of the song is thus transposed (generally up between a third and a fifth) as a result of the new starting pitch of the A phrase. The song continues at this higher tessitura, louder volume, and faster tempo until the song is over, the ending being marked by five hard beats in a row (again a clear sign for the dancers to adjust their choreography to end exactly on the fifth and final hard beat).[16]

Songs Distinguished by Use

The song categories described above are those that most Northern singers regard as essential for regular performance on the Northern circuit. These songs, with the exception of the Flag song, are all performed for dancers in accompaniment to the six basic dance styles, and are distinguished according to various musical features. There are, of course, a host of other song types that reflect the local and tribal song-and-dance traditions and that may be used at various powwows. Singers also identify a list of other song types that are distinguished not by musical features but social use, almost all of which exhibit the same musical characteristics as

Straight/Traditional or Word/Contemporary songs. These include Victory songs (sometimes called Veterans' songs), which are performed during all Grand Entry ceremonies directly following the Flag song. Honor songs (e.g., CD, track 9), are often performed during specials and may be composed specifically for a family, family member, or individual. The song is sung when the person being honored makes his or her rounds within the dance arena (see chapter 1). A Blanket dance song is performed while a blanket is placed in the middle of the arena or carried around the edges of the dance circle; money is placed on the blanket, usually in support of an individual or family who requires some form of help or charity.

Song Composition

CS: So what are the main differences in the styles? Is it speed of the drumbeat or . . .

Mike Esquash: Sometimes it's the speed, sometimes it's the beat itself that's totally different.

CS: Like Chicken dance . . .

ME: Yeah, it'd be a different beat altogether. Yeah, I guess just the tempo of the song. The style, the way you sing it, is different also. You have to match your song with the beat itself.

CS: So how does that work?

ME: It's gotta be in rhythm with each other. The drumbeat [taps on his leg] has to [pause] . . . as you say, actually the song you are singing has to match the drumbeat. You have a certain style of beat and you have to make a song with that beat. And some songs, like, sometimes when we make songs—we'll make a song and we won't even have a beat for it. You just sing it. And then what we'll do is the beat will come with it. You'll know it, you can hear it. Pretty neat stuff.

CS: So you're singing a melody and sometimes you'll hear a Round dance under it or a Chicken dance beat?

ME: Yeah, sometimes a Chicken, Crow Hop, you name it. It just comes with the song. Usually a song will tell you what kind of beat it is.

CS: So you usually come up with the melody first and then . . .

ME: Yeah, try to come up with the melody or tune first and then the beat will follow.

—MIKE ESQUASH interview (September 1999)

For drum groups who regularly compete in competition powwows, song composition is essential. Successful groups must create a number of new songs every powwow season. With the formalization of competition pow-wows, where there are multiple song types that are used for each dance category, drum groups and songmakers must now also make sure they have original songs of each song type so that they can perform any song asked of them during a competition.

Gabe Desrosiers has described for me three general ways in which songs are created. A songmaker most commonly composes a song actively and purposefully, often beginning with the lead phrase and deriving the other ensuing melodic phrases from its motivic material. These songs, he reports, are often the most difficult songs to make. Sometimes this active composition may happen as part of a group process as would be the case if a singer brought a lead phrase that he had composed to a group rehearsal (although this is rarely the case for Gabe's compositions). Some members of the group may then suggest other phrases to follow the lead phrase, which other members may accept or reject, although generally, the person who composed the lead phrase has final say as to the phrases that follow. In this way song composition may sometimes be a group activity.

A second way that a songmaker creates a song is through spontaneous inspiration. Songmakers have described to me that songs sometimes "just come to them" in their entirety. Song melodies may also be based on their acoustic environment. Mike Esquash has related to me that he has made songs based on the whistling of wind through windows and doors or in-spired by the sound of wheels on the highway (see Parthun 1978, 27–28; Powers 1990, 34; Vander 1988, 130 for similar accounts).

The third method is through divine intervention. Gabe Desrosiers has said that the most important and most sacred songs in his repertoire are those that come through dreams or visions. These songs are considered highly personal (and sometimes totally private) and are generally per-formed only during traditional powwows or religious ceremonies and not for competitive or unrestricted public events.[17]

Within the vast repertoire of powwow songs there is only a relatively small degree of formal innovation in composition. These innovations are always noticed and appreciated by singers and (sometimes) dancers. For instance, Eyabay was one of the first groups to have used "double leads," where two singers in succession will sing two halves of one exceptionally long lead phrase. Several other young drum groups have since emulated this practice (e.g., "Double Clutch" from *Red Tail: Volume 1* [AR-11262] or "Double Trouble" from *Red Tail: Volume 2* [AR-11432]). Another common alteration of form occurs in performance practice (as opposed to compositional practice). When solo singers perform powwow songs or other Plains-style songs with AA'BCBC forms on a hand drum, the A phrase is often omitted in performance. This is a matter of necessity more than aesthetic preference: it is difficult for singers to repeat the very highly pitched A phrase twice in succession (A followed by A'). It is also difficult to sing both A phrases by oneself because there is no room to breathe between the phrases. In group performances the A' phrase, sung by the seconds, overlaps with the A phrase. Because solo singing does not allow for this performance feature, singers will simply sing the A' phrase and move straight into the B and C phrases.

Performance Aesthetics

Bounce

Shonto Pete: You got to be singing with your beat, too. If you're off the beat it won't sound [*pause*] . . . you got to be with the beat. Every little turn, that should be, like, on that soft beat . . .

D. J. Menenick: Yeah, here's two styles here [*sings high and clear while tapping his finger on the table*]. Like that [*sings again*]. Singing with the beat. So you can tell what sounds good and what doesn't.

SP: Yeah, like there's a soft beat. A soft beat like [*starts tapping soft beat first then hard beat*] and like that.

CS: That's the drumming . . .

SP: Yeah, that's how you're supposed to drum. One soft beat and one hard beat. It's not really noticeable like a Round dance [*taps Round dance beat, emphasizing the down beat of the triple-meter pattern while tapping much softer for the pick-up beat of the pattern*]. Straight, just kinda—make that soft beat a little softer than [*pause*] . . . You've got to sing on that soft beat.

CS: So you match your . . .

DJM: Yeah [*tapping a straight duple beat*], that bounce too, when you're singing like that. For that vibe . . .

CS: So that's where the bounce comes from? The alternating . . .

SP: It keeps the beat lighter too [*continues tapping*]. Like singing on the beat would be like [*sings*] . . . this would be the right way [*sings with* displaced syncopation and with melodic phrases beginning on softer beats]. And the other part would be like [sings melody without displaced syncopation and beginning melodic phrases on the loud beats; everybody laughs hysterically].

CS: So that's bad singing.

SP: It's not bad but you know . . .

DJM: At least they're trying . . .

SP: Yeah they're trying. It's not bad, but they're singing on the wrong beat. It's just their way of singing I guess. But most people prefer to sing on the other beat.

CS: You start your singing on the soft beat.

SP: Yeah, you jump right in on the soft beat.

—RED TAIL SINGERS interview (March 2000)

The description given by Shonto and D. J. about proper singing and drumming technique synthesizes a number of aesthetic values and musical principles under the term "bounce," used by many singers in reference to many different aspects of musical performance. It functions for all as a positive term that denotes a certain ineffable quality of "groove" in pow-wow performances. For D. J., Shonto, and the members of the Red Tail Singers, bounce is generated from the synchrony between the vocal line and the drum pattern. As mentioned above, typical straight-beat drumming involves a drumming pattern in which very slightly louder and softer drumbeats alternate, with the louder beat only being obviously and audibly accentuated during the honor beats. All (or most) melodic phrases should begin on the weaker or softer beats. Melody and drumbeat thus share a kind of syncopated tension.

Bounce can also sometimes refer to the rhythmic energy created by the tension between the drumbeat and the melody (the latter sung "off the beat"). Bounce can also be created when all the singers in a group have a similar or almost identical sense of where the melody is placed over the drumbeat. When this happens, the singing of the melody also synchronizes and it feels as if the melody is floating effortlessly but firmly over the flow of the drumbeat. This not only feels good for the singers but for the dancers as well, who find songs that have bounce to be inspirational and effortless to dance to.

Finally, bounce can also refer to a very tight synchrony of drumbeat shared by all members of the drum group. When this occurs, bounce describes the easy snapping of the drumsticks off of the drumhead after every beat. It becomes much easier to drum when all in the group are hitting the drum in tight unison, causing the drumsticks to bounce back up off the drumhead with minimal effort by the performers, each stick responding to the skin of the drum by crisply snapping back from each synchronized stroke. This tight unison also results in a kind of visual synchrony where all the drummers' sticks bounce the same distance from the drumhead. These moments of rhythmic and visual synchrony are extremely pleasurable, making drumming (and singing) almost effortless.

Vibrato

CS: What about vibrato. . . . Is vibrato good in the voice, too?

Shonto Pete: Like how do you mean?

CS: Like your voice shaking.

SP: Yeah, some songs.

D. J. Menenick: Like [*sings with exaggerated vibrato; everybody laughs*]

SP: Yeah, those little vibes. All those got to be right with the beat too, otherwise it's gonna sound like not the right tune.

DJM: [*sings with correct vibrato*]

SP: Yeah like that.

DJM: [*sings with more exaggerated vibrato; more laughter*]

SP: High Noon . . . High Noon, they got some vibes.

DJM: Although sometimes they got too much vibes, I think.

SP: Yeah, but if you just sing it straight like [*sings with no vibrato*] you know it don't got that . . . [*sings with vibrato*]

DJM: Some guys will get creative and throw it in there somewhere [*sings with vibrato only on some phrases*].

SP: Yeah, the leads are always . . . all cool.

CS: So sometimes you use the vibrato and sometimes you don't?

DJM: Yeah, you know, show how creative you can be . . .

SP: [*interrupting*] Yeah, on your lead . . .

DJM: . . . how much skills we got.

—RED TAIL SINGERS interview (March 2000)

Vibrato is a common element of vocal style in northern Plains singing yet I encountered very few singers who talked about it as a separate and identifiable vocal mannerism. However, the interview excerpt above demonstrates that, like many other aspects of singing style, different uses and styles of vibrato are recognized by singers and understood in terms of individual and group style and expressed through analogy (drum group names given as examples of a specific vibrato style and use). While the depth and amount of vibrato used varies from group to group, I suspect all singers would agree with Shonto's comment that powwow singing requires at least *some* vibrato (especially on the Straight songs) and that absence of vibrato alters the music on a fundamental level.

Enunciation and Phrasing

> *Mike Esquash*: They [the singers in a drum group] work together as a group, eh. Smooth. That's very important. Clarity is important. You don't want—you want to hear what they're singing. If they're singing a word song, you want to know what they're saying. If they're singing just a Straight-up song [a song with vocables only], you want to hear them emphasize certain parts of that song. I think it adds to that song.
>
> —MIKE ESQUASH interview (September 1999)

Proper pronunciation and enunciation of words and vocables is an essential element of good singing. A large part of the technique that allows singers to sound "as one" comes from all singers clearly articulating and enunciating the lyrics of the song (whether they are vocables or lexical texts). Time and again when singing with the Spirit Sands Singers, Mike admonished me for not singing the proper vocables in a song or not singing them clearly enough. Clearly articulating and enunciating each vocable produces a more definite and clear rhythmic rendering of the vocal melody. Clearly sung vocables also help to create consistent melodic phrasing. Much of the subtle beauty of a powwow song's melodic line lies in the novel ways that larger melodic phrases are segmented into often rhythmically asymmetrical subphrases that are delineated through rhythmic stress on particular vocables (e.g., Ya weh HEY YA ya weh YA weh, as opposed to simply Ya weh hey ya ya weh ya weh).

Commitment to Dancers and Community

> CS: So what do you think makes a good performance? When are you guys happy with your performance?
>
> *John Morris*: What makes us the happiest? I don't know, probably the "props"

["propers" or appreciative compliments] that we get. Like when little kids come up and say, you know, "you're Eyabay," and they don't even know us. And people come up and tell us, you know, "my kids can't even talk but they can say Eyabay," and "I can put a tape on the bottom of a big box of tapes and they'll pull out every tape until they see the Eyabay tape." Just stuff like that, you know. And this woman told us, she was blind, and she used to dance but . . . she told us she could— she listened to all the drums in Winnipeg when we was up there [at the Heartbeat of Nations Powwow in September 1999] and they was all just singing and sounding the same. But when we sang, she said she could feel it from her chest and it just made her fingertips tingle. You know, just stuff like that. It made her feel like dancing 'cause, you know, she's blind, so she can't—can't dance. But just making them— making the sick forget their pain for just that little while that we're singing. That's good for us, you know. It don't matter—all the fame and glamour and all that stuff. I mean, that's a big part of it and stuff but we could do without that. We could—just as long as we're doing our job, what we're supposed to be doing.

—JOHN MORRIS interview (October 1999)

On the powwow grounds, drum groups and singers recognize that they have a distinct set of responsibilities and social functions. In my interviews with a number of different drum groups, I found consistent agreement that singing performances are judged by their success at powwows. The main gauge for success is whether or not the songs inspire the dancers to dance. A group will often judge the success or failure of a particular performance by the response of the dancers. In all cases, when I asked why they sing, they said it was "for the dancers." For powwow singers, the ability to perform a song well means performing it at a powwow and engaging the dancers. At the heart of the matter is the drum group's commitment to sing for the community that has invited them to perform.

In July 2000 I attended the Mandaree powwow on the Fort Berthold Reservation in North Dakota. The event was a medium-sized competition powwow that was fairly well attended, considering that the cash prizes were relatively modest and it was occurring during the height of powwow season. As was typical, Saturday night featured competitions in all the adult dance categories (Saturday night is usually regarded as the best night of dancing). The Adult Men's Grass dance competition was called

and the emcee requested a Crow Hop song. The drum group in line to perform for the dancers was comprised mostly of teenagers who appeared
to be relatively inexperienced singers. For whatever reason, they played
a Chicken dance song instead. The dancers, undaunted, danced out the
song. What followed after the dance was over was something that happens only very rarely at powwows, competition or traditional. The emcee exploded in an angry tone and admonished the young group for playing such a song, sternly commenting, "We don't play those songs on this
reservation. The Chicken dance is a dance from Canada and we don't have
that kind of dance down here!" He continued criticizing and lecturing
the singers for several minutes, both for playing a Chicken dance song at
the Mandaree powwow and also for not playing the song that he, and the
powwow committee, had requested of them. He then asked the host drum
group to perform a Crow Hop song so the dancers could be judged on the
dance requested by the judging committee.

Although somewhat extreme (I had never before, nor have I ever since,
seen an emcee publicly criticize a drum group in this way), this ethnographic moment exemplifies the importance and value placed on song appropriateness at competition powwows as an indication of a drum group's
responsibility to the dancers and the powwow committee. An appropriate
song is defined not only by tempo and drumbeat pattern (major stylistic markers distinguishing the categories) but also by what the emcee, in
consultation with the head judges and powwow committee, requests of
the group. Appropriateness of songs for the dancers is highly valued; the
best and most respected drum groups can always be counted on to play
an appropriate song. They become known as reliable performers who take
their responsibilities to the dancers and the powwow committee seriously,
and they will often receive invitations to more powwows either as an invited drum or as a host drum. Thus, the value of a group that shows the
ability and propensity for rendering appropriate songs is expressed not
only verbally, but monetarily as well (as host and invited drums are often
guaranteed money for a performance, usually much more than they would
receive for simply showing up and performing).

Commitment to the dancers and the community may also involve
performing under special, often less than ideal, circumstances. While
mistake-free performances at powwows are appreciated, small mistakes—such as the cracking of voices or sloppy, unsure entrances by the
seconds after a vocal lead—are generally laughed off as part of the busi-

ness of singing. This is most evident when a drum group is "whistled" by a Traditional dancer and the group is obligated to continue singing regardless of how tired they are or how difficult they may find it to keep going. In this instance, the singers are often forced to disregard technical evaluations of the performance because their main concern is their responsibility in honoring the Traditional dancer's request. Singers' performances at powwows focus on this kind of commitment to the dancers, the powwow committee, and the community for which they sing.

This commitment is what prompts the sentiments found at the opening of this chapter, the idea that anyone who "wants to sing" or "tries their best" or "picks up a drumstick" is a good singer. These kinds of statements speak not to musical aesthetics but social ethics. In terms of how communities value singing, "good singers" are indeed those who will sing when expected, sing when asked, and always render an appropriate song. Ethics and aesthetics merge in understanding that appropriate songs are often understood as songs that are also performed well. As Waterman (1990) points out (in the case of *Jùjù*), it is not important simply to sing but to sing well, and the quality of the performance often has a direct bearing on the degree to which a performance is judged as successful. Everybody wants to dance to a good song.

CS: So what does it mean to you to be a singer?

GD: To be a singer means to have respect for yourself. Like for me, when I sing, I think of my relatives who have passed on, my father, my grandfather who was a good singer, you know. Both of my grandfathers were singers on both sides. They both were traditional drum carriers. To me singing means to have respect, you know, have respect for the spirits and our alters, you know, our ceremonies, our ceremonial pouches. Those are the first things that come to mind when I'm a singer. Everything else is second. Like to win, it's nice to win but it's not the first priority in my mind. It's OK to lose. It's alright with me. Because I always remember as a singer, it was given to me to celebrate life and . . . Life giver—the drum is a life giver and that's where I gain my strength. Not only for myself but for my family and my relatives. So that's what that means to me.

CS: And when you sing at powwows, whom do you sing for? Do you sing for yourself, do you sing for the audience?

GD: I sing, ummm, for the audience. I think it's nice to share songs. I have a good feeling when I compose a song and people like it and enjoy it. But I never forget why I sing, and it's for the Creator first in my mind. But it's always good to sing for the audience. And sing for the dancers, because I always think of the dancers and I always—like as a dancer myself, I always want a good song to fire me up. And that what I try to do as a singer too, you know. (Gabe Desrosiers interview, October 1999)

The Ethics and Aesthetics of Singing

This chapter provided a detailed review of many of the aesthetic choices and values that guide powwow singers in their evaluations of their own and others singing performances in the context of competition powwow singing. Singing at competition powwows incorporates a complex hybrid of aesthetic values where competing aesthetic discourses are worked out: regionalism and standardization, traditional and contemporary, tribal and intertribal. These aesthetic and evaluative negotiations are constantly at play in a competition. The general effect, however, has been one of increasing standardization, as criteria for judging song performances become more decidedly fixed with each passing powwow season. The aesthetics of the competition powwow circuit have created new and stronger affective links between powwow participants as they interact and evaluate each other every weekend on the powwow grounds.

These aesthetic values have also come to deeply influence aesthetic choices within the powwow recording industry. While this point is taken up in far greater detail in part II of this book, here I want to point out that a central link between these two worlds is the group of people that participate in both: Native youth. As Smith, Burke, and Ward point out, "One implication of global communications technologies is the predominance of young Indigenous voices, which could seriously undermine the structural position and power held by elders" (2000, 16). The implication is that participation in communications technologies is a young person's game, and thus elders, traditionally held to be leaders in communities, do not have the same kind of voice. This is one way in which the emerging powwow industry is affecting how powwow song styles are performed and developed. Northern competition powwow culture has, in a very real way, become synonymous with Native youth culture. This is not to say that there is not multigenerational participation in the production and consumption of recordings and other powwow media. However the direction of the stylistic development of powwow music is dominated by the voices of youth. They are the ones who exhibit the highest degree of investment in the kinds of innovations in singing performances introduced on the competition powwow grounds and in recording studios.

CHAPTER 3

Drum Groups
and Singers

To rework the pattern of social relationships is to rearrange the coordinates of the
experienced world. Society's forms are culture's substance.
—CLIFFORD GEERTZ (1973, 28)

Being a singer, I think, is a lifestyle. You're on the road all summer. You're gone
weekends. You know, during the week you come home for a few days maybe, re-
pack, do washing, whatever, get ready again for next weekend. You know, so it's
time-consuming but it's worth it. You travel all over, you meet lots of nice people,
you get to see different parts of the country. You get invited places. People ask
you to come and sing for them. Things like that. You know, that's important. It's
really important when somebody says they'd like you to come sing. And you feel
honored. And it's not an ego trip either, it's not a, "oh yeah, I'm good." It's just
about that respect that these people want to hear you sing and you feel good from
it. The sense of feeling I get from it, you know, it's a positive one.
—MIKE ESQUASH interview (September 1999)

In this chapter I interweave the stories and experiences of two drum
groups as they traveled the Northern powwow trail in the summers of 1999
and 2000: the Spirit Sands Singers, led by Mike Esquash; and the Northern Wind Singers, led by Gabe Desrosiers. Both of these drum groups—
or "drums," as these groups are more commonly referred to by powwow
people—regularly traveled the northern Plains competition powwow circuit in the summers of 1999 and 2000, although each occupied a different place in the social order of the powwow world. There is a multitiered
system of prestige for powwow drums within the competition circuit, a

prestige structure unique to competition powwows.[1] One earns prestige within this circuit through consistent, cross-country travel to Northern (and sometimes Southern) competition powwows, competing in and winning singing contests (particularly winning or consistently placing at large, national competition powwows like Schemitzun, Gathering of Nations, and the Denver March Powwow), through hosting (or being invited to host) large competition powwows (often sponsored by casinos), and through an active and successful recording career. Thus, singers speak of "different kinds of drums." There are those who are considered "local drums," groups that might have good singers but who do not travel very much and so do not become well known beyond a local or regional level. Ranked above this group are a large number of drum groups that travel and compete on the Northern circuit with a modest degree of success. These groups are well known regionally and sometimes beyond. They will have recorded at least one tape or CD in the course of their careers and have a relatively stable core of singers. Within the uppermost echelon of drum groups are those that are well known internationally — particularly in Canada and the United States — for their consistent success at large and small competition events; they will also have several recordings to their credit. In 1999–2000 this collection of groups included Blacklodge, Blackstone, Southern Cree, Stoney Park, Northern Wind, Eyabay, Mystic River, and two newer groups with rapidly growing reputations, Midnite Express and Bear Creek.[2]

By 2000 the Spirit Sands Singers and the Northern Wind Singers were at different stages in their careers. At that time, the Spirit Sands Singers were still becoming established on the Northern circuit; they were a relatively new drum group in their fourth year of existence. Northern Wind had been active on the Northern circuit since 1991 and was already quite well known and well established. I interweave the experiences and social arrangements of these two groups in order to portray a range of variation within the social habits and structures of powwow drums and singers. The purpose of this exposition is to detail the unique social arrangements forged on the powwow grounds, a social order structured by the dynamic interplay of tribalism and intertribalism and specific to the structural requirements of competition singing. Just as competition powwows compel drums to commit to a set of formalized aesthetic and ethical standards, social arrangements are similarly structured through participation within the competition circuit. Key components of this structure include the social requirements of travel, the economics of singing, and the distribution of social power across standardized social roles within and surrounding drum groups.

Traveling Culture

James Clifford suggests that the "people studied by anthropologists have seldom been homebodies. Some of them, at least, have been travelers: workers, pilgrims, explorers, religious converts, or other traditional 'long distance specialists' (Helms 1988). In the history of twentieth-century anthropology, 'informants' first appear as natives; they emerge as travelers" (Clifford 1997, 19). The lives of powwow people are deeply affected by the practice of travel. In fact, one is generally a condition of the other. It is, of course, possible to be a singer and stay close to home (wherever that may be), but for those powwow drum groups that participate in competition powwows on a regular basis, summers are filled with time spent on the road. Learning about and working with powwow singers requires an understanding of the role of travel in the lives of the musicians. Examining a "traveling culture" involves an investigation of how specific "rooted" cultural practices travel through time and space. This requires an attention to the cultural ideas and practices that are unique to the powwow grounds and powwow culture, and how they travel from reservation to reservation across the continent. This can involve various kinds of transformations and moments of hybrid cultural practice. For example, the Jingle Dress dance regalia, nearly universally recognized as originally being an Ojibwa dance and outfit style, has been elaborated and transformed through the addition of new elements of dress (e.g., a vest has been added to the original simple cloth dress) and new, specifically non-Ojibwa styles of beadwork. These kinds of elaborations and transformations of the traditional Ojibwa style have led to other kinds of transformations in terms of discourse and practice, including the creation of old-style and contemporary-style Jingle Dress dance categories at many competition powwows. In these, old style is limited to the original or traditional regalia style and to more basic footwork patterns, while contemporary style encompasses all of the intertribal variations in the style of dress and dance that have developed over the last thirty years. Powwows are a rich arena for the study of how cultural practices and cultural artifacts "travel" across North America.

Studying powwows also requires an understanding the "culture of travel," the particular ways of living practiced by those who spend a large part of their lives on the powwow trail. The culture of travel refers to specific cultural practices, ideologies, and discourses that emerge and develop through traveling as a general mode of life. For many dedicated powwow singers and dancers, more than half the year is spent "on the trail." Within such a transient existence, certain values and practices emerge and become central to the powwow way of life. Of course, how "culture" travels and how a culture *of* travel develops are deeply interconnected. But what is involved in these kinds of practices? How do traveling practices—behaviors and ideas—differ from the practices of particular, stationary places? How do powwow people construct ideas of travel, mobility, and transience? And what are the material, emotional, and economic requirements of that mode of life?

Stories of travel are ubiquitous at powwows. In August 2002, I met up with Gabe and his wife, Dianne, at the Schemitzun powwow in Connecticut. Both Gabe and his wife were competing in the dance competition that year, Gabe in the Traditional Grass dance category and Dianne in the Traditional Jingle Dress competition. For the first time in a number of years, Gabe's drum, the Northern Wind Singers, was not performing at the competition. We met in a small café about three miles down the road from the powwow grounds just after midnight, soon after the evening dance session had ended. The café was one of the only places open in the area, apart from the vast Foxwoods Resort Casino complex, which was open twenty-four hours but quite expensive. Thus as a result of proximity and affordability, the little diner was filled to capacity with powwow people smoking, visiting, chatting, and laughing.

As is typical, we began speaking about other powwows we had been to that year, and different drum groups, which ones were sounding good this year (or not), and who was singing with which group these days. Gabe mentioned to me that this year the Schemitzun powwow was organized differently than in previous years. Sponsored by the Mashantucket Pequot tribe and funded by the luxurious Foxwoods Resort Casino, the powwow was well known to singers and dancers who traveled the competition circuit as one of the most potentially lucrative powwows of the year. In previous years, individual dance prizes were as much as $5,000, and singing contests could net a group $25,000 for a first-place finish. In 2002, however, a new committee chairman presided over the powwow, and the committee had scaled back the prize money considerably. In previous years there were as many as fifty different drum groups competing. This year there were only fifteen, all of them invited specifically. As a result, according to Gabe and Dianne, there were perhaps only half as many dancers at the 2002 event as in previous years. Schemitzun was expensive for many powwow participants. Travel to Connecticut alone was very costly for competition dancers living in the Midwest and in the prairies of Canada and the United States, home to many champion dancers. The Foxwoods resort and all of the surrounding hotels were also expensive. Without the potential for large cash prizes, many dancers simply did not think it was worth the drive or the expense.

In speaking about the challenges of traveling, Gabe recounted a story about a gig that the Northern Wind Singers had in Eugene, Oregon, a few years earlier. They were hired as the host drum for the University of Oregon's annual powwow. But as the powwow weekend approached, they found that neither Gabe's van nor the other van they used were in working condition. So Gabe (the drumkeeper) said that he would pay for a plane ticket to fly out there with the drum. The other members had to get out there by car, but only one of them had a car that was running at the time. So all seven of the other singers (and their luggage) piled into that one car. Because only six could fit in the front and back seats, each of them took turns riding in the trunk of the car surrounded by the luggage of all of the other singers. They drove this way, six in the car and one in the trunk, from their homes on the Northwest Angle Reserve in the Lake of the Woods area in Ontario, all the way to Oregon and back! "They said it was alright riding in the trunk until they had to stop for gas," Gabe said through barely controlled laughter. "Then they felt a little funny getting out and opening the trunk and having a guy get out. It drew a lot of stares from the other people at the gas station." We all began to laugh uproariously. *This* was a powwow story! What made this quintessential was its focus on, and celebration of, travel. As a travel story, it clearly delineated "home" and "away from home" as spatial and social fields, each composed of different activities, expectations, and possibilities. Each year come spring, powwow singers and dancers spoke eagerly about getting on the road in the summer: a life filled with singing, dancing, "snagging" (courtship and dating), and relative making.

The culture of travel is an essential and deeply embedded aspect of powwows that informs and structures social practice on multiple levels. This is especially true for competition powwows, participation in which requires constant travel in a way that is not necessary for participation in regional traditional powwows. The Northern competition circuit structures travel and interpersonal relationships in unique ways. Travel itself becomes a central organizing trope in structuring acceptable ideologies and forms of behavior. Exchange of people, ideas, and songs between drum groups is shaped by the transitory nature of the competition circuit; the terms and nature of this interaction take place on the powwow grounds as social categories of age, tribal affiliation, and gender are constructed and contested. Modern Native American identity and consciousness are forged in and through these intertribal social relationships as they are worked out every weekend at powwow celebrations.

Powwow Economics 101: "You Don't Get Rich Singing"

The economic hardship endured by singers is often expressed through the ironically understated lament that "you don't get rich singing." Extensive summer travel on the competition powwow circuit is a costly endeavor for a drum group. Basic equipment needs include access to a drum and a set of drumsticks; several working, reliable vehicles; and, if one is fortunate, a portable public address (PA) system. Each drum costs between $200 and $600, sometimes more, depending on the size of the drum and the materials used in construction, and is made to order by instrument makers. Drumsticks, also handmade, are $10–$20 per stick unless a group makes their own. While it is quite common for someone within the group to have the ability to make drumsticks, only a few drum groups make their own drums. The Spirit Sands Singers owned three drums, two of which they commissioned and one of which was awarded to them for their participation in the Heartbeat of Nations powwow, a large, urban big-money competition powwow held annually in Winnipeg between 1996 and 1999.[3] Spirit Sands carried two drums to every powwow for both practical and aesthetic reasons. Each drum had a different timbre, depending on its size and the kind of hide used for the drumhead: one drum had a moose hide, the other a deer hide. The former is a thicker and more durable hide but less resonant and ringing. The timbre of each drum also varied depending on weather conditions. Mike liked to keep his options open and would decide each day of a powwow which drum was sounding better or which drum he preferred to hear. There was also a practical aspect to carrying a second drum: it served as a backup in case a drum skin split during the course of the weekend. It is also not uncommon for drum groups to be given drums by other singers or groups. Northern Wind's first drum was given to them by a fellow singer. A few years later, a powwow committee gave them another as a gift for serving as a host drum.

As indicated by Gabe's travel story, transportation to and from powwows is always an issue, so much so that an entire genre of jokes has emerged on the powwow trail celebrating the "Indian car" or "powwow car," vehicles held together by duct tape, the mechanical expertise and ingenuity of their owners, and the power of prayer. Working vehicles are required for regular powwow participation, and a number of singers commented to me that their summer powwow travel plans hinged on the group's ability to find adequate and reliable transportation. There are multiple possible sources for vehicles: individual singers may be fortunate enough to own a van or truck; a drum group might petition reservation band councils for the use or purchase of a vehicle; or another community sponsor (usually a family relation of one or more of the singers) could provide transportation. Regular participation in competition singing requires that many singers hold seasonal or part-time jobs, employment that allows them a great deal of free time to travel in the summer months. As such, the difficulty of finding adequate transportation is indicative of the larger financial constraints under which many singers operate.

A number of drum groups that travel regularly own their own PA systems (which typically consist of a powered mixer, two speakers, and one or more microphones and microphone stands). The Spirit Sands Singers always traveled with their own system when participating in powwows in which they were simply competing in the singing competition as opposed to being a host or invited drum group. Some reservation-based competition powwows do not provide sound systems for the amplification of drum groups and as such, owning one's own system ensures a certain quality of sound and volume. The Spirit Sands Singers purchased their system using money earned from powwows, as well as through economic sponsorship from the Esquash family. The sound system was a source of pride for Mike, and good sound gear was a kind of marker of prestige on the powwow trail. For other drum groups and for powwow committees, owning and traveling with a quality PA system was a sign that a group possessed a certain degree of economic viability and was serious about sounding good when performing.[4] Conversely, Northern Wind never traveled with a sound system and rarely required one, because the group typically performed at powwows where a sound system was provided or where a sound system was not needed (as is often the case at many smaller traditional powwows). Age also played a role in the perceived value of sound systems. Drums composed of young singers (under thirty) typically valued the convenience of a personal PA more than older singers and groups, for whom amplification was considered a "modern" development in powwows. For example, I was constantly amazed (as a sound engineer) at the PA system regularly used by the Mandaree singers, a well-known and highly respected group of elderly singers from North Dakota. Their PA system was of such poor quality that it consistently distorted their singing and drumming and produced screeching howls of electronic feedback. I was never sure whether they simply could not afford a better system or whether they just did not want to bother with the technology.

Powwow singers may be characterized as semiprofessionals: they are paid for their performances but very few singers are able to make their living solely from powwow singing. Powwows are, generally speaking, one of the few venues in which drum groups and singers expect to be monetarily compensated for their singing. Drum groups and, more often, individual singers perform in a variety of social contexts without pay. For instance, Mike sang for funerals, weddings, Yuwipi ceremonies, sweat lodges, and other ceremonial contexts, as well as holding informal singing classes for the youth of Swan Lake, all without monetary compensation (or at least no compensation was expected or required). For Mike, these duties were simply part of the social and ethical responsibilities of being a singer.

There are several ways in which drum groups can be paid, each depending on their social role at a powwow. Groups may be hired as host drums, meaning that a powwow committee contacts the leader of the group and hires them to sing for the weekend. The host drum is paid a guaranteed amount of money for their performance, as well as being provided for in any number of other ways. The committee will very often feed the group, either through a series of committee-sponsored feasts, or through meal tickets that members can exchange at various concession stands at a powwow. At reservation powwows, the host reserve will sometimes run a concession stand of its own and may provide the weekend's meals for the host drum through this venue. At urban powwows or casino-sponsored events, a number of hotel rooms are usually provided to the host drum as part of the agreement. In 1999–2000, the amount of money paid to a host drum at a competition powwow usually ranged between $2,000 and $5,000, depending on the size of the powwow and the location.[5]

As the host drum, a group is responsible to the committee for singing whatever and whenever they are asked. Apart from singing during their regular turn in the drum rotation, host drums often start off singing Grand Entry songs as well as Flag songs and Victory songs. They are also required to sing any songs that are unexpectedly required during the course of events. For instance if another drum group in the rotation does not sing a proper song for a contest (i.e., a particular song style requested by the judges) — described in some detail in chapter 2 — the host drum will be asked to provide the proper song. Host drums will usually sing for local dance specials and will also provide Honor songs for giveaways.[6] Their role as the host drum, however, prohibits their participation in the singing contest. First-place prizes for singing contests may often be more money than the guaranteed payment for hosting, but most drums are happy to exchange the possibility of more money for the financial security of being a host. It is rare for a drum group to turn down an invitation to serve as host drum for a powwow, simply because it is an honor to be asked by a community to sing for its event. It is also somewhat of a breach of etiquette to decline an invitation, although sometimes a group may have no choice but to refuse because of prior commitments.

Groups may also be hired as "invited drums." As such, like the host drums, the powwow committee guarantees a certain sum of money for the drums (although generally it is less than the host drum payment). As invited drums, however, they have less responsibility to the committee and generally sing only during their turn in the drum rotation. Invited drums may also participate in singing contests. In some instances invited drums are not guaranteed any money apart from what might be earned through a singing competition, but in such cases there may often be as many prizes in the competition as there are invited drums. For example, if a powwow committee invited ten drums, only those ten groups would compete in the competition and there would be cash prizes awarded for first place through tenth place, with first place bringing the most money and tenth place the least.

At all powwows, except perhaps some of the very biggest competitions, drum groups are welcome and encouraged to simply show up and perform. Drums that participate in powwows (but not as host drums or invited drums) are paid "day pay," sometimes also called a "drum split." Powwow committees set aside a certain amount of money for a powwow to be paid to any and all drum groups that choose to travel to and participate in the powwow. The amount of the drum split will again vary according to the size of the event and the location. As with host drumming, drum splits at powwows sponsored by out-of-the-way northern reserves might advertise a large drum split in the hopes of attracting more drum groups. This lump sum of money is then dispersed equally to all drum groups that participate. Day pay for drum groups is intended to offset the cost of travel to and from the powwow as well as to provide money for food during the weekend. There are several other ways in which drum groups can earn money at a powwow. Selling tapes and CDs, if a group has any, is one very common way. During the weekend a singer or a family member (often small children) will circle the arbor holding up CDs and tapes for sale, often at times just before and just after the group has performed. When the Spirit Sands Singers sang at the Onion Lake powwow in central Saskatchewan in the summer of 2000, Mike brought a box of twenty-five CDs and had sold them all by Saturday night. A young man who introduced himself to the group on Friday night agreed to walk the grounds selling the CDs in exchange for being provided food for the weekend. As it turned out he was a talented salesman and quickly sold all the discs Mike had brought to the powwow.

During that weekend Spirit Sands was also asked to sing for two different Buckskin dance specials. Sponsors for the specials approached the group and offered tobacco and a small amount of cash ($150 for one special, $200 for the other) in exchange for agreeing to sing. The offer of money in these instances is customary but not required. Drum groups consider it an honor to be asked to sing, both because they are committed to singing for the community and because it is flattering to be asked, and such a request will never be refused. All of these economic opportunities combined often help a drum group simply break even for a weekend of travel. Drum groups will only turn a profit if they place in the singing contest. Even if a drum group comes out "in the black" for a weekend's singing, individual members of the group may or may not see any of the money. Some groups have agreements whereby any money generated from singing is used to finance their future goals, which might include buying a new drum, PA equipment, financing a new recording, or sometimes even paying for a new vehicle.

For the Onion Lake powwow Spirit Sands Singers had traveled approximately ten hours to the Onion Lake Cree Reserve in west central Saskatchewan. There was vehicle trouble, however, and both the van and Mike's truck broke down on the way. As Spirit Sands did not place in the competition, the drum split money was not enough to fix the vehicles. The group was stranded. Mike's parents, who drove separately, were able to drive the drum and PA system back with them but had no room for passengers. I drove separately as well, and so five of us piled into my small Geo Prizm. Three others lit out early on Monday morning and began walking home, hoping to hitch a ride along the way. Much of the money generated from the CD sales and singing for the specials had been used to feed the group for the weekend. The costs of the Onion Lake powwow were unusually high for the group because of the distance traveled and the vehicle trouble. However, life on the powwow circuit is filled with such unexpected expenses, making economics a constant source of concern and tension within a drum group.

Social Organization of a Drum Group

Powwow drum groups typically consist of five to fifteen singers, generally all male.[7] Many groups are formed according to kinship ties, and groups with membership consisting almost entirely of close and distant family relations are common. More than one singer has suggested to me that "the best drum groups are family groups" because a family grows up singing together. As a result of the close proximity of family members, family drum groups also have the opportunity to practice with a greater frequency, giving the group a further advantage.

Although many drum groups operate in an informal, somewhat egalitarian manner, as drum groups have become increasingly professional (as a result of their participation on the competition powwow circuit), several well-defined social roles have emerged. Each drum group will have at least one lead singer: someone who is responsible for singing the leads to all of the songs. Well-established and successful drum groups will have a number of members who are capable of singing lead. For example, when the Northern Wind Singers first began singing together in 1991, Gabe Desrosiers was the only lead singer, so he performed all the leads on all of their songs. In 1999–2000 the group had four lead singers, each of whom would sing one lead during a four push-up performance, with Gabe typically singing the first lead and the other three singers each performing another in turn.

A lead singer is defined as someone who has a strong, loud, and clear voice; who is confident enough to sing without the accompaniment of any other singers; and who knows the leads to songs without prompting by other singers. Simply having what is considered to be a "good sounding" voice is not enough to be considered a good lead singer. One also has to have a good musical memory to be able to lead songs. Singers have commented to me that the most successful drum groups achieve their success because of the large number of lead singers in the group (as leads are considered to be "better" singers than those who do not sing lead—i.e., the "seconds"). Thus when I have asked singers to speculate on the staggering popularity of the Ojibwa group Eyabay, the response was often, "everyone in the group is a lead singer," meaning that all of the singers have the *ability* to sing lead, even if they all do not *perform* the role of lead singer in the group.

Drum groups must also have a designated "drum carrier" or "drum-keeper" who is responsible for the care and transportation of the drum. The drum carrier may or may not sing in the group but is considered a part of the group due to the importance of his responsibilities. In the Spirit Sands Singers Mike's father, Gerald Esquash, served as drum carrier. While Gerald did not sing in the group he was nonetheless thought of as an integral member; he and his wife, Linda (who was a harmony singer), traveled with the group for almost every performance, typically transporting the drum and the other equipment (such as the PA system). It is the primary responsibility of the drum carrier to watch over the drum during a powwow (although all drum group members share in this duty), making sure it is never left unattended and always sufficiently protected from the elements.[8] The designation of a drum carrier speaks to the symbolic and spiritual importance associated with the instrument for powwow singers as expressed by Mike during one of our formal interviews:

> ME: [And so] you always take care of the drum. Keep it warm. You have to take care of your drum. Very important. You respect it as a living being. That's what that is. Every drum has a spirit. Without that spirit you wouldn't—you wouldn't have the spirit of the song. You wouldn't

have a dancer dancing. You can sing all you want but the drum [group] is not . . . the makers of it [the performance], you know.

CS: Is that why you burn sweetgrass for the drum?

ME: Yeah, the sweet grass is an activator. You know, kind of cleaning the drum, and respecting it. And it kind of tells it, like it kind of activates the spirit of the drum and says, "OK, we're gonna use you now and [we] ask you to take care of us." You pray, when you're doing that. (Mike Esquash interview, September 1999)

Mike's respect for and trust in the drum was tested at the Onion Lake powwow. The reserve is somewhat isolated, accessible only by winding gravel roads. Early Sunday afternoon, storm clouds appeared rapidly on the horizon, followed—alarmingly—by funnel clouds. The wind had picked up and the sky turned an eerie gray-green. The powwow grounds were flat and treeless, much like the majority of the surrounding reserve, and there was no shelter or low ground in which to seek refuge. The emcee announced that the funnel clouds were heading in the direction of the reserve but had yet to touch down. He recommended that parents find their children and seek whatever shelter they could find. Tents were quickly taken down before they were blown away. Remarkably, the competition dancing continued unabated while the stands emptied and the audience of non-dancers scattered. The Spirit Sands Singers' turn in the drum order was quickly approaching. Mike urged his singers to stay by the drum, insisting that "the drum will take care of you." He sat by the drum and made a tobacco offering and prayed. The elders at the powwow also gave a similar prayer and offering. Mike turned to me and said philosophically, "You know the reason you see a lot of Indian people standing around here? It's because if the Creator wants to take you, he will, and there's nothing you can do about it. Indian people know this."

Regularly competing drum groups must also have at least one song-maker among them, someone who supplies the group with new songs for each subsequent powwow season. The growth of competition pow-wows and the increasing importance of recording have made it important for drum groups to generate fresh material for their repertoires. When groups first start out, they don't need original songs. Singers will simply learn the songs of their favorite local or nonlocal drums, either through face-to-face interaction, bootlegged recordings, or commercially produced tapes and CDs.[9] But as groups become more involved in competition singing, there is more pressure on them to sing songs that are specifically theirs (meaning that their repertoire is created by members of the group or otherwise owned by that group, e.g., songs owned by a singer's family). Drums that regularly compete in singing competitions typically do so only with their own songs (or, in some instances, with songs they have been given permission to sing). Part of the growth and maturation of a powwow group entails the gradual development of a unique repertoire, as Mike Esquash's story in this interview excerpt reveals:

> Me and my brother kind of threw the idea out to some guys on the reserve: "Let's try to start a group, see how we do." So, first thing we had to figure out is how to get a drum, and we knew one guy had a drum on the reserve and he said he wanted to jam with us. So we got his drum, we borrowed it. And we just started learning the songs of other groups. Like the influential groups for us, they were like Mandaree, Porcupine [Singers], the old style of singing, the old Straight style. That was something I really . . . I remembered a lot, eh, and I really liked that. So [we] learned songs like that and it just kind of—the style just stuck with us. . . . We barely had [any of our own songs]—we may have had one or something, but not really much. So we just went there [to our first powwow] and sang a bunch of Straight songs and tried it out. (Mike Esquash interview, September 1999)

Not only is an original repertoire valued, but the *size* of the repertoire is also a measure of a singer's or drum group's accomplishment and ability. When I asked singers how many songs they knew, I would often get the answer "hundreds" or even "thousands." While I never tested the limits of an individual singer's proclaimed repertoire, these numbers are most likely an expression of the value placed on the size of a repertoire (and, by extension, the value of a highly developed musical memory for singers) rather than a literal reckoning. In my experience singing with Spirit Sands and observing other groups, a typical working repertoire (a collection of songs that are sung repeatedly during any one powwow season) is closer to twenty to thirty songs, of which perhaps 80 to 90 percent are new.[10] Thus it is likely that in the career of a singer he may indeed sing hundreds or even thousands of different songs, but most concede that one never is able to recall that many at any one time.

> ME: Now we maybe know . . . maybe forty, fifty songs. I can't always re-member all of them at the same time [laughs]. Sometimes you're

struggling, you're sitting at the drum, "Umm, what are we gonna sing?" You know, you try and . . . you learn as much as you can, so you're prepared. You prepare . . .

CS: So how many are your own songs and how many are other people's?

ME: If not . . . probably half if not more. Yeah. Because you learn everybody's songs. (Mike Esquash interview, September 1999)

In learning other people's songs, variation or alteration of the original song is usually frowned upon. There is no value placed on learning someone else's songs and then "making them your own" through idiosyncratic stylistic treatment. An effort is made to render as faithfully as possible another group's or another singer's song. While there is a spoken rhetoric of song ownership among drum groups, in practice there is a great deal of flexibility in the free exchange of songs. During the course of my fieldwork, just about every young drum group that I spoke with knew at least one Eyabay song, often more. These songs may or may not have been performed in public by the groups. A group certainly would not sing another group's song if that group were present at the powwow and competing in the singing competition.[11]

Whenever possible, if a group wants to add a particular song to their repertoire, singers will ask permission from the songmaker or the drum group to which the song belongs. But even this is not a hard and fast rule. At the Onion Lake powwow, where I was singing with the Spirit Sands Singers, we were asked by sheer coincidence to perform a number of Round dance songs. Mike had only made a couple of Round dance songs and so for one performance we sang a song by Art Moosomin, a well-known, well-respected Cree singer and songmaker who specialized in this genre. After the song finished, we turned around to see none other than Mr. Moosomin himself sitting behind the drum. The group was a little embarrassed at not previously being aware of his presence and immediately all rose to shake his hand. Mike gave him tobacco and thanked him for the song and for the honor of being allowed to sing it. Permission to sing his song was thus only sought and given *after* the performance, since Mike had originally learned the song from a recording. There was no animosity during the exchange, nor any hint that any protocol had been violated. Among singers there is a kind of unspoken agreement that powwow songs are public, and they will often travel with or without formal exchange or consent.

Among regularly competing singing groups, other social roles have developed within the performance setting. Northern Wind has designated members of the group to perform honor beats and add improvised cries, yells, and other sound effects during the course of performance. In the Spirit Sands Singers, much of the decision making about social roles in performance evolved during the course of singing together. Mike controlled the performance through a series of predetermined hand signals. Typically Mike would begin each song, taking the first lead. He would either perform each ensuing lead or he would signal to another singer during the last phrase of the push-up, indicating that it was now that singer's responsibility to take the next lead. This was generally accomplished through making eye contact and nodding. These singers had the option to refuse if they felt they did not know the lead well enough or if they did not feel their voice was strong enough to carry the song. Sometimes they would "shake Mike off" (much to Mike's annoyance), shaking their head as an indication that they were not willing or able to take the next lead. In this way, Mike served an important role as a singing teacher for the group. Mike was by far the most experienced singer in the group at the time, and he composed almost all of the original compositions of the drum. He knew the songs better than anyone and many times dragged the rest of the group through a performance with the sheer force of his will and the power of his voice. But he was also constantly monitoring the development of younger singers in the group, and when he felt that they were getting stronger he would occasionally point to them during the course of a performance to take a lead. If they accepted and performed the lead successfully, he would begin to call on them more regularly and these singers would begin to take on more singing responsibilities within the group. Conversely, the Northern Wind Singers had a much more rigidly structured set of social roles. Four singers in the group, including Gabe, sang the vast majority of the leads, typically each one taking one lead over the course of four push-ups, often in a predetermined order. Northern Wind had been together for over a decade with a fairly stable core membership. As veteran singers, they all knew their roles.

Finally, each regularly performing drum group has an informal band manager, a spokesperson who acts as the contact for host or invited drum work and recording. More often than not this person is also the de facto leader of the group, a lead singer, and often the founder of the group. Mike

Esquash and Gabe Desrosiers are both typical in this regard. Both men function as the decision makers for their groups, determining where they will perform each weekend and making sure enough singers are available for each performance. It is also expected that the leader of the group will "take care of his singers," ensuring that members of the group get to and from the powwow without incident, and seeing that they're all fed and have a place to sleep while traveling. The degree of control exercised by a group leader depends on the level of professionalization of the group. Drum groups that do not regularly compete and sing at competition powwows are far less likely to have a formal leadership structure. As a group becomes more active and established as a competition drum, a drum leader becomes a practical necessity.

While drum leaders are tacitly acknowledged by other singers, the level of power and control granted to that leader is specific to the character of the individuals in the group, as the two excerpts below indicate:

ME: Myself, I never say that "I'm the boss." Because I'm not.

CS: How does that work? You're the one who will call the practices?

ME: I guess I set up the practices, the songs. . . . I'm the lead singer and I handle the business end of it. Stuff like that. But usually it's a group decision. If I have something [e.g., a recording contract] to sign, I'll go up to the boys and say, "OK, I can't figure this out [alone]. You guys gotta vote on this. We've gotta agree—make an agreement on this." Because it's not good to be the boss. (Mike Esquash interview, September 1999)

I think a good singer is a person who doesn't use alcohol and drugs, because those things don't mix. And you see that a lot out there too. That's another thing about my drum group is that when we travel, see I don't use alcohol or drugs. And I stress that a lot. And I think that's another reason why some guys haven't lasted with us [laughs]. They don't like my policies. Because a lot of powwow drum groups are, you know, partying and stuff, and I don't do that. And usually those are my policies when we're traveling. You can't drink, you know. If you want to drink, wait till you get home. Don't bring it to the powwow and don't bring it on the trail with me. Party afterwards [laughs]. (Gabe Desrosiers interview, October 1999)

Rehearsal of Songs

I often asked drum groups how much they rehearsed. Generally, they responded by saying once a week or even several times a week. While this may be true for some groups, I believe many groups rarely rehearse outside of the context of a powwow, at least during the summer months when active drum groups are performing together almost every weekend. Midweek practices are deemed superfluous because each weekend is thought of as one long rehearsal. With Gabe Desrosiers and Northern Wind, the singers of the group hail from different reserves throughout Minnesota and Ontario; they learn new songs only on weekends at a powwow, which is the only time they are all gathered together. When Gabe first mentioned this to me I expressed incredulity. Gabe's songs in particular, to my ears, often feature subtly complex melodies that I imagined were difficult to learn. "Good singers can learn a song after only one or two push-ups," he insisted. "My guys are good singers." This fact was forcefully demonstrated to me during the recording of the Northern Wind CD *Ikwe Nagamonan*. The group gathered in the studio the night before the recording session to rehearse for the impending session. Gabe had composed twelve new songs for the CD, none of which the singers had ever heard before. The recording session the next day went quite smoothly with only a few songs that had to be repeated because of singing mistakes. The group had indeed learned all the songs in a very short time. In fact, Gabe insists that this CD is one of the best he has ever recorded and claims that he has received a good deal of positive feedback from the powwow community for this recording.

When asked directly in a formal interview, a number of groups reported that they practiced regularly through the summer months, at least once a week (midweek between powwows). Others said that they only practiced during the summer and that during the winter months, when powwows were less common, they occupied themselves with other things, such as family commitments and seasonal employment. In my experiences with the Spirit Sands Singers, there were very few formal midweek rehearsals during the summer or winter months.[12] Instead the learning of songs often took place around the drum at powwows as the group waited for their turn to sing. At a powwow, five or six groups down the line of the singing order, Mike would begin to count forward in order to try and calculate the dance category for which the group would perform. After determining the dance category, he would begin to think of an appropriate song, lowering his head, putting a hand over his ear, closing his eyes, tapping quietly on the rim of the drum with his drumstick. He would start singing quietly, almost under his breath, singing the whole song through (one push-up), making sure that he remembered the tune correctly so that he would be able to lead it strongly and confidently. Sometimes tunes do not so easily come to mind. Mike always carried a hand-held tape recorder and several tapes full of old and new songs. Some were recordings of the group; others were songs that he had recently made. If he couldn't bring a song to mind right away, he usually knew what song he wanted and where it was on the tape, and he would do a quick search, holding the tape recorder right next to his ear to hear the song. Coming up with songs under these conditions can sometimes be a difficult task. While Mike is trying to bring a song to mind there can often be another group singing, their song loudly playing through the PA system.

The social discourse between drum group members that occurs around the drum is, to a great extent, musical discourse. It is not uncommon for members of the Spirit Sands Singers to break spontaneously into song while watching a dance or waiting for the next dance, singing quietly while tapping a drumstick on their leg or the back of a chair. Another group member may also know the tune or else be able to "catch it" (learn it) quickly. In this way, small talk around the drum is often replaced by (or takes the form of) singing together or for each other. These kinds of informal performances might turn into more formal rehearsals of a song. If singers like the way the song sounds, they might try to use it during the course of the weekend if it's appropriate for the dancers for whom they are singing. There is thus a great fluidity between formal and informal singing, where singing practice could very quickly turn into a public performance.

Who Sings?

The rise and proliferation of competition powwows—resulting in greater opportunities for the personal accumulation of both economic and cultural capital—has created new and increased incentives for singing. In the early 1970s Thomas Hatton observed that the "number of young men who join singing groups is surprisingly few. Indeed, I have not heard of anyone being caught in the stampede of young men aspiring to become good singers" (1974, 125). By the 1990s however, singing had become an attractive option for many young male Native Americans. Despite the lament that "you don't get rich singing," the money earned by drum groups for winning competitions or hosting powwows is often more than enough to support a number of groups in their travels all summer long. So even if, at the end of the summer, a group has very little money in the bank for their summer of traveling and singing, they have been able to support themselves doing what they love to do.

There are a number of additional incentives as well. Singers are accorded a great deal of respect on the powwow trail. A fraternity of singers develops and social networks are renewed, solidified, or created anew. Singing becomes an arena in which personal reputations can be developed and enhanced among one's peers. Singing and traveling with a drum group for a summer on the powwow trail is also widely recognized as an opportunity to meet and court members of the opposite sex. "Snagging" is a favorite pastime for many singers and dancers of both sexes. Many long- and short-term relationships are born on the powwow trail, and at just about every powwow I saw several singers spend their time forging and then extricating themselves from a weekend romance.

The idea that certain people are meant to be singers and have a natural gift for singing is surprisingly common among powwow singers considering the equally frequent assertion that "anyone who wants to be a singer can be a singer" (see chapter 2). This seeming contradiction is worked out in distinguishing different levels of singers based on ability. Compositional ability, memory, and a clear, strong voice are all considered to be the gifts of good singers. While it is thought that these talents may be learned to a certain degree, more often they are the result of family inheritance, and singers often trace their singing abilities to relatives of a previous generation. Both Mike Esquash and Gabe Desrosiers believe that the gift of singing runs in their respective families and that they are simply carrying on a family tradition.

GD: I've been a singer since I was about—at least six years old. I remember going to my first powwow around then, back home. And they held it in a weird place too, back in the bush. Everybody had to drive down this little road to get there. I remember that, those first powwows I went to, the place was called Reed Narrows. I went over there, I don't know who I went there with, but I remember it was my first powwow. And I distinctly remember, when the powwow was over, I went home—I could sing those songs. I was just a kid but I remember that. That was the first time that I realized, at that age, that I was going to be a singer.

CS: So that's what got you interested in singing?

GD: I don't think interest has anything to do with why I'm a singer. I think I'm a singer because I'm supposed to be. You see my family is really into our culture and our tradition and our spiritual beliefs. And to me, I'm like that. And I think this [talent for singing] was kind of given to me, in a spiritual sense. My grandfather and his father before him, they were all singers, great singers. There was nobody in between except my uncle. And we have a large family and not one of the boys ever did sing like that. I was the one . . . (Gabe Desrosiers interview, January 2002)

Singing is also, however, something that can be learned; ability can be acquired. Through practice and experience one can learn to be a competent singer, and a number of singers have commented to me that learning to sing is often simply a matter of making the commitment to learn. For example Burt, one of the singers in Spirit Sands, said to me that he worked for a number of years training his voice to be able to sing in the open-throated "warbling style" that he preferred (Hatton 1974, 1986). Thus powwow singing ability is also a matter of vocation. Learning to sing usually begins with the decision to sit down around a drum and learn through experience. As such, most drum groups encourage open participation. Young boys are very often encouraged to sing, even if they have no previous singing experience, and many singers encourage their young boys to sing at very early ages (as early as four years old). One learns through firsthand experience. In a sense then, the belief that "anyone who picks up a drumstick is a singer" expresses the idea that everyone has the *potential* to become a good singer. While there is some recognition of musical talent—some singers just have strong, clear, loud voices and good musical memories—those who are dedicated to learning believe they will succeed at singing.

The decision to learn how to sing usually implies joining or forming an organized drum group. When the Spirit Sands and Northern Wind formed as singing groups, the majority of their personnel had no previous singing experience.

GD: . . . I told my brother, "I'm gonna start a new group, are you in with
       me?" And he said, "Damn right" [laughs]. And that's how the drum
       group started. The next month, August, we started.

CS: Where did you get the rest of your singers?

GD: Well I had this idea. I just got my other brother, who'd never touched
       a drumstick in his life, and I got my two nephews, they never touched
       a drumstick in their lives either, and they came on. And about eight
       other guys, including the Copenace boys. Those three brothers came
       on with us, along with some Kelly boys and a couple other members
       who never sung in their life, from Whitefish Bay [Reserve].

CS: Were they mostly people from Whitefish Bay or were there some from
       Northwest Angle too?

GD: Northwest Angle, you know, and Whitefish Bay. Guys who had never
       sung before. (Gabe Desrosiers interview, January 2002)

Learning to sing is a recursive process; the repetition is built into the
structure of a powwow song performance. Songs are learned during the
course of performance with successive repetitions of push-ups, allowing
singers to gradually learn songs "on the fly." One of the talents considered
to be indicative of a good singer is the ability to quickly learn a song after
only one or two push-ups. Learning to sing not only means learning repertoire but also internalizing the basic structural components of songs:
understanding where honor beats are placed and recognizing drumbeat
cadence patterns. The open, participatory nature of drum groups and the
repetition in performance allow singers of all abilities to join a drum and
gradually take on greater roles and responsibilities within the group. Once
becoming a regular member of a drum group, singers can gradually learn
to sing lead by occasionally trying it during a performance, as was the case
for the Spirit Sands. As a singer becomes more dependable in rendering
leads, he is counted on to sing more. Most lead singers begin singing seconds in any number of different groups before becoming a lead singer in
an already existing group or forming their own drum groups.

Regular travel and performance on the Northern competition powwow
circuit has created a web of regional and intertribal relationships among
singers. As singers form friendships and connections, drum group membership has become quite fluid. On a micro level this condition manifests
itself in the widespread practice of drum hopping, the practice of informally sitting in with a drum group for a single song performance during a

powwow. Etiquette for drum hopping generally requires that a singer joining a group should be able to perform at a level comparable to that of the group, but in actual practice this is not always the case. I have never seen someone turned away from singing at a drum; however, singers will typically only sit in with a group with whom they are familiar. Those singers who are sitting in are also typically expected to either know the song already or have the ability to learn it very quickly.

At large competition events I have seen extreme versions of this behavior, with groups stacking their numbers, for particular competitions, with a number of high-quality, well-respected singers who act as free agents and go out on the road with a drum for a summer, or perhaps only for a particular powwow. It is thought that these stacked groups have a much better chance of winning at big-money competition powwows. Sometimes the opposite of stacking might also occur: some popular drum groups may split into different units for a particular weekend, traveling to and performing at two different powwows. Drum groups will fill in their rosters with "hired guns," other free agent singers or friends who are willing to travel with them. But rather than enhancing the quality of a group, this practice can degrade the sound of the drum, because there are often a number of singers who are not very familiar with the repertoire of the group or who are not lead singers or even strong seconds singers. The practice of splitting up a drum group and performing at two different powwows on the same weekend typically occurs only with more popular or established drum groups who can rely on their reputation to procure host drum gigs. Drum groups rarely try to compete with a "pickup crew" like this because of the effect this has on their overall sound. But host drums or invited drums at a particular powwow may sometimes show up with makeshift personnel, especially if the group is not traveling regularly and many of its regular singers may be otherwise booked, sometimes for the entire summer.

Gabe once told me about a powwow he attended in Minnesota, where all the drum groups were invited and guaranteed a particular fee for singing that weekend. One of those invited showed up with only one lead singer from the original group, and the rest of the group consisting of pickup singers. The sole original member sang all the leads that weekend, not only because he was by far the strongest singer, but because he was also the only one who really knew the songs. Needless to say, the overall sound of the group suffered tremendously, much to the consternation of the dancers and especially the powwow committee, who had hired the group with the expectation of a certain level of quality and professionalism. For Gabe, the lesson was that drum groups that make a habit of showing up to hosting and invited gigs without full crews may soon find themselves with far fewer invitations. Showing up with makeshift crews and performing at a level below that for which a group is generally known is considered an expression of a fundamental lack of respect for the powwow committee and the community that hired the group.

On a macro level, fluid social connections between singers have led to the constant formation and dissolution of singing groups that have drawn their membership from any number of existing drum groups. These new groups may become permanent or may simply be temporarily formed by singers who wish to sing a different repertoire, or to sing with another group during the weekends when their regular group does not travel. One of the large-scale possible musical effects of such practices is the increased blurring of tribally defined or identified styles, as musical style becomes more regionally defined or simply generalized as the "Northern style." Drum groups may thus identify their group styles according to stylistic lineages rather than tribal or regional lineages (e.g., a drum may identify its style as "influenced by Eyabay" rather than saying "we sing in an Ojibwa style").[13]

Singing and Gender Roles
In November 2001 the Sweetgrass Road drum, a group comprised mainly of female Ojibwa and Cree singers from Winnipeg, Manitoba, traveled to the campus of St. Thomas University, a Catholic university in St. Paul, Minnesota, to participate in their thirteenth annual intertribal competition powwow. They had performed at the powwow the previous year under the name the White Turtle Women Singers, and while they did not register for the singing competition, they sang regularly for noncompetition events. Expecting to participate in a similar way in 2001, they registered their drum group on Friday night and the next morning began to set up at the edge of the arbor in anticipation of Saturday afternoon's Grand Entry and dance session. While setting up, they were approached by a member of the powwow committee who informed them that they would not be allowed to sing at the powwow this year because of the traditional "'Woodlands [Indian] policy' of not allowing women to sing at the drum" (Stinson 2002). In December 2001 the group filed a civil complaint against

St. Thomas University alleging "discrimination in an educational institution and public accommodations under the Minnesota Human Rights Act" (ibid.). St. Thomas countered by filing a motion to have the case dismissed on the basis of the First Amendment rights to free speech and freedom of religion. An attorney working for the university claimed, "We believe this is a spiritual event covered by the First Amendment. Native Americans planned this event and they should be allowed to decide how to run it. That it's a public place is irrelevant" (ibid.). In March 2002 Judge Louise Bjorkman denied the motion on the basis that the powwow is not "protected speech" and a trial was scheduled for March the following year. The university responded to Judge Bjorkman's decision by canceling the 2002 powwow as well as all future events. In October 2002 Sweetgrass Road dropped their suit against the university, claiming that their goal in the lawsuit was simply to be able to perform at the powwow and that since the powwow had been canceled, there was no further reason for continuing with the suit.

The controversy over this incident and the lawsuit it produced sent ripples through Indian country and set off yet another round of discussion about the role of women at powwows and in singing groups, the variable influence and importance of tradition at powwows, and the tensions that can emerge from the collision of tribal and intertribal practices and ideologies that often occurs at intertribal competition events. Gender roles are a particularly complicated aspect of the Northern powwow culture of travel, as locally defined and often deeply rooted normative gender roles and gender stereotypes are challenged, questioned, or sometimes reinforced in new tribal and intertribal contexts.

The participation of women within singing groups is one of the most hotly contested issues on the powwow trail.[14] At a fundamental level, men's and women's roles in singing are a social reproduction of the gender segregation that occurs in many other social domains within Native American communities. This occurs not only through the social organization of drum groups but through the very act of singing itself; both serve equally to "engender" performers (Sugarman 1997). In my own experience with the Spirit Sands Singers and with other drum groups I recorded and spoke with, women, even when acknowledged to be regular members of a drum group, behave in a very different way compared with the men of the group. The role that women singers traditionally perform is often called "harmonizing," demarcating their social position to the music (Hatton 1986). This term is consistent with the general view that women do not so much carry the melody as help the men to sing (Vennum 1989). Thus a powwow song could be rendered without women's accompaniment and still be considered a complete and valid performance. Women who participate in drum groups as harmonizers are very often either the relatives—sisters, mothers, grandmothers, wives—or romantic partners of male drum members. In a performance, women stand behind the circle of men singers and drummers to form a secondary circle, and they sing an octave higher than the men during the seconds part of the song. Women's role as harmonizers is widely accepted at powwows and is consistent with the historical role of women in Plains singing (Hatton 1986).

More controversial is the phenomenon of mixed gender and all-female drum groups. Hatton (1986) claims that the role of women within drum groups grew out of the increased interest women took in Grass dancing in the late 1960s (although ethnographic records show that women have participated in Grass dancing in a limited way since the beginning of the twentieth century). He further documents the formation of a number of mixed gender drum groups in the northwestern Plains in the early 1970s (mainly in Alberta and Saskatchewan in Canada, and in Montana, North Dakota, and Wyoming in the United States), suggesting that while women's interest in male dance styles faded, interest in singing steadily increased. Presently, mixed gender groups are generally received with less suspicion and controversy at a powwow than all-female groups. One possible reason for this is because almost all mixed gender groups are family based, and these groups typically are led by the male members, many of whom are the male heads of the family. Thus conventional gender roles (and concomitant distributions of social power) are maintained.[15]

At reservation-based competition powwows that I attended in the summers of 1998 through 2001, it was not uncommon to see a family-based drum group of mixed gender with both males and females sitting around the drum.[16] The only all-female drum group that I witnessed during this time was a Winnipeg-based group, the Little Spirit Singers, composed of a number of young girls (teens and preteens) who attended school together. Much like Sweetgrass Road, this group never competed in singing competitions and rarely sang for competition dances; however, they did take a regular turn in the drum rotation for intertribal dancing. While occasionally publicly praised by emcees for their interest and participation in singing, the general reaction from dancers and other singers was polite indifference. Their performances never attracted crowds of singers around the drum and generally did not inspire dancers to rush to the arbor. It is difficult to say how much of this was due to gender and how much was a function of the fact that they were young, inexperienced singers and sounded as such. A number of male singers commented that the Little Spirit Singers sang too "on the beat" (a hallmark of inexperience), and their drumming was sometimes sloppy and tentative. Thus their overall cool reception at powwows was generally consistent with that accorded other young, inexperienced drum groups (although perhaps not as welcoming or encouraging). These judgments, of course, were not gender neutral. Hatton (1986, 209–10) perceptively notes that singing styles of women (when sitting around the drum, as opposed to harmonizing) attempt to reproduce as accurately as possible the style of their male counterparts and are judged by others according to how well they are able to reproduce idealized male vocal production. There is as yet no "women's style" of powwow singing formulated or recognized on the powwow trail. On the northern Plains, powwow-style singing is, by definition, masculine. Thus gender is always implicated in judgments about musical ability and musical style.

I suspect that even if a group of women singers were considered by other dancers and male singers to be very good, they might not share in the same level of camaraderie that male singers typically share with one another. For instance, I have never seen (nor has it ever been reported in the literature) a female singer "drum hopping" and sitting around the drum with other male singers. Women are free to sing with multiple groups but only as harmonizers. Women who are experienced harmonizers are able to learn songs as quickly as their male counterparts, and within a few push-ups they are able to join in and sing for drums whose songs inspire them to sing (although, as is the case for men, it is quite uncommon for women harmonizers to join in on a song from a group with whom they have no pre-existing social connection, either as a friend or relative).

While women's roles as singers at "the big drum" are in a constant state of intertribal negotiation, singing in a powwow drum group is also influential in shaping male gender roles and gender identity. From my own experience, undertaking ethnographic research in powwow-singing aesthetics placed me squarely within a male-dominated social world. Many singers begin singing with drum groups when they are very young children. They grow up around the drum and thus around the company of older male role models. In the summer of 2000 one of the regular members of the Spirit Sands Singers was a young boy from Swan Lake who was known as "Little Ron," so named to distinguish him from another, older singer in the group who went by "Big Ron." Although not related, Mike took Little Ron under his wing, teaching him how to sing and taking him on the road with the group, traveling to powwows almost every weekend. Traveling meant long hours in a car or van exclusively with the other male singers in the group. These hours were often spent telling stories (some might even be true), telling jokes (almost always off-color and very often scandalously unrepeatable), "busting each other's chops" (gently and sometimes not so gently poking fun at the eccentricities and personal habits inevitably learned about each other through extended periods of living together in close proximity), and generally trying to crack each other up. Young boys learn about how to interact socially with other males in these strictly gender-segregated contexts.

Gender roles at powwows reveal the dynamic interplay of tribalism and intertribalism at these events. Vander (1989) reports that new, gendered musical roles and musical innovations for Shoshone women are more readily accepted at powwows—intertribal settings where the assertion of new musical gender roles may be ascribed to the development of a more generalized "Indian" identity—but not in the context of ceremonial events that are specifically Shoshone, where "traditional" gender relationships are more rigidly and conservatively defended. She writes that although "at their own powwow Shoshones do display elements of costume design, beadwork, and ceremony that are Shoshone, they are also just as apt to experiment with new and borrowed elements of costume, dance, and song. Shoshone identity is subsumed under the broader heading of Indian identity. As an intertribal event, the powwow is the ideal time and place to affirm this broader Indian identity. Shoshones have accepted new musical roles for women in this context" (10).

However, at specifically tribal events, such as a community giveaway ceremony, the participation of an all-female drum group can meet with more strenuous objection. Thus for the Shoshone, powwows and powwow singing have afforded opportunities to forge and explore new musical roles for women. However, Vennum (1989) reports the opposite case in Ojibwa communities, arguing that the adoption of Plains musical styles (through powwow participation) has served to attenuate female musical participation throughout the twentieth century. As powwow music becomes the dominant musical genre in these communities, other genres in which women participate on a more full and equal basis (such as *Midewiwin* ceremonies) are heard less frequently.

From Competitions to the Recording Studio

In this chapter I tried to detail some of the social and economic requirements of active participation on the Northern competition powwow circuit. Such participation resulted in the steady "professionalization" of drum groups. This was especially the case for younger groups, who attempted to emulate the economic success and notoriety of the drums popularized in the early and mid-1990s. Powwow music operates in a similar way to other forms of mainstream popular culture. There are upper echelon groups considered to be the top groups in their field: Eyabay, The Boyz, Midnight Express, and Bear Creek are drum groups considered to be some of the best Ojibwa drums currently performing. These are drums that win at the large, big-money competition powwows or serve as host drums: powwows like Schemitzun, Gathering of Nations, and the large casino-sponsored events in Ojibwa country like the Hinckley and Shakopee powwows. These groups are models for younger drum groups to emulate and aspire to.

The larger point is that participation in competition powwow culture establishes norms of behavior and aesthetic values that make the activity of recording a logical next step. Drum groups who wish to succeed on the competition circuit are expected to record not only to increase their own prestige within the circuit, but also to help finance the increasing economic demands of near-constant competition travel. The rapid economic growth and spread of competition powwows in the 1990s thus became the ground upon which the emerging powwow recording industry began to build and grow.

(TOP) Grand Entry at the Eighth Annual Hinckley
Grand Celebration Powwow in July 2000

(BOTTOM) The Esquash brothers, Michael (left)
and Kevin, at the Swan Lake First Nation Powwow,
July 2000

(TOP) Gerald Esquash, drum carrier for the Spirit Sands Singers, at the Swan Lake First Nation Powwow, July 2000

(BOTTOM) The Spirit Sands Singers' camping area at the Norway House First Nation Powwow, July 2006

The author (in a cap, to the right) sitting in with the Spirit Sands Singers at the Shoal Lake First Nation Traditional Powwow, July 2006

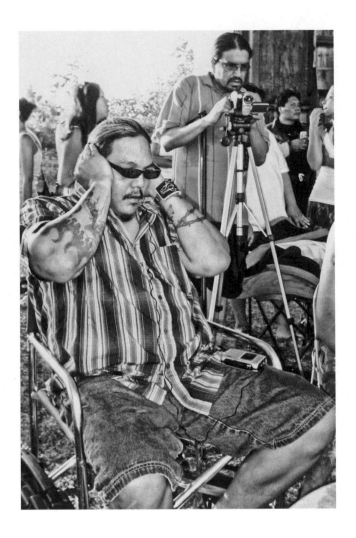

Mike Esquash listening through headphones to a recording that he just made of
the Spirit Sands Singers at the Shoal Lake
First Nation Traditional Powwow, July 2006

Studio 11 and the offices of Arbor
Records, 49 Henderson Highway,
Winnipeg, Manitoba, June 2000

(TOP) Brandon Friesen at the helm in the main control room of Studio 11, November 1999

(BOTTOM) John Marlow, sales manager for Arbor Records, working the phones, August 2000

(TOP) The Northern Wind Singers, cutting tracks for their CD *Ikwe Nagamonan: Women's Songs* in the main recording area of Studio 11, May 2000

(BOTTOM) The White Lodge Singers rocking the trailer during a remote recording session on the Fort Berthold Reservation, North Dakota, July 2000

Gabe Desrosiers in his Grass dance regalia,
performing on a hand drum at Michigan
State University, February 2010

(TOP) Arbor Records displays its wares at a vendor's booth, July 2006

(BOTTOM) Arthur Pearson, production manager for Arbor Records, in his office at the new Studio 441 office suite, July 2006

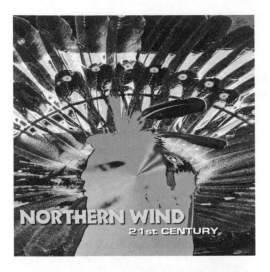

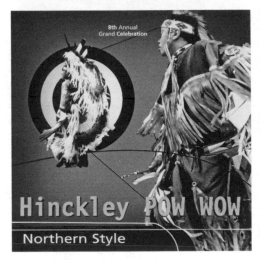

Cover art for the Northern Wind Singers' CD
21st Century (AR-11122)

Cover art for the Cree singer-songwriter Mishi
Donovan's CD *Journey Home* (AR-11192)

Cover art for the Spirit Sands Singers' CD *Sandstorm* (AR-12222)

Cover art for the Arbor Records compilation CD
Hinckley Pow Wow: Northern Style (AR-11162)

PART II

THE MEDIATION

OF POWWOWS

The Powwow Recording
Industry in Western Canada

Race, Culture, and Commerce

A number of anthropologists . . . have taught us to reconfigure the usual binary opposition [between indigenous and imperial forces, colonized and colonizer] as a triadic historical field, including a complicated intercultural zone where the cultural differences are worked through in political and economic practice. "The beach," as Dening calls it—though it could as well be the plantation or the town— where "native" and "stranger" play out their working misunderstandings in creolized languages. Here are complex "structures of the conjuncture," such as the alliances that cross ethnic boundaries and correlate oppositions within the colonial society to political differences among the local people.
—MARSHAL SAHLINS (1994, 385)

[When] a white guy shows me a contract, I stick a knife in it.
—ROBERT PEASLEY, owner of Rez Cue Records (August 2000)

Winnipeg is known as the River City, its very existence a result of the confluence of two major rivers that cut across the central part of the North American Plains. Winding north across Minnesota to Lake Winnipeg in Manitoba is the Red River, while the Assiniboine stretches across the Canadian Plains from west to east. These waterways played a significant role in the development of trade and commerce in the Canadian West, serving as important travel routes for Cree, Ojibwa, and Assiniboine groups before European contact, and later for voyageurs and the booming fur trade of the Hudson's Bay Company. Where these two rivers unite there evolved a meeting point of not only two bodies of water and two paths of travel, but two different peoples interested in cultural and economic exchange. At the confluence of these two rivers, as the story goes, Miles Macdonnell and three dozen other Scottish and Irish laborers founded the first Red River settlement in 1812. Later the colony took the name Winnipeg, an appellation stemming from the Cree words *win*, meaning muddy, and *nipee*, meaning waters. Winnipeg, historically and presently, is defined by these murky aquatic, cultural, and commercial intersections.

The 2006 Statistics Canada census reported the Aboriginal population of Winnipeg as 68,380 representing the highest urban Aboriginal population of any city in Canada and constituting almost 10 percent of Winnipeg's total population.[1] Much of the Native population resides in a lower-income urban sprawl located at the northern end of the city.[2] This large indigenous presence continues to leave its mark on a city that boasts a number of Aboriginal art galleries and numerous well-established Native Studies programs at post-secondary educational institutions (the two largest being the University of Manitoba and the University of Winnipeg). There is a plethora of outreach programs, Indian Friendship centers, and, as of 2001, an Aboriginal Resource Center. The city is also host to two non-Native-owned Aboriginal music labels.

The 1990s saw a blossoming of Aboriginal record labels on the Canadian Plains. During the bulk of my field research during 1998–2001, five record labels located in Manitoba and Saskatchewan were actively recording and distributing powwow music, either exclusively or in significant numbers.[3] Sweet Grass Records, owned by Ted and Darlene Whitecalf and based in Regina, Saskatchewan, has been producing powwow and hand drum (Round dance) recordings exclusively since 1993 and it has amassed a considerably large catalogue of tapes and CDs. In 1996 George and Kelly Parker started Turtle Island Records in Saskatoon, Saskatchewan, producing recordings by both powwow and "Contemporary Native" musical groups.[4] Wacipi Records, the smallest of these companies, was a reserve-based label run by Curtis Assiniboine, a well-known and well-respected powwow singer and leader of the drum group Horsetail. Created in 1998, this label produced and distributed powwow music exclusively.[5] All three of these record labels were owned and operated by people of Aboriginal descent. Conversely, Sunshine Records and Arbor Records, both based in Winnipeg, were under non-Native management and ownership. The first of these, Sunshine Records, is one of the longest running and most successful independent music labels in Canada. Started by Ness and Linda

Michaels in 1975, it has produced a wide variety of local music—including a large catalogue of Métis and Ukrainian fiddle music, Native and non-Native rock, folk, and country artists—and is responsible for one of the largest collections of powwow music available in Canada. Arbor Records, started by Brandon Friesen in the winter of 1999, is the latest addition to this group of labels.

My purpose in this chapter is twofold. The first is to describe and characterize the economic and corporate structure of powwow music labels generally, and Arbor Records specifically. The second is to examine how the discourse of race permeates and mediates a broad range of social relationships and structural divisions within Arbor Records, an arrangement producing a unique "structure of the conjuncture" (to borrow Marshall Sahlins's turn of phrase [1994]) in the creation and distribution of powwow recordings. In the first part of this chapter, I describe and characterize the structural features of the Aboriginal music industry in western Canada, briefly outlining some of the historic and current forces that have produced such a configuration. I then provide a general description of the corporate and contractual policy of Arbor Records in particular. In the second part of this chapter, special attention is paid to the kinds of cultural negotiations that take place at Arbor Records between non-Native record industry personnel and the Native musicians with whom they work. The detailed descriptions of Northern competition powwow culture provided in part I are intended to identify and describe the kinds of ideas and practices that powwow musicians bring to the recording studio and to the Aboriginal record labels. Within the industrial and social space of Arbor Records, the shared ideas, behaviors, and expectations of powwow performers were at times misunderstood and misconstrued by non-Native personnel. These negotiations were often framed within the shared discourse of race; that is, the tacit assumption that "racial" difference (meaning phenotypic traits) equals "cultural" difference (meaning ideologies and behaviors). Thus, while Native-owned companies are not categorically any more accommodating to powwow musicians or knowledgeable about powwow culture, they are often characterized this way by powwow singers. I want to suggest, however, that, in reality, the differences that sometimes separate singers and record producers are composed of a number of socially structured cleavages that cut across issues of race, class, gender, and age.[6] Powwow labels like Arbor Records are by and large "contact zones" (Pratt 1991) where competing commonsense notions about music, musical performance, musical ownership and authorship, and "normal" rules of social conduct and social relations continually rub up against one another. These dialectics have produced a hybrid corporate culture with concessions negotiated and established by both parties. The institutional structures and norms of this industry are under constant revision as both non-Native *and* Native record producers and industry executives attempt to find a middle ground between the commercial and social norms of the music industry and the logic of powwow musical culture.

Independents and Majors

The powwow recording industry presents an interesting case in industrial music studies because it exhibits a number of significant differences from larger, mainstream Canadian and international music labels.[7] First, this industry is small and bounded, and the vast majority of the record-buying public is Native; most powwow recordings are sold on the powwow trail (itself a unique kind of international market) through traveling vendors, and are rarely found in large national or international retail music chains. Despite the fact that companies such as Arbor Records often represent themselves as "world beat" labels, they have met with little success in their attempts to break into the mainstream world beat market with powwow recordings. Second, the majority of the target audience for these products consists of both producers and consumers of this music: powwow people who sing, dance, or are otherwise involved at powwows throughout the year. Third, because powwow recording companies are small and privately owned, the owners often become involved in numerous aspects of musical production, including not only recording and producing, but also packaging and marketing. It is this unique structural configuration — powwow participants who act as both performers and consumers, and industry executives who act as both businessmen and artists — that creates the terms of interaction not found in the mainstream music industry.

While these structural features distinguish the powwow music industry from the "majors" (Sony-BMG, EMI, Warner Music Group, Universal/ Polygram — often referred to as "the Big Four"), they overlap to a certain degree with a set of economic and aesthetic structures common to many small, independently owned record companies described within industrial and academic circles as "independent" labels (or "indies"). Independents have a long and important history within the music industry and the rise of indies has often been linked to significant musical innovations.[8] For example, Peterson and Berger (1975) have characterized the growth of the music industry as a series of cycles of production marked by moments of control by the majors (resulting in stylistic homogeneity) and competition between majors and indies (with accompanying musical diversity). The musical diversity fostered by the proliferation of independent labels has generally been attributed to the unique character of the indies, described as commercial ventures that foster a greater degree of innovation and musical creativity when compared to the more capital-driven major labels (Gillett 1996; Marcus 1990). Herman Gray (1988), who studied the rise and decline of Teresa Records, a small independent jazz label, further suggests that the differences between indies and majors are both structural—the size and scale of a company, musical diversity, catalogue size, access to capital and other cultural and economic resources—and ideological, influencing social organization, symbolic meaning, and aesthetic choices (Lee 1995). In other words, indies are not simply majors on a smaller scale but distinct corporate and creative entities.[9]

The structural configuration of the powwow industry shares many similarities with other indie labels. The bounded nature of the business is typical of indie labels that cater to other niche musical markets like jazz (Gray 1988) or alternative/techno music (Lee 1995). Within these "genre worlds" (Frith 1996; Negus 1999) many historically important labels have been independents, with some of the more successful indies eventually cutting distribution deals or in some cases being bought out by larger labels. Also similar to the powwow case, members of an indie-market targeted community are often both producers and consumers of the music: jazz and certain American folk music provide analogous examples. In addition, the division of labor found at powwow labels is typical of that found at many other indie labels headed by staffs of two or three people who are active as businessmen, producers, engineers, and graphic artists (Gray 1988; Rapaport 1979).[10]

Despite these similarities, powwow record labels differ from other independents in significant ways. First, this industry features unique methods of distribution; unlike other indies, powwow labels handle most of their own distribution, generally bypassing the need for independent distributors to get their music out to the public. Their public is found on the powwow trail and not in Barnes and Noble, Walmart, or other large international retail chains, where most independent and major distribution companies conduct business.[11] Second, ideologically, Aboriginal labels do not typically partake in the "ideology of independence" found at other indie labels (Gray 1989; Lee 1995), where label executives and musical artists both participate in the characterization of these institutions as "more concerned" with artistic freedom, creating an almost family-like loyalty to their artists, and proudly trumpeting their independence and difference from "the mainstream." By contrast, label executives at Arbor Records, recognizing the small scale of their market, welcome distributional and promotional ties to larger labels, and their marginalized status within the mainstream music industry has more often been lamented than celebrated.

Sunshine Records

Sunshine Records holds an important historical position within the development of the powwow recording industry in Canada and as such, I examine the history of this company in more detail than some of the other labels. Sunshine Records is an interesting case for two reasons. First, while Sunshine Records distributes a wide variety of Native *and* non-Native recordings (powwow music and Aboriginal popular music constitute approximately 75 percent of their sales [personal communication with Ness Michaels]), they have self-consciously and purposefully developed a corporate image as an "Aboriginal" music label. Sunshine Records has historically served as one of only a few stable musical institutions dedicated to servicing the Native and Métis populations in Winnipeg, in Manitoba, and in western Canada more generally. Through the course of its history it has become a nexus of urban Native musical activity where new Native musical styles are envisioned, constructed, and distributed. Second, in the often economically volatile world of the music industry, where independent labels come in and out of existence with alarming frequency, Sunshine Records has remained a relatively stable corporate entity. Eschewing the pursuit of a distribution deal with one of the major corporate labels, Sunshine has survived through the development of a catalogue of local "ethnic"—or niche market—musical acts. Sunshine's list of artists includes Native country musicians, folksingers, rock and rap artists, powwow drum groups, Ukrainian fiddlers and comedy acts, and a wide variety of entertainers with a limited local following in Winnipeg and the surrounding area. The freedom from larger corporate ties has allowed Sunshine Records to maintain a greater control (and freedom) over the kinds of music they are willing to record and the markets they are willing to serve.

Ness and Linda Michaels launched Sunshine Records from the basement of their home with the release of a recording by Winstun Wutunee, a Cree folksinger from Manitoba. Wutunee soon afterward suggested that Sunshine record and distribute a powwow drum group led by his friend Vic Thunderchild, and as a result the Big Thunderchild Singers became the first powwow group produced by Sunshine Records (SSCT-4012, the twelfth release). The label soon expanded into a variety of Aboriginal and non-Aboriginal music, particularly Ukrainian and Métis fiddle music: Reg Bouvette, a famed local Métis fiddler, was another important artist signed to Sunshine in their formative years.[12] The early years of Sunshine records were thus spent catering to small niche markets in western Canada, communities of Native Americans, Métis, and Ukrainians (Ness Michaels interview, July 1998).

In the early 1980s Sunshine expanded first into a 1,500-square-foot warehouse and then into an older two-story house where its first, relatively modest, recording studio, Sunshine Studios, was built. In 1990 Sunshine renovated an abandoned sewing factory in the northern end of downtown Winnipeg, and moved into its current location on Selkirk Avenue in the city's "historic district." Here Sunshine built two digital recording studios and later an in-house cassette manufacturing division. In 1992 Sunshine Records hired Brandon Friesen, a recent high school graduate, who began working part-time for the label, filling and shipping orders during the day and working as a recording engineer in the evenings. According to Friesen, by the early 1990s, while Sunshine had a large catalogue of local Aboriginal country, rock, folk and fiddle recordings, their powwow catalogue was still quite small.

> When I came on board his [Michaels's] catalogue number was 4060. So Sunshine had already done sixty releases before I started. When I first started at Sunshine they had one Whitefish Bay, one Sioux Assiniboine, the Vic Thunderchild, and two Plains Ojibway. These were the only powwow releases. And they also had a lot of local bar bands. They had Native bar bands. Like Louie Riel Rebels or some weird name like that. Just bar bands that played the Native bars in town. They recorded cover songs. I don't know how well he did, he probably sold, who knows, a few hundred. . . . So at that time Sioux Assiniboine had one [release] and Whitefish Bay had one . . . and I saw

his catalogue and I saw that powwow was the only thing that he was selling at that time. And he only had three or four releases. And so I said, "Come on, let's go to these powwows and let's record these groups." (Brandon Friesen interview, October 1999)

In the summer of 1993 Friesen began traveling the Northern powwow circuit, from Wisconsin to Montana and throughout the central Plains of Canada between northern Ontario and Alberta, visiting powwows that were within a day's drive or less from Winnipeg. Interestingly, according to Brandon, he first began recording powwows not through any special interest in promoting Aboriginal music but because he saw powwow music as an untapped market.

> BF: Did I know anything about powwows? Well I knew what an intertribal was and, like I knew the differences. But when I—the first powwow I recorded, I had no clue. I had no clue at all.
>
> CS: So you got interested in powwow music just because . . .
>
> BF: I just saw a market for it. I saw the possibilities. And I had to go to the Roseau River powwow [on a small reserve in southern Manitoba], and I brought along a Sunshine catalogue that had like twenty fiddle releases, and forty rock and folk releases, and five powwow releases and everybody said where can you buy this—these five powwow releases. They were flipping out over it and I couldn't believe it. So I realized there was something happening. (Brandon Friesen interview, October 1999)

Most of the powwow recordings produced for Sunshine by Brandon were made at powwows as he traveled the Northern circuit all summer long. Through the mid- and late 1990s he produced and released over ninety different powwow recordings and is responsible for the vast majority of the powwow music catalogue from that time. He worked at Sunshine until the fall of 1998, at which time he left to open his own recording studio, Studio 11.

The Rise of the Powwow Recording Industry in the 1990s

One might be tempted to read the development of the powwow recording industry in the 1990s as an outgrowth of the world beat and world music boom of the late 1980s. Indeed, Lawrence Martin, recording artist and part owner of First Nations Music (a now-defunct Aboriginal label that distributed both powwow and Contemporary Native American music), described the situation in the early 1990s in similar terms:

> EMI approached us and said, "If you guys [Lawrence Martin and Wawatay Native Communications] started up your own label, EMI would be able to distribute your products for you." So that's how we got First Nations Music off the ground. And so right away we became a Native label, but sort of a sublabel of EMI. We then began looking around for Native products. But as soon as we started doing that, we were getting calls from Sony and BMG saying, "Well, what's going on here? Where can we get *our* Native music?" (Lawrence Martin, quoted in Scales 1996, 43)

The powwow music industry, however, has always existed apart from world beat markets, and demand for the music is driven almost entirely by the North American Native population. The rapid development of the industry may instead be traced to a number of social and economic developments within Native communities, which led to the explosion of Sunshine's powwow catalogue in the early 1990s and the founding of several powwow labels on the Canadian Plains. Taken together, these developments helped to greatly expand and consolidate an identifiable market for powwow recordings. It is also important to note that these developments took place on both sides of the Canadian-U.S. border: the northern Plains powwow recording industry, while based mainly in Canada, is nonetheless inextricably linked to U.S. political and economic policies concerning Native Americans. By far the largest markets for the products of these Canadian companies are south of the border. The United States is home to almost all of the large, big-money competition powwows, most of the large vendor operations and "trading posts" that act as subdistributors to the hundreds of smaller vendors that travel the Northern and Southern powwow circuits, and a much larger Native population.

Indian Casinos

Hoxie and colleagues have suggested that "future historians might someday conclude that passage of the American Indian Gaming Regulatory Act in 1988 was the most significant event in Native American history during the late twentieth century" (2001, 468). The rise and spread of reservation-based Indian casinos in the United States throughout the 1990s affected the development of the powwow recording industry in direct and indirect ways. The economic impact that the rapid development of Indian casinos has had on tribal economies is difficult to overstate. The Indian Gaming Regulatory Act (IGRA) effectively legalized Class III gambling (lotteries, casinos, pari-mutuel racing) on tribal lands pursuant to tribal-state negotiation. This created a massive influx of capital into both new and established tribal casinos. Thus while tribal bingo revenues saw a relatively modest increase from $380,200 in 1989 to $435,300 in 1993, Class III revenues increased from $100,300 to $2,594,000 over that same period. In 1994 the total revenues from Indian gaming reached $4.4 billion (Mason 2000, 44). By 1997, 237 Indian-owned casinos were in operation, with gross revenues estimated at $6 billion annually (Jorgenson 1998, 163). Ten years later, the National Indian Gaming Commission (NIGC) announced that the 2007 net revenue for Indian gaming in America was $26 billion. Significantly, the provisions laid out in the IGRA ensure that tribal members maintain controlling interest in Indian casino administration. Further, Jorgenson suggests that "early evidence from the testimony of participants was that gaming was an economic development in and of itself and, as a multiplier, a source for further economic developments in areas surrounding the tribe which owned the casino. The revenues were being used to enrich Indian lives and to nourish Indian culture" (Jorgenson 1998, 159).

One very noticeable and public way that casinos were "nourishing Indian culture" was through the creation and sponsorship of large competition powwows. The Pequot Foxwoods Resort Casino in Connecticut, one of the largest and most lucrative Indian casinos, began sponsoring its annual Schemitzun Powwow and Green Corn Festival in 1992. By 1998 the powwow was offering in excess of $800,000 in cash prizes for singing, dancing, and rodeo competitions. In 2001 the drum group Blackstone won the competition categories of Best Northern Contemporary, Best Hand-Drum Singing, and Best Overall Drum Group, and walked away with $65,000 in prize money for a weekend of singing. Similar (although less extravagant) high-dollar competition powwows began to be sponsored by casinos all over Indian country. More than simply raising the sheer number of big money competition powwows, these casino powwows raised the stakes for non-casino-sponsored competition events on both sides of the Canada-U.S. border, as urban and reservation-based competition powwows began increasing their prize money for singing and dancing in order to attract the best singers and dancers. The amount of money guaranteed to host drums and invited drums also increased. The top competition circuit drum groups thus became accustomed to much higher monetary compensation for their performances. This had an impact on the relationship between drum groups and record companies, as drum groups began to understand the value of their singing and their popularity on the pow-wow trail in more basic economic terms. As Brandon Friesen described it,

> Eyabay started that whole money thing. Stoney Park, Eyabay. Once the pow-wows got richer. Like back then [the late 1980s and early 1990s] there were no Indian casinos. So all the powwows could afford to pay a group $500 to show up, at the most. Or they pay their travel or they give them food. Now with these Indian casinos—like Eyabay got $20,000 to show up here in Winnipeg [and function as host drum at the 1999 Heartbeat of Nations pow-wow]. (Brandon Friesen interview, October 1999)

On a more general level, the rise of big-money competition powwows created a large influx of cash into the powwow community. Singers, dancers, and powwow fans found themselves with more expendable income and could afford to buy more recordings. Casinos on some U.S. reservations also funneled money back into the reserve community through direct cash dispersals to every member of the tribal community, sometimes in excess of thousands of dollars per month. The injection of casino-generated capital into reservation economies created a potential source of expendable income for many reservation tribal members.

Larger casino-sponsored competition powwows also became opportunities for record companies to make several recordings of some of the most popular powwow drums all in one weekend, and in the 1990s companies began to release powwow compilation recordings. Beginning in 1993, Sweet Grass Records released annual "Best of Schemitzun" CDs, recordings that contained tracks from many of the top drum groups from the 1990s (e.g., *Schemitzun '93–'99: The Best of the Best*, SGS-91899). Arbor Records pursued a similar strategy in 2000, releasing compilations from the Hinckley Powwow, sponsored by the Grand Casino in Hinckley, which is owned and operated by the Ojibwa Mille Lacs Band in Minnesota (e.g., Hinckley Powwow Northern and Southern compilation CDs for 2000 and 2001—AR-11152, AR-11162, AR-11412, and AR-11422, respectively). More recently, powwow committees have started to realize the economic potential of recording, and a number of them have begun recording and distributing recordings of their powwows themselves. Tom Bee and SOAR

(Sound of America Records) won the first Grammy in Aboriginal music in 2000 for their release of a compilation of the Gathering of Nations pow-wow in Albuquerque (not directly linked to a casino but a high-profile and high-dollar competition powwow). The following year Gathering of Nations began to record and distribute a compilation CD themselves, locking out SOAR and all other record labels. Schemitzun has followed suit and now also releases its own compilation CDs.

The lasting effects of Indian gaming for tribal economic development and the Aboriginal recording industry remain to be seen. Brandon Friesen has predicted an economic backlash:

> Once that Schemitzun started and started giving away, you know, $25,000 for first place. That fucking completely screwed up the whole powwow industry. Completely. Completely. All of a sudden all the drum groups were expecting a ton of money. What's happening with powwow music now is just like 1980s rock. It's just got so big. In the 1980s you had bands like Motley Crüe getting something like forty million from their label to renew their contract. And where are they now? Well right now I think we're at the end of the powwow era. And things are out of control and it's bound to take a dive. Powwow will always be there, but it's bound to take a fall. (Brandon Friesen interview, October 1999)

However, to date I have seen little evidence of an economic slowdown in the prizes and stakes of competition powwows, or in the payments requested, negotiated, and often received by drum groups in negotiating contracts for their recordings.[13]

Bill C-31

In Canada, one of the most significant developments in the lives of Native Americans in the later half of the twentieth century was the passage of Bill C-31. In 1985 the Canadian government legislated the bill as "An Act to Amend the Indian Act," fundamentally redefining federal recognition of Indian identity. The major revisions set forth in the bill allowed for those people who had previously lost their federally recognized Indian status (through enfranchisement) to have their status reinstated. Under the previous tenets of the Indian Act, Indians were enfranchised in several ways, one of the most common being through intermarriage: an Indian woman who married a non-Indian man automatically lost Indian status for herself and her children. Bill C-31 effectively ended the sexual discrimination of the Indian Act and brought it in line with sections 15 and 28 of the Canadian Charter of Rights and Freedoms (Frideres 1998, 30). Just over a decade later, close to 100,000 Bill C-31 Indians — approximately 17 percent of the total Indian population of Canada — had been registered, resulting in unprecedented growth in the Indian population (from a 1984 pre-C-31 total of 348,809, to a 1996 total of 573,269) (ibid., 34).

This explosion in the Native population created a new and bigger market for the Aboriginal recording industry in Canada (as well as many other Aboriginal media outlets including newspapers, radio stations, and more recently, television stations and programming). Of course there is no simple and direct correspondence between increased population and an increased consumer base. For instance, many people who regained federally recognized Indian status might have already been participating in powwows and other tribal and intertribal cultural events before reinstatement. Gabe Desrosiers is one such example. Until 1985 he and his family were not "status Indians" (as their status had been stripped through enfranchisement) and as such, despite his family's long genealogical and cultural ties to the Northwest Angle Ojibwa community, they were not allowed to live on the reserve and were not able to avail themselves of any of the benefits and services guaranteed to those whom the government officially recognized as "Indian." While not "status," Gabe and his family still considered themselves to be Ojibwas, as did the mostly white community where they resided. While Gabe participated in powwow culture before 1985, subsequent to his reinstatement he and his family were able to move back on to the reserve, further facilitating and deepening his involvement in powwows.

Eschbach and Applebaum's (2000) statistical study of powwow attendance patterns revealed that "Indians' involvement in powwows increases with standard measures of acculturation, but declines with decreasing embeddedness in a homogenous ethnic community. . . . To be sure, rates of attendance are highest among college-educated white-collar workers. However, such an individual is most likely to attend powwows if he or she lives in an Indian community whose members tend to marry other Indians, and receives medical care [when needed] at a local Indian Health Service clinic" (2000, 79–80).

Those most likely to attend powwows are those who have ties to Indian communities but who have experienced or participated in a number of non-Native acculturative institutions, such as higher education and urban, white-collar careers. While this study was U.S.-based and predicated on statistics from the 1987 Survey of American Indian and Alaskan Natives (SAIAN), carried out by the Agency for Health Policy and Research among Native Americans in the continental United States and Alaska, this profile fits a large percentage of Bill C-31 Indians, whose reinstatement allowed urban Indians to reestablish reservation ties, many of whom moved back to the reservation and began to participate more deeply in tribal community life.[14] Powwows are an effective public way to reconnect with one's Indian heritage; I have witnessed many "specials" at powwows where families welcome long-lost family members back into the reserve and the tribal community.

Eschbach and Applebaum refer to this connection between identity and consumption as the "ethnic consumption model," which posits that "higher social and economic status increases the resources available to group members for cultural displays, and abates the costs of participation in such displays by reducing discrimination" (2000, 70). Further, "as group membership becomes less determinative of social roles and obligations, assimilated members of an ethnic group may choose to supplement diminishing ethnic social ties in daily life with participation in the cultural events sponsored by formal voluntary associations in order to give social form to personal identity" (70). For C-31 Indians who had been forcibly alienated from reservation life and tribal communities, participation in and consumption of powwows in the 1990s became an important "ethnic option" (Waters 1990).

Cassette Technology

Also significant to the boom in powwow recordings in the 1990s was Sunshine's switch to cassette tape as the predominant medium for powwow music. Sunshine's earliest recordings from the 1970s were released on LP and eight-track. In the 1980s, as eight-track technology disappeared throughout the music industry, cassette tapes became the predominant medium by which Sunshine's music was sold. According to Stewart Astleford, who was the head salesman for Arbor Records for much of the 1990s, 75 to 80 percent of Sunshine's Aboriginal sales were sold on cassettes throughout the decade (Stewart Astleford interview, August 1999). Cassette technology proved to be an economic boon for Sunshine Records. The company created an in-house cassette manufacturing division in the early 1990s that allowed them to manufacture their own cassettes in small numbers—to order—thus reducing production costs and giving them more economic flexibility. This arrangement meant that titles which sold slowly but steadily could be manufactured as orders for them were received, keeping inventory low. This meant less money tied up in manufacturing outside the company, since commercial manufacturers require minimum orders in the hundreds or thousands and represent large cash expenditures for the label. It could take the sales department of a small label years to recoup those expenditures.

The cassette format was central to the distribution of powwow recordings throughout the late 1980s and 1990s. Consumers of powwow music preferred it because cassettes were inexpensive, portable, and user friendly. Portability was a key feature for powwow singers and dancers who purchased this music. Cassettes could be transported on the powwow trail and played in the cassette players of cars and trucks traveling to and from powwows, as well as on the portable boomboxes that became increasingly popular in the 1980s. The durability of cassettes was also a positive feature for powwow musicians and proved to be convenient for drum groups to sell. During the early 1990s powwow drum groups would often receive a certain number of cassettes as partial or full payment for their recording. They then sold their cassettes during their travels on the powwow trail. Traveling with and selling vinyl LPs would have been a much more difficult task for powwow drums due to the fragile nature of the medium and vinyl's susceptibility to the temperature extremes of the powwow grounds. Tapes were small, lightweight, easy to pack and transport, and relatively durable.

Despite the fact that cassettes have virtually disappeared as a viable consumer product within the mainstream music industry, they continued to play an important role in the powwow industry throughout the 1990s and only began to decline in importance in the early years of the twenty-first century. The dominance of cassette technology in the 1990s was demonstrated to me by the role that it plays in the imagination of powwow singers, who in the late '90s continued to speak metaphorically about recordings as "tapes." In the same way that many rock and pop performers continue to refer to their recording activities as "making a record," and music retail stores that almost exclusively sell CDs are still referred to as "record stores"—referencing the now virtually extinct LP vinyl record—powwow singers in 2000 and 2001 still often referred to the activities surrounding the making of a commercial recording as "making a tape," even though by 2001 CDs had become a medium of equal, or perhaps greater, importance to the industry, and by 2004 tapes had disappeared almost completely.

Studio 11 and Arbor Records

In January 1999 Arbor Records opened its doors as the second Aboriginal music label in Winnipeg. Brandon Friesen left Sunshine Records in the fall of 1998 and opened up his own studio, Studio 11, with a friend and business partner, Paul Scinocca. Friesen and Scinocca purchased a derelict house located in a somewhat unfashionable district just east of and across the river from downtown, and significantly remodeled the interior. The ground floor was redesigned to house the small but well-equipped Studio 11, a recording facility that featured two studio control rooms that shared a large recording area. Studio A was the larger of the two and featured an ADAT (Alesis Digital Audio Tape)-based twenty-four-track digital studio with a series of rack-mounted effects processors located to the right of the mixing console.[15] Studio B was significantly smaller and housed a Macintosh-based Pro Tools recording system that recorded directly onto one of the four twenty-gigabyte hard drives that shuffled between Studios A and B. The second floor of the building, accessible by a small circular metal staircase, consisted of several offices that served as the administrative center for both Studio 11 and Arbor Records. Initially Studio 11 employed a full-time staff of three: Friesen and Scinocca, the owners who served as producer/engineers, and Brandon's sister Jamie, who served as the office secretary. As is typical with all recording studios, several part-time engineers/musicians came and went depending on the recording projects and the work available. For example, Justin Hartlooper (or "Dutch" as he was known in the studio), Brandon's friend and the keyboard player and saxophonist in a dance band they both played in, continued to be involved in a number of the studio's recording projects either as an engineer, producer, or musician. Dutch worked informally, often "on spec" (where payment for work on projects occurs only after the project is done and starts to make money), and was not on salary for the studio. Much of Studio 11's business involved recording local Winnipeg rock, jazz, and pop music groups, and occasionally bands from other parts of western Canada.

A few months after establishing Studio 11, Friesen formed a partnership with the former Sales Manager of Sunshine Records, Stewart Astleford (who had left Sunshine Records in 1998), and created Arbor Records. Because of Brandon's previous work with a number of Aboriginal pop and rock musicians, Arbor Records also recorded and distributed a limited number of Contemporary Native music products (see chapter 5), but the bulk of the catalog and the musical focus of the label consisted of powwow and other so-called traditional Native American music genres. Initially, Friesen was responsible for signing, recording, and packaging all of Arbor's artists while Astleford handled advertising and sales. In autumn 1999 Astleford left the company and was replaced by John Marlow, an independent record distributor in Winnipeg who had worked briefly at Sunshine Records in the late 1990s. John soon became the Studio 11 business manager while continuing to work as the head salesman for Arbor Records. Sharing the same corporate space and personnel, Studio 11 functioned as the in-house recording facility for Arbor Records.[16]

Signing Artists

Generally eschewing his own aesthetic preferences of "good" or "bad" powwow performers or songs, Brandon Friesen instead takes advice from singers in drum groups and pays attention to the logic of the market in choosing which drum groups to sign. He described this arrangement in speaking about one of Arbor's newest drum groups in 1999, the Southern-style group Sizzortail:

> I think Sizzortail will be the next big thing. Sizzortail and the Southern style. I'm banking on them. If I had to put my money on a horse, they'd be my horse. Because everybody I've talked to, Gabe of Northern Wind, Andy of Whitefish Bay, John Morris and Terry [of Eyabay], they all say Sizzortail is the shit. They're hot. They're great. They've all put in a good word. And Sizzortail, Steven the leader, Steve went to Gabe and said, 'What about Arbor, you know, what's this Brandon, who's Arbor Records?' And they all put in a word for me. So that's [how it works]." (Brandon Friesen interview, October 1999)

Not only does Brandon seek advice from powwow singers but he also pays attention to the winners at the big-money competition powwows that draw more people. Rather than relying on prediction, Brandon responds quickly to current trends, carefully monitoring the constantly fluctuating popularity of groups on the powwow trail. While he may have his own aesthetic preferences concerning particular drum groups, he is first and foremost interested in signing groups that have a good deal of commercial viability or potential. Therefore, the priority of Arbor Records is to sign drum groups who have a proven history of success and who intend to travel nationwide during the powwow season. The commitment to traveling the competition powwow circuit is crucial to the sales of a recording. Brandon cited Arbor's Battle River CD, *Couple for the Road* (AR-11032), as a prime example of this. An Ojibwa drum group from Red Lake, Minnesota, Battle River won first place in the Northern Straight category at Schemitzun in 1998. In Brandon's eyes, a first-place finish at a high-profile powwow like Schemitzun positioned the group as potentially one of the top powwow groups of 1999, so he signed them to a lucrative, multiyear contract. The sales for the recording, however, were disappointingly slow, in large part because the group simply did not travel to very many powwows in the summer of 1999 and therefore never became widely heard on the Northern competition circuit. According to Brandon, "If you're not out there singing every weekend, people just forget about you." Brandon had similar concerns about his longtime friends and collaborators Whitefish Bay, whose first Arbor CD, *Ndoo Te Mag* (AR-11022), also sold more slowly than anticipated. But in this case it was not because the drum group was not out singing every weekend, but rather because they were singing at small traditional powwows, serving as the host drum. That summer, they rarely participated in singing competitions and took part in very few competition powwows as hosts or invited drums. Thus, for recordings to achieve economic success, groups must not only travel, but must travel to the strategically correct powwows, which are the large competition powwows.

Brandon's comments about the signing of Sizzortail also indicates that—just as the reputation of the drum group is an important factor for labels—a recording company's reputation on the powwow trail is a key component of its success in both attracting and signing drum groups and in establishing lucrative working relationships with distributors, vendors, retail outlets, and other labels. Reputation is built almost entirely by word of mouth. There are few publications that actively review recordings of powwow music, and even fewer that attempt to distinguish between the different labels that produce this music. The magazines *Whispering Wind*, *Neechee Culture* (now defunct), and *Aboriginal Voices* (also now defunct) featured such reviews on a semiregular basis throughout the 1990s. Occasionally powwow music reviews may be found in Native American newspapers such as *Windspeaker* and *First Perspective* in Canada and *Indian Country Today* in the United States. Internet web pages and chat rooms will also occasionally broach the subject of recording companies. Pow-wows.com is one of the most frequently used sites, featuring discussion lists on a wide variety of powwow-related topics, including record companies. One post from March 2003 even asked for opinions regarding which record labels produced the "best sounding" recordings. Opinions varied and no consensus was reached.

While discussions of this nature are increasingly happening online, the reputation of a record company is still principally created and maintained in the same way that dancers' and singers' reputations are created: through word of mouth on the powwow trail and on the powwow grounds. There are a number of criteria by which drum groups judge record companies to be reputable and desirable. Above all else is their track record regarding financial arrangements with their stable of artists. How much money does a particular recording make for a group? Is there a signing bonus or money "up front"? Perhaps the most contentious issue is in the area of royalties. A constant suspicion and source of complaint among singers is that record companies are withholding royalties that are rightfully owed to drum groups. This is especially true for royalty rights for individual songs. It is a common practice for record companies to create compilation CDs and tapes that cull material from any number of past recordings. Depending on the terms of a contract, drum groups may not have any control over whether or not their music is compiled, and they may or may not be paid any extra royalties for the use of their songs in this new context. Record labels that do not pay royalties fairly and promptly to drum groups are quick to be disparaged by singers. Of course, innuendo is rampant on the powwow trail and the truth of the matter is often extremely hard to determine. There are many reasons, business and personal, for a drum group or a group of singers either to solidify or disparage the reputation of any particular label; oftentimes this may have very little to do with the status of contractual arrangements.

A recording label's reputation is also enhanced by the roster of artists they currently have under contract and, in particular, their association with other well-known and well-respected drum groups. While on a break during their first recording session, the lesser-known Lake of the Woods singers told me that the reason they decided to record with Arbor (*Honouring Our Elders*, AR-11244, and *Songs of Thunder*, AR-11372) was because the label was also working with other very popular drum groups, including Eyabay, Northern Wind, and Whitefish Bay (significantly, all Ojibwa groups popular in the Lake of the Woods area in western Ontario, which most of the members of the group called home). The roster of artists is considered by drum groups to be an indication of the success of a label. This axiom holds true for label executives as well. During an interview with Curtis Assiniboine of Wacipi Records, he took care to list for me the high-profile roster of artists that his label had under contract:

> Over the year and a half or fifteen months that we've been in operation, I know a lot of the singers, the main singers, and the drum groups. And some of them, they are the favorites and the top groups all across the United States and Canada. And I feel good that they've decided—and proving who I am, I guess, proving the kind of job I can do—they've decided to come with me and join my company. There are eight of them that are in now and three—well, all of them are champions in their own way, in their own composing. But you know, during the summer and springtime they have championships all over the United States and Canada, and there's three very big powwows that go on and we have those three top winners in the categories that they've been chosen as first place winners in our company so they've—so we've got pretty much the champions of 1997 in the company. (Curtis Assiniboine interview, July 1998)

John Marlow explained the competition between Arbor and other powwow labels as similar to a competition between "teams":

> They [Sweet Grass Records] have a roster of acts that are signed exclusively to them that are off limits to us. So it's up to them to promote those ones to sell them. And we have our set of groups. You know, I guess it's like a hockey team. You just find out what roster's better and that team wins. But you know, I believe with my future endeavors with radio and press we'll be that much further ahead than them. But I would rather work in conjunction with them, you know, because we have different assets and stuff like that. And people will definitely want one of theirs [another label's recordings] as much as they want one of ours. (John Marlow interview, February 2000)

The struggle among various labels to sign and record popular groups has allowed drum groups to have increasing control over whom they record with, and where and how they record. Top-selling groups such as Eyabay are able to jump from label to label shopping for the most lucrative contract before agreeing to record. Drum groups want to sign with labels who already have a stable of top sellers in order to enhance their reputation, just as labels want to sign top drum groups to enhance their own corporate reputation. The perceived stability of the label also plays a role. In 2003 the Ojibwa drum group Bear Creek turned down a better offer from a new and lesser-known U.S. powwow label and instead recorded their second CD with Arbor Records (*The Show Must Go On*, AR-11992).[17] They accepted Arbor's deal simply because Arbor was an established label and had a track record of producing quality CDs for a number of well-known groups.[18]

The reputation of the label is particularly important for Brandon because he rarely actively seeks out and signs drum groups but prefers to let them approach him. The powwow trail is filled with unspoken alliances and relationships, webs of connections between various singers, dancers, and record labels. Brandon's work at Studio 11 prohibits him from regular attendance at powwows, making his presence on the powwow trail far more limited than in the early 1990s during his years with Sunshine Records. Losing touch with the rhythm of the powwow trail has also meant losing touch with this constantly shifting set of relationships. As such, in order to avoid becoming entangled in any feuds through the pursuit of one drum group over another, he simply lets the drum groups approach him. Drum groups come to Arbor Records either through meeting Brandon at a powwow, or through the recommendation of other singers or other powwow people. Arbor also fostered a friendly working relationship with a number of different vendors who work the Northern and Southern powwow trail. These vendors occasionally recommended Arbor Records to particular groups who were interested in making a recording. These vendor connections played a particularly important role in Arbor's signing of a number of Southern drums, including Southern Boys and Sizzortail. As these drums perform within the Northern powwow circuit less frequently, they were less likely to meet a representative of Arbor Records on the powwow grounds. These vendors worked as informal "talent scouts" for Arbor Records:

JM: We so far have maintained very good relationships with groups that we have currently, which is to Brandon's credit. And those groups will talk to other groups about their good relationship with us. That's one way. Another way is we're out in the distribution field [with] our product, in a minor way, and so people that come across our music will phone us up to see what is available for them. And we also have non-exclusive agents of Arbor that do hype us to groups, too. For instance, there's a duo named Connie and Everett who are—who run Native American Winds [a commercial vendor of powwow music, among other commercial and craft items]—who brought us Sizzortail. They work out of Oklahoma and buy product from us and sell it at pow-wows.

CS: That's how you signed Sizzortail?

JM: That's how we got Sizzortail. I think that was in combination with a couple of other things but we'll give them credit for it. And apparently they're still doing this for us for other groups, too. They [Connie and Everett] don't sign a contract with us because we're not a big enough company that they could make money off us, and they're not gonna get into the sales agent group that I am in and so if something ever soured with the group at Arbor Records or whatever then they become a target also, and so we keep an arm's length away from each other. (John Marlow interview, February 2000)

When a drum group signs with Arbor Records, the structure of the contracts consistently involves three hotly negotiated components of artist reimbursement: signing bonus, free product (tapes and/or CDs), and royalties. The contractual relationships between drum groups and record companies are constantly developing as drum groups communicate with each other about the kinds of deals that they are able to procure. These negotiations have an impact on the constant redevelopment and refinement of corporate strategies as the industry makes structural adjustments, responding to how drum groups understand the industry. Increasingly, groups are learning that successful recording careers can help to further increase their economic and cultural capital within the field of competition powwows.

Funding Projects

One of the first projects I volunteered to become involved in at Arbor Records when I began regularly hanging out there in the fall of 1999 was to write a grant proposal to the Canada Council for the Arts in support of a Jingle Dress DVD project that Arbor wanted to produce in collaboration with Andy White of the Whitefish Bay Singers and members of the White family. The video would document the origins of the dress and dance as part of a healing ceremony, and the subsequent development and geographic dispersal of the Jingle dress outfit, dance style, and song style throughout the powwow world. The White family was the driving force behind the project because, according to the family's oral history, Andy's grandfather was the person who originally received instructions through a dream about how to make the Jingle dress. Not only that, but Andy's mother, Maggie White, was the first person to dance in a Jingle dress. While the project was never funded, it was my first introduction to the huge investment in time and energy that goes into grant writing at small, independent Canadian music labels, and the importance of Canadian granting agencies in Native music record production.

For the first years of their existence, Arbor consistently applied for Canada Council funding for a range of different audio and video recording projects, often applying in conjunction with recording artists. The Council is a funding agency created by the Canadian federal government in 1957 in order to financially foster and support Canadian artists and arts agencies and institutions across a broad spectrum of artistic pursuits. Of particular importance for Arbor and their artists was the Aboriginal Peoples Music Program, a collection of grants and prizes targeted specifically to promote Aboriginal artists and arts institutions. Because it was owned and primarily operated by non-Natives, Arbor Records was only eligible for some of these specifically targeted Aboriginal grants, but they were very active in assisting their Native American artists in applying for grants to help support touring, making videos, making demo recordings, and full length CD projects.

Eventually Arbor also became eligible for funds from FACTOR (the Foundation to Assist Canadian Talent on Records), a private, nonprofit granting agency created by various Canadian music industry organizations, primarily radio broadcasters and music publishers. FACTOR grants, as the name suggests, primarily support recording artists and independent record labels. In 2004, as they grew and became a more established and stable corporate entity, Arbor qualified for FACTOR "DBA" ("Direct Board Approval") status, which meant that the label was eligible to apply for larger grants (up to $25,000) in support of particularly costly recording or video projects. For Brandon and other administrative personnel at Arbor, grant writing was a never-ending but essential component of making records.

Constructing Markets

In the spring of 2000 Brandon and John were working feverishly in an attempt to forge a licensing deal with Naxos International. Cutting licensing deals with other labels and distribution companies is a way of creating capital influx and lessening the problems of cash flow for small indie labels like Arbor. These deals can be structured in one of two ways. Arbor can license a product (recording and packaging) to another label in return for a specified percentage of profit for each unit sold, structured in a similar way to a royalties contract. The licensee is then responsible for all subsequent manufacturing costs. Arbor has arranged this kind of distribution deal with Tom Bee and SOAR for a number of its recordings, particularly their Contemporary Native American titles within the catalogue. Alternately, Arbor may license a product to another label for a flat fee (without promise of future royalty payments), again with the licensee covering all manufacturing, advertising, and distribution costs themselves. The advantage of this latter arrangement for Arbor is that it injects a large amount of capital into the label without substantial overhead costs. Arbor is also free from the responsibility of keeping track of sales (wondering whether the licensing company is being honest in their sales reports to Arbor about the number of units sold). The downside of licensing arrangements is that Arbor loses all rights to future profits for that recording. In these deals, Arbor trades uncertain but potential large-scale profits for smaller but secure lump sums of money. Because the capital needed to break a popular music CD into the mainstream can put an enormous financial strain on the company, licensing deals are particularly advantageous to Arbor in their distribution of Contemporary Native American artists.

A licensing deal with Naxos was attractive to Brandon and John because it represented a new market for their powwow recordings: commercial retail stores in North America and possibly Europe. Naxos is a well-known classical music label with most of its catalogue consisting of familiar and popular classical compositions performed by relatively unknown orchestras and soloists. As such, Naxos CDs are sold at approximately half the price of a similar recording produced by the classical music divisions of the Big Four, which more typically market their recordings on the basis of the star power of conductors, orchestras, and soloists. Naxos has carved out a market share in the global distribution of classical music by catering to what they have categorized as first-time buyers: people who are learning about classical music and venturing the purchase of their first few CDs. Naxos nurtures this target audience by providing CDs with copious liner notes that explain the history and significance of the classical pieces performed, and by offering these titles at a fraction of the cost of the major labels and other European imports (John Marlow interview, February 2000).

At the time of the negotiations with Arbor, Naxos had recently opened a world music division and was tentatively marketing a limited number of world music recordings. John Marlow's position as one of the western Canada distributors for Naxos allowed him to pitch the idea of adding Native music to the world music catalogue. The proposal hinged on the ability of Arbor to provide finished products which would be packaged in a manner consistent with Naxos corporate philosophy, which meant clean, slick graphics and clear, plentiful liner notes that elucidated the musical and cultural significance of the various recordings.[19] This was a significant change from Arbor's typical packaging strategy. With the majority of its sales targeted to cultural insiders (powwow people), liner notes and CD inserts for Arbor's products—as well as the packaging of all of the other Aboriginal Canadian labels—were minimal, typically consisting of a photograph of the group, a listing of song titles and perhaps a paragraph written by the group, thanking various friends and family, tribal councils, powwow committees, and others who supported the group and facilitated the production of the recording. Products packaged and licensed to Naxos needed to be significantly different.

Arbor's interest and attraction to a Naxos licensing deal was fueled by the promise of a new market share, a demographic defined by two key features: non-Native and European. Brandon and John envisioned the European market as a Promised Land of sales, a market demographic of vast potential, and Brandon often spoke of the European market as a lucrative but untapped resource. European interest in Native music was thought to be high, offering far more potential sales than the non-Native North American market. Brandon mentioned numerous times his desire to tap the European market, once offering a joke he had shared with Darlene Whitecalf of Sweet Grass Records. Powwow recordings that they believed to be substandard or that did not sell well in North America could be salvaged for profit though marketing to Europeans. "Thank God we can dump it in Europe," was the joke, meaning that in the eyes of label executives, Europeans were simply hungry for this music and consequently were less discriminating about its quality.

The degree to which this reflects the reality of the market is questionable. The assumption is simply that, as cultural outsiders, the European public is less knowledgeable about powwow music but very open and interested in Native culture. The "thank God we can dump it in Europe" thesis posits that there is a non-Native audience who will buy product far more indiscriminately than the North American market, a market dominated by Native Americans. The assumption therefore is not that white Europeans know less about Native music than white North Americans but simply that white Europeans are far more likely to buy the music than their North American counterparts, and that all non-Native populations are equally unable to make intelligent (i.e., culturally or emically informed) distinctions between good and bad powwow performances.

Arbor's negotiations with Naxos illustrate the kinds of marketing strategies employed by the company, which imagined and constructed two separate and distinct markets: Aboriginal and non-Aboriginal.[20] Once imagined and formulated, these markets were then targeted through packaging, advertising, and distribution. Arbor Records' strategy for addressing the non-Native market involved the creation of crossover recordings. Even though the Naxos deal eventually fell through, Arbor ultimately realized their goal of developing crossover products with the creation of a line of CDs in 2002 called the *Native American Heritage Series* (NAH), a collection of music compilations thematically organized around intertribal and pan-tribal (both powwow and non-powwow-related) dance styles and musical styles. Some of the compilations feature the six standard powwow dance categories (Men's Traditional [AR-11732], Grass dance [AR-11702], Jingle Dress dance [AR-11722], etc.) while others were dedicated to Chicken dance songs (AR-11712), Forty-niner songs (AR-11832), Round dance songs (AR-11792), and Stick Game songs (AR-11742). This series is described in the 2002 Arbor Records product catalogue in the following way: "The Native American Heritage Series (NAH) was conceived to preserve the beautiful history and traditions of the Native American culture through music. . . . The result is an incredible series of never before released compilation albums filled with the unique sounds of traditional Native American music! The NAH series is presented in beautiful and highly descriptive packaging. Every album is unique in that they each represent a specific style of music found within Native American culture. All packaging contains a brief educational history of the drumming and dress style found on each album. The NAH series is the perfect blend of cultural preservation and entertainment. It's time to discover Native America!"

Clearly intended for non-Native consumption, these products used packaging strategies similar to mainstream practices of marketing world music. According to Negus (1999), the standard corporate strategy for marketing music specifically as "world music" involves "localizing" the music by stressing both geographical distance (this music is from far away) and specificity (this music is very different than the music we have "here"). Arbor followed a similar commercial strategy in the creation of these CDs, except that instead of geographical distance, tribal affiliation (often a sign of geographical specificity) was often obfuscated in order to emphasize *cultural* distance, which became a central marker of otherness.

The NAH CDs include liner notes that describe the history of each dance and musical style, current regalia and footwork styles, and symbolic/iconic meanings. For example, the CD insert for the recording *Stick Game Songs, Volume 1* (AR-11742) features the following text:

> The Stickgame is an ancient game within North American First Nation's [sic] culture that pre-dates contact from [sic] other cultures. The First Nations culture passed on its information orally through the use of story and song. Through the Stickgame, stories and song could [be], and still are shared. The Stickgame brought people together; people from within a tribe, and also from differing tribes. The gathering of people encouraged the exchange of stories, whether it was information about friends and relatives, passing on of myths, or information about the different tribes, the topics for conversation was [sic] limitless.
>
> . . . The singing that accompanies the Stickgame had connotations that were mostly of a mythological nature. The songs that were used were believed to have mythological powers, and if a group sang its songs and won the game then it was believed that the group had more power than the opposing group. Their powerful song was believed to have made them succeed. These songs were passed down many generations. The songs that were sometimes sung were also used to instill fear in opponents, and some songs were used in order to taunt a group. The drums are played to keep to the rhythm of the song or game, but this is a recent addition to the stickgame.

Further, in the Arbor Records 2002 catalogue advertising the CD, the copy reads: "Arbor Records proudly presents Stick Game Songs (performed by the McGilvery Family). We know you'll be entertained by these unique traditional songs. Have fun learning to play North America's First Nations' oldest and most popular game! *[Game instructions included!]*" (italics in original).

Noting the "ancient" nature of the game which "predates" European contact constructs the aura of exotic authenticity while effectively "othering" the product and guaranteeing for the customer that this music and game are indeed culturally distant from their own practices, historical continuity being a regular marker of cultural otherness in non-Native representations of Native culture (Clifford 1986). The connection to the importance of mythology (a hallmark of pre-modern oral cultures) serves to drive home the point further. The instructional nature of the CD ("Have fun learning to play")—unique in the NAH series—is perhaps the most obvious sign of the imagined market being constructed, as non-Native consumers are encouraged to learn about a pan-tribally constructed, generic "First Nations culture" through consumption.

Appadurai (1986, 44–45) suggests that one way to preserve the symbolic capital of prestige (luxury) items like CDs is to complicate the criteria for *authenticity*. Benjamin (1969) suggests a similar idea, noting that a work of art gains an aura of authenticity only after its mechanical reproduction within the context of modernity (as a historical moment). In the absence of such reproduction (mass production) there is little need to discuss authenticity. Such is the case for any creative work's relationship to industrial, capitalist circuits of production and distribution. Luxury works of art and musical performances not connected to these mass-mediated circuits are rarely questioned as being authentic. It is their entry into industry—mass production and mass circulation—that brings with it questions and discussions of authenticity, not only through mechanical reproduction (and thus much more varied and widely dispersed consumers) but through the intermingling of these aesthetic products with the practices and discourses of modern capitalism.[21]

Authenticity in the art world has to do with issues of expert knowledge, good taste, "originality," and social distinction (Bourdieu 1984, 1993). In the world of rock music, authenticity is earned through symbolic productions of individuality, honesty in self-representation and image, non-self-consciousness, and an attitude of distain for measures of success in the music business. In country music, authenticity is generated through embracing the music business and mastering its intricacies, and also by becoming symbolically and indexically linked to "the South," family (often Christian) values, patriotism, and blue-collar social class (Peterson 1997). In the marketing of powwow music (considered a "traditional" music by the industry), authenticity is constructed for non-Native audiences through the exoticizing discourses of "culture" and "tradition," and explicitly marked through the emphasis on both cultural and temporal distance. This may perhaps be evidence of Appadurai's (1986) suggestion that authenticity becomes an issue only as products become distanced from producers and consumers, creating gaps of knowledge that must be filled in with ever-expanding and labyrinthine mythologies of production and consumption.

The visualization and subsequent construction of the *Native* market requires a different strategy, a fact that accounts for the wide variance in packaging and marketing strategies for the two market demographics. It is not that authenticity is absent in Native American evaluations of recordings, rather the discourse of authenticity is differently constituted for Native and non-Native markets. At Arbor Records, powwow recordings intended for the Native market regularly cite the tribal affiliation of a drum group, their success at competition powwows, and their longevity on the powwow trail:

1. *References to tribal affiliation.* Brandon and the other executives at Arbor believe that there is a certain degree of local and regional pride for local powwow groups who have success on the competition powwow circuit and who have become popular enough to draw the interest of a recording company. As such it is believed that a recording sells in greater numbers in the region from which the group hails. This could have to do with expressions of regional loyalty or pride, or an expression of friendship and support as local communities choose to embrace "their own" groups.[22] Tribal affiliation is also an important style marker for other singers and dancers as powwow participants recognize and celebrate the differences between, for example, Cree and Ojibwa Round dance styles or Ojibwa and Sioux Side-step songs. Powwow dancers and fans also readily acknowledge that certain regionally or tribally defined singing styles experience runs of heightened popularity on the powwow trail. In the early '90s Ojibwa-style singing experienced a boom in popularity, followed by a wave of Cree powwow drums that became popular for a time. Thus tribal

affiliation not only marks a drum geographically, but also, to a certain extent, stylistically.

2. *References to a group's success at competition powwows*. This is a marker of prestige for groups and also a sign for singers and dancers that the group has successfully absorbed and articulated the aesthetic principles of successful competition singing. This is an important criterion for dancers who want to become familiar not only with the singing style but also the repertoire of active and successful competition drum groups, since there is a greater chance that these drum groups will be performing for them during dance competitions. Knowing the repertoire (or at least the compositional and performative tendencies) of certain groups is a definite advantage for competition dancers who are always trying to avoid "overstepping" and "understepping."[23]

3. *References to longevity on the powwow trail*. The number of years a group has successfully participated within the powwow circuit reflects their dedication and service to the powwow community; it is thus to be valued and respected. Longevity is also a marker of quality because it implies that the group knows all of the songs and styles required for continual participation in the competition circuit. If a group is relatively new, their freshness is valued. The relative "newness" of a group may also have marketing potential, as new groups bring with them a degree of excitement and anticipation. They are frequently marketed as the "next big thing."[24]

Circuits of Distribution

Gray (1988) has suggested that one of the central structural features that distinguish independents from majors is the tension and resulting financial instability between small indie record labels and the major (and sometimes independent) distribution companies that bring their products to the market. One of the greatest financial challenges faced by small record labels is meeting the financial demands of mass production required by distribution companies. Distributors and subdistributors act as middlemen between labels and the retail market, and the success or failure of a recording within mainstream music industry circuits depends to a large degree on proper and successful distribution.

Arbor Records and other powwow music labels do not labor under the same degree of financial and industrial pressure as do music labels that must deal with large distribution companies. Instead, all of the Aboriginal labels on the Canadian Plains engage in a good deal of direct selling, obtaining vendor space at large powwows, and setting up retail booths in much the same way as other craft and retail vendors who travel the powwow circuit. The summer of 1999 (Arbor's first year in existence), Stewart Astleford, the head salesman at the time, made it a priority to travel to a number of large competition powwows to establish an Arbor Records vendor's booth and sell products directly to customers.[25] In North America, record labels may also act as distribution companies. As such, Arbor distributes most of their powwow products themselves, either selling the product directly to the public or by selling wholesale to small craft vendors who travel the powwow trail, to large craft vendors who may also act as subdistributors to other smaller traveling vendors, or to independently owned retail stores (often located in small northern communities in Canada). Selling to traveling vendors is the route by which the majority of Arbor's product is distributed. These vendors travel the Northern and Southern powwow circuits year-round, visiting powwows, art shows, craft fairs, and other exhibitions where Native cultural products are commercially featured. Only a small percentage of recordings are sold through major and independently owned retail record stores, and these markets are carefully cultivated and targeted:

SA:　. . . I deal with a company called CD Plus, which is here in Winnipeg— formerly National Records—which now own 135 stores across Canada. They go by a number of different names: CD Plus, Music Baron, which is in town here, Music City, Music Plus, a company called Big K out of the east. They're changing all the names to CD Plus now. Now I deal with them in my Native product, but they don't send it to all 135 stores. We find out where their stores are, and we know that there are reserves in the area, and we know that there's a Native population, and they know it too. And then we sit down and put it [Arbor's powwow products] in thirty stores. And it's the same thing with HMVs [a retail chain no longer operating in Canada]. There's eighty-five or ninety stores. You'll wind up contacting them all, and you'll wind up with twelve of them. The main ones: downtown Winnipeg, superstore Toronto, superstore Montreal, Sault Saint Marie area, and that's how you end up dealing in the mainstream.

CS:　So what is the percentage of product that you sell through record stores and mainstream?

SA: Probably 10 percent. It's very small, and it's one hundred—or at least it's 95 percent CD. So that kind of tells you why you don't move a bigger percentage. The population of powwow is buying 75 percent cassette [in 1999], yet the mainstream is buying 95 percent CD from you because you walk into these stores, it's all CD and the mainstream public buys more CDs. So we have to, we actually have more success with the "one-stop," the independent, small store. (Stewart Astleford interview, August 1999)

One-stops are small, independently owned gift shops, "mom-and-pop" variety stores and gas stations, and trading posts that dot the Canadian prairies and service a local Native population. As Stewart mentioned, they are the other major distribution target. Constructing and maintaining this list of one-stop clients is an incredibly time-intensive task, as each store must be contacted individually for an order that usually only amounts to ten to twenty units (CDs or cassettes). However these nontraditional retail music venues are a crucial part of Arbor's distribution strategy; it is a segment of the market that is almost impossible to reach through mainstream major or independent distribution companies. According to Brandon, in servicing his one-stop client list, "You can't get rich, but you keep the lights on. You can get your bills paid" (personal communication, July 2006).

Arbor's distribution network mirrors their construction of the marketplace for powwow recordings, characterized essentially as both Native and peripheral to the mainstream music business. References to "the mainstream" surfaced often in my conversations with Arbor Records personnel as they repeatedly located their own position within the music industry as existing outside of or on the periphery of the mainstream. This self-conscious awareness of their own marginality within the international music industry was not celebrated—as it often is in the case of independent labels (Gray 1989; Lee 1994)—but lamented. These circuits of distribution were recognized and well established, but ultimately unique to powwow music and the powwow recording industry.

Contract Negotiations: Eyabay Bolts

In early April 2000 the Arbor office was buzzing in crisis. The staff had found out that Eyabay had recently cut a recording with Sunshine Records. Brandon sat in his office behind a rarely closed door, smoking. Everyone was in shock. This was a significant development. Since the mid-1990s the Eyabay singers—an Ojibwa drum group from Red Lake, Minnesota—had been one of the most popular groups on the Northern powwow circuit. Consistently winning singing contests wherever they traveled, by 1999 they were at the pinnacle of their popularity. Rarely competing anymore, they were in constant demand as a host or invited drum across North America. They were the jewel of Arbor's stable of artists and their recording *No Limit* (AR-11012) was the first CD produced by the label, released in May 1999. The group had originally worked with Brandon when they were both at Sunshine Records. When Eyabay heard that Brandon had started another label, they signed a lucrative, long-term contract with Arbor. The signing and recording of Eyabay (which means "big buck" in Ojibwa) gave Arbor instant credibility and guaranteed them a top-selling recording.

I walked into Brandon's office to venture a few questions. Brandon was staring at his computer screen. "You heard the news?" he asked, briefly looking toward me. I nodded. He said that he had found out about the recording after speaking with a member of the drum group. "He told me that Ness [Michaels, owner of Sunshine Records] offered them $3,000 dollars and they took it and did the recording. I told him, 'What's with *that*! I spent $10,000 on you guys last year! And you're under a *seven-year contract*!" Brandon went on to tell me that he had contacted a lawyer, one who specialized in artist contracts within the music business, to discuss what legal recourse was available to him. There were few palatable options. Eyabay was in clear breach of contract and Arbor could sue, but the end result would simply be that Eyabay would likely never do another recording with Brandon, and Arbor Records would quickly become known as the record label that sues powwow groups. It would spell the end of the company. All Brandon could do was cut his losses, rip up Eyabay's contract, and try to negotiate another deal with the group. As it turned out, this is exactly what happened, and in the summer of 2000 Eyabay came out with their second Arbor release, *Eyabay: Live 2000* (AR-11182). They have since released two others: *Miracle* in 2002 (AR-11612) and *Soldiers* in 2005 (AR-12192).

I came to recognize this crisis in artist relations with the industry as one in an ongoing series of "structural readjustments" in Arbor Records' corporate and contractual policy. These negotiations between the record label and the drum groups it records are conditioned by several factors:

competing understandings of "standard" recording industry policy and operating procedures; the job and responsibility of powwow singing; and the culturally conditioned expectations regarding the nature of the relationship between drum groups and record labels. Contract negotiations and the relationships—both formal and informal—between record labels and powwow groups are important arenas within which cultural difference is identified and negotiated.

In the early 1990s, during the formative years of the powwow recording industry in Canada, most powwow recordings were made with minimal formalized economic arrangements. Brandon referred to these conditions in describing his job as a recording engineer in the early 1990s:

BF: So the first powwow I recorded was Roseau River, here in Manitoba. And I recorded Blacklodge [Singers] there.[26] That was the first group I ever recorded. Blacklodge. And for free! For nothing. They just let me record them and there was no contract or nothing. So Sunshine's first Blacklodge release, they never paid a penny for it. I brought a DAT and a [mixing] board and backed my pickup truck right up to where they were and recorded them.

CS: And they were ok with that?

BF: Yeah, they didn't care. Back then it wasn't like it is now. Back then it was like, "whatever, go ahead if you want to make a tape."

CS: They didn't ask for any money?

BF: No, nothing.

CS: So when you started recording, were you having to sign contracts with these guys or were you just going out there and . . .

BF: No, the first couple—nothing. And then Winston Wutunee [a Cree recording artist for Sunshine Records] came up with this idea. He said, "You know, none of these powwow groups understand contracts. They don't understand royalties, they don't understand these things," which, I think, was true for a lot of them at the time. And so Winston said, "Offer them two hundred free tapes and that will be good enough." And fuck, sure enough it was good enough. Most of the groups that Sunshine signed from 1994 till . . . well, right until the day I left, with the exception of Eyabay and Whitefish Bay, got two hundred tapes and no royalties. That's all it cost Sunshine was two hundred tapes. And nowadays it's five hundred free tapes and cash, and other perks.

CS: When did that start happening?

BF: The perks and the money? Just in the last couple of years. But it's still the case with some groups. I mean, you can still get away with that [not paying royalties] with some groups. But in my case [Arbor Records] I've never even offered that. I've offered royalties on everything. Cuz I don't want to do that, you know.

CS: So you say Eyabay started that though?

BF: Whitefish Bay did. Cuz they were doing so well for Sunshine for so long. Andy [White, leader of Whitefish Bay Singers] said we want more. We want cash here, we want cash there.

CS: So they wanted cash up front for every release?

BF: All the time, yeah. Not every release. They just wanted to drop by and get a thousand bucks whenever they could. So Ness finally just said, "No, we're signing a contract if you want this kind of money." So he would give them the money whenever they wanted it, and got their releases. (Brandon Friesen interview, October 1999)

I believe powwow musicians accepted these early, informal, and sometimes highly asymmetrical economic arrangements for a number of reasons. In the 1990s it was already quite common for crowds of singers and dancers to gather around powwow groups and record their performances using hand-held tape recorders. Thus the relatively free and unfettered recording of a drum group's performances was a standard practice, typical of the way in which singers, dancers, and fans learned and familiarized themselves with the songs of a drum group. In the early years of the recording industry, many drum groups did not realize the economic potential of recording, nor the legal implications of Euro-American copyright law. However it should also be noted that, because many powwow recordings sold in very modest numbers, the money generated from the drum group's personally selling the two hundred free tapes provided by the label would likely exceed the money generated from royalties on the total number of units sold.

It is significant that the two most economically successful powwow drum groups changed the business practices of the industry. As Whitefish Bay and Eyabay grew to understand the earning potential of their recordings they became more keenly aware of their own power to change the economic arrangements between singers and record labels.[27] When Arbor began signing powwow groups in 1999, Brandon attempted to reconfigure the structural relationship between labels and singers, drawing on a "commonsense" model of contractual relations that was a product of his own cultural understanding of "fair" and "standard" recording industry practices. The first drum groups signed to Arbor Records entered into long-term, seven-year contracts which were structured to resemble standard contracts in the mainstream recording industry. These contracts locked drum groups into guaranteeing that Arbor would be the only label with whom they could legally record. And while the contracts guaranteed royalties to the group for every unit sold, production costs and a percentage of the promotion costs accrued by Arbor would be paid for out of initial royalties earned by the drum groups for every unit sold.

> Seven years is the standard length of a contract [at Arbor]. But, I mean, in the real world, if they [drum groups] call me and say, "We're absolutely unhappy, we want to go do this," I would let them. I don't care. Like right now Sweet Grass is chasing Eyabay and they recorded them at Schemitzun. And if they release it, I'll send them a contract and force them to take it off the market or get paid for every copy they've sold. And so Ted's wife called me and said, "Well, why don't you sign a release form and allow us to record one song for this compilation." And I said, "OK, I'll let you do that if you let me use Stoney Park [a group signed to Sweet Grass Records] for this release." And they said, "OK, we'll do it." 'Cause when I started, every contract was for just one album, one album only. When I left Sunshine, that's when they started tying people down to long-term and that's immediately what I started doing. And then Ted and Darlene from Sweet Grass said that all of their groups are under long-term contract now. And seven years is a long time. That's a career. (Brandon Friesen interview, October 1999)

While long-term contracts were becoming the industry standard by 1999, this arrangement did not last long, and Eyabay's defection to Sunshine was one of the first signs that long-term contracts were untenable within the powwow recording industry. Arbor Records (and others) tried to restructure the informal nature of powwow recording by introducing long-term contracts, but this failed because drum groups simply refused to recognize the validity of the arrangement. I believe the impersonal legalistic nature of contracts did not hold emotional or cultural force for drum groups; it was not the way that arrangements were made on the powwow grounds. When drum groups are approached and asked to sing for a powwow, either as host or invited drum, it is usually done in a face-to-face manner, with a handshake and an exchange of tobacco. Functioning relationships on the powwow grounds are not achieved through contractual negotiation but through continual maintenance and face-to-face interactions. Through Arbor's experience with Eyabay, Brandon learned that, in the powwow world, seven-year contracts are not worth the paper they are printed on. Drum groups, because of a kind of social power which artists in the recording industry do not typically wield, were able to influence changes in the kinds of relationships they forged with record labels.

Subsequently, in the years following Eyabay's defection, Brandon and Arbor Records no longer attempted to sign groups to long-term deals because it became clear that powwow groups did not recognize the legitimacy of these contracts. Ironically, contractual relations returned to a condition similar to that of the mid-1990s with single record deals and a guarantee of a certain number of free CDs and tapes to the group. A critical difference, however, was the continued assurance within the contract of royalty payments on units sold. This change in contractual policy may also have been influenced by the emergence of a new record label, Rez Cue Records, owned and operated by Robert Peasley, a record vendor who traveled the Northern powwow circuit throughout North and South Dakota, Minnesota, and Wisconsin. He started Rez Cue Records in 2000, recording and distributing mainly Minnesota Ojibwa drums. Claiming Native heritage, Bob maintained that he established the label because he wanted to empower powwow singers and protect them from being "ripped off" by white-owned powwow labels. As an urban-dwelling Native living in Minneapolis, Peasley was extremely outspoken about Native rights, once proclaiming to me in his typically colorful fashion, "[When] a white guy shows me a contract, I stick a knife in it." Peasley offered contractual arrangements with his groups whereby he recorded drum groups on a record-by-record basis, taking care of all recording and production costs, and delivering to the drum group a certain number of CDs and tapes *and* the master recording, guaranteeing that control and ownership of the recording would be in the hands of the drum groups. In this way drum groups would have total control over their music: how it was manufactured, how it was marketed, and how it was distributed. As well, by cutting out the middleman (the record company), they would enjoy a much greater profit margin on any CD they sold. And they never had to sign away their rights to any of their songs. In return, Peasley wanted a certain number of free CDs that he could sell out of his craft booth, the sales from which would recoup his initial investment in recording equipment.

Bob told me of his offer to these drum groups as he set up his recording equipment:

> I don't use contracts. That's not the Indian way. I tell my groups, "I'll record you, but you own the masters. I'll give them to you. All I want is a run of CDs I can sell at my booth." You know, I give the groups all the information I have access to. I tell them, "Here's the master, here's the place where you can get the CD manufactured, here are some graphic artists that I know that can design the cover for you." Brandon says to me, "Bob, you're giving away the farm, you're gonna put us all out of business." But you know what? The singers, they don't want to bother with it. They won't do it. (August 2000)

My own observations and experiences confirm Bob Peasley's assessment of singers' relationship to the industry at that time. Despite all the mistrust and complaining that singers may engage in regarding the dishonest nature of the powwow recording industry, most have virtually no interest in remedying the situation by starting their own companies and manufacturing their own products. There are many possible reasons for this. Foremost is the economic reality that most singers simply do not have the capital to fund the manufacture of a recording, which can cost thousands of dollars up front. Money that singers earn on the powwow trail is used to support further travel, and it is a challenge for most groups to simply break even by the end of the summer. Without established sales connections to music distributors, their only method of distribution is wandering the powwow grounds between performances selling copies out of hand. Add to this the simple truth that most singers simply want to travel and sing, and they have little interest in becoming entrepreneurial businessmen.

Race, Culture, Industry

The emergence of Rez Cue Records and the somewhat militant, Red Power–inspired rhetoric of its owner served to remind Brandon and Arbor Records of the politics of non-Natives who record and distribute powwow music.

CS: So have you ever gotten any hassles for being white and recording powwow music?

BF: For being a white guy? All the time. Well, only in the case of arguments. Like I pissed off [this one singer] one time. He called me and wanted to do a recording and we were talking about it for six months before we actually did it. We didn't do it until August and we were talking right from February. And it came to the point where we couldn't come to an agreement on a deal. Totally a money thing. And he said—he was really pissed off when he called me—he said, "You know what they say about fucking white people recording Indian music. You know what they say about that." He was trying to hold it over me. And I said, "Who cares, business is business. You could strike up a deal with Ted Whitecalf [Native American owner of Sweet Grass Records] or you could strike up a deal with me. It's all the same, it's money, right." And that's where we left it. (Brandon Friesen interview, October 1999)

Brandon often lamented that a central problem for Arbor was the fact that there were no regular staff with Native American heritage. Almost since the inception of the company Brandon had been searching for a Native business partner to work with Arbor, to go to the powwows and meet and sign drum groups, to do field recordings, and possibly even to run a vendor's booth selling Arbor's products. Several candidates presented themselves during my own tenure at Arbor but none of them really worked out. "Purple" (Derek Gerbrand) was one such candidate. Purple was connected to Brandon and Arbor Records through Paul Scinocca. He and Paul performed together in The Mollies, a hard-rock cover band that worked occasionally in Winnipeg and southern Manitoba. As the lead singer and front man of the group, Purple was a born entertainer and perhaps one of the most charismatic and naturally funny people I have ever met. He worked a day job as a teacher's assistant at a North End public school where he was responsible for a number of "problem children," kids who have displayed behavioral dysfunction in the classroom and who need extra out-of-class attention. Purple spoke warmly and affectionately about these kids, and it was clear that he genuinely enjoyed the challenges and rewards of working with them.

At the urging of both Paul and Brandon, Purple attended a course on studio production and recording techniques that Studio 11 offered on Tuesday nights, as a way of grooming him for a central position within

Arbor Records.[28] He was an ideal candidate in Brandon's eyes because, while identifying and being identified by others as Native American, Purple operated in social worlds familiar to Brandon and the Arbor staff. Brandon regarded his lack of knowledge about recording and powwow music as only a minor inconvenience. He could be taught these things. Purple had other attributes: he was personable, honest, a hard worker, and he was Native.[29]

TKO was another such candidate, a Winnipeg-based Native rapper Brandon had known as a friend for years. Brandon and TKO had also worked together musically when Brandon produced TKO's first CD at Sunshine Records a few years earlier (*Welcome to the Playground*, SSCT-4337). TKO was occasionally hired as a recording technician for large powwows; he was also asked to staff a vendor's booth and sell product. Both TKO and Purple were raised in Winnipeg and had few ties to their "home" reservations, with no desire to return there. Their association with Arbor was based on the same context shared by Arbor Records' and Studio 11's non-Native personnel: connections to, and aspirations within, the local popular music industry in Winnipeg. Significantly, both had less knowledge about powwow singing and powwow culture than Brandon himself, but because of their Native status they were able to function on the powwow grounds with greater ease than white recording technicians or salespeople. Purple often accompanied Brandon (or myself, when I worked there) to powwows for live recording projects. On the powwow grounds Purple encountered little resistance from powwow committees and other powwow participants as he worked within the dance arbor with a boom microphone and DAT machine, standing over drum groups as they sang. Purple was also young (in his late twenties) and extremely personable, and thus able to relate exceptionally well to most of the drum groups with whom Arbor worked, groups with singers under thirty. Ultimately, however, the very qualities that made Purple and TKO ideal candidates — Native who nonetheless acted and thought in a way similar to the commonsense worldview of many at Arbor Records — ultimately became their greatest liability: they lacked an essential *cultural* understanding of the powwow music world. Thus neither turned out to be a good fit for the company.[30]

The importance of having a Native presence at Arbor Records arose from the numerous moments of tension or negotiation between drum groups and record labels, where stereotypes of race (and accompanying assumptions about cultural difference) were employed as discursive tropes by each party in attempts to resolve differences. The power of the discourse of race lies in the power of this trope to naturalize difference based on phenotypic distinctions. I found that during my time at Arbor, at certain moments of tension and negotiation, racial differences (white vs. Native American) came to be understood as immutable markers of cultural difference. This in turn functioned to prioritize racial and cultural differences over other social distinctions such as class, tribal affiliation, region of origin, and differences between urban and reservation lifestyles and attitudes.

When Bob Peasley told me, "[When] a white guy shows me a contract, I stick a knife in it," he was making a statement about racial difference that had the rhetorical force of history behind it, implicitly referencing the colonial history between whites and Native Americans wherein Native Americans have repeatedly felt betrayed by a series of white-constructed contracts such as treaties and government policies. Strategically in opposition to white-owned companies like Arbor and Sunshine Records, Native-owned labels like Rez Cue Records and Wacipi Records have stressed a lack of formal, paper-driven relationships with their drum groups. The symbolic status of contracts is one way in which racial and cultural allegiance has been articulated. Curtis Assiniboine stressed this fact to me during an interview:

> Well, I feel very confident in what I do, so while we do sign a contract, all we do is we contract the songs that they decide to put on there [the recording]. I think part of the confidence that I have is not using the legal system to have the artists stay with me. To prove that—to try to prove the best that I can that we're trying to do the best we can on behalf of these individuals. And they make the decisions on the job that I do whether they stay with us or not. I think that's a fair way to do it. And after we've proven ourselves and they've made a decision, "Yeah, we're going to do another one and we've enjoyed what has happened," then we, at some point, we would like to have their name under the label exclusively. But until that time I leave it open. Nobody is under a contract where they have to stay with the company at this time. (Curtis Assiniboine interview, July 1998)

The obfuscation of racial and cultural difference is also implicated in forging trust relationships between recording artists and white record-label personnel that may or may not be contractually driven. This was forcefully demonstrated to me through an incident in early February 2000 in the offices of Arbor Records. Brandon's longtime friend Andy White from Whitefish Bay dropped by the office to pick up a box of CDs of *Ndoo Te Mag* (AR-11022) in order to sell them at a powwow his group was planning to attend; he also wanted to get an advance on royalties to help fund their travel. For powwow groups, record labels are useful because they provide CDs that the group can sell at powwows; they can also be a source of capital that helps to fund travel to powwows. Thus the number of CDs that a group is given, and the upfront cash advance they receive for a recording, are two central components of most powwow recording contracts. Because of Brandon's long-term association and friendship with Andy and Whitefish Bay (dating back to the early '90s and their time spent recording together at Sunshine), they have a trust relationship that transcends, to a certain degree, formal contractual arrangements. However on this day, Brandon was out of the office and so Andy instead had to deal with John Marlow, who had only recently been hired by Arbor as the sales manager. Trained in the world of commercial mainstream music retail, John joined Arbor records knowing very little about powwow music and culture, and certainly less about Brandon and Andy's long working relationship.

Andy and John disappeared into Brandon's office behind closed doors. Ten minutes later Andy stormed out of the room and quickly left the office, saying nothing. John walked out a short time afterward commenting sarcastically, "That went well." John complained that Andy was expecting money for royalties, and John countered by explaining to Andy that the recording costs and jackets for the group were all paid for out of the royalties for the CD. Whitefish Bay "got them for free" but the money was being paid out of their royalties. Thus under the terms of the contract, Whitefish Bay was not entitled to any royalty payments until all recording costs and other upfront costs accrued by Arbor—for advance payments and for the custom-designed jackets for every member of Whitefish Bay—had been recouped. Andy felt cheated and betrayed, accusing Arbor of lying to the drum group. John lamented that he could not make Andy understand that Arbor was a *business* and that they were in the business of making money and that this money had to come from somewhere. When John attempted to depersonalize the interaction by stating that it was "just business," Andy became enraged and accused Arbor of acting in a way typical of "white people" who were again trying to take advantage of Indians. Mark—an urban, Winnipeg-born Native and a part-time staff member for Arbor who was in the office at the time—suggested that the misunderstanding was a result of Andy being a "simple man [meaning, I think, straightforward and honest] who didn't know the business." Paul Scinocca, also in the office at the time, remarked wryly, "Of course he thinks that [you're trying to take advantage of him]! It's because you stole all his fucking land!"

Racial stereotypes and guilt—the types of race-based, socially imagined roles that are structured by the larger institutional treatment of Natives in Canada—provide the backdrop for many of the interactions between Native and white employees at Arbor. The white employees of Arbor were all very sensitive to the racial politics of which they were a part, and joked about it constantly as a way of dealing with the discomfort they experienced. Apart from Brandon, none had any real association with Natives, and they knew very little about either the traditional Native way of life or the culture and conditions of daily life on a contemporary reserve. This was not a business misunderstanding, resulting from Andy being a "simple man," but a *cultural* misunderstanding. The kind of relationship that John was trying to establish with Andy was both insulting and nonsensical; it was antithetical to the ways in which relationships are forged and maintained on the powwow grounds. It was not the kind of reciprocal relationship that Andy expected from a "friend" like Arbor Records. On the powwow grounds and the reservation, social relationships are maintained through continual and sustained interaction, through ritualized public events like giveaways and "relative making" and through informal networks of visiting. From a drum group's point of view, their music is valuable. It is highly valued at the powwows and they are honored in that social context for providing an important service. When they enter into a relationship with a recording company, these same drums are "giving" their music to that company. For drum groups, this exchange is not completed when a contract is signed but is part of a continuing relationship that must be maintained through the continued exchange of product for services. Brandon, having worked with Andy and other powwow singers for years, works hard to develop and maintain these kinds of trust relationships. When Brandon returned to the office and heard about what had happened, he took immediate steps to remedy the situation, phoning Andy to apologize and sending several boxes of CDs. This speaks not only to Brandon and Andy's long-standing friendship but also to the fact that maintaining good relations with Arbor's recording artists was essential to the continued success of the company as a business.

Keith Negus's excellent and continuous study of the corporate practices of the music industry (1992, 1996, 1999) rests on the central thesis that just as *industry* produces culture, so, too, does *culture* produce an industry (Negus 1999, 14). This provocative turn of phrase addresses how broader social divisions and ways of living intersect with corporate organization and practice. Negus suggests that "staff within the music industry seek to understand the world of musical production and consumption by constructing knowledge about it (through various forms of research and information-gathering), and then by deploying this knowledge as a 'reality' that guides the activities of corporate personnel" (1999, 19). Within culture industries such as the music business, production takes place within broader cultural formations and practices as personnel employ commonsense attitudes about how music and people operate and intersect within the world. This model for understanding corporate organization and production is the lens through which I have tried to describe the social dynamics of Arbor Records. Aboriginal record labels like Arbor may be understood as sites of struggle over material and symbolic resources, the terms of which are defined through commonsense ideas about race, culture, and capitalism. In this chapter I have outlined some of the structural features of the powwow recording industry generally—and Arbor specifically—in order to distinguish this industry from both mainstream and independent record labels and to highlight some of the distinctive characteristics of the Aboriginal music business. However, the deployment of the discourses of race and culture is not only important for Arbor's corporate image, but also gets played out in the microprocesses of production, a theme more fully explored in the following chapters.

CHAPTER 5

Powwow Music in the Studio

Mediation and Musical Fields

The ongoing debate within popular-music studies over the relative primacy of production and consumption has often precluded the analysis of what might be called the "logics" of particular musical terrains. . . . The specificity of these "fields" . . . is shaped in part by the "regions" they occupy, as markets and contexts of production, relative to a given set of cultural institutions.
—WILL STRAW (1991, 374)

Ethnomusicology's continuing engagement with the related phenomena of world music and world beat as they exist within and through the mass media has produced a great volume of work which details the various processes through which non-Western musicians and musics interact with and transform, or are transformed by, the multinational recording industry. Many of these earlier studies dealt primarily with employing musicological and textual analysis to illuminate the various political and cultural meanings semiotically embedded within the musical *products*. More recently, ethnomusicologists have begun to pay closer attention to the actual *process* of recording (see, for example, Austin 1993; Greene and Porcello 2005; Meintjes 1997, 2003; Porcello 1996, 1998; Théberge 1997; and Zak 2001). Shifting the focus of study from musical products to musical process, in this chapter I wish to explore both the activity of studio recording and the structural potentials and limitations of the recording studio as a unique site for Native American musical creation. In doing so, I attempt to understand studio processes and social interactions through "field" analysis. Pierre Bourdieu has suggested that the social world and all social collaboration may be understood in terms of how interactions take place within particular social "fields." He defines a field as "a network, or configuration, of objective relations between positions. These positions are objectively defined, in their existence and in the determinations they impose upon their occupants, agents or institutions, by their present and potential situation (*situs*) in the structure of the distribution of species of power (or capital) whose possession commands access to the specific profits that are at stake in the field, as well as by their objective relation to other positions (domination, subordination, homology, etc.)" (Bourdieu and Waquant 1992, 97).

Fields describe arenas of production and circulation in which various kinds of capital (cultural, economic, social, symbolic, etc.) are exchanged and contested. Each field is defined by its own set of aesthetic positions, goals, dynamics, ethics, and distribution of power. Two key structural components are common to all social fields: (1) they are arenas of struggle for control over valued resources (including the struggle over definitions of what forms of capital are valued within a particular field); and (2) they are spaces that are structured by dominant and subordinate positions, based on the control of different types and amounts of capital (Swartz 1997, 122–25).

Inspired by Bourdieu, I suggest that it can be illuminating to consider different recording sessions as taking place within different "musical fields."[1] While each field shares a similarity in structure, created by the tacit (and sometimes explicit) agreement between all parties that creating a commercial recording is something of value and worth pursuing in the first place, dominant and subordinate positions within these fields are under constant negotiation. In framing recording studio practices in this way, I want to emphasize that the recording studio is not in itself a site of any one particular kind of social formation or process, and there are a vast number of possible relationships and outcomes within any recording context. These differences in *process* are generated by unequal power relationships and structured by different market systems, differing claims about cultural authenticity, and varied perceived (and actual) levels of cultural fluency and expertise.

Despite Studio 11's close relationship to Arbor Records, with the exception of Brandon, the studio was populated with musicians and engineers who knew very little about Native musical styles or genres. All full- and part-time employees were non-Natives, and the majority of recording projects undertaken at the studio were completely unrelated to Arbor

Records. When Native musicians entered the studio, the field of inter-action between studio employees and Native recording artists was struc-tured through various discourses about cultural, economic, and racial dif-ference. This configuration made Studio 11 a unique site for the creation and performance of Native music.

My focus in this chapter is not concerned with a close examination of musical style itself, but an analysis of the *process* by which musical style gets created and defined in the studio, and how particular style features become articulated to genre classifications. This emphasis on process is intended to help frame "the recording studio" as a site of various forms of *mediation*. There are two senses in which I use the term "mediation" in this chapter. First, studio recording requires negotiations among people with differing aesthetic and commercial interests that may intersect and/or di-verge at different times. The process of recording is a mediation between different personal and social subject positions, different value systems, and different claims and stakes in the production of musically encoded Native identity. In the second sense of the term, it is the electronic pro-cess of recording itself that mediates musical performances. The acoustic and ambient sounds of voices and instruments are encoded as electronic and digital signals, which in turn may become the subject of further forms of manipulation and intervention. Collapsing these two meanings, Louise Meintjes has described mediation in the recording studio as that which "transfers but in the process it necessarily transforms. It connects and translates different worlds, imaginations, meanings, ideas of the real and the Other. . . . In other words, mediation is a form of intervention that is interactive and mutually transformative" (1997, 10). It is the transforma-tive and interactive nature of recording studio mediation that will be the focus of the following ethnographic examples.

Journey Home

In January 2000 while living in Winnipeg, I began to experience Cana-dian prairie winters in earnest: bitter cold, white, bright, and steadfast. Experiencing only two or three hours of daylight most days, I would wake past noon only to watch the sun begin to set by 3:30 PM. Come 5:00 PM I would head down to Studio 11 again and work until dawn. I had been working these hours for a few weeks, as Studio 11 was alive with activity almost twenty-four hours a day. A number of recording projects needed to be finished all at once: Studio A was being used around the clock recording various tracks for Mishi Donovan's new CD *Journey Home*; in Studio B Dutch was mixing down GQ Smooth's new CD. GQ was a local Native rap artist, the younger brother of TKO. Both of these recordings were being licensed to SOAR, and Tom Bee wanted the masters down in Albuquerque ASAP to send to the manufacturer. When Dutch was not in Studio B, I was there sifting through all of the Hinckley powwow recordings from 1999, looking for songs to feature on what would become the *Hinckley Pow Wow Northern Style* (AR-11162) and *Hinckley Pow Wow Southern Style* (AR-11152) compilations.

One day I poked my head in Studio A and found Paul and Rob messing around with percussion tracks for "Mahe'kun Waits for Me," which later would become the opening track of the *Journey Home* CD. They had pulled apart a drum kit and were playing a distinct rhythmic line on each individual drum and recording it to a separate track, in order to try to layer a drum groove that would serve as the rhythmic signature of the tune. Paul and Rob were both rock and pop music drummers by trade and it was clear they were having a good time working together, bouncing rhythmic ideas off of one another and experimenting with different microphone placements and timbral manipulations for each drum. I hung out for a while before bounding up the cramped spiral staircase to the upstairs offices to say hi to Jamie and see if Brandon was around. I found him in his office squeezing a stress ball. He had just received a fax from Steve of Sizzortail, one of Arbor's newest and most popular Southern drums. The group was upset because of a printing error on the inside of the CD insert and wanted some kind of monetary compensation, accusing Arbor of a breach of contract. Brandon was reluctant to comply but John was advising him to make an apologetic gesture; he suggested picking up the price of the jackets (custom made for the group) or "throwing some free product at them" (free CDs). I popped my head into his office and asked what was up. "I'm stressed. Fucking stressed," was all Brandon said, not taking his eyes from the computer.

Later that evening he almost exploded. At 2:00 AM one of the ADAT (Alesis Digital Audio Tape) machines chewed up one of the master tapes for Mishi's CD, one that had irreplaceable bed tracks: vocal, bass, and guitar parts. If Mishi's vocal parts were lost, the project could be set back indefinitely. Everyone in the studio fell silent as Brandon carefully pulled the machine out of the rack, removed the top casing and freed the tape from the jam. He put the tape in another ADAT machine and attempted a "data dump" from one machine to another. Brandon pressed record and LED lights began to flash: it was working. The tape only played right ONCE!! No tracks were lost, only precious time. It was now 4:30 AM and Brandon had neither the time nor the heart to do much else. He laid down a couple of guitar tracks, adding tremolo guitar to a few of the songs, re-recorded a Native flute solo using a flute sample MIDI-controlled by a keyboard, and then called it a night.

The last few weeks in January marked the culmination of several months' work on the *Journey Home* CD, a process that began in the fall of 1999. Mishi Donovan is a Chippewa Cree whose ancestors were renegades from the Turtle Mountain Reservation in North Dakota. When she is not touring, Mishi makes her home in Alberta. This CD would be her first since *The Spirit Within*, a recording Brandon produced while working for Sunshine Records. Brandon had been working with Mishi since the mid-1990s, producing all of her recordings. When Brandon started Arbor, Mishi approached him and asked him to produce her next CD. Mishi came to Winnipeg for six days in the early fall of 1999 and in this short time cut all the vocal tracks for the CD. The first four days of her stay were spent in the studio working with Brandon in arranging the fourteen new songs she wanted to record. Brandon described this collaborative process to me as one where Mishi sang her new songs for Brandon, accompanying herself on an acoustic guitar, and Brandon made suggestions about arrangements, including where to add bridges, the transposition of songs to different keys, and sometimes smoothing out or evening up verses that had an uneven number of measures or beats in them. Then in the following two days, Mishi recorded all the vocal parts, with only a sampled kick drum as a metronome and a "scratch" guitar part played by Brandon, in her headphones.[2] She then left town, and the next time she heard the recording was after the master had been burned to CD.

Brandon arranged the ensuing sessions, calling in the rhythm section of Groove Town, his regular on-again, off-again pop and dance band. Bass and drum tracks were recorded with another series of scratch guitar tracks. Brandon, like most producers, has a preferred methodology for recording rock and pop groups. Typically he records "bed tracks" (core rhythm section parts) by recording the whole band (drums, bass, guitar/keyboards) "right off the floor." The band plays together but every instrumentalist performs in a soundproof "isolation booth" to reduce the amount of "bleeding" (where a dedicated microphone picks up extraneous sound). The musicians hear each other through headphones only. All of these tracks serve as scratch tracks, which together provide a working structure of the song's arrangement. Then beginning with the drums, each instrument is recorded again, as Brandon pays meticulous attention to each instrumental part, listening for clean and mistake-free performances. The drums are the first instrument to be recorded in earnest because the drummer is the only instrument to play to a "click track," a metronome pulse fed into the performer's earphones. Click tracks are essential for pop music recordings like Mishi Donovan's because perfect metronome time is needed in order to add sequencer tracks to the songs after all the live tracks have been recorded.[3]

If the scratch drum track is relatively free of mistakes, then instead of re-recording the entire part, Brandon will simply direct the drummer to particular parts of the song and then "punch in," at particular times, recording over only the parts of the track where the drummer missed a cue or drifted off the click track. Generally, depending on the drummer, a drum track is created in two to four hours. After this, Brandon moves on to the re-recording of the bass track and the process begins again, followed by basic guitar tracks. On Mishi Donovan's CD almost every song also has a number of acoustic guitar bed tracks, performed by Brandon.

Brandon's recording method, while not unique, is not necessarily standard either, and every engineer and producer has a preferred method of working. For instance, Paul Scinocca, the other engineer/producer at Arbor, often simply recorded a number of entire takes of a particular instrumental or vocal part and then tried to edit together a master take out of the various flawed takes. One problem with this method is that one is still not guaranteed a mistake-free track. Brandon told me that he never records this way because it is too inefficient; it simply takes too much time. According to Brandon, being a good and efficient producer means making optimum use of studio time, which means being able to make a snap decision about a particular take. Find the problem, or decide if there is a problem, and fix it right away. Brandon is not afraid to discard an average take in order to try and get a better one, insisting that part of the job of the producer is to be able to gauge the talent, ability, and stamina of the performer (just how many good takes the performer has in him or her), and to know when to say, "Let's do it again" and when to say "That's great, let's move on." He once told me about a conversation he had with

Kim Spears, his girlfriend at the time and a professional country music singer in Florida. She phoned him complaining that she was making a demo recording but that the producer was not "producing." She would sing a take and the producer would ask her, "Well, what do you think of that? Do you want to do another?" She complained that the producer was not doing his job. "Production," in this context, involves constant input and back-and-forth dialogue between performer and producer, with the producer taking responsibility for deciding which takes to keep and which need to be done again.

With the bed tracks and Mishi's vocal tracks completed in the late fall, the project lay dormant for a number of months while other recording obligations were fulfilled. While Studio 11 operates as an in-house recording facility for Arbor Records, the studio stands on its own as a corporate entity, and Arbor projects do not necessarily get priority. But by January, during the final two weeks of this project, Studio A, the larger control room of Studio 11, was buzzing day and night as percussion, keyboards, more guitars (there were seemingly *always* more guitars), sequencing tracks, harmony vocals, and the fiddle and mandolin solo breaks and fills were all laid onto ADAT tape.

The progressive and piecemeal nature of these sessions—typical of pop music recording of this kind—resulted in a decision-making structure that, during the recording process, was rather haphazard and loose. The recording of these tracks happened in a number of ways. While Brandon was unquestionably the producer for the CD, he gave a great degree of freedom to Paul Scinocca to add percussion parts to any songs that he wished. Dutch, who was also the keyboard and saxophone player for Groove Town, was given a similar freedom in adding his keyboard and sequencing tracks. As both of these musicians were also engineers, they usually engineered their own sessions without Brandon's supervision or input. In their dual role as engineers and performers, these musicians were given a great deal of latitude over both the kinds of "sounds" that were acceptable—referring to timbral manipulation of instrumental and vocal sounds through microphone choice and equalization—as well as which performance takes were kept and which were done again.[4]

Brandon engineered all of the sessions in which he added guitar, sequencer, and keyboard parts as well as those that featured other local musicians. For sessions with other musicians, Brandon took on a much more expanded and active role in the recording process. At the beginning of a session, he and the performer would sit in the studio and listen to the song together and then Brandon would ask for or suggest ideas about the kinds of parts he would like to hear in the recording. During the recording of the tracks, Brandon would always have final say over which performances were successful takes.

The final "mixdown" of the CD was performed by Brandon in a series of three all-night sessions that would begin in the late afternoon or evening, each one stretching further and further into the early morning of the following day: 5:00 AM, 7:00 AM, and finally 8:00 AM. Mixdown began at 12:30 AM on the first night. While setting up the studio for the mixdown, Brandon flipped a copy of Loreena McKennett's *The Book of Secrets* (WEA CD-19404) into the CD player and played it loud through the main studio monitors. He was getting his ears accustomed to the sound of the recording. Brandon wanted to produce Mishi's CD in a similar way: densely layered mixes with instruments swirling in and out of audible focus; "wet" and "deep"-sounding reverbs surrounding every instrument and voice. Using other recordings this way, as references when creating new recordings, is a common technique used by studio producers and engineers throughout the recording industry.[5]

As Brandon was setting the levels on a Drawmer tube compressor that he had rented specifically for this mixdown, he said, "Mixing is where I am most comfortable. It's what I think I do best." Each of Brandon's mixes was a separate performance. He began with drums, adjusting the parametric equalizers on the mixing board's channel strips for every drum track until he found the timbre that he liked. Then he moved to electric bass, then acoustic guitars, vocals, and then all the other tracks. Digital reverbs were then added to the vocal tracks (the verses and the choruses each had different reverb settings) and the snare drum. Once all the general levels and timbres were set he started focusing on the specific mix of particular parts of the song: first the chorus, then the verses, the pre-chorus, bridge, instrumental solo, etc. Finally the whole song was given a rough mix as it played through in its entirety. Looking back in my direction he told me, "The first song usually takes about two or three hours to mix and after that the rest only take about a half an hour to an hour." The first song required special attention to every track in the mix. Subsequent mixes were completed more quickly because many of the equalization, compression, and reverb adjustments were already set. These settings became part of the homogeneous sound of the entire recording, contributing to a sonic signature of every song, part of what makes it sound like all of the songs belong together on the CD. Audio effects settings (reverberation, compression, equalization) for the drums and often the vocal tracks, once set, were generally maintained for the entire CD.

Brandon listened to each song a number of times before he began working on it. Each song presented a different set of problems. Instruments were often faded in and out of the mix on the fly, meaning that a number of tracks had to have their volume adjusted numerous times during the course of the song. The Studio 11 board at that time did not include any programmable automation features. More high-end mixing boards allow the user to program any number of subtle changes to volume or equalization adjustments throughout a song that will then automatically occur at particular points in a song every time the song is played. Lacking this higher-end board, Brandon asked me in several instances to manipulate a number of the faders, because the series of adjustments were too complex for Brandon alone to perform. After the first mix was completed and bounced through the Drawmer compressors to the two-track DAT master, he listened again a number of times to the entire song, first at louder volumes, then softer. Was the vocal line present enough? Was the kick drum too buried? Did the mix get too opaque and "messy" at quieter volumes or did it become clearer? If Brandon didn't like the answers to any of these questions, he went back and remixed it, a process that usually involved a large number of very small tweaks in amplitude and timbre to various tracks. Each mix was like a house of cards. One small adjustment to one part of one track could fix one problem but create three more.

Mediating Native Identity

At one point during the *Journey Home* mixdown session, Paul's girlfriend, Jules, stuck her head into Studio A and, upon hearing a few bars of the first track of Mishi's recording, asked, "So what's so Native about this CD?" Paul laughed and said it was "only the lead singer-songwriter. Otherwise, it's just a bunch of white boys." Several other joking comments followed, each one an attempt to use humor to address a level of discomfort—or at least confusion—that all who had worked closely on this recording, Brandon, Paul, Justin, had experienced. What *was* "Native" about this CD?

Steve Blum has written that the "definition of stylistic norms evolves from both the actual practice of performing musicians and the verbal statements, evaluations, [and] justifications which attach themselves to practice" (1972, 4). Following Blum, I would suggest that "Nativeness" becomes attached to a style element or to a piece of music or recorded performance through two specific articulatory practices: processual productions and discursive productions. Discursive productions of Nativeness happen after the fact, in judgments over "what is Native" in a piece of music that already exists. Jules hears a Mishi Donovan song and asks "What's Native?" because she hears no obvious indexical signs of Nativeness in the music: musical signs or standardized codes and norms of a genre—such as instrumental timbres, vocal mannerisms, melodic and rhythmic phrases—that iconically or indexically link sound to sentiment.

Processual productions of Nativeness occur during moments of creation, and they involve socially positioned actors engaged in the production of musical style. The musicians who performed for this CD were required to make decisions and judgments about their performances before, during, and after any given performance take. The creation of a track in the studio, a carefully crafted single performance, differs perhaps most significantly from other kinds of performance contexts in the high degree of evaluation and reflection required. This is embedded in the very procedure of creating a studio performance. A musician will listen to the existing tracks of a song a number of times before deciding on his or her own part. The creation of the part is itself often the result of a discussion and negotiation between musician and producer. The part is then performed and recorded and another series of evaluations ensue, engaging whether the take is acceptable technically and whether it works, or fits musically, with the other parts already recorded. Processual productions of Nativeness are the result of these discussions and negotiations and subsequent actions, and the degree to which Nativeness is inscribed in a particular recording is dependent upon the degree of investment each musician had in creating a "Native CD" and the degree to which that investment is translated into practical performance decisions.

Paul's comment was very close to accurate. Of the nine musicians who performed on the CD, only two were of Native descent. In addition to Mishi, Trevor Prairie Chicken was present at the original recording session, co-wrote one of the songs for the CD, and contributed some background vocals and traditional flute tracks. Mishi and Trevor were the only Native musicians who played on the recording. The rest of the performers were drawn from a pool of regularly working musicians that Brandon uses for many of his recording projects. Of all the "white boys" who performed or participated in the recording in the last number of weeks, only Brandon, as producer, had both an artistic and economic stake in producing a "Native CD," a product that would circulate in both the Aboriginal market and the much larger world beat market as a "Contemporary Native" recording. His concern was with adding *enough* indices of Nativeness to link this recording to the Aboriginal and world beat markets. The main source for these indices was a sample bank called *Voices of Native America* (Q20450-P), a commercially produced CD containing a large catalogue of sampled sounds of Native musical instruments: various flutes, rattles, drums, short snippets of native languages, and short sung musical phrases. Apart from Mishi's vocal performances and Trevor's flute solos, this catalogue of sampled sounds was the main source of "Native sounds," Native musical indices that Brandon placed more or less judiciously in every mix. A number of the traditional flute parts on Mishi's CD were played by Brandon on a keyboard, as were myriad Aboriginal drums and rattles. Brandon made countless unilateral decisions about the level of Native indices in the music, controlling the nature of the stylistic signs as well as their sheer number. These, of course, are not the only types of signs present in the music. The strong and poignant lyrics of Mishi's songs are also a central part of the communicative force of the music, lyrics in which many of her Native fans no doubt find reflections of themselves. But the musical framing of these lyrics has been, for the most part, generated outside of her control. Thus it was Brandon, Mishi's producer, who had final say regarding the musicians used, the arrangements, the song order on the CD, and the final mixdown and mastering of the recording. And it is during the mixdown that final decisions are made regarding which tracks are used and where they are placed in the mix. The voice and songs were Mishi's, and the instrumental performances were created by many different musicians, but it was *Brandon's mix*.

Honouring Our Elders

I arrived at Arbor Records in the early afternoon of February 20, 2000, just as the Lake of the Woods singers were hauling their drum into the studio and setting up in the large recording room adjacent to Studio A. Purple was there setting up microphones and stands according to Brandon's instructions. Brandon himself was upstairs in his office sifting through paperwork. This was going to be Purple's first studio recording project as engineer, and Brandon had given specific instructions regarding recording methodology. The microphone setup was standard for Brandon (and thus for Arbor Records) when recording powwow groups in the studio. Two AKG C 1000 S condenser mics were used as "overheads" and placed in an X-Y formation (where two microphones are mounted on the same stand and angled at 90 degrees at the capsules) approximately eight feet above the drum and singers; two Shure SM57 mics were positioned close to the lead singers, and an AKG D 112 was positioned under the drum. Each microphone was linked to a separate channel on the mixing board. These five channels were then mixed directly down to a two-track stereo mix and fed into a digital audio tape (DAT) machine.

After the microphones were in place and all the lines had been checked, Brandon came downstairs and took control of the session. He asked the drum to perform a warm-up song, and while they sang Brandon began working, first patching all of the channels through compressors. Brandon advised Purple that the overhead microphones were the most important, and as such they were fed into the best compressors in the studio. All of the compressors were set to a relatively high threshold, meaning that they would only engage during the check beats (hard beats), which are generally the loudest parts of any performance and can cause distortion on a recording. Brandon explained that the trick to setting the compressors was to set the levels so the listener never hears the compressor working. If the signal is compressed too much it begins to sound clipped.[6]

As the warm-up song continued, he began to work on each channel specifically, punching "solo" on each channel strip on the board to isolate the sound of a particular microphone while effectively muting all others. He spent the most time on the drum signal, adjusting the equalization by rolling back all of the high frequencies while boosting the bass to the point where all that was heard was a low and muffled booming. This was to counteract the sharp "slapping" sound that was being picked up by the overhead microphones as the drumsticks were hitting the skin of the drum. The sound of the overheads dominated the mix and Brandon wanted them to sound as natural as possible. Rolling back the higher frequencies on these microphones lessened the loud slapping of the drum but it also diminished the volume and presence of the singing and so he was careful not to get too heavy-handed in his equalization of the overheads. Brandon also applied a digital reverb to the two overhead microphone channels (and these channels only), a "large hall" reverb emulation that was deep and resonant and had a long and slow rate of decay. He "rolled off" all of the "high end" (decreasing the treble frequencies, those above 2K) on this reverb as well in order to minimize the sound of slapping from the drum that echoed sharply.[7] The other two vocal microphones, the SM57s, deemed least important by Brandon, were given the least amount of attention and were buried deep in the mix, used simply to raise the volume of the lead singers during their leads.

All of these manipulations were completed by the end of the fourth push-up of the warm-up song, after which time the group stopped singing. Brandon asked them for one additional verse which would allow him to fine-tune the settings, double-check the compression, and further evaluate the sound of the reverb he had chosen. Satisfied with the mix, he popped his head into the recording area: "Sounds good, let's do one." He explained the recording procedure to the group. Because no one in the drum group was wearing headphones, the only way for the engineer (Brandon and later, Purple) to communicate with the group was through hand signals that could be seen through the large, thick Plexiglas window separating the control room and the recording area. He instructed the drum group, "When I lift my hand, it means the recording is about to start. Get all of the coughing and throat-clearing out of the way. When I hear silence I'm going to hit Record and lower my hand. Then you start the song."

He closed the door, the drum group shuffled into place, Brandon raised his hand, punched Record on the DAT machine, and dropped his hand. The drumbeat began in a slow crescendo as the group launched into their first song. After the final push-up the group piled into the control room to listen to a playback of the song. "You guys sound good," Brandon said. "The singing sounds good." After listening to the playback the group agreed that the performance and the sound of the recording were both satisfactory, and they filed back into the recording area to ready themselves for the next song. Halfway through the second song, Brandon turned to Purple: "It's all yours. The levels are all set. Just do what I've been doing," and he left to go back upstairs, leaving Purple to finish the session.

The recording session went remarkably smoothly; the drum group was well rehearsed. The Lake of the Woods singers had performed semiregularly for several years, but only within the traditional powwow circuit in the Lake of the Woods area in western Ontario, the area from which all members originated and where most of them still made a home. This recording was part of a larger plan to go on the road the coming summer, and to sing at more competition powwows beyond their home communities. Like most powwow drums, their plans hinged upon the matter of transportation and a new recording that they could sell while on the road. Several members of the group were veteran singers. A few had sung with Horsetail, Curtis Assiniboine's drum, but that group had broken up the previous fall. Others in the group, including the leader (although not a lead singer) Mike Fisher, had previously sung with Northern Wind. There were two singers in the group who had never gone out on the trail before, and this was the first time they had been in a drum group.

After each successful take of a song, Purple would go into the recording booth and ask what that song was called and then write it down on the DAT cassette insert, along with the start and stop times for each. The group needed only one take for each song. The only song they wanted to perform again was the fourth song, an Honor song. Listening to the playback, they decided the performance was fine except for the tail, which was a little ragged at the start because some of the singers missed the entry. They asked Purple if he could simply edit it out in the final mix. Purple looked at me for guidance and I said, "Sure." I had a feeling that I was going to be the one mastering the recording.

The group took a short break following their fourth song. A number of them stepped outside for a cigarette and I joined them. We chatted idly. They asked about jackets and stickers as part of their promotional package. Arbor Records had furnished some of the best-selling and most well-known groups (Eyabay, Battle River, Whitefish Bay, Northern Wind) with free bomber jackets and stickers, custom-made with the drum group's name on them. They were not the first group to ask about jackets or stickers. Every drum group wanted them. These kinds of commercial consumer products served as symbols of prestige and were markers of success in the same way (although to a lesser degree) as the recordings themselves. They represented a degree of popularity and professionalism to the other groups and to powwow committees, which could in turn lead to more host and invited drum engagements. Symbolic capital transformed into economic capital.

After twenty minutes the group reassembled in the recording area and began discussing the next song. Each recorded performance was preceded by the same set of actions. They would talk over the next song and make sure everybody knew the arrangement: how many push-ups they were going to do, where the honor beats were, and who was taking the leads and in what order. They sang each song through quietly at the drum in hushed voices, drumsticks tapping on the rim. This is a practice that originates on the powwow grounds, where drum groups rehearse songs this way just before it is their turn to sing for dancers. Singing quietly and tapping on the drum ensures that they do not disturb the performance of the current group that is singing. In the studio there is no need to sing or drum quietly but it is the habit of the groups; it also helps to save the singers' voices. As the session wore on the breaks became more frequent, and the number of songs sung between breaks decreased. Singers rarely sing so many songs in such a relatively short period of time (the entire recording session took just over four hours). In this way, studio recording is quite unlike most powwow performances, where drum groups who are not hosting may sing four or five songs in the course of an entire day. In the studio, singers' voices are taxed in a way unlike any powwow performance.

During each break the singers would mill around, some outside, some inside, some listening to the playback of the songs they had just recorded and laughing at the random cries of some of the singers or the leads taken by others. When they had finished recording we sat in the control room while I burned a CD copy of the DAT for them to take home. They seemed happy with their performance and with the recording. While the DAT was being dubbed they looked over the song list and changed the names of the Shake song and some of the intertribals to more creative names. They also asked me if they could have a loon call added to the end of side two of the tape in order "to remind people where the group is from, the Lake of the Woods area." They wanted a sonic marker of place. I asked if they wanted that at the beginning and they said no, but how about a thunderclap instead? "What's the name of the tape?" I asked. Mike Fisher responded, "Call it 'Honoring Our Elders.'"

The Lake of the Woods recording session was typical of all the in-studio powwow recording sessions in which I was present as either a witness or an engineer. Recording sessions generally took between four and six hours, extraordinarily fast for an entire commercial CD to be recorded, and certainly fast compared to any other recording projects that happened at Studio 11. Powwow sessions proceed quickly because there is generally no need to mix down the recording. Once the initial recording levels are set, they remain fixed for the entire session. Every song is essentially performed in the same manner and so there is no need for mixing on the fly or for moving microphones between takes. Essentially, there is no producer for the session. Engineers (like Purple, for example) can record drum groups with little or no knowledge of how powwow singing is supposed to sound or how to distinguish between good and bad performances. The constant breaks and playbacks that are a common part of all powwow recording sessions allow musicians themselves to make judgments about the quality of particular performances and the validity of various takes. As such, powwow musicians are invested with a far greater degree of *cultural capital* within the "musical field" of powwow recording. Formally defined as "a form of knowledge, an internalized code or cognitive acquisition which equips the social agent with empathy towards, appreciation for, or competence in deciphering cultural relations and cultural artifacts" (Johnson 1993, 7), the cultural capital possessed by powwow musicians is a result of their perceived level of expertise in the performance and aesthetics of powwow music. The aesthetic disposition of powwow musicians is a form of cultural capital which, like other forms of capital within a social field, tends to follow unequal patterns of accumulation and distribution.

It is important to note that the structure of this powwow recording session was highly interactive throughout. Mike Fisher, and to a lesser degree the other singers in the group, had steady and continued input regarding which performance takes would be kept and which discarded, the order of the songs, and the overall equalization and mix of the recording. The session only began in earnest when the group was satisfied with what would end up being the "final mix" of the recording. Generally speaking, drum groups are able to maintain greater control of the mix (and thus the overall sound of the recording) because there is no mixdown stage that occurs after all the tracks have been recorded (as we saw with Mishi's CD); once the levels are set the songs are recorded directly to digital audio tape. The interactive nature of this session was typical of all the powwow recording sessions in which I was a witness or participant during my time at Arbor Records.

Producing Musical Styles

Understanding processes of studio recording in terms of musical fields allows one to map the specificity of social relationships within a larger structural context. It also shifts the focus of analysis from the musical product (a commercially produced and mass-distributed CD) to the musical process: the activity of musical creation and the constant negotiations and shifting asymmetrical social arrangements that are structural components of all social fields. In the process of recording these two commercial products, two very different social spaces—two different musical fields— were in operation within the same walls of Studio 11's Studio A. Different distributions of cultural capital structured the relationship between performer and producer: a relationship characterized by the association between the record producer and the commercial music market, and the knowledge the producer has about that market. Brandon's relationship to the business world of pop music and powwow music dictates his relationship to the recording artists. In the case of Mishi's CD, Brandon's high level of decision-making power and influence over the final recorded product was in part a result of his perceived level of cultural expertise in the arena of Aboriginal pop and world beat music. Similar to many non-Native performers, pop singers like Mishi work with Brandon because of his expertise in popular music production. He is a resource who has power, influence, and knowledge in the world of commercial music, a world in which they wish to succeed. For Mishi, and for other Native artists, Brandon's reputation has been enhanced significantly by his work on Mishi Donovan's second CD *The Spirit Within* (SSCD 4258), which garnered both Mishi and Brandon a Juno Award in 1998 for Best Aboriginal Recording. This award solidified Brandon's reputation within Aboriginal music circuits as a major figure in Native music recording. He is known as someone who can produce and deliver a successful Contemporary Native music recording.

Conversely, powwow singers came to Arbor and Brandon not because of his expertise in the aesthetics of powwow music but because he has technical expertise in recording and because he has established a reputation among powwow groups as someone who is fair and honest. Within this field of interaction the level of cultural fluency and expertise is reversed. It is the powwow groups who have something that Brandon values. Because of his years of experience, Brandon is well versed in the different styles of powwow music and is fully capable of making informed judgments about powwow music performances; however his own judgments mean very little to him and he will instead most often trust the aesthetic judgments and preferences of the powwow musicians he records. During the creation of the Lake of the Woods recording, Brandon was able to set levels and leave. His presence was not required because the drum groups themselves are afforded such a high degree of autonomy in the creation of a CD. It is the musicians themselves who are deemed the best suited to judge the quality and success of particular songs and performances.

Brandon has often expressed that he does not even consider himself a producer when he records powwow groups, repeatedly emphasizing his low level of involvement in powwow recording projects. He does this by contrasting his work in powwow recording with the work he does on recording projects such as Mishi Donovan's. The degree of involvement and investment in the final product of a CD like Mishi's is consistent with what Brandon considers to be the role of a "real" record producer.

CS: So what is the usual recording process when those guys [powwow singers] get in the studio. How much input do you have into . . .

BF: None. I don't interfere with any of their songs. Like, I don't arrange any of their songs.

CS: And you don't tell them, look we need one Crow Hop and a Round dance?

BF: Well, yes I do. I tell them that. But other than that, the rest is up to them. And they ask how many push-ups. And generally it's four, four push-ups. And that's it.

CS: That's your only input?

BF: That's it. Yeah there isn't any producing involved. Like Ted [Whitecalf of Sweet Grass Records] calls himself a producer. You know he records and pays for the recording and that's it. A real producer sits there and arranges the songs. Like, in any other industry [and here he is referring to other music industries like the rock or pop or rap music industries], the producer writes half of the songs. And all the parts. But it can never be that way with powwow, because it's like producing a classical guitar album. That classical guitarist is just going to interpret that piece the way he does it. It's my job to just capture it, the best I can, which, for powwow, means lots of compression, lots of Eqing [equalization], and lots of reverb. With powwow anyway . . . (Brandon Friesen interview, October 1999)

It is significant that while insisting powwow is qualitatively different than other recording contexts because of the low level of mediation involved, Brandon downplays the electronic manipulation that does take place: compression, equalization, and the addition of digital reverb. To Brandon, who considers himself, above all else, a pop and rock music producer, this level of electronic manipulation is considered noninvasive to the point of transparency. Brandon also minimizes the other kinds of roles he plays in creating the final product. For many of Arbor's powwow releases, he plays a part in choosing the material to be included, sometimes suggesting a certain number of songs, a certain length, or a variety of styles. He also typically designs or subcontracts the CD covers and packaging with the final design subject to his approval. Thus despite Brandon's significant role in the creation of the final recorded product, he considers himself to be simply a conduit. His job is to capture and present a powwow performance with minimal electronic or digital mediation. I believe that part of the reason for this seemingly contradictory position is that, despite his years and experience in powwow recording, he still considers himself an outsider in terms of understanding the aesthetics of powwow music.

Given the differing degrees of cultural authority granted to the social actors within these different contexts, these fields are also shaped by aesthetic preferences regarding the level of electronic mediation, and perceived levels of social power play a key role in final aesthetic decisions. In the case of Mishi's CD, it is Brandon who is granted this power; in the case of the Lake of the Woods recording (and in powwow recording in general) it is the singers. Mishi's CD features a comparatively high level of studio manipulation due to the level of control Brandon is granted over the process of recording. His preferred method of studio recording is constructivist: recording one track at a time over a long period of time. This process allows for the greatest amount of sonic control. By contrast, for powwow musicians the recording process is always understood to be a procedure whereby performances are captured "live" by audio engineers, with minimal technological intervention. Thus in powwow recordings Brandon relinquishes this control and cultural authority, and the level of mediation is, by mutual consent, in the hands of the performers.

Some of the differences in the power relationships between actors involved in the creation of these two recordings are the result of how gender roles are positioned within these different fields. To be sure, the world of studio recording is extraordinarily male-dominated, and attitudes among many studio professionals (including many who work at Arbor and Studio 11) are extremely patriarchal. In general, women like Mishi are simply less able to insert themselves into positions of authority within the highly masculine world of recording studios. That being said, the low level of control Mishi maintained in the production of her CD was consistent with the level of involvement for a majority of Contemporary Native music CDs (and most non-Native CDs) produced at Arbor for both male and female artists. For example, the records of two male Native rappers produced by Arbor Records during my tenure at Studio 11 were both created in a very similar fashion. The producers for the CDs (in both cases Dutch) called in the rap singer to lay down his vocal tracks only *after* he had completed all of the instrumental tracks for a particular song.

To be clear, I am in no way arguing that men and women experience the recording studio in a similar way. Indigenous women's experiences of and ideas about recording are unique and need to be understood within their larger cultural and gendered contexts (Diamond 2002, 2005). Men undoubtedly feel a greater entitlement to assert their authority within the masculine setting of the studio, and as in the case of the male rappers, may even understand their low level of involvement as a symbol of a greater (and not lesser) degree of social power. For example male rap artists may believe that their producers are in their service and that their instrumental tracks are created to serve their own, more important, vocal performances. For her part, Mishi has stated that a main concern for her during the recording process is not in the details of the process but the "atmosphere" of the sessions. She has stated, "The atmosphere in which we're creating our work has to be a good environment or I won't sing . . . that's just the way I am, the way I work, and it has to be something honored. If it's not, then the feeling won't be represented in the music" (Diamond 2002, 24). In her interviews with Beverley Diamond, Mishi has also emphasized that "trust" rather than "sonic control" governs her relationship with the musicians and producers with whom she collaborates in the studio (Diamond 2005). The very act of choosing Brandon as her producer is an important way that she exerts control over her recording; the choice speaks to a trust relationship borne of a long-term collaborative working relationship that she knows will help to create the right "atmosphere." However, I would still argue that regardless of the *meanings* attributed to the social positions, their *structural* position remains consistent. In other words, producers within the "musical field" of popular music, whether working with male or female artists, are still granted unique authority, power, and responsibility commensurate with that occupational role.

Finally, these two musical fields also create products that subsequently enter different commercial markets. Mishi's CD, once completed, was licensed to Tom Bee's SOAR Records and SOAR was given all U.S. marketing rights. Arbor did not have the financial resources to break a CD into the U.S. pop market, a process entirely different than selling powwow music. Hundreds of free copies must be sent to radio stations across the country, print advertisements need to be purchased in relevant magazines and newspapers, and large retail stores must be solicited. Production and distribution costs for such an undertaking were beyond the financial means of the label. Arbor Records did not even distribute the recording in Canada, and instead worked out a deal with Festival Records, a relatively small independent distributor. Sales for the CD were barely even tracked by Arbor. The licensing deal left Brandon unsure as to whether Arbor was going to break even on the project. From Brandon's perspective, the money was not important. If the CD was even a moderate hit in the United States, it meant that more people would get to hear his production work and he would be the producer/writer/arranger for a critically acclaimed record; as well, the profile of Arbor Records would be enhanced. That would be reward enough. The Lake of the Woods recording had an entirely different network of distribution. Most of Arbor's sales are generated by four U.S.-based Native arts, craft, and music vendors that act as middlemen or subdistributors to the myriad craft and music booths that work the powwow circuit. The audience for this music is almost entirely Native: powwow singers, dancers, and fans.

These different markets also influenced the manufacturing of the recordings in different playback formats. As an international Contemporary Native music and possible world beat recording, *Journey Home* was pressed in CD only with a tri-fold j-card insert that featured several professional photos of Mishi, lyrics to all of the songs, and a long list of musician and production credits. In contrast, *Honouring Our Elders* was released in cassette only. In 2000, when the powwow music industry was still transitioning from a cassette-based market to a CD-based market,

Arbor had a policy of manufacturing and releasing the initial run of recordings of lesser known drum groups on cassette only, both as a way of lessening costs for the company (and therefore reducing the financial risks of recording a more obscure powwow group) and also because cassettes were sold at a much lower retail price. The expectation was that consumers would be more willing to buy a lesser-known group if the price were lower. The cassette-only policy was also a reflection of the expectation that the recording would never cross over and be sold to more mainstream markets that demanded and expected the CD format.

Genres, Fields, and Mediation: Contemporary and Traditional "Genre Worlds"

The front page of the 2005 product catalogue for Arbor Records begins with the following text:

> Greetings,
>
> We are very pleased to share with you our catalogue of Native North American Music. Arbor Records is at the forefront of quality Traditional and Contemporary Aboriginal recordings.
>
> Our roster of award-wining albums features top drum groups like Bear Creek, Eyabay and Northern Wind as well as contemporary artists like Derek Miller (rock), Lucie Idlout (alt-rock), Team RezOfficial (hip hop) and newcomer Wayne Lavallee (alt-country).

In reading this introduction we are immediately informed that there are two broadly defined *kinds* of Aboriginal recordings: Traditional and Contemporary. This basic bifurcation is then immediately restated and refined in the very next paragraph, supplying the reader (and presumably the potential consumer) with examples of these two generic categories: Traditional music includes powwow drum groups, and Contemporary music includes a range of familiar North American popular music styles like rock, country, and hip hop.

The two recording sessions discussed in this chapter are, in many ways, archetypal representations of these two core music genres produced by the Aboriginal recording industry in general. Arbor Records, along with labels like SOAR and Canyon in the United States, organize the production and distribution of their Native musical products according to the genre classifications of Contemporary music and Traditional music. Music classified as Traditional typically includes both tribally specific music (e.g., *Yeibichai* songs of the Navajo, Stomp dance songs of the Creek or the Mohawk), as well as intertribally shared music, including secular genres such as powwow music, Round dance songs, Stick Game and Hand Game songs, and sacred genres like peyote music. "Contemporary Native" music (or "Contemporary Native American" music) is a broad genre category that encompasses a wide range of musical styles, but most typically it refers to music that blends stylistic elements from any number of popular music genres with tribal or pan-tribal musical styles and lyrics that reference the artist's indigenousness.

Simon Frith has suggested that the recording industry typically employs genre categories "to *organize the sales process*. . . . The underlying record company problem . . . [of] how to turn music into a commodity, is solved in generic terms. Genre is a way of defining music in its market or, alternatively, the market in its music" (1996, 75–76). The music industry's classifications of Traditional and Contemporary serve as marketing tools within the Aboriginal record business to help target particular recordings to particular market demographics. These terms, of course, were not invented by the industry, but rather have been co-opted, connecting with already existing discursive fields. In doing so, industry personnel actively elaborate or amplify certain connotative meanings associated with these terms while attenuating others, in an attempt to simplify the complexities of the market. The power of the categories of Traditional and Contemporary is that they exist outside of industry circuits and within the larger cultural discourses of both Aboriginals and non-Aboriginals in North America. In using these terms to classify musical styles, music industry personnel are also making claims about Aboriginal identity, and the relationship between Natives and non-Natives in North America.

I suggested in the last chapter that music markets are not so much discovered by industry executives as they are imagined and subsequently constructed (Hennion 1990; Negus 1992, 1996, 1999). As Richard Peterson notes, "What is most important in shaping the decisions of those in the culture industry is not the preferences of the population of actual or potential consumers, but rather their preferences *as these are understood* by decision-makers in the culture industry. Accordingly, we use the word 'market' to designate the audience as it is conceptualized by the culture industry" (1990, 111).

Markets are imagined using various forms of market research and information gathering combined with commonsense, culturally conditioned assumptions about the aesthetic preferences of different social groups and what kind of music they will listen to and like. These markets are then subsequently constructed through practices that take place at the level of production (choosing musicians, cutting tracks, engineering, mixing, etc.) and in a host of post-production activities, including packaging decisions and marketing strategies, decisions about media format (CDs, DVDs, music videos, cassette tapes), advertising (where advertising dollars will be spent most effectively), and distribution (which geographic and demographic markets should receive the most attention and concentration).

The theory of genre classification is that certain social groups will invest emotionally, aesthetically, and thus economically in certain genres of music more than others. The key to selling a recording successfully lies in properly identifying the genre and properly matching it to a particular social consumer demographic. Keith Negus (1999) has written about this practice, suggesting that genre categories spring from "genre cultures," constructed in and through the social and cultural conditions of music industry workers and their culturally constructed attitudes and ideas about social identity and how they map to musical categories. Genre categories thus go far beyond simply musicological definitions and instead operate as "social categories" (1999, 29). In a similar way Frith points out that, in imagining markets, one is really imagining idealized, *fantasy* consumers. He notes, "As fantasies . . . genres describe not just who listeners are, but also what this music means to them. In deciding to label a music or a musician in a particular way, record companies are saying something about both what people like and why they like it; the musical label acts as a condensed sociological and ideological argument" (1996, 85–86). Frith has used the term "genre worlds" to describe the complex webs of mediation that construct genre categories for industry, media, musicians, and fans. Frith's "genre worlds" (1996) and Negus's "genre cultures" (1999) are similar conceived social spaces where there are both real and imagined sociological and ideological mediations between musicians, recording engineers, record producers, salespeople, various media and broadcast industries, retail industries, and music consumers (fans).

Thus these two genre worlds are social fields that are structured not only by distributions of cultural and economic capital but particular discursive strategies and ideologies. The discursive universes of Contemporary and Traditional genre worlds work to impose commonsense under-standings not only of what is expected but of what is *possible* in the recording studio. When Jules poked her head into the studio during the *Journey Home* mixdown and asked, "What's so Native about this music?" a number of other analytical questions spring to mind: Who is asking such questions and why? What is the investment in markers of "difference" by different individuals and groups? What is the nature of that investment? Who has the power to make more or less definitive statements about the "Nativeness" of a piece of music? And how might particular music recordings complicate ideas about the "authenticity" of Native identity? Ultimately the ideas and arguments about the Native identity that are sonically encoded in the digital signatures of the *Journey Home* and *Honouring Our Elders* recordings are structured through the negotiations of the various musicians, engineers, and producers involved in the recording projects, and the uneven distribution and control of the different types of capital.

The creation of a commercial recording in the studio is a multistage process that involves a complex range of people, ideologies, aesthetic interests, and commercial interests; this process unfolds over what can be a very long time. Recording studios exist at the intersection of musical creation and commerce: a commercial institution in the business of creating aesthetic products. This intersection is further complicated when Native North Americans enter the studio to record and the studio then becomes a place of intercultural contact, a meeting ground where meaning is jointly constructed and contested. This mutual construction is embedded within typical "Fourth World" (Manuel and Posluns 1974) power relations, the power structure created by the studio as a corporate and creative entity, and by the distribution of capital within a particular musical field. Arbor Records does not act simply as a conduit between the artist and the market, nor is it a closed mechanical assembly line where musical products are simply transmitted from producer to consumer. Rather, Arbor Records *mediates* and thus is integral to the creation of the final musical product.

CHAPTER 6

Producing Powwow Music

The Aesthetics of Liveness

Electrical recording (and amplification) broke the previously necessary relationship between sound and the body; tape recording broke the previously necessary relationship between a musical object in space and a musical object in time. Recording perfection ceased to refer to a specific performance (*a faithful* sound) and came to refer, as we've seen, to a constructed performance (an *ideal* sound). The "original," in short, ceased to be an event and became an idea.
— SIMON FRITH (1996, 234, italics in original)

Having discussed the various social and structural arrangements of powwow studio recording in the previous chapter, I wish to further explore the aesthetic universe of powwow recording. Studio recording presents unique challenges to the aesthetic dispositions of powwow musicians, challenges that are worked out through negotiations with record producers and with reference to existing standard practices of competition powwow performances as they develop on the powwow grounds. In this chapter, through a detailed analysis of the production and post-production processes of two different Arbor Records powwow CDs (*21st Century* by the Northern Wind Singers and *Red Tail, Volume 1* by the Red Tail Singers), I identify "liveness" as a key component of powwow recordings. Liveness—which refers to an aesthetic discourse as well as a set of technological and methodological recording practices—is sonically marked on powwow recordings through specific timbral manipulations and nonmusical sonic events, some of which are the natural outcome of a particular recording method, while others are achieved through careful digital manipulation. Liveness is also elaborated through the discursive practices of powwow musicians, audio engineers, producers, and consumers (fans), articulating the idea of "sounding live" both to the perceived "cultural authenticity" of the recording and to powwow singers' more generalized imagining of Native American "tradition."

While different record companies have particular preferences in terms of specific recording procedures (choice, placement, and number of microphones; digital vs. analog recording technologies, etc.), all powwow recordings are made in one of three general ways (all of which were used at Arbor during my tenure there): live recording, studio recording, and remote recording. In *live recording*, engineers record powwow groups as they are performing at powwows. At Arbor, live recordings were made most often with a portable digital audio tape (DAT) machine and a stereo microphone positioned over the drum group. This method of recording produced stereo DAT masters that were brought back to Studio 11 then digitally processed and mastered. In *studio recording*, drum groups came to Studio 11 and performed in the main sound room, using a specific set of microphones and microphone placements, and mixed on the fly, again producing a stereo DAT master (see chapter 5). Alternately, drum groups whose members lived in the United States or in provinces distant from Manitoba and who could not afford to travel to Winnipeg instead made recordings at professional studios in their local areas. Arbor Records would pay for the recording session and have the studio ship the recording masters (the unmixed audio files) to Winnipeg for mixing and mastering. *Remote recording* refers to a method whereby drum group performances were recorded at a place other than the powwow grounds or the studio. This could be a room within a reserve community center or some other similarly quiet, out-of-the-way place. Remote recordings combine the procedures and equipment of live recordings with the methodologies of studio recording.

Live recording was the most common method by which drum groups recorded between 1999 and 2001, and this continues to be the most common recording environment to this day. The term "live" has a specific set of meanings within the context of powwow recording and these meanings are negotiated and shared among producers like Brandon and the drum groups he records. Despite the fact that most of the powwow recordings Brandon produced during the course of his career at Sunshine Records were done live at a powwow, this was not his preferred method of recording. Arbor Records' original mission statement described a plan to make "top quality traditional Aboriginal music," which according to Brandon meant "better masters, better recordings, better artwork." In order to create better recordings and better masters, Brandon strongly encouraged powwow drum groups to come to Studio 11 to record, insisting that the studio is *always* a preferable environment in which to create a recording because of the level of sonic control this context affords. As such, when he first started Arbor Records he attempted (unsuccessfully) to make most of his powwow recordings either in the studio or through remote sessions:

CS: So when you record powwow groups, are they mostly in the city [meaning in the studio at Arbor records] or are they mostly . . .

BF: Live.

CS: Is that the way Ted [Whitecalf of Sweet Grass Records] does it too?

BF: That's the *only* way Ted does it! No, actually that's wrong. He does bring some of them into the studio. For me it's half and half. Whether it's set up in the studio or a remote recording. I prefer not to record at powwows because it's an uncontrolled environment. But the majority of the Arbor stuff is in the studio or on a remote. Live at a powwow, I prefer not to do it—with the exception of the recordings I made for Sunshine. A lot of that was live. A *lot* of it. Probably ninety percent of the releases were live.

CS: Northern Wind and Whitefish Bay—they didn't go into the [Sunshine] studio?

BF: They were all in the studio. Everybody else was live. Now with the Arbor stuff the only live one right now [the fall of 1999] is Battle River. They were adamant about having it live. They didn't want to go into the studio. And the recording suffered because of it.

CS: Why didn't they want to go into the studio?

BF: They wanted the energy [of a live performance]. So we recorded them at a powwow in Bimidji, Minnesota, which is like, fifteen minutes from where they're from [the Red Lake Indian Reservation]. (Brandon Friesen interview, October 1999)

Battle River was not alone in their preference for live recording, and their reticence to record in a studio was echoed countless times in multiple contexts by many drum groups during the course of my research. For many powwow singers and drum groups, recording live is the *only* way to make a powwow recording. Liveness is a practice rooted in the historical development of powwow recording. During the flowering of the powwow music industry in Canada in the early 1990s, recording powwow music necessarily meant that recording engineers were obliged to travel to pow-wows. At that time, very few drum groups had even considered recording with a commercial record label, and many of those who did desire to make a recording had very little knowledge of standard studio recording procedures. Entering the studio to perform a powwow song was simply not something that occurred to most drum groups, and as a result almost all powwow recording was done on the powwow grounds.

But "liveness" is not simply a recording habit; it is both an aesthetic ideal and a discursive trope that articulates a constellation of meanings and discourses, linking recordings (as a sonic text) to the ideologies of "tradition" and "culture" (see Meintjes 2003, 109–134). The Mandan Mid-winter powwow was the first recording assignment I was given by Arbor, where I was the only recording engineer. It marked a turning point in my relationship to the label and to Studio 11, the moment I went from being someone who hung around the studio and helped out on recordings, to someone who was counted on to work independently, recording and producing CD projects. I was sent to Mandan, North Dakota, to make a recording of Eagle Ridge, a drum group composed of singers from a number of other groups, most notably the Mandaree Singers and Battle River. Upon meeting, the leader (and one of the lead singers) of the group was quick to mention, "Brandon wanted us to come into the studio, but we have to play live. The songs don't sound the same without the dancers there. You need those bells [on the dancers' outfits] or it just doesn't sound like a powwow song." As is often the case when making live recordings, Eagle Ridge was unable to sing enough songs during the course of the weekend to fill a CD; by Saturday night we realized we were not going to have enough recorded material once the powwow was over. So after the flags were danced out and the dancers and crowds had left the building, we stayed in the gymnasium where the powwow was being held and recorded a number of extra songs. Listening to these performances on the headphones after we had recorded three songs, the lead singer shook his head in dismay. "Can you overdub the sound of some bells? Just record some people dancing and put it behind these songs."

This singer's concern about the sound of bells as a central element of what made a recorded powwow performance *sound* like a powwow song goes beyond issues about recording context (at a powwow or in the studio) and recording process. Many of the drum groups I worked with did not want to record in the studio and preferred live recording, citing for me, as they did for Brandon, the "energy" that singers are able to summon on the powwow grounds, an energy they felt they were unable to reproduce in studio or remote recording contexts. But *this* singer was concerned with the *product* of the recording process and with the aesthetic dimensions of liveness, not as a method of recording or even a context, but something that can be actively and purposefully produced through technological intervention: the overdubbing of bells and the sounds of dancers. For this singer, liveness was not simply an ideal performance context, but something that is embedded in the actual *sound* of the recording. Liveness is a central part of the aesthetics of powwow recording, and certain sounds function as indices of liveness whether the actual performance was captured live at a powwow or not.

For many singers who record, a powwow song is ideally indexical of a powwow event. That this singer from Eagle Ridge wanted me to add bells to a recording in which they were not audibly featured is a strange kind of technological accommodation: an admission that a recording may not be authentically "live" but can be manipulated through studio mediation to "sound live," indexically linking the recorded music to the powwow grounds and the authenticity granted to that performance context. The overdubbed addition of bells is but one of the many ways in which liveness may actually be produced in the studio as an audible sign, and many other more subtle studio manipulations are also employed to produce this effect. The liveness that is heard on record is not the liveness that was recorded on site but a liveness that is produced in the studio. Powwow musicians value liveness to such a degree that even singers who regularly record in the studio insist on the importance of liveness in the post-production process, and they want their studio recordings to sound as "live" as possible.

Brandon, like many recording engineers and producers, is of course well aware of the technological and methodological techniques for the production of liveness. Sitting in his office one day in the early spring of 2000, we were discussing the preference many powwow singers have for live recording. He compared powwow singers to many rock musicians he has worked with over the years, as both groups of people were similarly invested in the ideology of liveness as an index of authenticity. He complained that rock musicians always wanted their recordings to be representative of music that they could reproduce live in concert. Brandon laughed because he knew that the recording studio is a place where liveness is produced or not produced. He said, "They don't want to overdub any guitar tracks because they say they won't be able to play it live. But the song would sound better with twelve guitar tracks and there's nothing stopping us from doing that. You can still make it *sound* as live as you want to."[1]

21st Century

In the fall of 1999 Arbor Records released *21st Century* (AR-11022), the Northern Wind Singers' debut CD on the label. The members of Northern Wind are veterans of studio powwow recordings; previous to this release they had made fifteen CDs over the course of nine years, working with different labels on the Canadian Plains. Gabe Desrosiers is unique as a singer and songmaker: no stranger to studio experimentation, he is far more willing than most powwow musicians to avail himself of the full range of musical possibilities of the recording studio. *21st Century* is worthy of note because it makes use of an unusually high level of electronic studio manipulation. This recording is extraordinary on two counts. First, it features the use of unusual digital effects applied to the lead vocal phrases of two different songs, which, while admittedly subtle, is nonetheless an extremely rare practice. The first song on the CD, "Side Windin' (Dianne's Song)" (e.g., CD, track 10), features an effect achieved through the use of a Pro Tools–based digital pitch correction program overdriven to the point of distortion. Denizens of Arbor Records refer to this as the "Cher" effect because a similar effect was used on Cher's 1998 radio hit "Believe."[2] Another track on the CD, "Dancin' 2000" (e.g., CD, track 11), also uses an unusual vocal effect, in this case a reverse reverb (referred to by Brandon as the "Pearl Jam" effect), which was applied to every vocal lead of the song.[3] Both of these electronic effects were applied to the recording during post-production.

The second unique feature of this CD is that it made use of multiple-take, temporally displaced multitracking during the recording process, a practice almost unheard of in powwow recording. Brandon spoke to me about this recording in the context of a formal interview:

> BF: Their [Northern Wind's] most recent recording [*21st Century*], it's different because I actually overdubbed background vocals [the seconds]. They were fucking amazed at it. They sang the whole song and then I

played it back to them and I had a speaker in the control room. And they listened to it and they sang all the seconds again. So I multi-tracked all the seconds [*laughs*]. So instead of sounding like ten guys it sounds like twenty. They were blown away. But you know, they made me swear to secrecy [*laughs*]. Cuz they consider it cheating, right.[4]

CS: And they were able to do it and it sounds really blended?

BF: Pretty much. It took them awhile. It took them about an hour to get the hang of it. They didn't use headphones. There's too many guys for headphones—there's like twelve guys. So I just played it through a little guitar amp and they could hear it and hear the lead and I'd gate it and then they would come in and sing. Bang and they were just . . .

CS: Oh, OK, so because of the gate you don't actually hear the amp?[5]

BF: Yeah, it was neat. And they just sat where they normally sit in front of the drum, but they didn't drum though [perform on the drum]. They did that on all the tunes, every one [*laughs*]. It's cool, I've always wanted to try that and they were open-minded enough to try it so . . .

CS: It sounds like they were *really* open-minded if they wanted you to do all this.

BF: Yeah. That's Gabe. He's getting the bug. He's always asking me, "How can we sell more records? How can we do this? What can we do that's different?"

CS: So Northern Wind is really the only one [where you would call yourself a "producer"] . . .

BF: Well, even that one I didn't *produce*. Like, Gabe recorded the [initial] songs [at another studio]. And we were talking about these effects ahead of time, that we wanted a Cher effect, like the vocoder effect, and the Pearl Jam effect, the reverse reverb coming onto the attack of the melody. And so I explained how the effect worked and then they rearranged the song so that . . . the effects would work. But it didn't always. Like they wanted the Cher vocoder effect on every lead. But the problem is because it's live, because it's recorded live [meaning single take performances using overhead mics], the lead vocal mic picks up a lot of the drum. So to put the vocoder effect on the lead vocal it actually changed the timbre of the drum. So we could only use it on the parts when the drum was not as loud.

CS: But that was just something that happened later anyway.

BF: Yeah. All the songs were recorded. We listened to them, and I did it from there.

CS: And that's the way they wanted it, too, they wanted it as live as possible? Or don't they care?

BF: They don't know any different. Like, there is no concept [among powwow singers] of just recording the drum and then recording the vocal [as separate, temporally displaced tracks].

CS: So no group has ever asked for that?

BF: No group could even conceive that! Which is too bad. It could work. (Brandon Friesen interview, October 1999)

I also interviewed Gabe about the *21st Century* session and the degree to which it differed from some of his previous recording experiences:

CS: So can you tell me a little bit about the recording of *21st Century*? You went into a studio to record it?

GD: Yeah. I was talking to Brandon, I told him how we were getting tired of doing live tapes. And that's what our last two recordings were, [the last] two or three. And I told him I wanted to get back into the studio and do a studio tape for a change.

CS: What's the difference between studio and live?

GD: The main difference for me is you get a third, fourth, fifth chance at the song [*laughs*]. You can make a mistake. And whereas live, obviously if you make a mistake it's—you know, you can't change it. And another thing I like about studio recording is that you can put in your own special effects wherever you want them and you have a choice how to format them. You have more control like that. I enjoy more the studio tapes as well because the sound quality is better. You know, the sound is just a lot better than hearing a live tape. Although I don't mind hearing a live tape every once in a while, it just doesn't sound the same.

CS: Do you think the energy is the same or . . .

GD: Live tapes have the energy because you can hear a real powwow going on. But then again, if you make a studio tape you can just make as much energy as you want [*laughs*]. Yeah, this last tape we did [*21st Century*], I'm really pleased with it. A lot of people are.

CS: So looking at this [CD jacket], it looks like you didn't record it at Studio 11. You recorded it somewhere else.

GD: We recorded at another studio, one of Brandon's friends. That was in late August. We went in there and we recorded. Brandon had something else going on over there [at Studio 11] at the time. I think there was a session going on there on the same day we were, you know, supposed to come in and do the recording. Plus, they're in the process of building a bigger [recording] area. Cuz I went to the studio and it's not that big. There's hardly any room. Especially to fit twelve guys and a big drum. And it worked out fine.

CS: And so when you recorded in this other studio did you all just sit around the drum and sing through the songs?

GD: We all just sat around the drum. And I usually take a tape with me [with all the songs the group wants to sing]. I usually get ready by formatting the songs how I want them. And usually I'm the decision maker.

CS: What do you mean formatting the songs?

GD: In what order we're gonna sing them. And I thought of the theme of the tape, the album. I sort of pondered on it for a while. And I try to be original, as much as I can be. And just to keep up sometimes with the times. So I thought of *21st Century* since it was going to be the end of the millennium coming up. And I thought it would be a great idea to release an album right before and call it *21st Century*. And then just, you know, have songs that reflect the times like that. You know, name the songs even towards the millennium. And, I don't know, it's just fun to do different things.

CS: So you did some interesting effects on this one too.

GD: Not a whole lot. We did a couple things. Like the beginning of the album, that first song ["Side Windin' (Dianne's Song)"] where I altered my voice, I wanted something different to make me sound like some kind of robot or something. You know, just to be different. But I don't try and—we just did it once, and, when we do stuff like that, we don't overdo it. You know, like to take away from the whole idea. Especially you don't want to take away from the singing, you know. You want to stick with cultural values I guess you could say, or tradition, I guess. But it's alright to just do a little bit. And there's one song there where there's—just before the lead there's an explosion of sound on one straight song [a reverse reverb effect that begins the song "Dancin' 2000"]. That's pretty cool, you know, that's not overdoing it, it's not too bad. We don't try and do too much on all the songs.

CS: Was that the first time you've tried something like this?

GD: These effects? We've done a couple of them before on our other albums with Brandon. But, you know, little things like rain and thunder. And even one time we brought in a flute player [for the Sunshine Records recording *Northern Wind Vol. 10* (SSCT-4319)]. That was done with Brandon as well. The flute player played—I do a solo [lead phrase] without the drum, and the flute player would play his flute, what I had just sung. We'd go back and forth. Then I'd come in with the [regular] lead and then the whole drum starts in.

CS: So was it your idea to try and come up with—to try and do some other effects for this *21st Century* album. Did you go to Brandon and say, "I want to do something different?"

GD: Yeah, well you see, when we get ready to do an album, me and Brandon spend a lot of time on the phone, you know. Or, you know, if we come up with something, I'll call him or he'll call me. But a lot of times I'll tell him this would be a great idea to do. And when we were at the studio then he would come up with something. Maybe this [effect]. And then he would suggest something. But basically I'll say this is what I want. And Brandon's there too, you know, because he has ideas too, you know, so I don't control everything. He knows the effects. I don't know if he has an effects library somewhere, I don't know where he gets them but he knows what I'm talking about, what kinds of effects I want.

CS: So how do you think of the difference between recording in the studio and playing live? Do you think of those as different things, playing at a powwow and playing in the studio, in terms of what you want to do with a performance?

GD: No, it's not different, you know. In comparing both, basically what I feel about that is—basically me and my singers are there to, first, never to forget why we're singing. And never to get away from what the whole reason behind singing is. And whether we do it live or in the studio is no different. We always come down to earth on that. And when we travel, even—sometimes we're not home for three or four weeks at a time. Once we have these commitments [to sing at powwows] we go around all summer. And every once in awhile we'll sit around and I'll talk to them about the whole meaning of why we're doing this. That's how we've been surviving, you know, by believing in what we do. (Gabe Desrosiers interview, November 1999)

These lengthy interview excerpts reveal strikingly different attitudes about live and studio recordings. Whereas Brandon celebrates the creative possibilities of studio recording and laments the habits and preferences of powwow singers for live recording processes (which limit these possibilities), Gabe expresses a deeply ambivalent attitude toward the creative potential and problems of the studio recording process. While intrigued and excited by the opportunities for sound manipulation afforded by the studio, Gabe is also somewhat distrustful of these kinds of actions because they are a threat to the "traditional" values associated with singing. In framing studio recording in these terms, Gabe is very intentionally linking recording practices to the discourses of culture and tradition and negotiating new spaces for the expression of "authentic" Native American identity. His careful reminder that "we didn't do too much" electronic manipulation is an expression of a larger concern that the greater the level of studio-assisted electronic mediation, the further one gets from the traditional meanings associated with singing.

Three different and separate aspects of studio mediation are considered in the above discussion, each delineating a different acceptable level of electronic manipulation: (1) "live at a powwow" performances are distinguished from single-take, in-studio performances, (2) single-take studio performances are distinguished from multiple-take multitracked studio performances, and (3) the process of multiple-take multitracking is distinguished from the process of adding effects to single-take performances. While recognizing the advantages of studio recording as a means of controlling the final product, Gabe and Northern Wind originally recorded all of the songs for the album as, essentially, a series of single-take performances. The difference between a live and a studio performance in this case is not found in how a song is actually performed in real time, but only in the circumstances in which the song is rendered. The group performed all of the songs on the *21st Century* CD once through in their entirety, simulating a performance "live" at a powwow. Interviews with a number of different drum groups reveal a consistent agreement that powwow performances are judged by their success at powwows. The main criterion for success is, "Do the songs make the dancers dance?" A group will often judge the success or failure of a particular performance by the response of the dancers, and powwow singers insisted repeatedly that the main reason for singing is "for the dancers." Thus the preference for low mediation in recording powwow songs is linked to the authenticity imbued in a live performance. The liveness of a powwow performance is important because it is linked both to what is considered to be the normal context of powwow songs, which is the powwow as an event, and also with what singers consider to be traditional Native values, those which associate singing with service and commitment to the dancers and, more generally, to the community for which they sing.

This preference for liveness is typical of almost all powwow recordings. In all powwow recording contexts (live at powwow, in the studio, or on remote location), the songs are performed from beginning to end in one take. The process of constructivist, piecemeal, multitracked recording common in rock and pop production methods has never been considered an option. Recording the drum separately from the vocals as well as recording multiple vocal parts are not part of the current practice of powwow recording. For most drum groups, live recording and single-take performances are the only ways to capture the energy of a powwow song. Because of this, studio manipulations such as multitracking are considered to be a form of "cheating" and Gabe has commented to me that he has felt "funny" about this recording because it is not a true reflection of what his group "really sounds like." As Brandon indicated, this powwow CD is the only one I know of that uses multiple-take multitracking on every song. In all the songs, the seconds (the vocal parts sung by the entire group in response to the lead phrase which is sung at the beginning of every push-up) were sung once as a single take and then sung again on a second set of tracks, which was then mixed with the first take.

The electronic effects added afterward, such as the Cher effect found in "Side Windin' (Dianne's Song)," were not thought to have the same degree of inauthenticity as the practice of multitracking because they did not disrupt the standard process of powwow performances (singing a song straight through as a single take). As a result, Gabe was much more willing to talk about and celebrate the use of these audio effects, but only to a point. While the vocal effects were subtle, they were the result of obvious studio manipulation. In using those digital effects, Gabe is positioning himself as an indigenous performer, trained as a traditional singer, who is nonetheless open to studio experimentation and comfortable with twenty-first century recording technology. The recording is not only a statement about modern indigenous identity, but about his relationship to Brandon, whom he describes as a collaborator ("Brandon's there too, you know, because he has ideas too, you know, so I don't control everything"), rather than a producer. In the words of Louise Meintjes, the "audible traces of the means of production are also traces of the relations of production" (2005, 39).

The multitracked seconds, however, are an imperceptible form of studio manipulation and thus give the impression that what is being heard is what was captured during the recording of a live or single-take performance. Not surprisingly, it was Brandon who lobbied for this particular studio recording technique. Multitracking masks the means of production, which is, in part, why Gabe was more ambivalent about it. In other words, multitracking breaks the rules, formulated and agreed upon by both parties, as to what it means to make a powwow recording: that is, recording as a conduit, and recording as a means of *capturing* a live performance.

It is also worth noting that the digital effects were applied *only* to the vocals and not to the drum. This is perhaps not at all surprising given the respect afforded the instrument as a sacred item. As such, I suspect that digitally altering the natural sound of the drum would be an egregious act of disrespect, something quite far indeed from the traditional values of singing. Porcello (2005b) has suggested that the stylistic conventions and norms of styles and genres are established in part through decisions about which parts of recordings are considered "documentary" and which parts may be digitally altered and sonically manipulated. For instance, in rock recording the voice is an instrument most likely to be treated as "documentary." Because rock singers are expected to actually "feel" the emotions they are singing about while they are singing, digital manipulation of the vocal line represents a disruption of the authenticity of the emotional state of the singer. When the pitch or timbre of a singer is digitally altered, rock music fans begin to question the authenticity of the singer's very identity. Conversely, as the *21st Century* CD suggests, with powwow music it is the vocals that are subject to alteration, while the main instrument, the drum, must remain as unmediated (or as documentary) as possible. The Cher effect is applied only to the lead vocal part of "Side Windin'" because the song is a Jingle Dress Side-step song composed, according to Gabe, in a traditional way. As such the song begins with a lead vocal without drum accompaniment; the drum enters when the seconds enter. As a result, this digital effect could be applied to the lead vocal alone without altering the sound of the drum or the other singers. When the drum and the seconds enter, the vocal effect is no longer used.

The sacred and traditional nature of drums prohibits the kind of sonic experimentation that singers will sometimes indulge in when making a studio recording. Since the release of *21st Century*, many singers, especially younger groups, asked me about the possibility of adding similar sonic effects to their voices; none have ever inquired about the sonic manipulation of their drum sound, nor have I ever encountered a recording by any singing group on any label where drum sounds were digitally manipulated to sound like anything other than a drum. This is not to say that drum sounds are not digitally manipulated, only that these timbral adjustments are all in the service of creating a documentary sound: recording technology in the service of making the drum "sound as much like the sound of the drum" as possible.

Post-production

Somewhat obscured by the authority granted to live, single-take performances are the electronic mediations of liveness that occur *after* the performance has been recorded. "Post-production" refers to a series of sonic manipulations that occur after all the tracks for a recording have been mixed down to a two-track (stereo) master. In post-production, final audio effects may be added before the recording is ultimately mastered (a process whereby yet another set of equalization and compression effects are applied). A good deal of my time spent at Studio 11 and Arbor Records was spent in post-production, readying powwow recordings before they were finally sent to the manufacturer for pressing. The production of liveness through technological intervention in the studio happens largely in post-production and in the mastering process.

The "entrance trope" has become a ubiquitous feature of ethnomusicological and anthropological literature, Geertz's Balinese cockfight being one of the best known. Entrance tropes are rhetorical devices that attempt to bestow a sense of authority to ethnographers; in short, they communicate to the reader, "This is how and when I got in," gaining access and acceptance in the field site community. In ethnomusicological literature, part of the entrance trope often involves acceptance into performance circles, becoming "bimusical" through musical participation. Competence within a musical tradition or style is to a certain degree an index of the degree to which one has gotten "inside" that tradition. Learning a musical tradition, however, serves many purposes apart from its ethnographic usefulness as a rhetorical device. Learning and performing become opportunities for a special kind of feedback interview analysis. Gauging one's competence and understanding of a musical tradition involves asking teachers, "Is this the correct way to perform? How about this way?" Learning to compose in a specific musical tradition functions in a similar way. The degree to which our teachers accept and/or reject and correct our attempts at bimusical composition and performance provide us with important information about our own understanding and comprehension of specific musical styles and practices.

My participation as a member of the Spirit Sands Singers was a field experience typical of many ethnomusicologists working to gain competency in a "foreign" musical style or genre. However, working at Studio 11 and Arbor, my apprenticeship was somewhat unusual. I was faced not only with certain musical challenges (how should a powwow recording sound?), but also a great many technological hurdles (what on earth is a stereo multiband peak limiter and what do all these knobs do?). My understanding of powwow music production, and my eventual acceptance in the studio as a recording engineer and producer, was measured in part by the degree of competence I gained in producing powwow CDs. Near the end of my full-time tenure at Arbor Records, I had become the powwow recording specialist, responsible for the post-production of almost all powwow recording projects. Given the opportunity to play a larger role in the recording and production of powwow music, I was required to become familiar with the technology of Studio 11: various mixing boards, "outboard" effects (effects processors not located on the mixing board itself), sound processors, and a Macintosh-based Pro Tools digital recording suite. The challenge was twofold. First, I had to learn how to use the equipment, understanding how different effects and programs worked on a practical level as well as a theoretical level. Knowing practically how to use a digital compressor to achieve a desired effect (e.g., to achieve this particular sonic effect I need to push this button and turn this dial) is different from knowing in the abstract what a digital compressor does — what acoustic effects it exerts on an audio signal. Second, and more importantly for my research and my own success as an audio engineer, I had to understand how these technologies could be used in creative, musical, and culturally appropriate ways.

By late April 2000 my habit was to spend the major part of most evenings and early predawn mornings working at Studio 11. I had graduated to a level of technological sophistication that allowed me to work almost exclusively in Studio B, the Pro Tools studio. During this time, among other projects I worked on a recording by the Red Tail Singers, an intertribal drum of young singers (mostly teenagers) from Lapawai, Idaho. The recording eventually became *Red Tail, Volume 1* (AR-11262). The Red Tail CD was one of the first recording projects in which I took part in every step of production. I had engineered the two-day remote recording session in Idaho a few months earlier and now was charged with the task of mastering it. This process required a number of steps: downloading the DAT recording master onto the computer, removing extraneous room noise from "spoken word" parts of the recording (the Red Tail Singers had prefaced a few of the songs on the CD with brief, humorous, playful interchanges between singers), and experimenting with adding a vocoder effect to some of the lead vocals. A number of the singers had heard the *21st Century* CD and loved the studio effects, requesting that I emulate the effects on their recording. Because they were recorded remotely and not in the studio, the masters were "dry," meaning free of any effects or audio manipulations. As such, the stereo masters had to be loaded into Pro Tools in order to add reverb and compression, and to tweak the equalization, emulating Brandon's standard formula for powwow production.

My methodology followed Brandon's exactly. When he first explained the basics of Pro Tools to me and set me up in the system, he advised that I start by using a Drawmer compressor plug-in, then add a reverb plug-in of my choice (there were several reverb options available), and then finally to add whatever equalization was necessary. "Plug-ins" are digital effects processors that are integrated with digital audio workstation (DAW) software systems like Pro Tools. They are pieces of software that try to emulate commercially available, rack-mounted "outboard" digital and analog effects processors. They are also many processors that offer unique operational configurations and possibilities for sound shaping that are not based on any analogous hardware device. Commercially produced outboard effects processors each have their own sound signature, created by the particular configuration of electronics within the unit and the interface design (which establishes the control parameters for the user). Because the audio signature of every unit is different, it is common for recording studios to have a number of different effects that ostensibly do the same thing. Multiple reverb and compression units are most common because each one has its own unique sound that is applicable and appropriate to particular recording situations. Studio 11's Pro Tools suite was equipped with an extraordinary array of plug-ins: various kinds of reverbs, compressors, equalization units, time shifters, sound modules, guitar effects units, speaker emulators, noise reducers, noise gates, noise generators, and so on. The list seemed endless.

Brandon began by setting the Drawmer compressor to a high gain threshold (meaning that the compressor would only affect the signal when the recording reached a certain, rather loud volume) and a high compression ratio (around 6:1) in order to compress only those signal spikes generated by the check beats, but to compress them in a rather significant way so they would not jump out audibly in the mix.[6] Ideally, the compressor should also kick in during the third and fourth push-ups of a song when the drumming usually gets consistently louder. Next Brandon added the reverb, because the type of reverb used and the settings of the reverb unit would effect any equalization that was done to the stereo signal. Adding reverb second in the effects chain allows for better control over how the reverb affects different parts of the sound spectrum. Brandon suggested a reverb with a "low pass filter" that would act as a kind of frequency spectrum gate, limiting the frequencies to be affected by the unit. Setting the low pass filter at around 800 Hz allows only frequencies below this threshold to be affected by the reverb. Brandon explained that adding digital reverb tended to dampen or cut high frequencies, rendering them less audible. In powwow recordings, the higher frequencies are where the voices have their "presence"; adding too much reverb to the higher frequencies serves only to deaden and flatten the sound of the vocals. Cutting the high-end frequency response of any reverb also limits the amount the reverb unit can respond to the high "slapping" sound of the drumsticks hitting the drum skin. Adding reverb to this part of the frequency spectrum only ends up accentuating this noise and creating a "pinging" sound on the recording.

For the Red Tail CD I chose Waves Audio's TrueVerb plug-in, a somewhat complex reverb with a large number of control variables that took me a good deal of time to fully understand and operate. The advantage of this reverb unit was that it had a fairly precise set of interface controls that governed frequency response (mapping the range of frequencies to which the reverb would respond and also controlling the frequency spectrum of the reverb itself). In this way the reverb could sound either "bright" or "dark" by cranking, respectively, either the high end or low end of the frequency response. Upon loading the reverb into Pro Tools I found that there was a program preset already saved in the program's memory called "Lake Vermillion verb." Waylon Wityshyn, another engineer at Studio 11, had used this plug-in when he had mastered the Lake Vermillion Singers' CD *Onamani Zaaga-igan* (AR-11042) in the spring of 1999. This reverb sounded big and boomy, like a very large "concert hall" reverb with a medium decay time, but a fairly low mix level (meaning the level of reverb that was mixed into the signal). Waylon had set up the reverb to have a big but subtly applied echo. To my ears it seemed similar to the reverb setting that I had heard Brandon use for the Lake of the Woods recording. I started with Waylon's preset and began cranking the low end of the frequency spectrum while knocking out the high end, experimenting with the program and creating a reverb that was not quite as big, but that sounded much darker.

I then used the Waves Audio Q10 Paragraphic Equalizer plug-in. As the name suggests, this functioned as a hybrid of a parametric and a graphic equalization unit.[7] Using this plug-in, it was possible to raise and lower the amplitude of specific frequencies while shaping the degree to which the frequencies on either side of the peak frequency were affected. I started out by boosting the low end slightly (around 80 Hz) and then tried to pinpoint the frequency of the slapping sound of the drum as much as possible in order to remove those frequencies without dulling the vocals too much and taking all "presence" and brightness away from the recording. Brandon had often said that this was an inherent problem with two-track recordings gleaned from live or remote recordings. Because there is no track separation between the drum and the vocals, it is very difficult to get both the vocals and the drum properly balanced and equalized; their frequency spectrums work at cross-purposes.

After completing all these manipulations, I still felt as if I were stumbling around in the dark. I had no idea if this was how a powwow CD *should* sound. Recalling Brandon's habit of listening to specific CDs before beginning a mixdown, I went down to the basement where all the Arbor Records stock was stored and picked out a handful of play copies in order to listen to what other Arbor powwow recordings sounded like. One of the CDs that stood out for me was Northern Wind's *21st Century*. The drum sounded deep and resonant, the vocals were loud and powerful (no doubt in part because of the double tracking), and the reverb was big and dark. Compared to that CD, the Red Tail recording sounded small and flat. No depth, no power, and no dynamic range. I went back and re-equalized it, cranking the volume of all the frequencies at around 80 Hz to get a more booming drum, and I was more aggressive in removing the "slapping" frequencies before boosting the volume of the frequencies at around 4 kHz (4,000 Hz) in order to give the vocals more volume and presence. I also changed the reverb dramatically. Waylon's Lake Vermillion reverb was set to be subtle, while Northern Wind's reverb was high in the mix and dramatically present, making the whole recording sound more powerful. I tried to duplicate the heavy reverb by boosting it in the mix to make it more noticeable, making it less "big" but more "deep" (smaller hall but a longer decay, more "live"). I dragged both Justin and Paul into the control room and played both mixes for them, the one with the "Lake Vermillion reverb" and the one with the "21st Century reverb" (my attempts at mimicking the sound of those reverbs). They both liked the darker reverb of the latter mix and so we went with that.

Next I applied the Waves Audio L1 Maximizer plug-in, a "limiter" plug-in that was typically used during the final mastering process in all Studio 11 projects. The L1 program further helped to compress (limit) the drum signal while bringing the vocals up in the mix. It further smoothed out the signal by compressing peaks and raising the lowest decibel levels of the signal, which in turn raised the overall volume of the recording. After digitally creating all the fade-ins and fade-outs in Pro Tools, I then copied each song (with all the plug-ins and effects added) as a new stereo track file, ordered the files in a master list in the same order that they were recorded during the remote session, and finally burned a CD.

When it was done, I took the CD home with me in order to listen to it on my own stereo, something that Brandon had also advised. It is important, once a CD is mixed and mastered in the studio, to play the recording on a number of different audio systems. Every audio system is different because each has a different set of frequency responses that result from particular combinations of amplification and speaker technology. Studio monitors are usually quite expensive and ideally have a "flat" frequency response (where no parts of the frequency spectrum are accentuated or biased over any others). Stereo systems and speakers, boomboxes, and car stereos all have a wide range of frequency responses. Testing the sound of the CD by playing it on different types of stereo equipment is a way of testing how a CD will sound in the "real world," that is, how the CD will be used by the consumer. Brandon often played his own tentative mixes of rock bands on a relatively cheap boombox in the Arbor Records main reception area. It was a more "biased," and thus more "natural" playback source than the studio.[8]

The Red Tail CD had been mastered in Studio B, which housed speakers that reproduced bass frequencies far more accurately than most home stereo units. I took the CD home to see how it would sound on my own stereo, with speakers that were far less expensive and thus less accurate. Much to my disappointment, when I listened to my mastering job the next morning, it sounded dull and flat. Worse than that, the drum was loud and booming while the vocals sounded small, thin, and distant in the mix. I listened to Arbor's *Hinckley Powwow Northern Style* CD (AR-11162) on my own stereo for the sake of comparison. Sure enough, the Hinckley Northern CD was mastered in such a way that the vocals were far more present in the mix. Both the Hinckley recordings and the Red Tail stereo masters were done with the same two-track setup (a pair of Shure SM57s into the Tascam portable DAT recorder), so it was not just that the microphones recorded the drum louder than the vocals, it was something I had done in the equalization process. I took the CD back into the studio that afternoon and tried to re-equalize it in Studio A (which had smaller, less bass-heavy speakers), using the Hinckley recording as a comparison CD because I wanted to match the mix of the drum and the vocals on that recording. I dragged Brandon down and asked him what he thought of the recording as I had re-mastered it. Not wanting to trash my work, he said it sounded, "OK . . . except it's a little dull." He suggested adding more 4 kHz (increasing the volume of the frequencies around 4 kHz) in order to brighten the CD and give the vocals more presence. Following his suggestions, I recopied all the tracks with the new EQ and burned another CD. I took that one home and played it on my stereo and it sounded much better. The next day I handed the master to Brandon to be sent to the manufacturer.

The methodology for mastering powwow recordings that I used for the Red Tail CD was one that other engineers used prior to my working there. To the best of my knowledge, this methodology continues to be used to this day. During a typical mastering process, several audio manipulations were applied to powwow recordings, each of which was designed to create a CD that sounds as "live" as possible. Brandon's formula (and thus Arbor Records') for powwow production and post-production was remarkably consistent: it always involved the addition of reverb, compression, and equalization. For Brandon, each of these operations functioned as a core sonic index of liveness.

The addition of reverb is perhaps the most obvious of these operations. Audio engineers describe reverb as functioning to "naturalize" the sterile and unnatural acoustical ambience of the recording studio. The addition of digital reverb is essential in attempting to mimic the ambience of powwow performances as they occur on the powwow grounds. When I presented a paper at the national conference of the Society for Ethnomusicology (SEM) some years ago that described the production process of powwow recordings and how a discourse of liveness was developed through the interactions of performers and record producers and engineers, a member of the audience commented during the question and answer session that it seemed only natural that reverb would be added to a studio performance because that was the "normal" way that powwow music was heard: at powwows where the music is experienced by listeners as reverberating through the acoustic environment of the powwow grounds. This audience member's observation that powwow music *should* sound this way forcefully struck me as further proof of the essentially ideological nature of liveness. On this point, it seems, powwow singers, ethnomusicologists, and powwow record producers agree. Powwow music should index powwows because that is the natural context within which powwow music is heard.

The digital manipulation of ambience—adding reverb—is one of the key sonic markers that links singing performances to the powwow grounds. Reverb is a central component of a powwow recording's "spaciality," a term Peter Doyle (2005) coined to call attention to the historical role that echo and reverb have played in invoking "spaces" and "places" in pop music recordings. In particular, Doyle was interested in the ways in which echo and reverb were sometimes used in "classic" rock and roll and pop recordings with the intention of engendering quite specific "affective outcomes" (2005, 5). His arguments hinged on a relationship between "spacio-acoustic conditions" and a performer's "sense of self" or, more specifically, of a personal sense of "self-in-place." Thus Doyle provocatively suggested that through the use and manipulation of echo and reverb in recordings, the "social, the personal, the geographic, the demographic, the physico-spatial conditions of [performers'] lives (and of life in general) were rendered into aesthetic effects" (2005, 7). Similarly, the digitally produced ambience of a powwow recording creates affective connections between the powwow grounds as an acoustic space and as a very specific place where dancers, family members, and fans of powwow music all share in the powerfully emotional experience of powwow participation. Reverb places powwow performers in their natural setting, thereby emplacing listeners on the powwow grounds as well.

Equalization is typically applied to powwow recordings in order to create a greater sonic separation and clarity between the sound of the drum and the sound of the vocals. Because powwow recordings are always created by "capturing" live performances (either on the powwow grounds or in the studio) an engineer's job is made only marginally easier by using three, four, five, or more microphones. For example, I conducted an informal interview with George Parker, a co-owner of Turtle Island Music, who told me that the standard practice for recording studio powwow performances at his studio was to place a microphone on the drum as well as in front of every singer, thus dedicating a separate track for every singer in the group. Because my conversation with him occurred at a time when he was well aware that I was working full-time at Arbor Records, I was never able to witness whether this was actually the case or not. From my own experience, that kind of arrangement would not only make it extremely difficult for the singers to be able to sit comfortably around the drum, but would also present numerous problems in mixing. Because of the close proximity of singers to each other and to the drum itself, "bleeding" would occur with every microphone, where the sounds of the drum and the other singers would "bleed" into what was supposed to be a track isolating the voice of a single singer. This would make the kind of vocal separation that is the ideal aim of such a microphone configuration a near impossibility. Thus the central challenge of creating the right balance between the vocals and the drum is not often a matter of mixing, or even necessarily of microphone placement, but rather a matter of equalization. This often involves boosting frequency ranges that add "presence" to the vocals (allowing them to stand out in the mix) without altering the sound of the drum in an audibly detrimental way.

Compression (and "limiting") are applied to a two-track (stereo) master as a way of flattening the dynamic range of the recording so that the volume of the entire CD can be raised without distortion occurring at particular spikes in volume (typically the honor beats). This has the effect of raising the level of the vocals in the overall mix, as the vocal lines rarely spike the signal in the same way that the drum does. Thus the vocals remained uncompressed (or at least the compression that does take place is not that audibly noticeable). Compression is applied in the most transparent way possible, so that the listener never hears when the compression kicks in. In this way, compression works to correct the imperfect response of microphones in handling extremely high sound pressure (volume).

Compression and equalization work in tandem to recreate the ideal listening situation at a powwow. It is now a common phenomenon at large competition powwows to find a large group of people, many of whom have hand-held tape recorders, who stand around a drum group as they perform, listening and recording. From the listening position of singers who are sitting around the drum and audience members who crowd around the edges of the drum circle, one hears a particular balance between the volume of the drum and the volume of the singers. Imperfect tools for recording powwow music, a microphone positioned in a similar position to these listeners will often pick up much more of the sound of the drum than the singers. As I have illustrated in great detail, audio engineers recording powwow groups strive to recreate an ideal balance between singers and the drum through the application of compression (which has the effect of lowering the volume of the drum, especially during check beats) and equalization (which typically raises the volume level of the voices). Importantly, this process of "naturalization" is rarely thought of as invasive; rather it is typically framed as a series of manipulations that attempt to "remove" the technical impediments of capturing a "live" performance—hence Brandon's insistence that powwow recordings "have no producer."

Liveness and the Grain of the Recording

Referencing the "sound" of other CDs—as Brandon had done when mixing Mishi's CD and as I did in the creation of the Red Tail CD—is a practice that brings to a listener's/producer's focal awareness something that I will call the "grain of the recording," a concept inspired by Barthes' well-known discussion of the "grain of the voice" (Barthes 1977). Recording technology allows for the manipulation of the complete sonic structure of a musical performance, sonically "coding musical time and space" (Tankel 1990, 34). This code has a dual nature. Barthes was concerned with the "dual production" of the voice, identifying how different elements of a singing performance operate at distinct semiotic levels:

The *pheno-song* . . . covers all the phenomena, all the features which belong to the structure of the language being sung, the rules of the genre, the coded form of the melisma, the composers idiolect, the style of interpretation: in short everything in the performance which is in the service of communication, representation, expression . . . [and] which takes its bearing directly on the ideological alibis of a period ("subjectivity," "expressivity," "dramatism," "personality"). The *geno-song* is the volume of the singing and speaking voice, the space where significations germinate "from within language and its very materiality"; it forms a signifying play having nothing to do with communication, representation (of feelings), expression; it is that apex (or that depth) of production where the melody really works at the language—not at what it says, but the voluptuousness of its sound-signifiers, of its letters—where melody explores how the language works and identifies with that work. It is, in a very simple word but which must be taken seriously, the *diction* of the language. (Barthes 1977, 182–183, italics in original)

The concept of the dual production of the voice maps well onto the sonic code of recorded musical texts—such as those created during the production of powwow recordings—identifying and naming sonic elements that producers concern themselves with when recording, mixing, and mastering CDs. Put rather crudely, we may consider powwow songs as they exist apart from their recorded form (lyrics, melody, drumbeat patterns, compositional idiosyncrasies, etc.) as the pheno-song, or perhaps pheno-recording, to borrow the term from Tankel (1990, 35) and the engineering, production, mastering, and all technologically induced sonic manipulation of the entire audio spectrum as the geno-recording or the "grain" of the recording. Of course, this analytic transposition is neither simple nor neat. There is a physical, bodily aspect to the grain as described by Barthes. He writes, "the 'grain' is in the body of the voice as it sings, the hand as it writes, the limb as it performs" (Barthes 1977, 188). In recorded music, the grain is not just physical but also technological. Listening to CDs of the Red Tail Singers or the Northern Wind Singers, it is not the bodily grain of their voices that we, as listeners, respond to, but a *recording* of their voices, electronically and digitally manipulated during the recording and post-production process, and further altered as it is reproduced during playback on the radio or compact disc player and amplified through speakers or headphones.

What is gained by such an analytic posture is not only a clearer understanding of the duality of recorded texts but also insight into how the technological grain functions in the aesthetics of sound recording practices. In both the Red Tail and Northern Wind recordings discussed above, the production of the geno-recording—the "grain"—involved mediations (between producer and musician and between the producer and the technology with which he works) in order to create various degrees of liveness. Distinguishing pheno- and geno-recordings—naming the grain of a recording—allows one to understand the process of mediation in its technological specificity. All grains, even grains of liveness, must be actively produced in the studio through technological intervention. However, these technological interventions are still governed by the relationship structures of the social space. In the creation of *21st Century*, both Brandon and Gabe use similar metaphors in constructing this terrain, agreeing that capturing liveness, real or simulated, is at the heart of powwow recording. Both parties construct mutually agreed-upon social roles for the other. Brandon is cast as the outsider, a white producer and capitalist who acts as a conduit through which powwow recordings are created and distributed, linking the world of powwow singing to the world of the commercial music industry. The Northern Wind Singers (and other drum groups) are the insiders, as both creators and consumers, to the aesthetics and values associated with powwows and with singing in general. They provide that which is captured and redistributed to other powwow people like themselves. The metaphor of capture, however, obscures for both parties the active creation of the grain that, while both parties speak of it obliquely, is never overtly discussed or acknowledged. My interpretation of this mutual agreement of omission is that both parties are guided by deeply felt beliefs about the link between the aesthetics of liveness and the authenticity endowed to powwow singing as a "traditional" and Native "cultural" practice.

Edward Kealy (1990) has generalized three historically situated modes of collaboration between sound engineers and producers and musicians. The first is the craft union mode, which arose in the years directly following World War II. A producer's job at this time was to use the acoustic design of the studio (or concert hall) to full advantage. Microphone placement and mixing was done in an attempt to capture, as best as possible, the sound of the performance in a particular space at a particular time. The acoustic space of the location of the performance was an integral part of the recording. The recording aesthetic was one of "concert hall" or "documentary" realism, what Kealy referred to as a concern with "high fidelity." High-fidelity recordings are those that reproduce, with as much accuracy and clarity as possible, both the performance itself and the sonic signature of the performance space. With the invention and subsequent popularization of magnetic tape recording, audio technicians entered what Kealy termed an "entrepreneurial mode" (1990, 211). The relatively cheap method of tape recording resulted in a dramatic increase in the number of recording studios that were creating and releasing recordings. Many of these smaller studios did not have the financial resources to create a high-fidelity recording, so they instead tried to create their own unique "sounds": they began to experiment (e.g., Sun Records or Stax are often referred to as having their own unique "sounds," meaning that all of the recordings done at these studios had similar recording "grains"). This period (from the late 1950s into the 1960s) was marked by a more open collaboration between engineers, producers, musicians, and marketers. The third mode of collaboration, which began in the later part of the 1960s with the development of multitrack recording, was termed by Kealy the "art mode." This mode was characterized by the development of a "recording consciousness" by musicians. The recording process became an integral part of aesthetic expression for musicians who began to become increasingly involved in the aesthetic and technological decisions of the recording process.

While these practices and aesthetic values grew out of historical practice, all three continue to operate presently within different recording contexts. Liveness as an ideological discourse operates within a number of different "genre worlds" (Frith 1996, Negus 1999), and is often tied to the aesthetics of high fidelity. Brandon, when first discussing powwow recording practices with me, tellingly equated the process to the parallel practice of recording classical music. In each case the job of the engineer was to "capture" a live performance. For Brandon, liveness in powwow recording is generated in a similar way to liveness in classical music recording. James Badel (1996) has published interviews with a number of world-famous conductors regarding their experiences making recordings. He noted that many of those interviewed likened a recording to a photograph: "Any recording, even a heavily edited studio product, represents an artist's interpretation of that work at that moment in time. In essence it is an audio snapshot" (3). The text that draws our aesthetic attention is the music itself (the pheno-text). While CD reviews, especially those in audiophile magazines, may concern themselves with the way an art music recording "sounds" (the quality of production), usually the comments are restricted to the fidelity of the recording, how accurately the recording reproduces the unique performance of the musicians. The medium of transmission (the recording process) remains quite distinct from the text (the performance) and the recording process lies outside of any aesthetic considerations about how successful or beautiful a recorded performance may be. The "aura" of the artwork remains intact. Even the obsessive and endless tape manipulations of Glenn Gould do not disturb the aura of the music he is performing. While his performance may be a simulacrum (a perfect copy for which there is no original), the piece of music is not. The text to which the listener addresses himself remains the music composed by a particular individual and performed by another individual.

Brandon addresses powwow performances in a similar way, guided by an ideology of high fidelity.[9] Significantly, his concern with fidelity—the accurate and detailed sonic reproduction of a performance—is only partially shared by the powwow musicians whom he records. For Brandon, me, and many other recording engineers and producers, creating a grain of liveness on a powwow CD was the result of high-fidelity recording processes (combined with various post-production manipulations) and guided by an aesthetic of documentary realism. Producers want the "best-sounding" recorded performances. Powwow singers are also interested in grains of liveness, but for them liveness functions as an audible indexical sign linking recorded powwow performances to the powwow grounds. As such, "nonmusical" sounds that are anathema to the goals of high-fidelity recording—the sounds of bells, the sounds of dancers, the sounds of the emcee and the crowd—become important elements of recorded performances (and, some powwow musicians would argue, "crucial"). By insisting on the importance of liveness as a way to indexically link recorded singing performances to the powwow grounds, singers are guided by a belief in "sound making as place making" (Feld and Brenneis 2004, 465). Powwows are sites for the construction of a uniquely Native American sound environment. It is not only the sound of powwow songs, but the sound of the entire powwow (the "noise" of the crowd, the emcee, the ringing bells of the dancers) that evokes so many indexical emotional connections to the powwow grounds and the joy of that social and musical space, and this is key to understanding the preference for liveness in recordings. The sound of the powwow is really what needs to be captured.

The transformational aspects of mediation are always downplayed and the "authenticity" of the performance is valorized in the live recording. "You need those bells or it just doesn't sound like a powwow song."

It is not that powwow musicians are unconcerned with high fidelity; they are. However, the fidelity of a powwow recording functions, to a large degree, as an important sign of technological intervention. Fidelity is a concern for many singers because it is often sound quality alone which distinguishes a commercial recording from the myriad recordings singers make of different drum groups themselves, using small, hand-held tape recorders. These tape recorders have become standard equipment for drum groups. While many singers and dancers engage in the practice of this bootleg taping, no one would confuse these recordings with commercial recordings, and it is superior sound quality (high fidelity) that is the central feature of distinction. In Gabe's words, "live tapes are all right, but they just don't sound the same."

This chapter has been concerned with three ways in which liveness can be understood: as a performance practice, as a technological practice, and as an ideological discourse. Liveness is not something that simply happens passively when somebody places a microphone over a drum group and records a performance from beginning to end. The practice of recording is always an active form of technological intervention and mediation; liveness must be actively produced. In other words, through various processes of technological manipulation (and this can vary from microphone choice and placement or recording location to the use of myriad kinds of digital effects processors), recordings are very purposefully made to *sound* more or less live through the production of specific recording *grains*. But the liveness captured during a performance or produced through technological intervention is also the expression of a series of ideas about how a powwow recording "should" sound. As such, it is an ideological construct that is worked out discursively through language and through recorded sound itself. Powwow performance and recording practices are guided by an ideology of liveness, and powwow musicians explicitly position themselves relative to this discourse when they choose how and where to record (at powwows, in remote locations, in the studio) as well as when they make requests and recommendations about how the recording should sound ("Let's use the Cher effect," "Can you put the sounds of dancers behind our singing?" "We have to record live!").

Central to the creation of grains of liveness is the issue of social power:

who has the power to decide what liveness sounds like and how it is produced? Liveness and high fidelity express aesthetic decisions about recorded objects that have changed through history and across different social groups; what it means to "sound live" or to display a degree of high fidelity has changed over the course of the twentieth century. What is significant about the case of powwow recording is that while white record producers and Native musicians share in the use of the liveness trope, this sharing produces multiple outcomes, multiple ways of attaching meaning to the sonic markers of liveness. The practice of producing powwow music is negotiated through this trope of liveness, standardizing recorded powwow performances as live performances.

CHAPTER 7

Powwows "Live" and "Mediated"

Any Indian music of which we have recordings is, by definition, in a new context from that of traditional culture before Anglo contact. There was once no Native American identity in need of preservation. Perhaps the only perspective in American Indian music today that is not "new" is that of the traditionalist who refuses to record the ceremonies he has learned or even to countenance the presence of outsiders at their performance. This view is by no means uncommon in Native North America and has, if anything, become more prevalent in recent times. It is matched these days by a new respect for the Native point of view on the part of folklorists, anthropologists, ethnomusicologists, and even some small part of the general public. Three hundred years of Indian resistance have finally begun to teach the Anglo world a new perspective too.
—DAVID MCALLESTER (1981, 443)

Imagine for a moment that while walking through the Manitoba bush you catch a glimpse of an animal darting through the forest. A fox perhaps, but it is impossible to be sure. It was there only for an instant and then it was gone. You continue on your way.

Now imagine that instead of catching a fleeting glimpse, you managed to capture and cage the animal. Caging the creature puts it under the control of its captor, creating a very different kind of power dynamic. The animal is now more pliant and open to manipulation according to the wishes of its captor. Now the animal will go wherever the captor wishes it to go. It will eat whenever the captor chooses to feed it. This state of capture also serves to "freeze" the animal in time and space. One is able to remove the animal from its "natural" habitat and place it into other environmental, social, and cultural contexts according to the desires of the captor, perhaps on display for others in a zoo. At the zoo the fox is "consumed" by visiting families and tourists, the paying customers. At the zoo the identity of the fox undergoes a semiotic shift as the animal moves from "token" to "type." On display, the animal ceases to have a unique identity within the local floral and fauna and becomes an "example" of a fox: *Vulpes velox*, the swift fox, an animal native to southern Manitoba's mixed-grass prairies; for zoo patrons this is an "example" of the animal that one might typically find in its "natural" habitat. Taken out of time and space, a particular fox becomes an example of "A Fox" in the same way that a particular Zuni cradleboard with its own social life and family history might become an example of "A Zuni Cradleboard," on display for onlookers in the National Museum of the American Indian.

Now imagine that you have just witnessed the drum group Dakota Travels bust out a newly composed Grass dance song, performed for the adult men's competition on Saturday night at the 2001 Shakopee Mdewakanton Sioux annual powwow in Prior Lake, Minnesota, on a warm August evening. A crowd gathers around the drum; the dancers are dancing hard, pulling out all of their best moves; and standing over the group you can feel the power and volume of the drumming pounding at your chest. An inspired performance. But this performance has also been "captured" by a recording engineer's microphone and "caged" as one of the tracks on a mass-produced, commercially available CD. The track now has the potential to become a good example of "a Grass dance song," used by a teenage Grass dancer to practice his steps and work out new moves in his basement during the winter, or by a college professor who plays the track for his class of undergraduate students in order to teach them about some of the general style features of Northern powwow songs. The track might be used by an Aboriginal music-label employee who needs one more recording of a Grass dance performance to complete the latest compilation of Grass dance songs for release in the spring, the start of a new powwow season, or as background music for the "Dakota, Sioux" display at the National Museum of the American Indian. Perhaps in forty years it might be discovered by a Dakota university student attending the University of Minnesota, who finds the song on a Grass dance compilation CD at her university library and recognizes it as "her grandfather's song."

Clearly, we are dealing with a very different "animal" than the one we saw and heard fleetingly at the Shakopee powwow on that warm August evening. Powwow recordings are unique cultural texts with unique "social lives" (Appadurai 1986). The social and cultural value of these texts continues to be worked out in sometimes very different ways and using very different strategies and cultural interpretations than other instances of powwow performances (e.g., "live" at a powwow). This final chapter is dedicated to the investigation of some of these linkages and to understanding the relationship between powwow singing performances that are "live" and "mediated." I have structured this book in two large sections: the first describes practices of the powwow grounds; the second, the practices of the studio. I constructed the work this way because I wanted to explore the production and consumption of powwow recordings as a kind of closed loop, each context feeding into and becoming increasingly dependent upon the other.

The problem with such an organization is that it perhaps artificially separates these two worlds; it is not necessarily an accurate representation of how powwow singers experience performing, recording, and the general business of singing. It may also encourage an understanding of powwow recording practices as rigidly divided along racial lines: white record companies and Native musicians. While both industry personnel and powwow musicians may actively forge and strategically deploy this discourse in pursuit of various economic and cultural goals, the reality of the relationship is far more complex. Asking questions about the social life of recordings necessarily involves not only an analysis of the circulation and symbolic meanings embodied in recordings as cultural products, but an understanding of the similarities and differences between recordings and powwow grounds performances. More fundamentally, this answers the central question that, in a way, has motivated this entire study: "Why record?" Understanding the symbolic status of recordings as unique cultural texts is crucial for tracing the links between powwow recordings, competition performances, and indigenous modernity.

Why Record?

When I first began this research, I routinely asked musicians why they wanted to record. This question was inspired by my own initial understanding of powwows as, essentially, community-building endeavors; why, I wondered, would one want to introduce commodity exchange and the capitalist practices of the music industry into what was and continues to be a vibrant and healthy community musical event? Certain themes surfaced regularly in formal interviews and informal conversations with singers, most of which revolved around the social and economic requirements of participation in competition powwows.

Money

Making money is a big part of it. Once we get, you know, a little royalties and then we get free tapes and stuff and we sell them and it gives us extra funding. Cuz singing, you don't sing to get rich, you know. You know, we're one of the best paid drums around and we're only making like five thousand a powwow. Split between, you know, twelve, fifteen guys.
—JOHN MORRIS interview (October 1999)

The requirements of travel, including time and money, are fundamental to participation in present-day competition powwows. Some of the most successful groups travel all summer long, singing every weekend, which prohibits singers from maintaining full-time employment during the summer months. Singers must not only earn enough money to fund constant travel but, in many cases, enough to support families. Because of this, recordings are highly valued as one more source of income. Money earned from royalties on sales are modest; however, the free tapes and CDs given to groups (as a signing bonus) provide singers with a much-needed opportunity to increase their earnings at a powwow. Between 1999 and 2001, Arbor Records routinely supplied anywhere from 200 CDs or tapes for a standard contract to 1,000 for their top-selling groups. Singers selling these CDs at powwows (at $15 to $20 a CD) stood to make a considerable amount of money from the personal sales and promotion of their recordings. Thus the financial requirements of participation in competition powwows have made the activity of recording almost a necessity.

Reputation and Prestige

> GD: I think what makes a good drum group is the ability to make people dance. How—I know when I first started [my own drum group], when I left Whitefish Bay, that was the year they won first at all the major powwows. They won at Albuquerque, and, you know, all over. And

that summer, that's when I, you know, I went my own way. And when I went my own way that fall, I knew it was important for me to release a tape right away, because it promotes the drum. But not only that, if people know you out in the powwow world, powwow country, they're gonna know who you are right away and . . . and releasing tapes is just one way.

CS: So it just helps to get your name around.

GD: Yeah, releasing tapes makes your name get around, plus your reputation. That's what makes a good drum group. If you have a good reputation and you release tapes and they sound relatively good. And most importantly when they see you at a powwow and how you conduct yourself, your singers, other singers, is what makes a drum group successful.

CS: So you think you've got to have recordings to be successful?

GD: Oh yeah, definitely. Especially in the contemporary world, contemporary [competition] powwows. That stuff doesn't matter at traditional powwows. They [traditional powwow committees and dancers] don't care who you are. But if you want to get a name out in the contemporary world like Schemitzun or Albuquerque . . . [you need recordings].

CS: Why did you have to make a tape right away [as soon as you formed your drum]?

GD: I felt at the time it was important to have people hear us—what we sing and what songs, what kind of style that I have as a composer. And kind of make them [powwow people] believe that I was the one composing those other songs over there [in my previous group, Whitefish Bay] and to kind of compare and contrast with that style.

—GABE DESROSIERS interview (January 2002)

A drum group's desire to forge a reputation on the competition powwow circuit is another common response to the question: why record? The reputation of a drum group can lead to more frequent and higher-paying invitations as a host or invited drum at a powwow. Recordings are also symbolic of the dedication and success of a drum group within the competition powwow circuit. For Gabe, making recordings was particularly important for staking out stylistic territory and marking the unique sound of his new drum group (the Northern Wind Singers) as distinguishable from his previous drum.

Preservation of Culture and History

For an individual singer, I've had those [Jingle Dress] songs for years. I've been singing ever since I was nine, maybe even earlier. There was a need as an individual to try and preserve the culture that way. Cuz I feel like if nobody does it now, who is going to do it when the years go by. At least there will be a part of me there that people will say, "Gabe composed these songs in the old style and it's good that we see that." And it's good that we release this tape [*Ikwe Nagamonan* (AR-11282)] in that way to try and preserve and maintain the culture of the dance.
—GABE DESROSIERS interview (May 2000)

Many powwow groups see their songs and their role as singers and song-makers within a larger historical context. Songs become understood as cultural items to be treasured, memorialized, and recognized as existing within the flow of history. As songs become recorded, they move from being thought of as items of an individual or family history to items of cultural patrimony—invaluable artifacts of tribal and intertribal cultural history. In this way powwow music moves from the realm of direct participation and performance to the realm of representation and commoditization; from a "participatory" activity to a "presentational" one (Turino 2008).

The concerns and motivations that compelled powwow singers to record were reminders of the essential link between the competition powwow grounds and the recording studio. However, as my research continued, I realized that the question I really wanted answered was not "Why record?" but why powwow singers were recording *in the way* that they were—that is, why some practices were valued over others and why powwow recordings *sound* the way they do. These questions were intimately connected to *how* a recording is produced and evaluated.

Powwow Singing "Live" and "Mediated"

Powwow recording practices and aesthetics are linked in multiple and complex ways to the powwow grounds. Having examined various musical practices and discourses in the recording studio and at competition powwows throughout this book, we can now attempt to draw some general conclusions about powwow musical aesthetics "live" and "mediated" (Keil 1984). As drum groups move from the reservation to the studio, from community participation to sound booth isolation, and from powwow committees and dancers to engineers and record salesmen, this new set of performance contexts carries with it a specific set of social relationships and aesthetic negotiations. The emergence of the powwow recording industry and the rise of "recording culture" have created new social and economic conditions, which in turn have generated novel and distinct ways of performing and evaluating powwow songs. The aesthetic concerns of powwow singers are significantly different when addressing and evaluating recorded powwow performances as opposed to live powwow performances. What is interesting to note is that this is an aesthetic discourse that is specific to *commercial* recordings only. As I have already detailed in other chapters, audio (and, increasingly, video) recording is ubiquitous on the powwow grounds. Since the widespread commercial availability of portable, hand-held tape and digital recorders, singers and dancers have crowded around drum groups as they perform. Powwow singers make dozens of these kinds of recordings every summer. But the rules governing the value and evaluation of these kinds of recordings are quite different from those that govern commercial releases: for powwow singers, dancers, and fans, the social life of commercial recordings is imbued with a unique symbolic status.

The Importance of New Songs and Originality of Style

It is generally agreed among powwow singers that commercial powwow recordings must have all new material in order for them to be popular and accepted. There are a number of reasons for this. Foremost is the expectation of the dancers.

> CS: Did you know what songs you were gonna record when you [went into the studio to record *No Limit* (AR-11012)]?
>
> *John Morris* (singer for Eyabay): We usually just sing the new ones that we're gonna come out with during the year, you know. And then, see, everybody kinda gets used to them on tape and then by the time they hear us sing them they already got favorites and what not. (John Morris interview, October 1999)

It is a common practice for most dedicated competitive powwow dancers (i.e., those who compete at competition powwows for large cash prizes) to practice dancing to powwow recordings during the winter months when there are fewer powwows to attend. It is also important for these dancers to be familiar with the new songs of a group, because during dance competitions, points are deducted for "overstepping" (continuing to dance after the song has ended) or "understepping" (stopping one's dance steps before the song has ended). Part of a dancer's prowess is demonstrated in understanding the form of a powwow song. Dancing well to a song means choreographing one's dance moves to match the formal structure of a song and linking certain movements with important structural moments (e.g., knowing when the honor beats occur and how many honor beats there will be). Dancers who have a familiarity with a drum group's repertoire will thus have a greater competitive advantage.

A second reason for the value placed on new songs is purely economic. Both the drum group and the record company are invested in creating a recording that will be commercially successful. Dancers, singers, and other powwow people who make up the majority of the target sales audience for recordings have a limited amount of money to spend on new CDs. I have often seen dancers and other collectors of powwow music carefully scan track lists of compilation CDs to see what songs they already own, being very reticent to spend money on a CD that contains songs they already possess. In this way, the powwow recording industry functions in a similar way to the mainstream music industry. As a form of popular culture, there is a value placed on "newness." Certain songs and certain drum groups go in and out of fashion every year. Drum groups that do not consistently come up with new material quickly lose their appeal with other singers and dancers. The emphasis placed on new repertoire is often framed within the discourse of "continuing the tradition": the creation of new songs that are consistent with accepted (i.e., traditional) styles of powwow singing and powwow song genres.

Originality of style is also linked to the desire for the originality of songs. On the powwow trail, drum groups are appreciated for having their own unique style of singing. This originality is valued even more by drum groups who consider recording. Drum groups who are not considered to have a unique style will generally not make a commercial recording.

Song Ownership

When we record we just record our own songs that I compose. That's the only right thing to do.
—GABE DESROSIERS interview (November 1999)

Linked to issues of originality are concerns about song ownership, an important and highly contested issue for drum groups who make recordings. Native musicians (and nonmusicians) will often have songs that they claim belong to their family; they are some of the most treasured songs in their repertoire. Powwow singers also compose their own songs, which are also considered to "belong" to them. One may choose, however, to share one's songs with others; more secular, public-oriented songs, such as powwow songs, are usually shared quite freely. But if singers and drum groups wish to sing songs that do not belong to them, they are typically expected to ask permission from the song's original owner. Complicating this protocol, however, is the ubiquitous practice of taping and bootlegging on the powwow trail. At large competition powwows like Heartbeat of Nations in Winnipeg, or the Hinckley powwow in Minnesota, the crowd of people recording a performance is usually four or five persons deep. Many of the tapers are other singers and dancers. Singers will learn other people's songs from these recordings, and do not explicitly ask for permission when doing so. This is not considered "stealing" the song but is thought to "honor" the songmaker:

CS: What about if you're at a powwow and you've got people crowding around the drum group with their hand-held recorders and you're singing somebody else's song, is that OK by you?

GD: That's OK by me. Usually if somebody likes our song like that, it kind of gives us a little boost too, you know. People really enjoy our songs and that's the whole purpose why we sing. And why I sing really. And usually it's a common—how should I say that—it's common with Indians that if they're gonna sing your song, usually they'll come up and give you tobacco and ask you in a good way; and tell you that "I really like that song and I offer this to you," and get your permission to sing it. Or a lot of times they come up with tape recorders and say, "Can you put a song in there for me? And is it OK for us to sing it?" And usually that doesn't bother me at all. The only thing that would bother me with that is if they just went ahead and recorded us and went to another powwow and changed the song totally [laughs] and claimed it. That would bother me then. But generally it doesn't. (Gabe Desrosiers interview, October 1999)

Other scholars (Hoefnagels 2002; Vander 1987) have suggested that powwow musicians from areas more peripheral to the central Plains have used noncommercial recordings, (specifically cassette recordings) in order to learn new repertoires and bring new songs to their home communities.[1] Thus cassette recordings have for some time been employed to disseminate musical styles and genres. The advent of the widespread availability of commercial recordings has amplified this practice exponentially. Commercial recordings further compromise "traditional" ideas and protocols of song ownership as drum groups relinquish control and distribution of their songs. Replacing these ideas of informal, face-to-face arrangements and interactions is a concern with copyright, as any commercial use of the song by the record company must be monitored. In these cases, use is exchanged for money.

Naming of Songs

In the early years of powwow recording, CDs and tapes were filled with song names that reflected a song's function at a powwow: "intertribal," "Jingle Dress song," "Contest song," "Honor song," and so on. The renaming of powwow songs is a practice that has only recently begun to emerge. Informally scanning hundreds of cassettes and CDs, I have found that this practice began to appear in the mid-1990s. While Browner (2000, 215) has suggested that urban-based drums are more likely to give names to their songs than "rural" (i.e., reservation-based) drums, I have not consistently found this to be the case. Rather, age is the most salient factor in the practice of song naming. While older groups, like the Mandaree Singers or Whitefish Bay Singers, continue to simply name songs by their traditional use or function at a powwow, younger groups will almost always name their songs. For instance, when recording two CDs with the group Red Tail, whose members range in age from eighteen to twenty-six, the group spent a good deal of time coming up with names for their songs, often cracking each other up with countless joke names before finally coming up with ones that they would keep. Song titles can be generated from a wide variety of sources. They can be a joking play on words ("KFC" is the name of a Chicken dance song on Northern Wind's *21st Century* CD [AR-11022]) or refer to a structural component of the song ("Double Clutch" from Red Tail's *Volume One* [AR-11262] is a reference to the lead phrase of the song, which is split between two different lead singers, a rather unique compositional and performance technique for a powwow song).

The use of slang, often borrowed from hip-hop culture, is another common feature in song naming, and the drum groups Eyabay (a reservation-based group from Red Lake, Minnesota) and The Boyz (an urban-based group from Minneapolis-St. Paul), both of whom are extremely popular groups, use slang names regularly on their CDs: for example, "Thugs-N-Harmony" from Eyabay's CD *Thugs-N-Harmony* (SSCD-4332), "Thuggin N' Snugglin" (a Round dance song, the name being a play on the association between Round dances and courtship) from the Arbor Records compilation *Champion Round Dance Songs* (AR-11082), and "Wolf-Pac" and "Boogie Dayz" from The Boyz's CD *Worldwide* (NRC-090). I believe that Eyabay was one of the first groups to consistently give names to their recorded songs. The ubiquity of the practice now may be due in no small part to the staggering popularity of the group in the 1990s. Not only has Eyabay's style of singing become widely popular and widely emulated, but the group itself has also become a model of a successful and trendsetting powwow group.

Naming can also be more simply a matter of crediting a composer, or honoring a person by including their name in a song's title. Song names can also reflect particular places or experiences of singers. Names also sometimes are a product of the lyrics of word songs or simply a phrase of the lyrics translated into English (or sometimes left in the original Native language). Naming songs is generally a product of the process of recording. At a powwow I have never heard a song referred to by the name given to it on a recording. Instead, songs are identified by the lead melody. When song leaders call out a song to be sung, they do so by singing the lead of the song or by other indexical markers such as, "Let's sing that new one that Mike just made," or "Let's do that Blackstone song." Thus the practice of naming has yet to filter back to the powwow grounds to become part of the regular practice of singing during powwow events. The practice of naming recorded songs speaks to a song's ontological change in status from something that exists only in specific manifestations—unique moments of performance—to something that exists as a commodity. As a commodity, a recorded song's use and use value are different from a song as it exists during a performance at a powwow.[2]

Technical Perfection
Technical considerations play a much larger part in the evaluation of studio performances than they do on the powwow grounds. Evaluations concerning the level of technical perfection in the performance (i.e., the number of "mistakes") are common among the drum groups with whom I have recorded or spoken. Drum groups who record in the studio gener-

ally sing one or two songs at a time and then stop to go into the control room to listen to playbacks of the recordings. Mistake-free performances are left alone while those that contain even minor flaws are performed and recorded again. This differs considerably from performance evaluations at powwows, where singers' commitment to the dancers and the community may involve performing under special, often less than ideal, circumstances.

Peter Manuel has similarly noted that one possible outcome of transforming local "folk" musics into mass media forms is a standardization of performance practice, generated through a consistent preference for "talented, professional-quality performers." Record labels typically look for those who can perform "'ideal' renditions [of particular folk genres] rather than an 'authentic' one" (1993, 162). While there is no question that the powwow recording industry prioritizes "professional" and polished performances, the degree to which we can speak of these performances as "inauthentic" is less clear. Many singers I spoke with readily characterized the vocal performances of groups like Eyabay or Bear Creek as "*real* powwow singing," meaning that they thought it was powwow singing the way it was "meant to be performed." Certainly there are many traditional drums that perform almost entirely at traditional powwows and that do not approach the level of professionalism of these successful competition groups. However, labeling competition groups, who regularly make recordings, as somehow less "authentic" than the traditional drums, who rarely record, would be highly misleading, and I suspect that very few singers or dancers would ever make such a statement.

The coexistence of traditional and contemporary powwows in the twenty-first century speaks to a different kind of musico-aesthetic arrangement. Native Americans have carved out separate and unique aesthetic spaces for different kinds of musical and social practice. While some elders may attach similar judgments about the variable authenticity and inauthenticity of competition and traditional powwow musical practices, a great many powwow participants understand them as simply addressing different audiences and fulfilling different social needs. This holds true for the powwow recording industry as well, although the preference for polished, "professional sounding" drum groups on the part of record labels is also a preference shared by competition powwow circuit participants. Indeed, the entire notion of competition is built on the valuation of powwow drums as professional entities capable of performing at a consistently high and polished level. It is worth mentioning again that this is not the case at traditional powwows where all drums are equally valued and welcome to sing. Some drums may be preferred or enjoyed more than others by the dancers but the emphasis on open participation overrides any other aesthetic preferences.

Related to concerns of technical perfection in performance are evaluations of recording fidelity. These evaluations revolve around the audibility of the lead vocals, the balance between the lead and the seconds, the balance between the singers, and the overall sound quality of the recording of the drum. Fidelity is an important sonic marker of commercial recordings and one of the central ways in which professional recordings are distinguished from private, bootleg recordings. Riding home from a powwow in Saskatchewan with four other members of the Spirit Sands Singers, we sang or listened to powwow tapes throughout the nine-hour drive. Burt threw in a commercially produced tape that he had bought at the powwow. The hiss of the tape was loud and obtrusive; the drum sounded muffled and boomy. When the lead came in it was barely audible. Burt listened for about two push-ups of the first song before slamming the eject button and throwing the tape on the car floor in disgust: "That was a fucking waste of money!"

Sound Effects

During my tenure as a recording engineer, many groups who made recordings requested that particular sound effects be added during post-production. Similar to the addition of digital effects added to vocals, the addition of sound effects was considered an acceptable form of technological intervention because it did not disturb the practice of single-take "live" performances, either in the studio or during a remote recording session.[3] Sound effects are generally inserted directly before or after a song: environmental sounds such as thunder claps (Young Grey Horse, TP-*Creepin'* [AR-11302]), sounds of loons (Lake of the Woods, *Honouring Our Elders*) or brief, often humorous conversational interludes. Related to these studio manipulations are unusual renderings or arrangements that would not typically be heard at a powwow. For example, the opening song of *Northern Wind 10*, produced by Brandon Friesen and Gabe Desrosiers at Sunshine Records in 1997 (SSCT-4319), featured a Women's Traditional Round dance song (side A, track 5) which opens with a duet between Gabe and Traditional flute player Brian Akipadryan. Gabe opens the song singing through a push-up with only rattle accompaniment.[4] The flute then enters and doubles the melody heterophonically, before the solo flute plays a push-up. After this introduction the drum enters and the song is sung in typical fashion (leads and seconds accompanied by the big drum). These kinds of studio-produced performances exist only in recorded form, and such arrangements would never be heard during a powwow (neither competition nor traditional). These kinds of technologically inventive productions presently mark the outer boundary of accepted practices of recorded powwow performances.

....

Emerging from this discussion is a complex set of relationships between values generated and fostered through participation within the competition powwow circuit, and those generated in recording practices. Many of the same principles that guide the aesthetic practices of competition powwows are reproduced in the practice of powwow recording. The requirement for clean, mistake-free performances, new and original songs, and the high value placed on individual style, are all aesthetic preferences carried over from competition powwows. However, in the process of recording, new kinds of aesthetic choices are made and new preferences developed.

Put very coarsely, three different sets of aesthetic dispositions currently exist between the nexus of the competition powwow grounds and the recording studio. The first is the aesthetics of the powwow grounds, rooted in a drum group's commitment to the dancers and to the community. Second is the aesthetics of the studio, whereby singers consider recordings to be aesthetic objects in their own right, and where the performances are not tied to a particular place or time. These CDs often feature audible and noticeable studio manipulations, including sound effects before and after songs that would not typically be heard at a powwow, or in rare instances, digital audio effects added to a song. In these recordings, singers are concerned with the fidelity of the recording and the technical perfection of the performance, elements of performance that can most readily be controlled in a recording studio. The third mode of evaluation, the one that is by far the most widespread, is the "aesthetics of liveness," functioning as a middle ground between the powwow grounds and the studio and used by drum groups who still insist on live recording and refuse to enter a studio to perform powwow songs. These singers want their recordings to be "audio snapshots" of their performances at a pow-wow.

I see these emerging aesthetics as the direct result of the development of the powwow recording industry. This industry presents an interesting case in the kinds of aesthetic transformations that are possible when an essentially oral/aural musical tradition interacts with the technology and economy of a mass media industry. These shifts in aesthetic preferences are a reflection of the ongoing attempts of powwow singers to negotiate the new technologies and performance processes of recording with traditional values and responsibilities of singing. The aesthetic of liveness exists at the intersection of technology and "tradition," a "middle ground" (White 1991) between the powwow grounds and the recording studio.[5]

The idea of a "middle ground" not only characterizes the kinds of aesthetic accommodation engendered by the activity of recording, but also accurately describes the historical conjuncture of the powwow recording industry at the turn of the century. As I have tried to portray in part II of the book, Native and non-Native participants in the powwow recording industry are currently meeting and interacting on a middle ground. Musical (aesthetic), economic, and social arrangements are forged at Arbor through a series of mutual accommodations and misunderstandings, which generate new practices and ideologies surrounding the business of powwow singing. Interactions between Native musicians and the powwow record industry are guided by discourses of Nativeness and non-Nativeness and the relationship between "liveness" and authenticity. The ways in which the production of powwow music interacts with ideas of authenticity/mediation and culture/tradition may be represented in the following table.[6]

Live	Mediated
powwow grounds	studio
Native culture	white culture
tradition	modernity
authentic	inauthentic

Certain recordings, certain methodologies for recordings, and certain ideologies about recordings can be graphed along this continuum, with different CDs appearing at various points between these two idealized (and in some ways purely theoretical) poles. Through sonic indexical and iconic relationships to the powwow grounds, mediated forms of powwow music become powerful signs of modern indigenous identity, and mediate between the discourses of modernity and tradition. Powwow recordings are a sonic mediation articulating powwow songs to the discourses of authenticity, tradition, and culture. The power and importance of powwow recordings and the powwow recording industry lies in the very fact that these recordings function as a middle ground between the authenticity of the powwow grounds and the "contemporary" postcolonial world in which both Native Americans and the Aboriginal recording industry operate. Musical and social values developed and disseminated through competition powwows merge with Aboriginal recording industry practices as the competition powwow and recording industry create a feedback loop of ideologies and discourses, naturalizing modern indigenous identity through iconic and indexical productions of (Native) self and (non-Native) other.

Powwow musicians, when contemplating the activity of studio recording, locate themselves and their affective affinities through explicit and implicit allegiance to the aesthetics of liveness, mediation, or both. Just as participation and affective investment in traditional and competition powwows is an expression of a drum group's commitment to local tribal values (in the case of traditional powwows) or intertribal or pan-tribal values (in the case of competition powwows), so too are singers' social and aesthetic values expressed in how and why a drum group makes a recording. The central importance of recordings lies in this medium's ability to synthesize a variety of aesthetic values and social positions. Powwow musicians express their value of and commitment to ideas about "tradition," "authenticity," and "culture" in creating recordings which fall somewhere along the continuum from live to mediated musical performances. When powwow musicians decide to make a recording, they do so by grappling with these very discourses. In choosing *how* they make recordings, they are weighing in on the liveness-authenticity debate, stating a particular political allegiance through their affective allegiance to the ideology of liveness and to acceptable levels of mediation. Increasing levels of *recognized and identified* electronic mediations that result from the recording process are understood to represent increasing movement *away* from tradition, or at least a radical "reinterpretation" of tradition. In the same way that competition powwows allow singers and dancers to celebrate tradition and innovation at the same time, so too does the discourse of liveness provide a middle ground for powwow singers to create recordings that take advantage of contemporary recording technology and the machinations of the music industry, while linking their music and themselves to the cultural authenticity of the powwow grounds.

The aesthetic links between competition powwows and the recording industry are not surprising. Competition powwows have helped to develop a standardized set of aesthetic criteria by which powwow music is judged as "good" or "bad." These aesthetic judgments are intimately connected to (and are a product of) cultural values as they are negotiated and generated on the powwow trail. The highly intertribal nature of competition powwows has created a context within which intertribal values and ideologies—values that all participants can feel equally attached to—are developed and disseminated. Successful competition singing groups come to record labels and recording studios expressing the aesthetic values of the competition powwow grounds. Powwow singers' engagement with the technology, politics, and culture of the recording studio reflects this investment in the culture of competition powwows.

Aesthetic allegiance to the stylistic norms and values of competition are the foundation upon which "affective alliances" (Grossberg 1992, 86) or "communities of sentiment" (Appadurai 1996) are constructed and structured. Allegiance to a particular aesthetic ideology may be articulated through a particular set of social values and ethics; in turn, these articulated ethical and aesthetic ideologies may then serve as the articulating principle for larger projects involving the politics of indigenous identity. As Grossberg suggests, "It is the affective investment . . . that explains the power of the articulation which bonds representations and realities . . . which enables ideological relations to be internalized and, consequently, naturalized" (1992, 83). Modern indigenous identity, a complex hybrid of the discourses of modernity and tradition, is made to feel "real" and "true" in the hearts and minds of powwow participants through this kind of affective investment. It may seem somewhat obvious to ethnomusicologists that music may function politically, given that there are a host of ethnographies and histories that all describe the link between politics (either identity politics or protest) and music. What is less well documented is the "politics of pleasure." For it is the pleasure engendered through musical performances and the experiences of listening that is the true site of political significance. Music only has political potential in its ability to produce pleasurable responses and pleasurable experiences for listeners, performers, and other participants. Thus, to speak of the political functioning of music is not to deny its aesthetic value but rather to place aesthetics and pleasure at the center of the discussion.

Powwow recordings are the concrete, material effects of these aesthetic allegiances and affective alliances. The powwow recording industry is predicated upon the ability of powwow musicians, powwow recording engineers, and record producers to "imagine" a particular audience for their commercial products. This imagined audience is wide and varied, including many different tribal groups and even non-Natives (although not always). The very idea that anyone would want to buy the recording suggests that musicians imagine an intertribal group of individuals who are interested in powwow music for similar reasons. The genre of music known as powwow music is by its very nature intertribal. When Gabe says, "Out there, in the contemporary [powwow] world, you need CDs," he is making an explicit assertion that there is indeed a supratribal "world" that is somehow "out there" that can be "reached," "contacted," "connected," and ultimately "articulated" through powwow recordings.

Indigenous Modernity and the Discourse of Tradition

At the 2005 conference for the Society for Ethnomusicology, the society's fiftieth anniversary, I presented a paper that discussed my work as a recording engineer and record producer for Arbor Records. A scholar in the audience who has published extensively on issues of music, technology, and mass mediation, asked a question about whether, and how, I thought that recordings and recording technology were implicated in "modernizing" powwow music. This scholar's comment has stuck with me for a number of reasons. Part of what was so striking about the comment is that a great many Native Americans also struggle with how to make sense of powwows and powwow recording practices, and a great many use the very same discourses of tradition and modernity in trying to describe and qualify the current social world of powwows. These discourses are reproduced across several cultural domains and in multiple contexts. The traditional and the contemporary are marked on a fundamental level in the designation of traditional and competition powwows. Within competition powwows, singing styles are categorized as either Traditional or Contemporary and are evaluated as such in singing contests. With ever-increasing frequency, dance styles are being similarly marked as either Traditional or Contemporary, and it is now common to find competition categories for "old style" (or "Traditional style") and "Contemporary style" Grass dancing, Jingle Dress dancing, and Traditional dancing. As these styles of song and dance become stylistically elaborated by new generations of powwow performers, new discourses of authenticity are being developed to describe and mediate the aesthetic choices of performers. Record companies are following suit in their industrial genre classification of Traditional and Contemporary musics, developed as a marketing tool to try to target particular recordings to particular market demographics. As a marketing tool, it is effective precisely because it is also a categorization that resonates, and is thus accepted, by both Native and non-Native consumers.

The binary structure of the modernity/tradition discourse across these multiple domains of music making is difficult to ignore, and signals a deeply felt working out of the issue by Native Americans who participate in present-day powwow culture. Speaking more generally, I would go so far as to suggest that one of the central challenges for colonized indigenous peoples in North America is how to make sense of and mediate between the discourses of modernity and tradition, and I would cautiously suggest that this is a central issue for a great many Fourth World indigenous groups. One of the challenges for scholars and students of indigenous expressive practices is how to untangle our own discourses of modernity and tradition from those with whom we study. In other words, are these terms still of any use to us as scholars, either theoretically or descriptively?[7]

We can begin to answer this question by reminding ourselves that the discourses of tradition and modernity are not of indigenous origin but have been adopted by Native Americans in the twentieth and twenty-first centuries as a form of social and political mobilization and cultural consolidation. Used as a "resource," tradition, which is linked to authentic, precontact, non-European cultural practices and ideologies, is conceived of and used as a form of political resistance. For example, Emma LaRocque, a Canadian First Nations scholar, suggests that "traditions can and must be used in a contemporary context in such a way as to bring meaning to our young people, justice and equality to women, and safety and human rights protection to everyone" (1997, 91–92). The "tradition as resource" strategy calls for a reinterpretation of modernity within Fourth World contexts, using Native "tradition" as a social and political tool toward very "modern" ends. As musical ethnographers and analysts however, we have a responsibility to separate emic uses of the terms "traditional," "modern," and "contemporary" from our own analytic constructs. Both are problematic.

For indigenous groups, the adoption of these discourses potentially hinders both decolonization and indigenous peoples' negotiations with colonizing forces by categorically placing traditional (i.e., tribal or other colonized) cultures somehow outside of the modern world. This in turn is used as a basis for erroneous and harmful imaginings of indigenous peoples on the part of colonizers, and these have devastatingly real social and political effects (see Berkhofer 1978; Churchill 1992; Clifton 1994; Deloria 1998; Dyck 1991; Francis 1992). Despite the fact that tradition is most often constructed and specifically designed to serve particular cultural and ideological purposes in the modern world, one of the risks of using tradition as a defining marker of indigeneity is that when indigenous political groups organize and mobilize for "indigenous rights," often embracing modern telecommunications networks and existing global political channels, they are often accused of inauthenticity, of becoming too "assimilated" and thereby losing the power to claim these rights on the basis of cultural difference (Levi and Dean 2006).

David Samuels suggests a similar critique of the articulation of tradition and Native identity in suggesting the usefulness of the "pun" as a metaphor for the ambiguity involved in meaning making, cultural practice, and identity production. He offers: "I think the interesting question here is not, 'Why are San Carlos Apache identities fluid?' but rather, 'Why does the fluidity of Apache identity make people uncomfortable when the fluidity of other identities doesn't?' The ability to choose and refashion one's identity is a privilege accorded to some, but not all" (2004, 234). Samuels's question is an ethnographic restatement of Marshall Sahlins's wry observation regarding the "invention of tradition": "What else can one say about it, except some people have all the historical luck? When Europeans invent their traditions—with the Turks at the gates—it is a genuine cultural rebirth, the beginnings of a progressive future. When other people do it, it is a sign of cultural decadence, a factitious recuperation, which can only bring forth the simulacra of a dead past" (Sahlins 1994, 381). The "traditional Native" articulation is precisely what the Chippewa "crossblood" academic and novelist Gerald Vizenor writes against in coining the phrase "postindian survivance" (1994) as a way of grappling with the complexity of indigenous modernity and the legacies of domination that Native Americans continue to work through in their social lives, including, importantly, their artistic and musical practices. Being "postindian" involves leaving behind some of the dead ends offered to indigenous peoples by their would-be colonizers regarding the creative construction and envisioning of Native identity.

Without the (English) vocabulary to express culturally specific responses to changing global forces and relations, our native informants say things like, "Our tradition is a very modern tradition" (Waterman 1990) thus sending ethnographers scrambling for their notebooks. Our informants have just given us the language to express what the discourses of modernity and tradition make theoretically impossible: that the culturally meaningful force of tradition is created within, and is indeed wholly dependent upon, the structural conditions of modernity. While the "tradition as resource" strategy is politically expedient, my reservations about this strategy are that using these two mutually exclusive conceptual categories fails to capture the complexity of indigenous cultural and social circumstances. It boxes Native peoples and communities into social categories that time and again have betrayed them, particularly in tribal-state negotiations for land, Aboriginal rights, cultural autonomy, etc. It's a Faustian bargain.

For social theorists and analysts, the discourse of modernization is often linked to a narrative of "tradition and change": in the case of powwow music, recordings become just one more of the many current changes to the powwow music tradition. However, as I have argued consistently throughout this book, we cannot and should not understand powwow recordings as a kind of synecdoche of powwow musical style more generally. The relationships between powwow recordings and the larger cultural practice of powwow music performance is far more complex. Indeed, the whole point of studying the Aboriginal recording industry is because it is unique and different from other instances of powwow performance. Instead of thinking about powwow recordings in terms of continuity and change in some imagined historical progression of powwow musical style and practice, I have tried to show how live and mediated instances of powwow music are related but unique fields of cultural performance (Turino 2008) and that powwow recordings are distinct cultural texts. The social and cultural value of these texts continues to be worked out in very different ways, and using very different strategies, than cultural interpretations of instances of other powwow performances (e.g., live at a powwow).

To state the obvious, powwow performances and CDs of powwow performances are just different things. Our habit as ethnographers is to assume that they are essentially linked because of how we think about recording. We may also be tempted to think of the two as linked because many powwow performers, powwow recording engineers, and record producers do as well. But these links, these articulations, are always culturally generated and socially enacted. Rather than just assuming they are linked, we must investigate *how* they are linked, trying to understand the processes *by which* they are linked (if they are at all—and there is no guarantee that in other cultural or social contexts such links are ever attempted, achieved, or maintained).

Recording Culture and Ethnomusicology

In working with Gabe Desrosiers, Mike Esquash, Brandon Friesen, and many other singers, engineers, and record producers, documenting how they wrestle with the aesthetic implications of recording technology and the problems and possibilities inherent in mass media commoditization regarding powwow music, I came to realize that ethnomusicologists should perhaps begin to follow their lead in our own academically inspired audible cultural texts, questioning our own commonsense ideas of record production and consumption. Within ethnomusicology, recording technology has often been characterized as central to the development of the field (Abraham and Hornbostel [1904] 1976; Blacking 1995; Kunst 1955; Nettl 1964; Shelemay 1991). Recordings provide us with fixed "texts" to be analyzed and understood; this is one solution to the many problems inherent in musical transcription. But what is the nature of such a text and what are the implications for its study? Under what social and cultural conditions are these recordings created and how are they then reinserted into social and political life? The "postmodern turn" in the social sciences, initiated in the 1980s, continues to produce critical debate and new experimental procedures regarding the representational practices of ethnography. Inspired by this body of literature, ethnomusicologists continue to grapple with the problematic implications of "writing culture"; however, the field has been far less engaged in critical debates surrounding the issue of "recording culture," specifically, our own commonsense, institutionally and theoretically conditioned ideas about the business of recording. During the course of my fieldwork and employment at Arbor

Records, I was forced to confront some of these ethnomusicological habits of mind, body, and technology.

At this point, I hardly think my experiences working to produce commercial recordings are unique to ethnomusicologists. More and more we are now engaged in the process of creating specifically *commercial* CDs, as opposed to the "scholarly ethnic recordings" (to borrow Kay Shelemay's [1991] term) of previous generations, recordings that sold in quantities of three-digit numbers and were of interest mainly to scholars and academic libraries. This increased participation in the music industry has developed, in part, as a result of the emergence of world music and world beat as viable commercial genres in the 1980s. It is also a product of a growing and increasingly sophisticated CD-buying public in the ethnic and cultural communities within which we work.

My work at Arbor Records brought to light some of the conflicts between the competing social roles of ethnomusicologist and record producer. Just what kinds of recordings was I making? And what made them so? Was I an ethnomusicologist moonlighting as a for-hire engineer, or vice versa? And was it even possible for me to escape the culturally and institutionally conditioned ideas about records and recording processes that years of ethnomusicological training had made common sense to me? My work at this label also brought me into contact with competing ideas about what commercial recordings *should* sound like, as the indigenous communities within which I worked had sometimes very specific aesthetic criteria for how powwow recordings should *sound*.

In March 2000 I hopped a train out to Lapawai, Idaho, to engineer a remote recording session for the Red Tail Singers (see chapter 6). Red Tail had arranged for this session to take place in the large video production studio of a nearby community college, a room filled with video cameras, props, lighting, and construction equipment. As this was the first commercial recording for the group, on both days of the two-day session this space was filled with excited and supportive family members, including many small children who were brothers, sisters, and cousins of the singers. These children, of course, had little concern for the standard procedures of remote recordings, which included silence in the recording area while a live take was being performed. As a result, the general playing, fidgeting, and banging noises of the children ruined a number of takes and made the day much longer than it might otherwise have been. Yet despite these constant interruptions, the children were not once asked to leave and were only gently and mildly reminded that they should try to be quiet while the group was singing.

I was playing the role of engineer that weekend, which made these sessions an exercise in frustration for me. Why were these children being allowed to ruin perfectly good takes? It was not that the group was unconcerned about the quality of the CD. On the contrary, they were an extremely dedicated and professional group that had high hopes of working their way up the ranks of the competition powwow circuit. It was only after returning to my motel room at the end of the first night that I began to process the day's events properly. As an ethnomusicologist I found these questions to be compelling, and as an ethnographer of powwow music the answer was clear. Of course you would never ask children to leave during a powwow singing performance. Powwow singers are role models for children to look up to. Participating in powwow practices helps to keep you on the "Red Road," a life of spiritual and physical well-being. Powwow performances are not something to be sequestered away in a sterile and controlled acoustic environment. They should be the *cause* of family gatherings and good times, not an inhibitor of these things. The larger lesson of the experience is one that Beverley Diamond (2002, 2005) has remarked upon numerous times in her writings on the practices of indigenous performers of popular music. Process matters. Culturally conditioned ideas about how and why music should be recorded are important areas of concern for ethnomusicologists.

My dual role as ethnomusicologist and recording engineer was further complicated when I was confronted with the recording aesthetics of indigenous musicians and musical groups. In learning about the aesthetics of liveness and the discourse of authenticity attached to such an aesthetic position, it occurred to me that this discourse is both very similar to and very different from ideas about recording held by many ethnomusicologists. Authenticity for ethnomusicologists is often expressed through a concern that recordings are indexically linked to their "real" contexts of performance. The recording should sound just the same as the live performance. Powwow musicians are also concerned with linking recorded performances to the powwow grounds, but some singers do not hesitate to suggest technological intervention to ensure that the recorded performance accurately reflects what a powwow song *should* sound like, including the many extraneous—and what many sound engineers would consider "nonmusical" or "extra-musical"—sounds of the powwow.

As an ethnomusicological documentarian and recording engineer, I had to confront the discrepancy between my own "similar but different" aesthetic preferences and those of powwow musicians, and this brought into relief certain ideological tendencies on my part. Powwow singers' insistence on a particular form of technological intervention (mediation for the purpose of sounding live) rubbed up against my own aesthetic: a recording engineer's preference for high-fidelity sound quality, and an ethnomusicologist's predilection for documentary realism. There is of course *no* recording technique that is completely transparent. No process can document what a performer or performance "really" sounds like, regardless of what definitions or discourses of authenticity one subscribes to. Whether I am an engineer making a recording or an ethnomusicologist writing an ethnography, I am a mediator of musical practice. As an engineer, I am in the position of making intellectual and aesthetic decisions about how recordings sound and how recordings *should* sound. Thus in making a recording one becomes a creator or co-creator and not simply a documentarian. Striving for high-fidelity documentary realism is a very particular and specific aesthetic choice, and only one among many others. In many recordings by ethnomusicologists, whether in our field recordings, our carefully packaged "scholarly ethnic recordings," or in our more commercial ventures, we perhaps often labor under similar discourses of "high fidelity," as do participants in the Aboriginal recording industry: the fetishization of liveness as an index of authenticity, an assurance that what we hear in the recording is what they (the "natives") really sounded like.

In evaluating recorded texts in *Ethnomusicology*, the journal of the Society for Ethnomusicology, much of the commentary found in reviews evaluates the accuracy of liner notes and the politics of representation: when commercial record companies have no academic "higher authority" to answer to, they may play fast and loose with the facts in order to package world music material in the most commercially attractive way. I have suggested that one of the central reasons for particular packaging strategies is the specific ways that record company producers and marketers "imagine markets" (chapter 4). In this light, criticizing record companies for not "getting it right" in their liner notes somehow misses the mark. Many record executives would no doubt argue that the degree to which they are "getting it right" is reflected in sales figures, because the degree to which they have accurately and successfully imagined and constructed their markets will be reflected in these economic indicators. In other words, what it means to "get it right" differs a great deal for ethnographers, academics, record industry personnel, and powwow singers.[8]

Despite this fact, many ethnomusicologists are quick to call for liner notes that should be held to the same rigorous academic standards as other ethnographic publications. Their concern is with the problematic texts that accompany the unproblematic recordings. And recordings themselves remain unproblematic until the common practice of high-fidelity documentary realism (and the accompanying discourse of liveness) is challenged. Two examples spring immediately to mind. In 1991 Steve Feld and Mickey Hart produced and released *Voices of the Rainforest* (RCD-10173), a recording that, through painstaking audio manipulation of field recordings in the studio, presented a hyper-real simulacrum of a Bosavi soundscape: twenty-four hours in the aural life of the Kaluli, magically condensed into a one-hour "piece." In 1995 the ethnomusicologist Louis Sarno and the producer Bernie Krause created a similar soundscape in an elaborate recording for Ellipsis Arts entitled *Bayaka: The Extraordinary Music of the Babenzélé Pygmies* (CD-3490), a work that blends a number of different musical genres and ceremonies together, interspersed with the overdubbed sounds of birds, frogs, insects, and other sonic markers of the central African rainforest.

These kinds of experimental commercial texts have met with mixed reviews in the academy. For example, Michelle Kisliuk, in a thorough and thoughtful review of Sarno's recording, nonetheless dismisses these audio manipulations as mere "theatricality" that needs to be "offset" by liner notes which discuss the "real context" of the musical recording (1997, 172). Similarly, Feld has been accused of deliberate misrepresentation in constructing a soundscape that systematically excludes sounds of airplanes, mission schools, tractors, Bible readings, and hymns, all of which are a common part of modern Bosavi life (Feld 1991, 1993). These kinds of audio texts stand out in the history of the production of ethnomusicological "scholarly ethnic recordings" precisely because they challenge the discourse of documentary realism so common to the genre: a discourse that links liveness to authenticity. Instead, these recordings are part studio performances and part audio texts, an audio analog of what ethnographers (musical and otherwise) have been performing on the page for a century: the manipulation of field data in order to construct a coherent narrative argument. As I have previously noted, having become quite comfortable performing with the written word, we continue to engage in a lively and open academic discussion about the nature and representational implications of *writing culture*. However we have not been nearly as attentive as we might be in grappling with the implications of *recording culture*. Ethnomusicology is a field that is becoming increasingly intertwined with recording technologies and mass mediation, both as topics *of* study and also as tools *for* study. Given this, I would suggest that we need to pay more critical attention to our own schizophonic (Feld 1995, 1996; Schafer 1977) endeavors.

There are several larger ethnomusicological lessons that I learned in my experiences as recording engineer and record producer. At every stage of the recording process, aesthetic choices are being made. These choices involve considerations about who the intended audience for the recording will be: Cultural insiders? The general public? Academics? As Antoine Hennion (1990) suggests, all recording engineers and record producers make decisions based upon an imagined consumer audience. And we imagine these different social groups according to commonsense ideas about who these people are and what they might like or are supposed to like in a recorded performance. These choices should also take into account the very sophisticated ideas of musicians and musical communities about what they want from recordings, how they expect the recording process to proceed, and specific aesthetic preferences about what recordings should and could sound like.

Finally, there may be certain opportunities afforded ethnomusicologists in making explicitly commercial CDs targeted either for a specific social group (as in the case of most powwow CDs) or the broader general public. In making commercial CDs we are freed somewhat from the discourse of documentary realism so common to the genre of "scholarly ethnic recording." It may encourage us to produce, or at least consider the idea of producing, more experimental kinds of recorded audio texts. This is not to suggest that we should abandon the practices of documentary realism, but simply to acknowledge that this is only one choice among many, one that is historically and culturally bound.[9] My work at Arbor Records revealed that we must always engage critically in recording as both a process and a text that produces knowledge, theory, and argument. In so doing we may understand "recording culture" as one of the many different ways in which we can engage in the practice of ethnomusicology.

CODA

Recording Culture in the Twenty-First Century

On the first weekend of July 2006 I attended the Sisseton Wahpeton Oyate Wacipi in Sisseton, South Dakota. I was back on the northern Plains for a summer to stay with friends and catch up on recent developments in the powwow recording industry. I was visiting with Gabe and Dianne Desrosiers and their family. They were all involved in the powwow that weekend. Dianne and the kids were all dancing, although, because it was their "home" powwow, none had registered in the dance competition. Local community members rarely compete at their own home powwows because of the controversy that would ensue if any of the local dancers placed in the competition. There would immediately be suspicion among the competitors that the powwow committee had rigged the judging to favor local dancers. Gabe was working as the head singing judge that weekend. The powwow committee was trying something new this year. In previous years they simply alternated each year between holding a traditional event and a competition powwow. This year the powwow was a combination of both. Dancers could either sign up for day pay (traditional) or sign up for the contests and dance for prize money. But if you signed up for the contest, you would not be eligible for day pay. The singing contest was run in a similar fashion. Drum groups could choose between singing for a share of the drum split *or* singing for the contest. Contest drums filled the perimeter on one side of the arena while the "traditional" drums lined the other side. The contest committees made sure that only competition drum groups sang for the dance competitions, to ensure that the dancers would get high-quality songs to dance to. The traditional drum groups handled all of the intertribals as well as the Junior and Tiny Tot contest categories. A lot of the "heavy hitter" Northern drum groups were competing: Mandaree, Bad Nation, Midnite Express, Lakota Tribe, Eyabay, Battle River,

Dakota Hotain, Young Kingbird, and Bear Creek. It was a big-money event with five prizes for the singing contest: $10,000, $6,000, $4,000, $2,000, and $1,500. The competition powwow circuit has continued to grow and flourish throughout the first decade of the twenty-first century. As more and more reservation casinos open up every year, the stakes continue to grow for singing and dancing competitions. When I first began attending competitions, a $10,000 first-place prize for a singing contest was an extraordinary sum of money. Now it has almost become a standard amount at any decent-sized competition powwow.

The Sisseton Wahpeton Oyate Wacipi was the start of about eighteen straight days of powwow participation for competition dancers and drum groups. First Sisseton, then a midweek powwow in Red Lake, Minnesota, followed by another the next weekend in Prairie Island, Minnesota. After that there was a powwow in Tama, Iowa, before everyone headed up to Sioux Valley in Manitoba for the third weekend in July, then over to Carry the Kettle in Saskatchewan for another midweek event. For competition singers and dancers who are serious—those who derive a significant part of their income from powwows—this was prime-time powwow season. I was skipping out on this circuit after Sisseton Wahpeton Oyate Wacipi and heading up to Winnipeg to hang out at Arbor Records and sing with the Spirit Sands Singers at their home powwow at Swan Lake, then travel with them to some smaller traditional powwows in the Lake of the Woods area. Mike Esquash had recently moved to Winnipeg, and Spirit Sands had a whole new crop of singers, mostly urban-dwelling Natives who were still learning to sing and learning about powwow culture.

Cruising the vendors' area at Sisseton Wahpeton, I came across a number of booths selling CDs. There were some Arbor products, a few releases from Sunshine and Canyon, and a number of CDs from a host of new labels: Wonksheek Records, run by a vendor who travels the Northern circuit; Drumgroups.com, an online record label and distribution company started by George Parker (former co-owner of the now defunct Turtle Island Music) and singers from Walking Buffalo, Blackstone, and Wildhorse; Drumhop Productions, a label started earlier that year by a veteran Grass dancer and professional graphic artist named Rusty Gillette and Everett Moore, a long-time singer with the Minneapolis-based intertribal drum group The Boyz; and War Pony Records, another brand-new label owned and operated by none other than my good friend Mike Esquash. All of these new labels were being run by powwow participants, and all but one (Wonksheek) involved singers. I immediately began to wonder whether the powwow recording industry had become less of a "contact zone" and more of a media infrastructure that was owned and operated almost entirely by powwow people themselves?

A few days later, in Winnipeg, I found myself sitting and chatting with Brandon one evening on the back patio of a downtown bar. From our vantage point you could still see the lights on in the fourth-floor windows of a building across the alley: the new administrative offices and recording studio for Arbor Records. In 2005 Brandon sold Studio 11 and moved Arbor Records to a new downtown location, complete with an expanded recording facility. The new office is located on the top floor of an old administrative building in the Exchange District, a trendy warehouse district that is slowly being transformed by incoming art galleries, coffee houses, hipster bars, funky fusion restaurants, and a repertory cinema. The first two floors of the building are home to a gay and lesbian dance club named "Desire," while the third floor houses a competitor's recording studio. The fourth floor is 441 Studios, a suite of office spaces and audio production units. When you walk out of the elevator you are greeted by a secretary sitting at a desk at the front of a long hallway of offices. To the right is a lounge with a pool table, a few slouchy leather sofas, and a semi-finished kitchen area. As you walk down the hall, the first door on your left is a large room that serves as the Arbor Records warehouse. Next to that is the main office, although one of the desks in the room is shared with the manager for Race Day Promotions, a promotion company for local popular music acts. The next room down is the Pro Tools production suite that also houses a desk for Shawn Schibler, Arbor's new sales manager.[1] The workstation is usually manned by Phil Deschambeau, an engineer, producer, and song writer. Phil spends about 60 percent of his day working on Arbor projects, but he also works on his own recording projects with various local musicians. In the summer of 2006 Phil was still relatively new to Arbor and learning the ropes. At the end the hall were two more studio control rooms equipped with digital audio workstations, mixing boards, and various banks of outboard audio gear. These were the control rooms for Paul Scinocca and Brandon, the two original owners of Studio 11. Occupying most of the right-hand side of the hallway was the main sound studio, one of the largest in Winnipeg, complete with a grand piano and various amps and guitars. The sound studio was patched into all three control rooms. A small room next to the sound studio housed

Strongfront productions, a Native-owned production company that does a lot of local work in film and video post-production. The three businesses (Arbor, Strongfront, Race Day) and record producers (Paul, Brandon, Phil) all have their own client lists; each company is responsible for bringing in enough money to pay for the space it rents on the floor. They all chip in to pay the secretary's salary.

From its humble beginning in spring 1999, Arbor Records has grown into one of the largest producers and distributor of indigenous music in North America, approaching—and by some measures surpassing—the catalog and infrastructure of the two largest American-based Aboriginal labels, the traditional Native American music specialists Canyon Records and the fast-growing and generically eclectic Sound of America Records (SOAR). Sitting with Brandon on the patio, I expressed my amazement at Arbor's rapid six-year rise through the ranks of Native American music labels, especially considering the fact that on national and international levels, the recording industry has been going through an extended period of massive contraction. I asked Brandon what he thought the central challenge was in being successful within the Aboriginal recording industry and how it might be different from the mainstream music industry. He paused, furrowed his brow while taking a drag from his cigarette, and offered: "I don't know, Chris. Is there . . . ? I mean, I don't know if there is much *of* an Aboriginal recording industry. What do you mean by that? Can you define it better?" Shocked by his answer, I blurted out a jumbled question about what he thought the differences were between independent labels that catered specifically to the North American indigenous market and those labels that targeted the North American "mainstream." But his initial response gave me pause. How could he doubt the existence of the very industry that he had been a key player in creating? From my perspective, there has been a remarkably steady growth over the last twenty-five years in the media infrastructure that is supportive of North American indigenous music.

However, Brandon's answer reflected the hard-headed pragmatism of a record label executive in the "post-Napster" age. In the decade that has followed my first engagements with powwow music and Aboriginal record labels at the turn of the century, the North American music industry (and the global music industry more generally) has undergone a number of tectonic shifts. In a time of regular, annual losses in CD sales, record industry personnel across the spectrum—from the largest multinational "major" label to the smallest independent and DIY outfits—are scrambling for new business models and working to find new revenue streams to replace those destroyed or disrupted by the new technological and economic realities of the twenty-first century. The biggest game changer, of course, has been the proliferation of the MP3 file format, which is increasingly becoming the predominant way that music fans (Native and non-Native) purchase, collect, share, use, and experience music recordings. This format has, in turn, led to a decade of widespread online music "piracy" (the illegal sharing of copyrighted content through peer-to-peer network Web sites such as Napster, Grokster, Limewire, Piratebay, etc., and more recently bit-torrent sites), and to a gradual shift in the music industry toward online sales of MP3s through legal sites (most notably iTunes and Amazon.com). This shift in the preferences and behaviors of music consumers toward online piracy and purchasing led directly to the collapse of the CD-based retail market and the disappearance of most of the major CD megastores across North America, including Tower Records in the United States, and Virgin Records, Sam the Record Man, and HMV in Canada. Even bookstores like Borders and Barnes and Noble in the United States, and Chapters in Canada, which were once major and reliable outlets for music sales, have over the past decade steadily shrunk their music inventories, replaced in many cases by the growing DVD and Blu-ray markets. With the disappearance of these music retail stores, finding CDs of powwow music anywhere outside of a powwow was an increasingly difficult task. Finding powwow music online, however, has never been easier, and all of the major Aboriginal music labels have online purchasing strategies, with consumers able to download MP3s either directly from a label's Web site or from iTunes and Amazon.com.

The increasing amount of time, energy, and money spent online by the music-buying public has also been enhanced by the relatively recent emergence of Web 2.0 communications technologies (social networking sites, blog and vlog sites, YouTube, Vimeo, and other user-generated-content sites) which have created many more opportunities for powwow participants to share content with each other and interact in the digital domain. Several highly trafficked Web sites are dedicated specifically to powwows, the most important being Powwows.com, Pow Wow TV (www.tv.powwows.com), and Native American Tube (www.natube.magnify.net). Just about every powwow drum group who wants to be taken seriously on the competition circuit now has pages on MySpace and Facebook, and perhaps even a YouTube channel.

Brandon's comment, questioning the very *existence* of an Aboriginal recording industry, was driven by these massive millennial changes within the larger global music industry, and much of our conversation that evening (and many conversations since) revolved around the place of powwow music within this new business environment and industrial context:

CS: So do you think major labels are now more like . . . just kind of like major distributors? I mean you were saying earlier they don't have any A&R departments anymore so they're just cutting all these fifty/fifty deals with all these indies now.

BF: Well, that's the indies cutting those deals with artists. Then the majors are doing regular distribution deals with indies. And the way that works is, the indies are taking all the responsibility for publicity, all the marketing. . . . They're called P&D deals. Pressing and Distribution. So the independent label goes out and finds the artist, signs the artist, makes the record, pays for the marketing, hires a third party for publicity, and has a distribution deal with a major label and that major label will go, "OK, what do you need, you got our team at your disposal." And the indie says, "I need a street team in Chicago, because, you know, there's a lot of fans up there and radio, radio is supporting the band. Universal will go, "OK, you've got our street team. OK, do you want to do pricing and positioning?" "Yeah we want to do that." That means you get your CDs right in front of the door when people walk in. But you pay extra for that. And that means the independent pays for it. But the major will gladly lend you the money to do it. And lend you the manpower. But it's all being billed back to the indie. If you don't sell enough records and, you know, a bunch come back, you're left holding a bunch of product you can't get rid of and a big bill from your major. So it's—it's a tricky game.

CS: So all the majors really have is a whole bunch of capital at their disposal to front you money . . .

BF: Capital and infrastructure. Infrastructure is the key. They have a marketing and record retail guy that's in Chicago that's on salary for Universal Artists. "Well there's not enough Universal Artists coming through right now so let's get some independents on there, so that we can keep him employed. We can generate enough business to keep him employed." And that is kind of the big picture.

CS: So how do you think the Aboriginal record industry fits into this structure? Is that very different from the way any other indie label works? I mean, does it fit into the industry in any different way?

BF: Umm . . . there are two sides to that. Being an Aboriginal label marketing Aboriginal artists that are trying to *be* Aboriginal artists, the mainstream won't embrace it. Certain pockets of the mainstream will. The gift shop market will. Tourism, the whole tourism trade, will. But the major label infrastructure doesn't know what to do with it. And until you have videos on Much Music or MTV or VH1—

CS: Do you ever see powwow music ever getting any bigger or is it just going to be . . .

BF: It will always be what it is. Powwow will never get big. I mean it just can't. I mean there's . . . you know I laid some records on a company in the UK. And every year we put together a powwow record based on a dance theme. And they, you know, they sell like two or three thousand copies of it worldwide. And they have fantastic distribution. Another thing is, like, Somerset [Entertainment]. I'll license six records a year to them. Somerset is—like, when you walk into a drugstore and you see a listening post, or you walk into Costco or any airport. That's Somerset—they own all of those posts. Like, 95 percent of those. They're huge. I've been in Charles de Gaulle Airport in Paris and saw my records in Paris and saw them in Germany. Powwow records scare people. You know, unless you grew up in powwow. But to the average guy [in Europe] who's interested in Indian music from North America, he will listen to a powwow record and go, "Holy shit. This sounds ridiculous." And then he'll listen to a New Age flute with keyboard record and he'll go, "Ahhh, I want that. Cuz I can sip wine to that." And the numbers prove it. I mean, Mishi Donovan's record and Longhouse's [one of Arbor's latest New Age recording groups] records outsell powwow records 25 to 1 in those listening bars. And that's where the customer has a choice to decide on what he wants because he can listen to every song.

CS: And so you've tried to put the powwow stuff on those posts . . .

BF: . . . On the listening posts? Like, we put Bear Creek on there. And we sold like 700 copies of Bear Creek, 5,000 copies of Mishi Donovan. Through those listening posts. You know, and Bear Creek was the *best* one that we did. That and Eyabay. So [the market demographic that buys music from listening posts], they're cool with themed records, like these are Snake dance songs, these are Grass dance songs, these are War dance songs, or whatever. Some theme that they can relate to, that's what they want. Which just gets you right back to the gift shop market. That [thematic, anthologized CD of a particular powwow music/dance genre] *is* the gift shop market. But powwow groups? You can't sell them by saying, "Hey here's an artist. Here's, like, the best powwow group in the powwow world, the best in powwow country." And they'll say, "What does that mean to me in Germany?"

CS: So by "gift shop market" you mean . . .

BF: Umm, you know, you have mom and pop stores, you have little gas stations by reserves that want to buy your product and that are willing to pay you for that product, whereas a major label doesn't have that [they won't pay upfront for CDs]. But they—at the same time a major label has a massive network that's waiting for the next Britney Spears or the next whatever, right? And by marketing an Aboriginal artist *as* an Aboriginal artist cuts you out of that scene. So as a little indie—as a little indie Aboriginal label, we can stay alive by servicing the mom and pop stores and the little traditional stores that I don't think a lot of other labels service.

CS: Can you stay alive doing that? Can you make enough money just by marketing to . . .

BF: You can't get rich but you can keep your lights on. You can keep your bills paid. You can keep your salaries paid. Yeah, but you can't get rich at all. But at the same time it's steady, you know what I mean. Whereas a mainstream artist costs a lot of money to market and you're rolling the dice. Cuz if it doesn't work out and everybody's not doing their job, then you're screwed. You've just spent—it's easy to spend a hundred thousand dollars on an artist. Easy! *Really* easy! And to make back a hundred thousand dollars you've got to sell at least eighty thousand records. So, how do you sell eighty thousand records, you know? (Brandon Friesen interview, July 2006)

Powwow recordings, and in particular, powwow CDs (as opposed to MP3s or other formats) have been able to maintain a small but structurally secure place within this larger marketplace because of these niche markets: gift shops, mom and pop stores, and powwow vendors. For all of these markets, CDs are still the predominant medium for selling music. While it is true that most powwow people, aided by the file-sharing technologies of the Internet, now have much larger collections of powwow songs on their MP3 players, many still continue to buy CDs of their favorite drum groups, if only as a gesture of support.

When I asked Brandon about the recent emergence of all of these new powwow labels and what it meant for Arbor Records, he appeared only mildly concerned. He reasoned, "There are always new labels springing up, started by powwow people. They do well for a few years and then they drop out of sight." It was hard to argue this point. Curtis Assiniboine's label, Wacipi Records, folded years ago. Bob Peasley's Rez Cue Records folded only a few years after it started. Even Turtle Island Music, a relatively stable corporate entity in 1998–2000 during my first visits to the Canadian Plains, was no longer in business. Brandon chalked it up to marketing. "They start off promising drum groups the world and then when they can't deliver on their promises, they [the drum groups] all start to fall away."

Brandon's lack of concern for the emergence of these new powwow labels was also an expression of the new corporate and artistic direction for Arbor Records. Later that same evening, after Brandon and I had closed the bar, we walked back to the 441 Studios and hung out in Brandon's control room, where he started playing tracks from some of his recent work. While Arbor still released several new powwow CDs every year, the fastest growing part of its catalog was "Contemporary Native music." He had just finished a new Derek Miller CD, *Music Is My Medicine* (AR-11842), which contained a number of scorching blues rock numbers. He could barely contain his excitement as he cued up some rough mixes of Pura Fe's new recording. She was a founding member of the popular Contemporary Native vocal trio Ulali, and this was going to be her first solo CD since the group disbanded. All of the tracks had been recorded months ago in Toronto by Derek Miller, but he asked Brandon to mix because he wasn't comfortable enough with studio production to finish the CD. The CD was a hybrid of blues, R&B, and soul. Brandon marveled at Pura's vocal performances as he soloed the voice, punched up an EQ plug-in, and began messing around. "I've never worked with someone who can sing like this." Her pitch was bang-on without the use of a pitch corrector. Her blues-inflected phrasing rode perfectly and seamlessly over the instrumental backing tracks. Her voice crackled and growled with every note. In short, the performances were inspired. "I'm taking my time with this. This is a special recording. I've been working with the voice, trying to give it a signature sound. Too bad about the recording . . . it's not a great vocal mic."

Over the last several years Arbor had invested heavily in Contemporary Native music acts. Along with Derek Miller, its 2006 catalogue featured rock and country CDs from Chester Knight, Eagle and Hawk, Lucie Idlout, Wayne Lavalee, Ray St. Germain, and a new release from Mishi Donovan. It also included four Native hip-hop acts, Team Rezofficial, Slangblossom, Stryker, and War Party; some Métis fiddle releases by Ryan D'aoust and Sierra Noble; and a new a cappella vocal trio from Alberta called Asani. During that summer Arbor employees also spoke proudly and anxiously about the upcoming release of Susan Aglukark's *Blood Red Earth*, her debut release with the label. In a musical style reminiscent of the Canadian contemporary pop icon Anne Murray, Aglukark's songs are a blend of country, folk, and pop styles and often feature a mix of English and Inuktituk lyrics. Previously signed to EMI Music Canada, Aglukark was a proven, top-selling, mainstream Aboriginal artist. This kind of musical catalog and roster of musicians was a far cry from the original vision for Arbor Records.

CS: So did you have a mission statement when you started Arbor Records?
BF: Yes, I did. It obviously changed quite a bit [*laughs*]. Initially it was . . . ahh shoot. It was long and I can't tell it to you verbatim. It was structured around being a producer of top quality Aboriginal music in that . . . it was more geared towards traditional Aboriginal music. Powwows, powwow music and flute music and things like that. That original idea, what I wanted to do was I just wanted to create better masters, better recordings, better artwork and then market—and actually market them more in a mainstream fashion. That obviously changed when I realized that the mainstream will only take so much of it. . . . I had a misconception that the more product you stick out there the more you'll sell of it. That's not true at all. You know, you got to make sure you have customers in those places to buy them. And there's only so many customers for traditional recordings. There's, you know, the powwow people and the "novelists" [people looking for something new or novel] that are interested in it. But putting powwow records or flute records in HMV on Younge Street [in Toronto] or Tower Records

on Sunset Blvd. [in Los Angeles] is not going to work, because those customers are not going to buy them. So that's the only way it's changed. I mean, but it's metamorphosized into something bigger, I think. You know, from being around for so long and putting out good records and developing careers and artists—the company grew from that.

CS: So what would the mission statement look like now, if you were to re-draft it?

BF: What's gonna change now? Well, I can give you a little bit of a road-map. I'm going to turn Arbor into what Motown [Records] was. I'm going to package tours with artists. And we just got approved for a TV show. So we're working on a TV format, I want to improve on the Web format. Make it all-encompassing. And I just want to cre-ate more vehicles for my artists. And I want to start doing deals with my artists where they are more development deals and not just flat record contracts. And that includes management, you know, book-ing, everything else. And by doing that properly I need outposts. So, you know, the plan is to set up an office in L.A., and put an office in Toronto in the EMI building. And staff it with experienced people who have been doing it for years and years in the business. And England, too, we've got an opportunity to do that in London as well. But what will happen is what happened in Motown. You had all these Black artists in Motown that couldn't play a lot of venues that were used to having, you know, non-Black performers and non-Black audiences right. But eventually by Motown signing great artists who—you know, they just carved out their own niche industry, that out of every couple of artists that Motown would sign, one or two of them would become Stevie Wonder, or Smokey Robinson, the Supremes, you know. Mo-town signed a lot of artists. And one out of every ten popped. The same thing will happen with Arbor when you sign—you know, if I take a Derrick Miller and Keith Secola and put them on tour with a Stevie Salas and a Robbie Robertson, then they're playing in front of massive audiences. And then I do the next tour with them [Miller and Secola] headlining, and two new kids opening up. So that's the whole—what's being worked on right now. (Brandon Friesen interview, July 2006)

When I asked Brandon what precipitated this change in direction he gave several reasons, mostly having to do with the current economic conditions throughout the music industry. But his first response was telling. He said simply: "Politics." For Brandon, this was convenient shorthand that referred to the level of commitment and attention to the shifting social relationships of the powwow grounds that was required to work with powwow groups. In other words, being part of a record label dedicated solely to powwow music required one to submit to, and work within, the cultural logic of the powwow trail.

Perhaps the emergence of these new labels—Drumhop Productions, Drumgroups.com, and War Pony Records—was in part precipitated by Arbor's shift in musical focus and the demise of labels like Rez Cue, Turtle Island, and Wacipi; the new labels were filling a void in the market. But it might also signal a gradual shift in powwow "recording culture." All of these labels are very purposefully and deliberately presenting themselves as unique and distinct from other, more established powwow labels, like Arbor Records, Canyon Records and Sunshine Records, citing their close ties to the powwow social world. In doing so, these new labels are attempting to transcend racial discourses of whiteness and Nativeness and instead are trying to emphasize their *cultural* affinity to singers and drum groups. As part of the same larger powwow social world, the owners of these labels are able to establish and maintain social relationships with other singers and dancers and fans of powwow music. And they claim that it is their identity as powwow people that, to a certain degree, guarantees an honest and ethical relationship with drum groups. For example, during a formal interview with Mike Esquash for a Powwows.com podcast, he told me:

> I guess what happened was for us we just wanted to find a way to—I guess take care of powwow people. You know me and my wife had the idea to figure out the best way we can utilize the things we've learned over the years to take care of our own people. For me it was a personal thing because of my own singing group. I think there's a lot of good companies out there that take care of groups. And they do the best they can. But many times a lot of them, you know, they don't sit at a drum, they don't travel to powwows every weekend. It ain't part of their lifestyle. So they really don't get as far into understanding what groups are seeking when it comes to recordings, or when it comes to, you know, having a good, honest, truthful and fair deal given to them. And at the same time a deal that protects their rights and protects the music itself. (Mike Esquash interview, July 2006)

Their distinction from other powwow labels is also marked by a different kind of business model. Rusty Gillette, in another podcast interview for Powwows.com (that I was not a part of), suggested that Drumhop Productions should not even be considered a "record label" but instead a kind of "community resource" for drum groups who are interested in making recordings. Their Web site makes a similar claim, stating the following:

> We started this company because we felt we had the talents and the resources to help our powwow drum groups become more influential in their business decisions. We wanted to give them a sophisticated means of controlling their own music without sacrificing ownership of their own music. We are a production company, not a record label. We are only a link between our singers and the powwow public. The songs belong to the drums and the people who sing them. It is Drumhop's main goal to keep the copyrights with the drum and provide its singers with avenues to market their talents. We as a production company are sensitive to these issues and want to create long lasting successful working relationships with powwow singers, record labels, vendors and distributors across the United States and Canada. (www .drumhop.net/aboutus)

In distancing themselves from the corporate model of the "record label," Drumhop is attempting to signal to drum groups that they are operating within a new and different kind of business practice, one wherein songs will "belong to the drum and the people who sing them," and not the record label, or so they state.

The larger discourse being constructed by these new labels positions powwow music as a uniquely Native American cultural artifact that must remain firmly in the control of its creators. In other words, "recording culture" is a practice best left to powwow people. This overt concern with ownership and control of powwow music is a direct result of the culture of recording that has permeated powwow culture more broadly. Since the early 1970s, a time marked by the increased availability of hand-held tape recorders, powwow singers and fans have recorded powwow music for their own private consumption. Indeed, recordings were an essential part of the spread of powwow musical style across the northern Plains and beyond (Desrosiers and Scales, 2012; Hoefnagels 2002). This kind of electronically mediated exchange was relatively straightforward. On the powwow trail, singers have developed formal and informal protocols that govern the rights of ownership and the rights over performances of powwow songs. Importantly, these protocols have been developed (and continue to develop) without primary reference to the kind of formal economic and legal arrangements that govern song ownership and control in the Aboriginal music industry (mechanical royalties, publishing rights, licensing arrangements, etc.). Rather, they have been independently negotiated between singers and communities, and typically reference local and sometimes regional systems of song ownership or standard cultural practices that have governed the exchange of all kinds of intellectual property (like particular religious or healing ceremonies) historically. The discourse of these newer labels suggests that they are offering powwow singers relationships with their record labels that will be governed in a similar way to those developed on the powwow trail. The business models of these labels revolve around a promise that the ethical self-policing that occurs on the powwow trail—with regard to song ownership, and by extension the ethical values that guide powwow people themselves—will inform and structure the relationship between drum groups and powwow record labels.

The practice of producing, distributing, and selling commercial powwow CDs continues to pose a number of challenges for both powwow musicians and commercial record labels regarding the moral, legal, and cultural status of powwow recordings. While it is uncertain just how viable the business models of these new labels are, it is clear that competition powwow practices and recording culture continue to be deeply intertwined, and this entanglement will continue to produce moments of creative tension and inspiration as powwow participants work through new ideas and discourses about Native identity, culture, and community.

APPENDIX

Notes on the CD Tracks

1. Traditional/Original Song: "November Winds" [4:36]
(*November Winds*, Arbor Records, AR-13032)

This song features medium tempo straight-beat drumming appropriate for intertribal dancing or Men's and Women's Traditional contest dancing. Note that both the tempo and the volume of the drumming increase subtly at the beginning of the third push-up, initiated by some unison check beating at the end of the second push-up. This is a standard dynamic shape for many powwow song performances. More unison check beating is heard on the A′ phrase of the fourth push-up, initiating another increase in drumming tempo and a rise in volume. The drumming becomes increasingly louder until the final hard beats at the end of the fourth push-up, when all but the singer performing the honor beats dramatically decrease the volume of their drumming. The final phrase is delivered with forceful drumming once again before concluding with a three-hard-beat drum cadence. The "whistling wind" sound effect heard at the beginning of the song is typical of the kinds of studio-produced "nonmusical" sounds found on many powwow music recordings.

2. Contemporary/Word Song: "They're Coming In" [2:31]
(*Dance With Us*, Arbor Records, AR-11392)

This song is also rendered in a "straight beat" at a tempo that makes it appropriate for a Grand Entry song (the activity referred to in the title) or to accompany and inspire some energetic intertribal dancing. Typical of many word songs, the A and A′ phrases consist only of vocables, while the BC phrases feature Native-language text (in this case, the language is Ojibwa). Note again, as in "November Winds," the use of unison check beats during the A′ phrase of the final push-up, a performance decision that adds dramatic shape to many of the Northern Wind's songs.

3. Sneak-up Song: "Attacking" [3:10]
(*Dance With Us*, Arbor Records, AR-11392)

This song features a common drumming arrangement for Sneak-up songs: tremolo drumming throughout the AA′BC sections of the push-up followed by straight-beat drumming for the BC repetition and honor beat drumming featured during the repeat of the B phrase. This pattern is repeated for the next three push-ups. During the fifth push-up the tremolo drumming is abandoned and a straight beat is heard throughout, dramatically increasing in speed during the end of the A′ phrase and continuing until the end of the song. Most renditions of Sneak-up songs follow this dramatic arc, where straight-beat drumming replaces the tremolo drumming for the final push-up or final two push-ups. "Attacking" also features a trick ending with the drumming stopping abruptly at the end of the C phrase without the hard-beat cadence pattern heard at the end of the earlier push-ups.

4. Round Dance Song: "My Better Half" [3:00]
(*21st Century*, Arbor Records, AR-11122)

Unlike many Round dance songs, which often feature a mix of vocables and humorous and mildly erotic English-language lyrics, "My Better Half" features vocables throughout. Both the tempo and the absence of English lyrics make this song particularly suitable for Women's Traditional dancing. Unlike many of the straight-beat songs heard on this CD, the tempo of this song remains fairly consistent throughout. Note how the drumming drops out completely during the repetition of the BC phrases of the third push-up, before returning during the A′BC phrases of the fourth push-up. Round dance songs often feature this drumming arrangement because it is during the repetition of the BC phrases that one sings the English-language lyrics; in order for the words to be audible and clear, the drumming is typically either performed very softly or stopped altogether. In "My Better Half" this drumming convention is maintained even in the absence of English-language lyrics.

5. Crow Hop Song: "Bells" [2:59]

(*Dance With Us*, Arbor Records, AR-11392)

This Crow Hop song is also a "word song" that mixes Ojibwa text (heard during the AA'B phrases) and vocables (heard during the C phrase). The lyrics encourage the audience to listen to the beautiful sound of the bells on the dancers' regalia as they perform in the dance arena. Notice how each push-up features a different improvised pattern of honor beats heard during the repetitions of the B phrase. This song also features a "surprise ending" with no hard-beat cadence pattern to let the dancers know when the piece will end.

6. Jingle Dress Side-step Song: "Zig-Zag" [3:06]

(*Ikwe-Nagamonan: Jingle Dress Songs*, Arbor Records, AR-11282)

An interesting and technically difficult lead phrase begins this Side-step. Gabe has described this song to me as composed in a "traditional way," with an opening lead phrase performed without drum accompaniment and a "tail" (a cadential repeat of the BC phrases instigated by a single hard beat on the drum and then a slow drum crescendo) completing the final push-up. This is also an excellent example of the "in between" rhythmic feel of Ojibwa Side-step songs, where the drum pattern sits ambiguously between duple and triple meter. Gabe and the Northern Wind Singers are famous throughout the powwow world for their excellent renderings of these unique, Ojibwa-style songs.

7. Chicken Dance Song: "KFC" [2:34]

(*21st Century*, Arbor Records, AR-11122)

This song features an interesting drumming arrangement, beginning with a tremolo drumbeat (similar to a Sneak-up song) before converting, during the A' phrase, to the typical strong-weak drum pattern that distinguishes Chicken dance songs. During the third push-up, after the initial lead phrase, the drumbeat switches again, this time to a straight-beat pattern. Finally, during the fourth push-up, the Chicken dance beat resumes and the song ends with a tail (with straight-beat accompaniment), once more initiated by a single drum stroke at the end of the fourth push-up. This mixing of the Chicken dance and straight-beat drum patterns is quite common in many Chicken dance songs, although the timing and order of the alternation varies considerably.

8. Trick Song: "Shake, Rattle & Roll" [2:13]
(*21st Century*, Arbor Records, AR-11122)

This fun and challenging Trick song features a mix of several different drumming patterns and clever deviations from the standard powwow song form; such compositional choices are intended to confuse Men's Fancy dancers. The tremolo drumbeat at the beginning of the song suggests a Shake song (referenced in the song title) but rather than converting to simple straight-beat drumming for the BC repetition (as one would expect) the drum group skips to a truncated version of the C phrase accompanied by a very quick series of drumbeats. The second push-up features a return to tremolo drumming for the A and A′ phrases before unexpectedly changing into a Crow Hop beat for the BC phrases and then once again singing a truncated C phrase instead of the expected repetition of the BC phrases. The same drumming pattern and formal irregularities featured in the initial push-up are repeated in the third push-up. The fourth push-up gives the dancers a false sense of hope and security by finally giving them a "normally" rendered verse with the A and A′ phrases accompanied by a tremolo drumbeat that gives way to a straight beat for the BC phrases and (heard for the first time!) the D phrase. The dancers' hopes are soon dashed as none of these phrases are repeated and instead the singers transition smoothly into a fifth push-up, this time with straight-beat drumming continuing to accompany the AA′BCD phrases. Finally, the group finishes the second half of the push-up (for the first time in the song) by repeating the BCD phrases, although the drumbeat again is altered and we hear unison check beating continuing through all of the phrases (giving the impression of a quasi–Crow Hop beat) before ending the song abruptly with another series of quick drumbeats.

9. Honor Song: "Rita's Way (Honor Song)" [3:23]
(*Campfire*, Arbor Records, AR-11572)

Like other word songs we have heard, this song features vocables for the A and A′ phrases and Ojibwa-language lyrics for the BC phrases, although the end of the C phrase returns to using the same vocables featured in the opening phrases. The song was made and performed in honor of Rita Hollybull, Gabe's adopted sister, who passed away in November 2001.

10. "Side Windin' (Dianne's Song)" [2:03]

(*21st Century*, Arbor Records, AR-11122)

Notice the subtle vocoder effect added to Gabe's opening lead vocal. This is the only time the effect is used because it is the only point in the song where the drum does not accompany the vocals. Despite the subtlety of this digital effect and its use, many singers (especially young singers) were struck by its uniqueness and requested similar effects on their own CDs. This song, like all songs on the *21st Century* CD, also features overdubbed "seconds" that were performed by the Northern Wind Singers at a separate recording session and then mixed into the original "live" two-track recording.

11. "Dancin' 2000" [4:13]

(*21st Century*, Arbor Records, AR-11122)

Unlike the vocoder effect of the previous example, the reverse reverb effect is heard at the very beginning of every push-up, applied to the opening lead.

....

All of the songs on this CD were composed by Gabriel Desrosiers and performed by the Northern Wind Singers.

The Northern Wind Singers are:

> Gabriel Desrosiers (lead singer) (all tracks)
> Elliot Desrosiers (lead singer) (all tracks)
> Nate King (lead singer) (all tracks)
> Tommy Hunter (lead singer) (all tracks)
> Daniel Buffalo (lead singer) (tracks 1–5, 7–8, 10–11)
> BJ Copenace (lead singer) (tracks 1–3, 5, 9)
> Rodney Crow (all tracks)
> Bruce Crow (all tracks)
> Farrell Desrosiers (tracks 1–8, 10–11)

Cory Joseph (tracks 1–5, 7–8, 10–11)
Archie Paypompee (tracks 1–8, 10–11)
Gabe "Misoon" Desrosiers (track 1)
Beemus Goodsky (track 1)
Nate King Jr. (track 1)
Travis DeBungee (track 1)
BJ Paul (track 1)
Phil Gavere (track 1)
Justin Handorgan (tracks 2–11)
Harvey Goodsky (tracks 2–8, 10–11)
Shannon Copenace (tracks 4, 6–8, 10–11)
Mike Fisher (tracks 4, 7–8, 10–11)
Ronnie Goodeagle (tracks 4, 7–8, 10–11)
Terry Goodsky (track 6)
Daniel Big George (track 6)

Introduction

1. Throughout this monograph I use the terms "Native," "Native American" (used mainly in the United States), "First Nations" (used mainly in Canada), and "Indian" (used throughout North America, most often by Native Americans themselves) somewhat interchangeably. All these terms refer to the same segment of the larger indigenous population in North America. Importantly, the terms "indigenous" and "Aboriginal," which are also used interchangeably with each other, are used to refer more broadly to *all* of the different indigenous groups in North America. The Canadian Constitution identifies three distinct cultural communities that qualify for "Aboriginal Rights" in Canada: First Nations (Native American), Inuit, and Métis. Thus I use the phrase "Aboriginal recording industry" quite deliberately to refer to labels that potentially produce music by and for all three indigenous groups.

2. I first came across this wonderful story in Erika Brady's excellent monograph *A Spiral Way* (1999, 92–93).

3. Throughout this book I speak of "powwow culture" in terms consistent with the way participants use and understand the concept: sets of ideas and practices that are considered to be central to participation in a powwow. In this way we can speak of the cultural practices and cultural values of powwows as those that are endorsed and accepted by powwow participants. The boundaries surrounding these practices and values are under constant construction, revision, and negotiation as different communities and intertribal gatherings of people try to erect and enforce borders that define what is and is not part of a powwow event and powwow culture. There are official and unofficial borders. For instance, a central policy for all powwows is the prohibition of drugs and alcohol. Thus, officially, powwow committees and powwow people do not support or engage in the use of drugs and alcohol. However, to say that drugs and alcohol are not a part of powwow culture would be misleading, because, in truth, some powwow participants engage in the use (and sometimes abuse) of both. Forty-nine dances (more often simply referred to as forty-nines or forty-niners)—events in which drugs and alcohol may be routinely found—are a regular part of the powwow experience for many participants, and at many powwows, as the night wears on, talk begins about where the forty-nine will be. These events take place after the comple-

tion of an evening dance session or after the entire powwow is over and are usually found outside of the regularly recognized boundaries of the powwow grounds (for example, on reserves they often take place in the bush outside the natural clearing of most powwow grounds). Drinking or drug use may also take place *on* the powwow grounds, although usually late at night and always covertly and with discretion. While powwow participants readily acknowledge these activities, they are rarely referred to as "part of a powwow."

4. Hatton (1974), Vennum (1980), Lassiter (1998), Ellis (2003), and Browner (2000, 2002, 2009) provide detailed descriptions and analyses of tribal styles, while Hatton (1986), Powers (1990), and Ellis, Lassiter, and Dunham (2005) focus on the regional diversity of music and dance practices. Academic studies concerned with "identity construction" include early works that generally described powwows as functioning as a means of pan-tribal social and cultural integration (e.g., Corrigan 1970) or as a forum for the construction and maintenance of ethnic boundaries (e.g., Campsi 1975), as well as more recent research that has treated powwows as sites for the "negotiation of identity" (Herle 1994, Learch and Bullers 1996, Mattern 1996, Rynkiewich 1980, and Toelken 1991). It is clear that identity construction is a particularly salient aspect of powwows for Native Americans, and these authors have added much to our understanding of the process of identity formation. However, such studies regularly suffer from paradoxical problems. First, too many of them are very local in focus, studying unique community traditions without placing those specific powwows within the larger discourses and practices of powwows as they are performed throughout North America. Paradoxically, within these works powwows are treated as monolithic entities; as such, there is little consideration given to the great plurality of powwow practices that exist, the variety of which has serious implications for the kinds of identity construction that can and does take place.

Powwow research has also been bogged down in the past by (sometimes heated) arguments over the characterization of powwows as quintessentially *Pan-Indian*, a term that has attempted to convey its somewhat unique position in Native North America as a widely dispersed and shared set of cultural practices and ideologies. For the most part, I do not directly engage this issue in my discussion of powwows, and when I do, I use the more descriptively accurate terms "intertribal," "pan-tribal," or "supratribal." Howard's original formulation of Pan-Indianism (1955) was intended to theorize some of the new and original practices in dance and dress at powwows in Oklahoma in the 1950s, practices that had no tribal affiliations or antecedents and that, in his opinion, had come about as a result of large-scale intertribal contact. Originally linked to theories of cultural evolutionism, Howard's Pan-Indian thesis posited that these dances and regalia represented the last stage in the acculturation process, and he predicted that Pan-Indian practices would slowly but inevitably replace tribally specific music and dance and the loss of all tribally specific Native identity. While I believe Pan-Indianism is useful as a *descriptive* term, giving name to particular practices or ideologies that have obscure or nonexistent specific tribal or community origins, as a *theoretical* device it has met with near universal condemnation from powwow scholars, most forcefully from Powers (1990), Jackson and Levine (2002; see also Jackson 2005), Browner (2002), and Ellis, Lassiter, and Dunham (2005). These scholars, among others, suggest that Howard's theory is troublesome on three counts. First, in overemphasizing intertribal homogeneity Pan-Indianism fails to explain the persistence and in fact the increased development of tribally specific musical practices. As Powers notes, "Many anthropologists have been quick to apply Howard's definition to all tribes. But in emphasizing the postulated homogeneity of 'Pan-Indianism,' they have failed to recognize tribal distinctiveness" (1990, 52). Learch and Bullers (1996) have similarly found that participation in Pan-Indian events like powwows does not preclude participation in more tribally specific activities. Cornelius and O'Grady (1987) have published on the Soaring Eagles of Oneida, citing how participation in a powwow drum group led members to search out and discover more about specifically Iroquois musical genres and practices. In short, Howard's thesis does not explain the complex relationship between Pan-Indianism and tribalism, as the adoption of Pan-Indian practices has often functioned to *promote* and stimulate the performance of other tribally specific music and dances.

Second, Pan-Indianism is often dismissed as an inappropriate analytic tool for understanding intertribal social dynamics because it fails to take into account complex community interactions, which, as Jackson and Levine point out, complicate assumptions of primordially defined sociocultural boundaries and ignore the "capacity of communities to consciously maintain distinctive local practices in interactionally complex settings" (2002, 302). Finally, Pan-Indianism's stress on homogeneity denies the reality that supposedly Pan-Indian events like powwows actually display a wide variety of differences in both form and content across North America (Browner 2002; Ellis, Lassiter, and Dunham 2005). While powwows throughout Canada and the United States may share many of the same general characteristics in terms of music and dance styles, general protocols, and types of events, there is a good deal of regional variation as well. Powers (1990) has published a number of articles detailing the differences between Northern and Southern powwow singing and dancing styles, also noting differing orders of events, and the variable inclusion or exclusion of different genres of music and dance within a powwow (hand games, forty-niners, Gourd dance, Stomp dance). Browner (2000, 2002, 2009) has also suggested that these differences are significant and need to be acknowledged. Because powwow research is still in its infancy, we still do not know what other types of regional variations might exist in other musical/culture areas in North America and what local dances and singing styles are regularly incorporated into powwow events.

Not only is the term "Pan-Indianism" deeply troubling for scholars, it is also almost universally disliked by powwow people themselves, in large part because of the word's associations with non-tribally based and thus "inauthentic" kinds of ideologies and practices. For most powwow people, singing, dancing, and attending powwows is an opportunity for them to deeply "feel" Native American (Valaskakis 2005) in forceful and genuinely "authentic" ways.

5. The inaugural Grammy for Best Native American Music Album was presented to Tom Bee and Douglas Spotted Eagle, who were the producers for the recording *Gathering of Nations Powwow 1999* (SOAR S-200). In 2011 the National Academy of Recording Arts and Sciences undertook a major restructuring of its category system, which included eliminating fifty-two separate categories. Many of these were merged to form new, larger categories, including the Best Native American Music Album. Under the new category structure, Native music recordings, along with Hawaiian, polka, cajun, and zydeco CDs, will be considered under the much more broadly defined Best Regional Roots Music Album category.

6. Antonio Gramsci (1971) distinguished between "conjunctural" and "organic" historical forces, describing the latter as the more permanent and enduring aspects of any historical analysis, for example capitalism or colonialism. Conjunctural forces, in contrast, refer to particular events that give historical moments a kind of singularity or specificity. An analysis of a particular historical conjucture thus requires the "coming together" or connection of particular historical elements at a particular time. Thus, my analysis of powwows and the Aboriginal recording industry involves an examination of how these particular forces come together and interact at a particular historical moment, but also considers the larger organic social forces (Native Americans' historically marginal social and political position within Canada and the United States) that have shaped the life experiences of indigenous North Americans.

7. In describing "indigenous modernity" as a kind of "social formation" I am borrowing from the writings of both Antonio Gramsci and Stuart Hall, who use the term to invoke "the idea that societies are necessarily complexly structured totalities, with different levels of articulation (the economic, the political, the ideological instances) in different combinations; each combination giving rise to a different configuration of social forces and hence to a different type of social development. . . . In 'social formations' one is dealing with complexly structured societies composed of economic, political and ideological relations, where the different levels of articulation do not by any means simply correspond or 'mirror' one another, but which are—in Althusser's felicitous metaphor—'over determining' on and for one another. . . . It is this complex structuring of the different levels of articulation, not simply the existence of more than one mode of production, which constitutes the difference between the concept of 'mode of production' and the necessarily more concrete and historically specific notion of a 'social formation'" (Hall 1986, 12).

8. The Northern powwow trail does not recognize the forty-ninth parallel as a national border, and many singers and dancers who travel this circuit do not distinguish between Canadian and U.S. powwows (unless they are considering prize money— some singing groups and dancers will dismiss Canadian powwows because a sometimes weak Canadian dollar makes Canadian prize money less attractive). Further,

the major markets for Canadian-based record labels are south of the border and most of the sales for Canadian-based labels are generated from U.S.-based distributors and subdistributors, simply because there are more people and more powwows in the United States. Because of climate, the outdoor powwow season is also longer south of the border. In Oklahoma and the surrounding southern states, powwows and craft shows continue throughout the year.

9. The "Arbor Records" trademark was actually filed and registered by Brandon Friesen years earlier, and he ventured a few independent powwow releases under this name in the early 1990s; however, it was not until 1999 that Brandon committed fully to the label and opened up an office dedicated to the production of powwow music on a large scale.

10. Anthologizing became the way in which I initially proved my worth. Brandon knew I was writing a book about powwow music, traveling to powwows, and conducting interviews with powwow singers, attempting to understand the various song styles, genres, and aesthetics of powwow performance. As such, I was the only person working at Arbor at that time, apart from Brandon himself, who was familiar enough with powwow music to be able to sift through hours of recorded powwow material, pick out specific song types, and make reasonable judgments about "good" and "bad" performances (or at least what I *thought* powwow people would think were good and bad performances—see Hennion 1990).

11. My apprenticeship at Arbor Records/Studio 11 was typical of how I observed others learn and eventually find employment there. Basically, I "hung out" until they started giving me things to do. This is not an atypical strategy. Rob Shallcross, one of the part-time engineers at Studio 11, started in a similar way. He learned about Studio 11 working with Waylon Wityshyn (another part-time engineer at the studio), laying down drum tracks and helping to produce his band's new CD. Taking an interest in the technology and technique of recording, he began to frequent the studio more regularly to observe recording sessions in a fashion similar to my own method of learning. He and I were given free rein to learn how to use the recording gear, the only condition being that we could not interfere with any scheduled recording projects. Neither of us was paid for our time. My research grant allowed me to dedicate a good deal of time to learning while Rob was collecting unemployment insurance and procuring the occasional gig as a drummer. As we learned we were eventually given small tasks: "burn that CD," "download this DAT into the computer." As we gained familiarity with more and more equipment and digital recording programs, our roles expanded and our jobs became larger and more frequent.

12. This "high-context" (Hall 1977) way of communicating, using personal, autobiographical narratives to describe historical chronology, has a great deal of precedence in anthropological literature. See, for example, Cruikshank (1990) and Vander (1988), among many others.

13. The "umms" and "ahhs" have been edited except where I have interpreted them to be significant to the points being made by an interviewee. For example, if they

occur during moments when interviewees are struggling to find the correct word or if they have been stumped or confused by the way in which I have asked a question, these instances of "umm" or "ahh" seem to me to be relevant to the analysis and interpretation of their responses.

14. One anthropologist has suggested a musical metaphor for the role of the ethnographer, and despite the awkwardness of the metaphor, as a student and performer of stringed instruments, it is nonetheless evocative. He suggests that ethnography involves bringing together a number of different stories, ideas, and people, each one like the various strings of a guitar. The ethnographer should act as the plectrum, sometimes playing single strings, sometimes playing chords, bringing together several voices and stories, creating a unique configuration. In this ethnography, the sonorities are mine, both the harmony and the discord. The voices of those with whom I have had the pleasure and honor to work, are used with kind permission, and while I use their stories in my own design, I hope and trust that they nonetheless feel fairly and accurately represented.

Chapter 1: Powwow Practices

1. Albers and Medicine (2005) argue for a similar "model" of northern Plains powwows, describing a continuum of practices clustered around two archetypal events that they termed "in-group" ("traditional") and "Pan-Indian" or "intertribal" ("competition").

2. For example, many large competition powwows feature contest categories for both traditional and contemporary Jingle dress dancing as well as old-style and contemporary-style Grass dancing and Traditional dancing. These different styles are marked most noticeably by the structure and decoration of a dancer's regalia (outfit) and by choreography. For example, old-style Grass dancing is often characterized by both simplicity and symmetry in movements; dance steps and movements performed by the right foot or right half of the body must immediately be followed by the same steps and movements on the left side. According to Gabe Desrosiers, the practice of splitting dance categories along these lines was started by the Schemitzun powwow, one of the largest and most lucrative competition powwows on the East Coast.

3. The 1980s saw the concepts of tradition and culture in the academy become more complex with the publication of a number of works that described or investigated the "invention of tradition," part of the larger trend of postmodern critique in anthropology and folklore studies that characterized a great deal of scholarship at that time. Hobsbawm and Ranger (1983) defined an "invented tradition" as a recently created or emergent practice constructed through formalization and ritualization, and they further distinguished tradition from "custom" (for example, custom refers to what judges *do* while traditions include the use of the gown and gavel). According to these authors, "old" traditions could be distinguished from "invented" ones by virtue of their social effects. The former strongly bind social action whereas newer invented

traditions are more general in nature and inculcate vague values like "patriotism" and "loyalty." Handler and Linnekin (1984) challenged this theoretical characterization by suggesting that *no* tradition is authentic; rather, tradition is always selective, preserving certain elements of the past to serve present conditions. In this way, all traditions are recursive in that they are symbolically mediated in the present. The invention of tradition is not limited to self-conscious ideological projects but is an essential facet of all social life. Thus, there is no difference between a genuine and a spurious tradition. "Old" (genuine) and "new" (invented) traditions both are consciously constructed visions of the past and utilize the past as a legitimating and affective force that can be used in projects of group identity formation. This is not to suggest that certain practices do not have a "real" history. There is a great deal of historical and ethnographic evidence supporting the claim that the Omaha dance (which has historical ties to the modern-day Grass dance) has been practiced for a much longer time than the Oklahoma Fancy dance. However, the articulation of the Grass dance to the discourse of "tradition" or the articulation of the Fancy dance to the discourse of modernity are instances of larger social strategies that use "tradition" as a trope for "authentic" individual or group identity, the legitimacy of which is guaranteed by the rhetorical force of history.

4. Assiniboine groups are also sometimes referred to as Nakota or, less often, Stoneys. According to the reserve Web site, Carry the Kettle was established after Chief Cuwkencaayu signed an adhesion to Treaty 4 on September 25, 1877. "Prior to this event the tribes of Chief Cuwkencaaya and Chief Long Lodge resided in Cypress Hills along with other Cree tribes of Payepot and Little Pine. The Assiniboines then moved from Cypress Hills and settled in the area around the Indian Head district. In 1891, after the death of his brother Cuwkencaaya, Cegakins was appointed Chief and relocated to the present location" (www.carrythekettle.ca).

5. Typically, powwow committees like to schedule their annual events around the same time every year. This allows for a certain consistency in the larger powwow schedule and makes it easier for dancers and singers to schedule their summer travels. This practice also is a way to "claim" a particular weekend to avoid conflicting with other powwows, which would only serve to lessen attendance at all competing events.

6. At competition powwows each business must pay a fee for a space in the vendor area. According to various vendors with whom I spoke, the craft, food, and vendor booths each are charged a different amount by powwow committees. Vendors' booths, because they sell commercially produced products (like CDs), are charged more by powwow committees than craft booths—upwards of $500 for some powwows between 1998 and 2001.

7. "Indian time" refers to the idea that events should unfold naturally and not according to a preset schedule. The term is used both with pride—to distinguish Native American conceptions of time from Euro-American (i.e., more rigid) conceptions—and as a form of gentle (self-) mockery. Those who are always late may be jokingly chided for operating on "Indian time."

8. The inclusion in every Grand Entry of a "Flag song," a "Victory song," and an Invocation or prayer rendered by a local or visiting elder or veteran are standard components of every Grand Entry at both competition and traditional powwows across the northern Plains.

9. The CTK competition form on Saturday featured six categories for judging, each of which was scored on a scale of 1–5: (1) drum beat, (2) clarity of sound, (3) rhythm and harmony, (4) the song itself, (5) clean around the dance area, and (6) dancer participation.

10. Being "danced out" means that it is the last dance that a competition category dancer is required to dance. Dancing out the adult categories is a common practice during the afternoon dance session of competition powwows because the afternoon sessions are generally dominated by competition dancing for seniors, juniors, and teens.

11. A great deal of attention has already been paid to dance styles and dance outfits in the ethnographic literature. As such, only very cursory descriptions of these dance styles will be presented here. For further details, see Browner (2002), MacDowell (1997), and Powers (1966) among others; www.powwows.com also features reliable and accurate descriptions and photographs of the different regalia styles. While a high degree of variation is the norm, both between tribally and regionally specific styles and in accordance with the tastes of individual dancers, some general comments can be made. Many of the footwork patterns for the dances derive from a basic form: a four-beat pattern in which the right foot moves forward, taps the ground and then lands flush to the ground and weight is shifted onto that foot. The left foot then follows exactly as the right foot did: tap-step, tap-step.

12. In the summer of 1999 these dancers were present at a number of powwows that I attended across the Canadian Plains. The dancers were part of a professional touring dance troupe that was supposed to have performed across Canada. According to the head of the troupe, when they arrived at Vancouver they found that most of the dates on their planned tour had been canceled. In response, the group began performing at powwows on a number of reservations and a few cities. The troupe had previously performed at Winnipeg's Folklorama folk festival and the previous weekend at a powwow on the Sioux Valley Dakota Indian Reservation in Manitoba. At that powwow, the leader of the troupe made a speech likening powwows to Australian Aboriginal *Corroborees*, and he emphasized that all the powwow participants were welcome in Australia and would be taken care of from the moment they got off the plane to the moment they left. I interpret their presence and formal speaking at powwows as an explicit expression of Fourth World pan-Aboriginalist discourse (Manuel and Posluns 1974). At Carry the Kettle, as at Sioux Valley, they entertained the crowd with a brief (twenty-five-minute) dance performance. During the presentation four powwow princesses carried a blanket around the outer rim of the dance circle, requesting donations for the group (it was later announced that the donations totaled just under three hundred dollars).

13. Giveaways serve a number of social functions. Exegetic explanations of give-aways highlight their purpose in "honoring" specific community members, family members, or groups of dancers or singers. In this way ritualized gifting practices such as giveaways help to forge and maintain social alliances while simultaneously repli-cating the social divisions between groups (Mauss 1924). Giveaways also function to enhance the social standing of those who host them: material wealth is exchanged for social prestige. Through the act of the giveaway, the individual or family helps to strengthen social position and prestige within the community. Finally, giveaways also serve as a method of wealth redistribution within reservation communities — particularly at traditional powwows where the majority of participants and spectators are local community members (Moore 1993). This form of wealth redistribution has a long history in Plains cultures as well as among other Native groups across North America.

14. See Thomas Vennum's excellent ethnohistorical work (1982) for more details on this type of Ojibwa "traditional" drum.

15. The pipe is smoked by either the drumkeeper alone, or it is shared among the drumkeeper and any other persons who are sitting and singing around the drum at the time.

16. Densmore (1918, 471) describes a similar practice in her 1918 monograph of the music of the Teton Sioux as related to the performance of the Grass dance, suggest-ing that this has been practiced for at least a century by some Plains tribes. Vennum (1980, 69–70) suggests that the Ojibwa adopted this practice from the Sioux for their powwows through the contact of urban Ojibwa dancers with urban Sioux in Minne-apolis and St. Paul and through their mutual attendance at Sioux powwows in the Dakotas. Regardless of origin, it has become a standard aspect of powwows on the northern Plains with all tribal groups and communities recognizing its significance.

17. The Waywayseecappo Ojibwa First Nation Reserve is located in southwest Manitoba, a few miles from the southwestern corner of Riding Mountain National Park.

18. As explained in the article, spot checks refer to the practice of randomly check-ing the arena for dancers to evaluate the degree to which dance competitors are par-ticipating in noncompetitive events like Grand Entry and intertribals.

19. The role of competition in the historical development of powwows and related tribal and intertribal celebrations is a source of constant debate on the powwow trail. My concern here is not with establishing a verifiable historical narrative of when and why competition powwows began but of how the idea of competition is currently framed within discourses of tradition and culture, and how competition is reconciled or rejected as a component of authentic "Indian" identity.

20. Herzfeld suggests that the power of such essentialisms rests on "creating the semiotic effect technically known as iconicity, the principle of signification by virtue of resemblance. . . . Iconicity seems natural and is therefore an effective way of creating self-evidence. But it is in fact culturally constituted in the sense that the ability to rec-

ognize resemblance depends to a large degree on both prior aesthetic criteria and the politics of the situation" (1997, 27). The transformation of indexical signs into iconic signs is part of the work of powwows. The kinds of ideologies and practices expressed at powwows operate as indexical signs that, through rhetorical strategies of emcees and others, become iconic of "Indian" identity. Giveaways, public forms of generosity, and sociality (concern and commitment to community) become reified (essentialized) as iconic of Indianness. In this way powwows become worlds in which "Indianness" is practiced and learned, involving the "selective manipulation of stereotypes" (Herzfeld 1997, 30) that become "good to think" for both Natives and non-Natives.

Chapter 2: Powwow Songs

1. Other scholars have shown that this dearth of technical specialized musical language is not the case in various indigenous languages. See, for example, Nettl (1989) and Powers (1980).

2. I use the term "symbolic" here in the strict Piercian sense; that is, as a general category of sign that is related to its object through language (rather than through *iconicity* [resemblance] or *indexicality* [co-occurrence]) (Turino 1999).

3. My thinking on this matter has been greatly clarified through discussions with Tom Turino who, against my initial protestations, has always maintained that all theoretical knowledge exists in the symbolic realm of language (Turino 1999, 2000).

4. Interestingly, musicians and engineers in recording studios use these same kinds of rhetorical strategies when trying to establish a common frame of reference for communicating about some of the more ineffable, difficult-to-communicate-with-words qualities of timbre and "groove." See chapter 5 for a discussion of the "Cher" effect and the "Pearl Jam" effect; see also Porcello (1996) for an extended discussion of this phenomenon as it exists in recording studio settings.

5. Powers notes that for the Oglala (and perhaps other Sioux groups), "in normal [singing] practice the leader starts the song on one tone and is seconded by a singer who slightly raises the pitch. The conscious raising of pitch is considered good singing technique" (1980, 32). I did not encounter a similar aesthetic preference during my discussions with singers; at least it was never stated as such. However, much of my work was with Ojibwa groups and such a preference simply may not exist within these tribal communities.

6. Several scholars have already discussed the historical development of powwow song forms and styles and so I only briefly outline the basic elements here. Most agree that the Heluska (*He'thu'shka*) song form was the basis for both the Northern Grass/Omaha dance songs and the Southern O'ho'ma Society songs, both of which served as formal models for current Northern and Southern powwow song forms, respectively. See Browner (2000, 2002), Hatton (1974, 1986), and Vennum (1980) for a more exhaustive treatment of the history and development of Plains song forms.

7. According to Powers, the Oglala term for "to begin or lead a song" is *Yawankicu* (*ya* [action performed by means of the mouth] + *wank(a)* 'upwards' and *icu* 'to cause to, to take') (1980, 28–29). He further notes that "since approximately 1974, the Oglala have begun to call in English this particular seconding effect 'push ups.' The term is used to determine the number of renditions of a war dance song each group will sing, one 'push up' being equivalent to one rendition" (1980, 31).

8. The number four is imbued with symbolic and spiritual meaning for many Native American groups in North America, particularly among northern and southern Plains tribes. The number four manifests itself in a number of cultural domains: four directions, four sacred colors in a medicine wheel, and so on.

9. Hatton (1974, 129–30) reports that in the early 1970s there were two common practices of using honor beats, categorizing them as "the traditional method" and the "hot-five method." The former consisted of all drummers participating in the striking of alternate beats (which may extend from five to nine beats) with these beats occurring at variable places within the BC repetition. The latter method involved one drummer striking the hard beats at once to signal the beginning of the beats and then four more repetitions. This hot-five method, which Hatton reported as a relatively new phenomenon, appears to have become standard practice for almost all Northern singing groups.

10. For example, Snake dance songs and exhibition dancing were featured at the Shakopee powwow, August 2001, put on by the Wisconsin Dells drum of the Ho-Chunk nation.

11. The term "War dance" continues to be used at Southern powwows as a general term for both Straight- and Fancy-style dancing and to distinguish these styles from Gourd dancing (the other common song-and-dance style found at Southern powwows). See Lassiter (1998).

12. It is interesting to note the consistent connection between triple-meter songs and either women's or mixed gender couples dance genres. This link appears frequently in both the intertribal and tribally specific repertoires of a number of Plains tribal groups.

13. The Whitefish Bay Singers also released a CD in 2002 (Sunshine Records SSCD-4439) that features songs and interview excerpts of a discussion with Maggie White, reported by many to be the first person to wear Jingle Dress and dance in that style, as well as songs composed and performed by Andy White and the Whitefish Bay Singers that are specifically made for Jingle Dress dancing. The CD also features excerpts of singing by the late Frank White, who was an important and respected traditional singer in the Lake of the Woods area. The CD is fascinating not only for its archival material but also as a document that represents an attempt by the White family to lay claim to the Jingle Dress story and legacy. The liner notes are careful to specify that "Maggie shared her "odih iziwin" [loosely translated as his or her own—referring to the dress and dance] with the people she had met all over North America. What is also

interesting to point out is that this is *her* story, our peoples [*sic*] story from the Ani-shinabeg of Lake of the Woods." [italics added] (from the liner notes of *Anishinaabe Meenigoziwin*, SSCD-4439).

14. Skinner (1914) reports that the Cree also had a traditional ceremony in which the actions of breeding prairie chickens were reproduced in dance: "Only the men danced, generally in the summer, one man dancing at a time, the ceremony ending at sunset. Both men and women sang. The head dancer wore a fringed leather shirt and an eagle cap that was donned by each dancer in turn. Small hand drums were used, those seen being painted with red circles with radiating lines in the center to represent the sun" (1914, 531).

15. At Schemitzun 2002 I also witnessed the emcee inviting the Northern drum groups in attendance to sing a Southern-style song and for Southern drum groups to sing a Northern-style song. The emcee announced these songs as "Switch songs." Mystic River (the Northern host drum) carried their drum to the center of the arena and performed a Southern Straight song (originally made and sung by the well-known Southern drum group Cozad) as a singing exhibition for the audience, and not as an accompaniment to dancing.

16. This extremely terse description of Southern-style singing identifies only the coarsest stylistic elements of War dance songs and I am by no means suggesting that Southern-style singing is any less complex or varied than its Northern counterpart. See Lassiter (1998, especially chapter 11) and Browner (2002, 85) for more detailed descriptions of the myriad Southern song and dance categories and genres.

17. Gabe's tripartite categorization of compositional process reflects Nettl's general discussion of learning and composition in Native American cultures wherein he describes emic conceptions of compositional process as existing on a continuum: "At one end of the continuum is the conception that songs somehow exist in the cosmos or the real world and that they are put together—in some instances, laboriously—by humans. . . . At the other end of the continuum is the body of tales and myths, particularly of Plains cultures, that present songs as being already in a developed state at the point at which they are provided to humans [through dreams and visions]" (Nettl 1989, 96). Powers similarly reports that the Oglala make lexical distinctions between "religious" and "secular" compositions in terms of compositional process, the former being "learned" or "given" from a supernatural source, the latter being "made" by humans (1980, 33–34).

Chapter 3: Drum Groups and Singers

1. A drum group may become known and well respected by competition singers without success or regular participation at competition powwows. For example, many singers cited the Mandaree Singers as a group they respected and admired. The respect was earned not through Mandaree's participation or success in competitions but because of their longevity as a singing group, providing a model for many young

singers and drums, as well as for their generally agreed upon expertise in singing Northern old-style Straight songs.

2. Who belongs in this upper echelon is, of course, a constant topic of conversation and disagreement among singers and dancers. Those listed here are the groups who were consistently praised by singers whom I spoke with between 1999 and 2002. However, when I returned to the field in the summer of 2006, these groups were still considered to be top drum groups, particularly Bear Creek and Midnite Express. This list also represents certain regional biases (i.e., this list contains several Ojibwa or Ojibwa-dominated groups). These are the popular groups in the area of the Northern circuit in which I was working. Such a list may look different in Alberta, in Michigan, or in South Dakota, reflecting regional preferences for singing styles.

3. Due to large financial losses at the 1999 powwow, the event was canceled the following year.

4. Groups who travel regularly to reservation powwows know that the quality of PA systems at various powwows varies widely (if there is even a sound system provided at all). Thus owning one's own PA system and traveling with it has become more and more common.

5. For example, powwows held on remote reserves in northern Manitoba often offer large amounts of money to drum groups because of the difficulty of travel.

6. Generally, the sponsoring family of the dance special or giveaway chooses which drum group they want to sing for their special. However, the host drum is often chosen simply because it is a well-respected and reliable drum group. Sometimes the hosts also have community ties and as such are connected in some way to the families sponsoring the specials.

7. It should be noted that this discussion of social relationships of singing and singers is limited to *powwow* singing. Within reserve communities there are other singers who may only participate in singing ritual or religious music for ceremonies and who may or may not participate in powwows. For instance, Mike Esquash often insisted that, for him, a large part of being a singer meant being able to participate in religious ceremonies as a ritual specialist. This required knowledge of an entirely different repertoire of songs, and the ability to distinguish proper songs for proper occasions and contexts.

8. The role of a drum carrier in a competition drum group like the Spirit Sands Singers is somewhat different from a drum carrier who owns a traditional drum.

9. See Hoefnagels (2002) for a description of the politics of song ownership and sharing among powwow singers in Southwestern Ontario.

10. Judy Vander (1988, 230–31) tracked the repertoire of Lenore Shoyo (a regularly performing powwow singer) over a number of years, and her work reveals similar data in terms of the number of songs in a typical working repertoire in any given powwow season and the percentage of those songs that were newly composed.

11. At a traditional powwow, singers are more inclined to sing whatever they like and will more often sing songs that do not "officially" belong to them.

12. Having said this, many "informal" singing opportunities occur in the day-to-day lives of musicians. For example, Mike and other members of the Spirit Sands Singers regularly hung out together during the week and would often sing together during these occasions.

13. This is my own interpretation regarding the arc and development of powwow singing styles. Gabe Desrosiers offers another point of view in Desrosiers and Scales (2012).

14. My own experiences trying to address this issue have convinced me that the ethnographic research of powwows (like most ethnographic research) is itself a highly gendered activity. Native men and women occupy separate and very different social worlds, and it would be difficult for me as a male to do significant participant-observation ethnography within the female social world.

15. Similarly, Vander (1988) has stated that "when the Big Wind Singers [a mixed gender Shoshone family drum] sing at a powwow or for my tape recorder, Wayland [the elder brother], as lead singer, is in control. 'Wayland will do the song the way he wants,' Helene adds, 'the old way or new way. He has certain kinks in certain songs, and it's up to the whole drum group to try to follow through" (164).

16. Vander (1988) discusses at some length the role of Helene Furlong as a participant in a mixed-gender family drum group. According to interview transcriptions with Ms. Furlong, her inspiration for sitting and singing around the drum came from a Canadian mixed-gender group that was also composed of immediate family members. The mixed-gender family group was active from 1972 to 1979, and Ms. Furlong claims that the group was the only one of its kind in that area at that time (123–27).

Chapter 4: Powwow Recording in Canada

1. According to the 2006 Canadian census, Winnipeg's total population is 686,035 (Statistics Canada 2006).

2. The North End is qualitatively different than any other part of the city, severely economically depressed in some neighborhoods, and known to be dangerous at night.

3. There are also a number of much smaller record labels that produce only a few recordings per year, but these are generally vehicles for singers or groups to record and distribute their own music. The five labels listed here all distribute the music of a number of different drum groups.

4. I use the term "Contemporary Native music" as a genre category consistent with its use in the Aboriginal recording industry. Musical products are generally categorized as being either "Traditional" (which include powwow recordings, hand drum songs, and forty-niner songs, among others) or "Contemporary" (which include all styles of Native-produced, Euro-American, popular music styles or stylistic hybrids including country, rock, new age, heavy metal, rap, etc.)

5. The label folded in 2003.

6. Of all the labels I studied, only Curtis Assiniboine, a well-known powwow singer

and songmaker and owner of Wacipi Records, could be said to be a true cultural insider, sharing to a large degree the habitus of powwow people and powwow singers.

7. There is precedence in the ethnomusicological literature for the structural study of small-scale music industries in other countries (Gronow 1975, 1981; Racy 1976, 1977, 1978; Wallis and Malm 1984).

8. Scholars have identified two major booms in the growth and proliferation of independent record companies in American popular music: the first between 1947 to 1957 (giving rise to bebop, R&B, and country and western), and the second from 196/ to 1977 (with the development of reggae, disco, punk, rap, and hip-hop) (Chapple and Garofalo 1977; Peterson and Berger 1975).

9. Alternatively, Simon Frith (1981) has argued that too much is made of the differences between indies and majors, suggesting instead that *all* labels may be characterized as businesses out to make profit. He further points out that the romantic celebration of indies as somehow more noble in intention than majors is not an entirely accurate depiction, since some of the most blatant exploitation of artists has come at the hands of these smaller labels. The degree to which indies and majors do or do not differ within mainstream industrial circuits, while significant, is only tangentially relevant to the central argument of this chapter. More important for my purposes is that the Aboriginal recording industry shares a larger number of structural similarities with small independent labels than with large multinational majors, and these structural characteristics have a significant impact on practice.

10. Label divisions for the majors are quite often run by current or former record producers as well (Pierce 2000). The difference is that, as producers within the mainstream music industry take on administrative positions, their producing activities are often curtailed. Work at an independent label requires concurrent involvement at several levels of production, sales, and distribution.

11. "Independent" distributors are distribution companies that do not have corporate ties to major record labels like Sony or Polygram. "Major" distribution companies are those that operate as divisions within the corporate structure of major labels. All of the Big Four have at least one—and sometimes multiple—distribution divisions that distribute these labels' (and subsidiary labels') products.

12. Western Canada is home to a large population of first-, second-, and third-generation Ukrainian families, and historically Winnipeg has had a thriving Ukrainian community.

13. Although, as of 2002, the prize money for the Schemitzun powwow, routinely one of the most lucrative on the powwow circuit, had been reduced considerably. I do not think this was due to any financial hardship on the part of the tribe or sponsoring casino, but rather to a change in the direction and philosophy of the powwow that itself resulted from a changing of the guard in the powwow committee.

14. It is reasonable to assume a certain correlation between Canada and the United States, given the similarities in the structural and institutional relationships between the indigenous populations and the federal governments of the two countries. I have

no statistical data for the emergence of this pattern in Canada, but instead a wealth of anecdotal evidence, as many friends and acquaintances I met on the powwow trail fit this profile.

15. This was the technical configuration during the time I was employed there. In 2001 the studio converted completely to hard-drive recording technology.

16. In spring 2003, John Marlow left the company and Stewart Astleford briefly returned as the head of sales. Several other personnel changes have taken place at both Studio 11 and Arbor Records since my full-time employment there ended in the late summer of 2000, an employment turnover rate typical of smaller independent labels and recording studios. The only consistent personnel are Brandon (who lists himself as president of the company) and his sister Jamie, who has slowly taken over more of the administrative operations of Arbor Records; she is listed in Arbor informational packages as the accounts manager. Family relationships played a key role at all five of the Aboriginal labels I encountered during my fieldwork. These labels were owned and operated either by spouses (Sweet Grass, Wacipi, Sunshine) or other family relatives (Arbor, Turtle Island Music).

17. Personal communication with Kevin Syrette, leader of the Bear Creek drum group.

18. Negus makes a similar observation, noting that musicians often look at the roster of artists for major labels when choosing where to sign, believing that "a company '*is*' its artists'; the artists on the roster provide an index of the entire organization and its [corporate] culture" (1999, 69).

19. This is not a unique practice in the marketing of "world music" by international music corporations. For instance, CDs in EMI's "Hemisphere" series contain detailed explanatory liner notes and maps (Negus 1999, 165–66; Pacini Hernández 1993).

20. See Negus (1999) for a related discussion of how markets are imagined and constructed within the mainstream music industry, particularly his juxtaposition of "international" recording artists versus "world beat/world music" recording artists.

21. See Buchanan (1997) for a similar account of how the marketing and packaging of Bulgarian women's choirs in the early 1990s relied on similar tropes of exoticism, through the emphasis on and intermingling of cultural, historical, and temporal distance.

22. For example, Red Tail, a group of young Yakima singers, expressed to me a great deal of pride about their geographical relationship to Blacklodge (a Blackfeet group), another drum group that hailed from the same general region. Similarly, young Ojibwa drum groups eagerly follow the careers of Eyabay and Bear Creek.

23. These terms refer to the competition criterion in which dancers must take their last steps at the same time as the last drumbeats. To stop dancing before the song is completely finished is referred to as "understepping," while continuing to dance after the last stroke on the drum is termed "overstepping."

24. These marketing strategies are employed not only at the level of packaging, but advertising as well. Print and radio advertising for powwow recordings, while

minimal, typically targets the Native market because only Native newspapers and reservation-based radio stations feature advertising for these products.

25. Arbor's presence at these events in the first years of its existence also allowed craft vendors to put a "face" to Arbor Records and allowed Astleford to establish face-to-face contact with other craft vendors who work the Northern powwow circuit. He often sold Arbor's product to these vendors right there on the powwow grounds.

26. Blacklodge Singers have recorded numerous albums and CDs with Canyon Records and have enjoyed a long and productive career as a singing group. Since their inception in the 1980s, they have been recognized as one of the top Northern singing groups in the powwow world.

27. It is also worth noting that these early economic practices have had long-lasting effects in structuring current and future relationships between singers and labels, and fostered a growing distrust of all recording companies on the part of powwow singers.

28. As another way to generate income, Studio 11 ran a series of concurrent ten-week recording courses on both Tuesday and Sunday nights. The classes, taught by Paul and Dutch, ran for three hours at a time with a maximum of four people per class. Most of the people taking the class were musicians from different bands that had recorded at the studio previously, and who wanted to know more about digital audio production. At that time Studio 11 was one of the best-equipped studios in the city; it was a good place to learn this trade. Purple started taking the Tuesday night classes as part of his training.

29. Purple's story is a familiar one, and one that I heard countless times while living in Winnipeg and interacting with the Native community there. Purple is a full-blooded Ojibwa by birth who was adopted at a young age by a white family; he was consequently raised as an urban white kid in Winnipeg. His parents made no attempt to interest Purple in his genealogical roots, and as a result he grew up knowing very little about Ojibwa people or his home community culture, although as a young adult he began to search out and explore his Native heritage in a variety of ways. The practice of the adoption of Native children by non-Native families has a long and tragic history in Canada (Frideres 1998).

30. There are also pragmatic economic and material incentives for non-Native-owned record companies to hire Native employees. Certain granting and funding opportunities are available in Canada specifically for First Nations peoples. For example, in summer 2000 Arbor Records sent TKO to represent the label at the Albuquerque powwow (one of the biggest powwows of the year) because he had received a grant from Manitoba Film and Sound to fund his travel to the powwow to perform and promote his own CD, *Welcome to the Playground* (SSCD-4337).

Chapter 5: Powwow Music in the Studio

1. In a more careful application of Bourdieu's conceptual terminology, different recording contexts might be labeled "sub-fields," each one part of the larger social field of the international recording industry. My use of Bourdieu and his theory of social fields differs substantially from Turino (2008), who builds upon Bordieu's ideas to develop a typography of music making based on the particular structural characteristics of four specific "musical fields." While there is a certain kinship between the recording contexts discussed in this chapter and Turino's "High Fidelity" and "Studio Audio Art" fields, my application of Bourdieu is much more narrow and less ambitious, intended simply to point out that particular "genre worlds" (Frith 1996) are defined in large part by the distribution of different kinds and amounts of "capital."

2. A "scratch" track refers to any track (instrumental or vocal) that is used as a "guide" track for further recording and is then discarded (scratched) or re-recorded for the final version of the song.

3. Sequencers are hardware devices or software applications that record, edit, and play back musical information in various formats and through various input methods. The most common way that a sequencer was used in Arbor Records recording projects was to record and play back MIDI data that were typically performed in "real time" on a keyboard.

4. See Porcello (1996) for a lengthy description of the typical occupational roles of engineers and producers.

5. See Porcello (1996).

6. A signal sounds clipped when you can actually hear the compressor kicking in and working on a signal. When this happens, the signal volume is audibly reduced the instant after the initial attack of the instrument, and then the volume jumps back up again when the compressor releases the signal.

7. Many digital reverb units allow the user to manipulate the timbre of the reverb being generated by the unit through similar kinds of controls that one finds on typical parametric and graphic equalization devices. These controls allow producers and engineers to control not only what frequencies or frequency ranges the reverb unit responds to, but also the timbre of the resultant reverberations.

Chapter 6: Producing Powwow Music

1. The idea of "liveness" has drawn the attention of a number of scholars in the last decade. Auslander (1999) makes an argument similar to Brandon's regarding typical rock music production styles. He notes that "few rock records foreground the artifice of their studio construction; most are made to sound like performances that could have taken place, even if they really didn't (and couldn't)" (64). Tom Porcello (2005a) also provides some of the details of studio-produced "liveness" in an article describing the creation of "the Austin sound." Louise Meintjes (2003, 2005) has written ex-

tensively about the discourses and technological practices of "liveness" as it pertains to the production of South African Zulu musical styles. Turino (2008, 66–92) includes a discussion of liveness that liberally refers to the work of Porcello and Meintjes, as well as his own experiences as a recording musician, in his elaboration of his "High Fidelity" and "Studio Audio Art" recording fields.

2. *Believe* (WEA CD-47121).

3. The "reverse reverb" effect is achieved through a process whereby a mirror image of the sonic reverberations produced by the lead singer's vocal line is created in post-production, and then that sonic event is placed *before* the lead singer actually begins singing the vocal line.

4. I have since spoken with Gabe Desrosiers and obtained his permission to include this information in my writing.

5. "Gating" the amplifier, in this case, meant that a "noise gate" sound processor was used to control the signal response of the microphones used for the overdubbed vocals. A noise gate unit works to measure the sound pressure exerted on the microphone's diaphragm and functions like an on-off switch, effectively blocking a microphone signal below a certain amplitude threshold and preventing that signal from being recorded. Only sounds of a certain volume are "let through the gate," while those sounds below a certain level are registered by the microphone, but the signal is shut off and thus not recorded. In this instance the gate was set to suppress ("gate") the audio signal from the amplifier while allowing the audio signal of the vocals to pass through the gate to be recorded.

6. The threshold level of the compressor sets the point at which the compressor activates and begins compressing the audio signal. A high threshold level means that the signal must reach a relatively high amplitude before being affected by the compressor. The ratio control sets the amount of compression that is applied to a signal once it is activated. For example, a 6:1 ratio reduces the decibel level of an effected signal by a ratio of six to one.

7. Graphic equalizer units typically feature a series of faders, each of which controls the amplitude of a specific, preset frequency within the overall frequency spectrum. Moving the faders up increases the decibel level of a specific frequency, while moving it down decreases the amplitude. Parametric equalizers consist of a series of paired dials. Within each pair, one dial allows the user to choose the frequency to be affected while the other dial controls the amplitude level of that frequency (typically within a range of ±12 db).

8. For example, after he finished mastering the Mishi Donovan CD Brandon took it home that night and came back the next day, saying the mix was fine but the CD needed to sound brighter. He went back into Studio B and re-equalized it and remastered it with more top end.

9. The link between liveness, high fidelity, and authenticity is negotiated in numerous other genres as well. For example, Frith (1996) discusses a similar phenomenon in folk music recording practices: "Kenneth Goldstein comes to similar conclu-

sions [about production methods] from his experience as a folk record producer for the Riverside, Elektra, and Folkways labels in the 1950s and 1960s: 'I had to figure out what my responsibilities were to (1) the public, which is a record that is good to listen to, easy to listen to, straight through; (2) to the folklorist, an actual representation, an ethnographic record, if you will; and (3) to the singer, which is the best that he bloody well can do, which is what the singer wants to present to the world.' Goldstein quickly identified primarily with the singers: 'They had heard records, all of them had heard records. They didn't hear background noises on those records. That became the standard for them for what a good record was.' The singers, in short, wanted the best possible sound in formal terms (Keil's perfection), and 'there was never a question to me about splicing if it made the performance better'" (233).

Chapter 7: Powwows "Live" and "Mediated"

1. See also Desrosiers and Scales (2012).

2. Tony Issacs, the owner of Indian House Records, offered an alternate explanation about the origin of song naming during an informal conversation. He suggested that the practice was originally encouraged by Tom Bee of SOAR, who suggested to the singers recording with his label that naming each song with a unique title was the easiest way to then file for publishing rights. It would be much easier to register the songs with ASCAP or BMI if they had unique titles rather than registering a dozen different songs that had the name "intertribal."

3. Studio and remote sessions were the only two contexts in which groups requested sound effects. "Live" recordings had their own sound effects already built into the recording: the sounds of the powwow grounds.

4. The use of the rattle is itself an unusual instrument choice, even for a Round dance song. Typically these songs are sung to the accompaniment of hand-held frame drums or, when performed at a powwow, the big drum.

5. Richard White introduced the provocative notion of a "middle ground" to describe a particular historical conjuncture in Native and non-Native relations. White used the term specifically to speak about a moment within the history of the fur trade when Native Americans still had enough social, cultural, and economic capital to be relatively equal partners in this interaction. He states: "The middle ground is the place in between: in between cultures, peoples, and in between empires and the non state world of villages. . . . On the middle ground diverse peoples adjust their differences through what amounts to a process of creative, and often expedient, misunderstandings. . . . They often misinterpret and distort both the values and practices of those they deal with, but from these misunderstandings arise new meanings and through them new practices—the shared meanings and practices of the middle ground" (1991, x).

In White's historical account of the *pays d'en haut*, this middle ground was upset when Euro-Americans began to wield a greater degree of social and economic capital, maintaining increasing control over valued goods and services which eventually led from a relationship of mutual equality and interdependency to a relationship characterized by inequality and exploitation.

6. This visualization of studio practices shares a certain consistency with Turino's (2000, 2008) continuum of participatory–presentational–high-fidelity–studio-art musics; another way of describing the numerous gray areas occupied by musicians between the discourses surrounding live and mediated musical performances.

7. The project of working in and working through the discourses of modernity and tradition shares a certain theoretical kinship with postcolonial scholarship that speaks of the creation of "alternative modernities," as well as nationalist literature that deals with instances of "modernist-reformism" (Turino 2000). Each of these intellectual fields attempts to get at the same kinds of issues and make use of the same discourses of tradition and modernity, wrestling with the same problems that the discourses impose on us when we try to explain complex social situations.

8. Furthermore, it seems a little disingenuous for academics to simply sit back and complain about the sloppiness of the industry in packaging and presenting these sounds and images. Part of my discomfort is the assumed authority of the academy as the final arbiter of accuracy of truth in representation. Certainly the "postmodern turn" of the 1980s should have produced a healthy skepticism of our own authority to represent Others.

9. As Erika Brady (1999) points out in her excellent historical study of recording practices in anthropology and folklore, there was a great deal of discussion and disagreement among ethnologists of the first part of the twentieth century over the effectiveness of the phonograph as a successful and accurate ethnographic tool. Many British folksong collectors felt that *true* collecting should be done through transcription and that the "real truth" of a folksong was best "captured" through the interpretation of the trained musician/transcriber and not the supposedly objective ear of a phonograph or microphone.

Coda

1. Shawn left the job in 2007 and was replaced by Paul Scinocca. As of this printing, Paul continues as the sales manager for Arbor.

Abraham, Otto, and E. M. von Horbostel. [1904] 1976. "Über die Bedeutung des Phono-graphen für die vergleichende Musikwissenschaft." In *Hornbostel Opera Omnia*, edited by Klaus P. Wachsmann, Dieter Christensen, and Hans-Peter Reinecke. Translated by Bonnie Wade, 183–202. The Hague: Martinus Nijhoff.

Albers, Patricia C. and Beatrice Medicine. 2005. "Some Reflections on Nearly Forty Years on the Northern Plains Powwow Circuit." In *Powwow*, edited by Clyde Ellis, Luke Eric Lassiter, and Gary H. Dunham, 26–45. Lincoln: University of Nebraska Press.

Appadurai, Arjun. 1986. "Introduction: Commodities and the Politics of Value." In *The Social Life of Things*, edited by Arjun Appadurai, 3–63. Cambridge: Cambridge University Press.

———. 1996. *Modernity at Large: Cultural Dimensions of Globalization*. Minneapolis: University of Minnesota Press.

Arbor Records. 2002. *Arbor Records Product Catalogue*. Winnipeg: Arbor Records.

Auslander, Phillip. 1999. *Liveness: Performance in a Mediatized Culture*. New York: Routledge.

Austin, Leslie. 1993. "Rock Music, the Microchip, and the Collaborative Performer: Issues Concerning Musical Performance, Electronics, and the Recording Studio." PhD diss., New York University.

Badal, James. 1996. *Recording the Classics: Maestros, Music, and Technology*. Kent, Ohio: Kent State University Press.

Barthes, Roland. 1977. *Image-Music-Text*. Edited by Stephen Heth. New York: Hill and Wang.

Bauman, Richard. 1977. *Verbal Art as Performance*. Rowley, Mass.: Newbury House.

Benjamin, Walter. 1969. "The Work of Art in an Age of Mechanical Reproduction." In *Illuminations*, edited by H. Arendt, 217–51. New York: Schocken.

Berkhofer, Robert. 1978. *The White Man's Indian*. New York: Alfred A. Knopf.

Blacking, John. 1995. "Music, Culture, and Experience." In *Music, Culture, and Experience*, 223–42. Chicago: University of Chicago Press.

Blum, Stephen. 1972. "Music in Contact: The Cultivation of Oral Repertories in Meshed, Iran." PhD diss., University of Illinois.

Bourdieu, Pierre. 1977. *Outline of a Theory of Practice*. Translated by Richard Nice. Cambridge: Cambridge University Press.

——. 1984. *Distinction: A Social Critique of Taste*. Translated by Richard Nice. Cambridge: Harvard University Press.

——. 1993. *The Field of Cultural Production: Essays on Art and Literature*. Edited by Randal Johnson. New York: Columbia University Press.

Bourdieu, Pierre, and Loïc Waquant. 1992. *An Invitation to Reflexive Sociology*. Chicago: University of Chicago Press.

Brady, Erika. 1999. *A Spiral Way: How the Phonograph Changed Ethnography*. Jackson: University of Mississippi Press.

Browner, Tara. 2000. "Making and Singing Pow-Wow Songs: Text, Form, and the Significance of Culture-Based Analysis." *Ethnomusicology* 44, no. 2, 214–33.

——. 2002. *Heartbeat of the People: Music and Dance of the Northern Pow-wow*. Urbana: University of Illinois Press.

——. 2009. "An Acoustic Geography of Intertribal Powwow Songs." In *Music of the First Nations: Tradition and Innovation in Native North America*, edited by Tara Browner. Urbana: University of Illinois Press.

Buchanan, Donna A. 1997. "Bulgaria's Magical *Mystère* Tour: Postmodernism, World Music Marketing, and Political Change in Eastern Europe." *Ethnomusicology* 41, no. 1, 131–57.

Campsi, Jack. 1975. "Powwow: A Study of Ethnic Boundary Maintenance." *Man in the Northeast* 9, 33–46.

Chapple, Steve, and Reebee Garofalo. 1977. *Rock 'n' Roll Is Here to Pay: The History and Politics of the Music Industry*. Chicago: Nelson-Hall.

Churchill, Ward. 1992. "Fantasies of the Master Race: Categories of Stereotyping of American Indians in Film." In *Fantasies of the Master Race: Literature, Cinema and the Colonization of American Indians*, edited by M. Annette James, 231–43. Monroe, Minn.: Common Courage.

Clifford, James. 1986. "Introduction: Partial Truths." In *Writing Culture: The Poetics and Politics of Ethnography*, edited by James Clifford and George Marcus, 1–26. Berkeley: University of California Press.

——. 1988. "Identity in Mashpee." In *The Predicament of Culture: Twentieth-Century Ethnography, Literature, and Art*, 277–348. Cambridge: Harvard University Press.

——. 1997. "Diasporas." In *Routes: Travel and Translation in the Late Twentieth Century*, 244–78. Cambridge: Harvard University Press.

——. 2000. "Taking Identity Politics Seriously: 'The Contradictory, Stony Ground . . . .'" In *Without Guarantees: In Honour of Stuart Hall*, edited by Paul Gilroy, Lawrence Grossberg, and Angela McRobbie, 94–112. London: Verso.

Clifford, James, and George Marcus, eds. 1986. *Writing Culture: The Poetics and Politics of Ethnography*. Berkeley: University of California Press.

Clifton, James A., ed. 1994. *The Invented Indian: Cultural Fictions and Government Policies*. New Brunswick, N.J.: Transaction.

Cornelius, Richard, and Terence O'Grady. 1987. "Reclaiming a Tradition: The Soaring Eagles of Oneida." *Ethnomusicology* 31, no. 2, 261–72.

Corrigan, Samuel W. 1970. "The Plains Indian Powwow: Cultural Integration in Manitoba and Saskatchewan." *Anthropologica* 12, 253–77.

Cruikshank, Julie. 1990. *Life Lived Like a Story*. Lincoln: University of Nebraska Press.

Deloria, Phillip. 1998. *Playing Indian*. New Haven: Yale University Press.

———. 2004. *Indians in Unexpected Places*. Lawrence: University Press of Kansas.

Densmore, Frances [1917] 1968. "Incidents in the Study of Ute Music." In *Frances Densmore and American Indian Music: A Memorial Volume*. Edited by Charles Hofmann, 40, Contributions from the Museum of the American Indian, vol. 43. New York: Heye Foundation.

———. [1918] 1968. *Teton Sioux Music*. Bureau of American Ethnology Bulletin 61. Washington: U.S. Government Printing Office.

Desrosiers, Gabriel, and Christopher Scales. 2012. "Contemporary Northern Plains Powwow Music: The Twin Influences of Recording and Competition." In *Perspectives on Contemporary Aboriginal Music*, edited by Anna Hoefnagels, M. Sam Cronk, and Beverley Diamond, 89–108. Montreal: McGill-Queens University Press.

Diamond, Beverley. 2002. "Native American Contemporary Music: The Women." *The World of Music* 44, no. 1, 11–40.

———. 2005. "Media as Social Action: Native American Musicians in the Recording Studio." In Greene, *Wired for Sound: Engineering and Technologies in Sonic Cultures*, edited by Paul Greene and Thomas Porcello, 118–37. Middletown, Conn.: Wesleyan University Press.

Doyle, Peter. 2005. *Echo and Reverb: Fabricating Space in Popular Music Recording, 1900–1960*. Middletown, Conn.: Wesleyan University Press.

Dyck, Noel. 1991. *What Is the Indian "Problem": Tutelage and Resistance in Canadian Indian Administration*. St. John's: Institute of Social and Economic Research, Memorial University of Newfoundland.

Ellis, Clyde. 2001. "'We Don't Want Your Rations, We Want This Dance': The Changing Use of Song and Dance on the Southern Plains." In *American Nations: Encounters in Indian Country, 1850 to the Present*, edited by Frederick Hoxie, Peter Mancall, and James Merrell, 354–73. New York: Routledge.

———. 2003. *A Dancing People: Powwow Culture on the Southern Plains*. Lawrence: University Press of Kansas.

Ellis, Clyde, Luke Eric Lassiter, and Gary H. Dunham. 2005. *Powwow*. Lincoln: University of Nebraska Press.

Eschbach, Karl and Kalman Applbaum. 2000. "Who Goes to Powwows? Evidence from the Survey of American Indians and Alaska Natives." *American Indian Culture and Research Journal* 24, no. 2, 65–83.

Feld, Steven. 1984. "Communication, Music, and Speech About Music." *Yearbook for Traditional Music* 16, 1–18.

———. 1991. "Voices of the Rainforest." *Public Culture* 4, no. 1, 131–40.

———. 1993. "The Politics of Amplification: Notes on 'Endangered Music' and Musical Equity." *Folklife Center News* 15, no. 1, 12–15.

———. 1995. "From Schizophonia to Schismogenesis: The Discourses and Practices of World Music and World Beat." In *The Traffic in Culture: Refiguring Art in Anthropology*, edited by George Marcus and Fred Myers, 96–126. Berkeley: University of California Press.

———. 1996. "Pygmy Pop: A Genealogy of Schizophonic Mimesis." *Yearbook for Traditional Music* 28, 1–35.

Feld, Steven, and Donald Brenneis. 2004. "Doing Anthropology in Sound." *American Ethnologist* 31, no. 4, 461–74.

Francis, Daniel. 1992. *The Imaginary Indian: The Image of the Indian in Canadian Culture*. Vancouver, B.C.: Arsenal Pulp.

Frideres, James. 1998. *Aboriginal Peoples in Canada: Contemporary Conflicts*. Scarborough, Ont.: Bacon Canada.

Frith, Simon. 1981. *Sound Effects: Youth, Leisure, and the Politics of Rock 'n' Roll*. New York: Pantheon.

———. 1996. *Performing Rites: On the Value of Popular Music*. Cambridge: Harvard University Press.

Geertz, Clifford. 1973. *The Interpretation of Cultures*. New York: Basic Books.

Gillett, Charlie. 1996. *The Sound of the City: The Rise of Rock and Roll*. New York: Da Capo.

Goertzen, Chris. 2001. "Powwows and Identity on the Piedmont and Coastal Plains of North Carolina." *Ethnomusicology* 45, no. 1, 58–88.

Gramsci, Antonio. 1971. *Selections from the Prison Notebook of Antonio Gramsci*. New York: International Publishers.

Gray, Herman. 1988. *Producing Jazz: The Experience of an Independent Record Company*. Philadelphia: Temple University Press.

Greene, Paul D, and Thomas Porcello, eds. 2005. *Wired for Sound: Engineering and Technologies in Sonic Cultures*. Middletown, Conn.: Wesleyan University Press.

Gronow, Pekka. 1975. "Ethnic Music and Soviet Record Industry." *Ethnomusicology* 19, no. 1, 91–99.

———. 1981. "The Record Industry Comes to the Orient." *Ethnomusicology* 25, no. 2, 251–84.

Grossberg, Lawrence. 1992. *We Gotta Get Out of This Place: Popular Conservatism and Postmodern Culture*. New York: Routledge.

Hall, Edward. 1977. *Beyond Culture*. Garden City, N.Y.: Anchor.

Hall, Stuart. 1986. "Gramsci's Relevance for the Study of Race and Ethnicity." *Journal of Communication Inquiry* 10, 5–27.

Handler, Richard, and Jocelyn Linnekin. 1984. "Tradition, Genuine or Spurious." *Journal of American Folklore* 97, 273–90.

Hatoum, Rainer. 2002a. "On the Developing Notion of Song Categories in Powwow

Music." Paper presented for the 47th Annual Meeting of the Society for Ethnomusicology, Estes Park, Colorado. Unpublished.

———. 2002b. "Eine Auseinandersetzung mit Fragen der kulturspezifischen Wissensvermittlung, Sinkonstruktion und Identität." PhD diss., Johann Wolfgang Goethe-Universität Frankfurt am Main.

Hatton, O. Thomas. 1974. "Performance Practices of Northern Plains Pow-Wow Singing Groups." *Yearbook of Inter-American Musical Research*, 10, 123–37.

Hatton, Orin T. 1986. "In the Tradition: Grass Dance Musical Style and Female Powwow Singers." *Ethnomusicology* 30, no. 2, 197–222.

Helms, Mary. 1988. *Ulysses' Sail: An Ethnographic Odyssey of Power, Knowledge, and Geographical Distance*. Princeton: Princeton University Press.

Hennion, Antoine. 1990. "The Production of Success: An Antimusicology of the Pop Song." In *On Record: Rock, Pop, and the Written Word*, edited by Simon Frith and Andrew Goodwin, 185–206. New York: Pantheon.

Herle, Anita. 1994. "Dancing Community: Powwow and Pan-Indianism in North America." *Cambridge Anthropology* 17, no. 2, 57–83.

Herzfeld, Michael. 1997. *Cultural Intimacy: Social Poetics in the Nation-State*. New York: Routledge.

Hobsbawm, Eric, and Terence Ranger, eds. 1983. *The Invention of Tradition*. New York: Cambridge University Press.

Hoefnagels, Anna. 2002. "Powwow Songs: Traveling Songs and Changing Protocol." *The World of Music* 44, no. 1, 227–36.

Howard, James H. 1955. "Pan-Indian Culture in Oklahoma." *The Scientific Monthly* 81, no. 5, 215–20.

———. 1983. "Pan-Indianism in Native American Music and Dance." *Ethnomusicology* 27, no. 1, 71–82.

Hoxie, Frederick, Peter Mancall, and James Merrell. 2001. "Indian Activism and Cultural Resurgence." In *American Nations: Encounters in Indian Country, 1850 to the Present*, edited by Frederick Hoxie, Peter Mancall, and James Merrell, 329. New York: Routledge.

Jackson, Jason Baird. 2005. "East Meets West: On Stomp Dance and Powwow Worlds in Oklahoma." In *Powwow*, edited by Clyde Ellis, Luke Eric Lassiter, and Gary H. Dunham, 172–97. Lincoln: University of Nebraska Press.

Jackson, Jason Baird, and Victoria Lindsay Levine. 2002. "Singing for Garfish: Music and Woodland Communities in Eastern Oklahoma." *Ethnomusicology* 46, no. 2, 284–306.

Johnson, Randal. 1993. "Editor's Introduction: Pierre Bourdieu on Art, Literature and Culture." In *The Field of Cultural Production*, Pierre Bourdieu, edited by Randal Johnson, 1–25. New York: Columbia University Press.

Jorgenson, Joseph. 1998. "Gaming and Recent American Indian Economic Development." *American Indian Culture and Research Journal* 22, no. 3, 157–72.

Kealy, Edward. 1990. "From Craft to Art: The Case of Sound Mixers and Popular Music." In *On Record: Rock, Pop, and the Written Word*, edited by Simon Frith and Andrew Goodwin, 207–20. New York: Pantheon.

Keil, Charles. 1984. "Music Mediated and Live in Japan." *Ethnomusicology* 28, no. 1, 91–96.

Kisliuk, Michelle. 1997. "Review of Bayaka: *The Extraordinary Music of the BaBenzélé Pygmies*." *Ethnomusicology* 41, no. 1, 171–74.

Kunst, Jaap. 1955. *Ethno-Musicology: A Study of Its Nature, Its Problems, Methods and Representative Personalities to Which Is Added a Bibliography*. The Hague: Martinus Nijhoff.

LaRocque, Emma. 1997. "Re-examining Culturally Appropriate Models in Criminal Justice Applications." In *Aboriginal Treaty Rights in Canada: Essays on Law, Equity, and Respect for Difference*, edited by Michael Asch, 75–96. Vancouver: University of British Columbia Press.

Lassiter, Luke E. 1998. *The Power of Kiowa Song: A Collaborative Ethnography*. Tucson: University of Arizona Press.

Learch, Patricia Barker, and Susan Bullers. 1996. "Powwows as Identity Markers: Traditional or Pan-Indian?" *Human Organization* 55, no. 4, 390–95.

Lee, Steven. 1995. "Re-examining the Concept of the 'Independent' Record Company: The Case of Wax Trax! Records." *Popular Music* 14, no. 1, 13–32.

Levi, Jerome, and Bartholomew Dean. 2006. "Introduction." In *At the Risk of Being Heard: Identity, Indigenous Rights, and Postcolonial States*, edited by Jerome Levi and Bartholomew Dean, 1–44. Ann Arbor: University of Michigan Press.

MacDowell, Marsha, ed. 1997. *Contemporary Great Lakes Pow Wow Regalia: "Nda Maamawigaami (Together We Dance)."* East Lansing: Michigan State University Museum.

Manuel, George, and Michael Posluns. 1974. *The Fourth World: An Indian Reality*. New York: Macmillan.

Manuel, Peter. 1993. *Cassette Culture: Popular Music and Technology in North India*. Chicago: University of Chicago Press.

Marcus, George and Michael Fisher. 1986. *Anthropology as Cultural Critique: An Experimental Moment in the Human Sciences*. Chicago: University of Chicago Press.

Marcus, Greil. 1990. *Mystery Train: Images of America in Rock 'n' Roll Music*. New York: E. P. Dutton.

Mason, Dale. 2000. *Indian Gaming: Tribal Sovereignty and American Politics*. Norman: University of Oklahoma Press.

Mattern, Mark. 1996. "The Powwow as a Public Arena for Negotiating Unity and Diversity in American Indian Life." *American Indian Research Journal* 20, no. 4, 183–204.

Mauss, Marcel. 1924. *The Gift: Forms and Functions of Exchange in Archaic Societies*. New York: W. W. Norton.

McAllester, David P. 1981. "New Perspectives in Native American Music." *Perspectives in New Music* 20, nos. 1–2, 433–46.

Meintjes, Louise. 1990. "Paul Simon's Graceland, South Africa, and the Mediation of Musical Meaning." *Ethnomusicology* 34, no. 1, 37–73.

———. 1997. "Mediating Difference: Producing Mbaqanga Music in a South African Studio." PhD diss., University of Texas.

———. 2003. *Sound of Africa! Making Music Zulu in a South African Studio.* Durham: Duke University Press.

———. 2005. "Reaching 'Overseas': South African Sound Engineers, Technology, and Tradition." In *Wired for Sound: Engineering and Technologies in Sonic Cultures*, edited by Paul D. Greene and Thomas Porcello, 23–46. Middletown, Conn.: Wesleyan University Press.

Moore, John H. 1993. "How Give-aways and Powwows Redistribute the Means of Subsistence." In *The Political Economy of North American Indians*, edited by John H. Moore, 240–69. Norman: University of Oklahoma Press.

Negus, Keith. 1992. *Producing Pop: Culture and Conflict in the Popular Music Industry.* London: Edward Arnold.

———. 1996. *Popular Music in Theory.* Hanover, N.H.: Wesleyan University Press.

———. 1999. *Music Genres and Corporate Cultures.* New York: Routledge.

Nettl, Bruno. 1964. *Theory and Method in Ethnomusicology.* New York: Free Press.

———. 1989. *Blackfoot Musical Thought: Comparative Perspectives.* Kent, Ohio: Kent State University Press.

———. 2005. *The Study of Ethnomusicology: Thirty-one Issues and Concepts.* Urbana: University of Illinois Press.

Pacini Hernández, Deborah. 1993. "A View from the South: Spanish Caribbean Perspectives on World Beat." *The World of Music* 35, 48–69.

Parthun, Paul. 1978. "Conceptualization of Traditional Music Among the Ojibwe of Manitoba and Minnesota." *Anthropological Journal of Canada* 16, no. 3, 27–32.

Peterson, Richard A. 1990. "Why 1955? Explaining the Advent of Rock Music." *Popular Music* 9, no. 1, 97–116.

———. 1997. *Creating Country Music, Fabricating Authenticity.* Chicago: University of Chicago Press.

Peterson, Richard A., and David Berger. 1975. "Cycles of Symbolic Production: The Case of Popular Music." *American Sociological Review* 40, 158–73.

Pierce, Jennifer Ember. 2000. *Off the Record: Country Music's Top Label Executives Tell Their Stories.* Lanham, Md.: Madison.

Porcello, Thomas. 1996. "Sonic Artistry: Music, Discourse, and Technology in the Sound Recording Studio." PhD diss., University of Texas.

———. 1998. "'Tails Out': Social Phenomenology and the Ethnographic Representation of Technology in Music-Making." *Ethnomusicology* 42, no. 3, 485–510.

———. 2005a. "Music Mediated as Live in Austin: Sound, Technology, and Recording Practice." In *Wired for Sound: Engineering and Technologies in Sonic Cultures*, edited by Paul D. Greene and Thomas Porcello, 103–17. Middletown, Conn.: Wesleyan University Press.

———. 2005b. "Afterword." In *Wired for Sound: Engineering and Technologies in Sonic Cultures*, edited by Paul D. Greene and Thomas Porcello, 269–81. Middletown, Conn.: Wesleyan University Press.

Powers, William K. 1963. *Grass Dance Costume*. Summerset, N.J.: Pow-wow Trails.

———. 1966. *Here Is Your Hobby: Indian Dancing and Costumes*. New York: G. P. Putnam's Sons.

———. 1980. "Oglala Song Terminology." In *Selected Reports in Ethnomusicology* 3, no. 2, edited by Charlotte Heth, 23–41. Los Angeles: Program in Ethnomusicology, University of California, Los Angeles.

———. 1990. *War Dance: Plains Indian Musical Performance*. Tucson: University of Arizona Press.

Pratt, Mary Louise. 1991. "Arts of the Contact Zone." *Profession* 91, 33–44.

Quequesah, Ruth. 2002. "Reflections from the Pow Wow Trail." *IndianCountry TodayMediaNetwork.com*, August 15, 2002.

Racy, Jihad. 1976. "The Recording Industry and Egyptian Traditional Music: 1904–1932." *Ethnomusicology* 20, no. 1, 27–48.

———. 1977. "Musical Change and Commercial Recording in Egypt 1904–1932." PhD diss., University of Illinois.

———. 1978. "Arabian Music and the Effects of Commercial Recording." *The World of Music* 20, no. 1, 47–57

Rapaport, Diane. 1979. *How to Make and Sell Your Own Record*. New York: Quick Fox.

Rynkiewich, Michael A. 1980. "Chippewa Powwows." In *Anishinabe: 6 Studies of Modern Chippewa*, edited by J. Anthony Paredes, 31–100. Tallahassee: University Press of Florida.

Sahlins, Marshall. 1994. "Goodbye to Tristes Tropes: Ethnography in the Context of Modern World History." In *Assessing Cultural Anthropology*, edited by Robert Borofsky, 377–94. New York: McGraw-Hill.

Samuels, David. 2004. *Putting a Song On Top of It*. Tucson: University of Arizona Press.

Scales, Christopher. 1996. "First Nations Popular Music in Canada: Identity, Politics, and Musical Meaning." Master's thesis, University of British Columbia.

———. 2002. "The Politics and Aesthetics of Recording: A Comparative Canadian Case Study of Powwow and Contemporary Native American Music." *The World of Music* 44, no. 1, 41–60.

Schafer, R. Murray. 1977. *The Tuning of the World*. New York: Alfred A. Knopf.

Seeger, Charles. 1977. *Studies in Musicology 1935–1975*. Berkeley: University of California Press.

Shelemay, Kay Kaufman. 1991. "Recording Technology, the Record Industry, and Ethnomusicological Scholarship." In *Comparative Musicology and Anthropology of Music: Essays on the History of Ethnomusicology*, edited by Bruno Nettl and Philip Bohlman, 277–92. Chicago: University of Chicago Press.

Skinner, Alanson. 1914. "Political Organization, Cults and Ceremonies of the Plains-Cree." *Anthropological Papers of the American Museum of Natural History* 11, 520–51.

Smith, Annie C. 2002. "More Reflections from the Pow Wow Trail." *IndianCountry TodayMediaNetwork.com*, August 15, 2002.

Smith, Claire, Heather Burke, and Graeme Ward. 2000. "Globalization and Indigenous Peoples: Threat or Empowerment?" In *Indigenous Cultures in an Interconnected World*, edited by Claire Smith and Graeme Ward, 1–27. St. Leonards, New South Wales: Allen and Unwin.

Statistics Canada. 2006. *Profile of Canada's Aboriginal Population*. 2006 Census of Canada. Ottawa: Industry, Science and Technology, Canada.

Stinson, Daune. 2002. "Redefining 'Tradition': A Women's Drum Group Files Civil Complaint for Sexual Discrimination." *The Circle: News from an American Indian Perspective* February 28, 10.

Stokes, Martin. 1994. "Introduction." In *Ethnicity, Identity and Music: the Musical Construction of Place*, edited by Martin Stokes. Oxford: Berg.

Straw, Will. 1991. "Systems of Articulation, Logics of Change: Communities and Scenes in Popular Music." *Cultural Studies* 5, no. 3, 368–88.

Sugarman, Jane C. 1997. *Engendering Song: Singing and Subjectivity at Prespa Albanian Weddings*. Chicago: University of Chicago Press.

Swartz, David. 1997. *Culture and Power: The Sociology of Pierre Bourdieu*. Chicago: University of Chicago Press.

Tankel, Johnathan David. 1990. "The Practice of Recording Music: Remixing as Recoding." *Journal of Communication* 40, no. 3, 34–46.

Théberge, Paul. 1997. *Any Sound You Can Imagine: Making Music, Consuming Technology*. Hanover, N.H.: Wesleyan University Press.

Toelken, Barre. 1991. "Ethic Selection and Intensification in the Native American Powwow." In *Creative Ethnicity: Symbols and Strategies of Contemporary Ethnic Life*, edited by Steven Sterns and John Allan Cicala, 137–56. Logan: Utah State University Press.

Turino, Thomas. 1999. "Signs of Imagination, Identity, and Experience: A Piercian Semiotic Theory for Music." *Ethnomusicology* 43, no. 2, 221–55.

———. 2000. *Nationalists, Cosmopolitans, and Popular Music in Zimbabwe*. Chicago: University of Chicago Press.

———. 2008. *Music as Social Life: The Politics of Participation*. Chicago: University of Chicago Press.

Valaskakis, Gail Guthrie. 2005. *Indian Country: Essays on Contemporary Native Culture*. Waterloo, Ont.: Wilfred Laurier University Press.

Vander, Judith. 1988. *Songprints: The Musical Experience of Five Shoshone Women*. Urbana: University of Illinois Press.

Vennum, Thomas, Jr. 1980. A History of Ojibwa Song Form." In *Selected Reports in Ethnomusicology* 3(2), edited by Charlotte Heth, 42–75. Los Angeles: Program in Ethnomusicology, University of California, Los Angeles.

———. 1982. *The Ojibwa Dance Drum: Its History and Construction*. Smithsonian Folklife Studies Number 2. Washington: Smithsonian Institution Press.

——. 1989. "The Changing Role of Women in Ojibway Music History." In *Women in North American Indian Music: Six Essays*, edited by Richard Keeling, 13–21. Bloomington: Society for Ethnomusicology.

——. 2002. "War Whoops, Hisses, and Animal Cries: Extra-musical Sounds in Traditional Ojibwe Song Performance." *Papers of the 33rd Algonquian Conference*, edited by H. C. Wolfart, 414–32. Winnipeg: University of Manitoba.

Vizenor, Gerald. 1994. *Manifest Manners: Postindian Warriors of Survivance*. Hanover, N.H.: Wesleyan University Press.

Wallis, Roger, and Krister Malm. 1984. *Big Sounds from Small Peoples: The Music Industry in Small Countries*. New York: Pendragon.

Waterman, Christopher. 1990. *Jùjú: A Social History and Ethnography of an African Popular Music*. Chicago: University of Chicago Press.

Waters, Mary. 1990. *Ethnic Options*. Berkeley: University of California Press.

Whidden, Lynn. 2007. *Essential Song: Three Decades of Northern Cree Music*. Waterloo, Ont.: Wilfred Laurier Press.

White, Richard. 1991. *The Middle Ground*. Cambridge: Cambridge University Press.

Wissler, Clark. 1913. "Societies and Dance Organization of the Blackfoot Indians." *Anthropological Papers of the American Museum of Natural History* 11, no. 4, 369–460.

Zak, Albin J. III. 2001. *The Poetics of Rock: Cutting Tracks, Making Records*. Berkeley: University of California Press.

Discography

Battle River. 1999. *Couple for the Road*. Arbor Records AR-11032.

Bear Creek. 2002. *LIVE*. Arbor Records AR-11512.

——. 2003. *The Show Must Go On*. Arbor Records AR-11994.

Bear Creek and Sizzortail. 2006. *When Worlds Collide*. Drumhop Productions DHOP-0200.

The Boyz. 1999. *Worldwide*. Noon Records NRC 090.

Cher. 1998. *Believe*. WEA 47121.

Donovan, Mishi. 1998. *The Spirit Within*. Sunshine Records SSCD-4258.

——. 2000. *Journey Home*. Arbor Records AR-11192.

Eyabay. 1997. *Thugs n' Harmony*. Sunshine Records SSCD-4332.

——. 1999. *No Limit*. Arbor Records AR-11012.

——. 2000. *Live 2000*. Arbor Records AR-11182.

——. 2002. *Miracle*. Arbor Records AR-11612.

Knight, Chester. 2003. *Standing Strong*. Arbor Records AR-11872.

Lake of the Woods Singers. 2000. *Honouring Our Elders*. Arbor Records AR-11244.

Lake Vermillion Singers.1999. *Lake Vermillion Singers*. Arbor Records AR-11042.

McKennitt, Loreena. 1997. *The Book of Secrets*. WEA CD-19404.

Miller, Derek. 2003. *Music Is My Medicine*. Arbor Records AR-11842.

Native American Heritage Series. 2002. *Stick Game Songs, Volume 1*. Arbor Records AR-11742.

Northern Wind Singers. 1997. *Northern Wind Volume 10*. Sunshine Records SSCT-4319.

———. 1999. *21st Century*. Arbor Records AR-11022.

———. 2000. *Ikwe Nagamonan*. Arbor Records AR-11282.

Red Tail. 2000. *Red Tail, Volume 1*. Arbor Records AR-11262.

———. 2001. *Red, Tail Volume 2*. Arbor Records AR-11432.

Sizzortail. 2000. *Enuff Said*. Arbor Records AR-11142.

Spirit Sands Singers. 1999. *Sacred Ground*. Arbor Records AR-11072.

TKO. 1998. *Welcome to the Playground*. Sunshine Records SSCD-4337.

Various Artists. 1991. *Voices of the Rainforest*. Rykodisc RCD-10173.

———. 1995. *Bayaka: The Extraordinary Music of the Babenzélé Pygmies* Ellipsis Arts CD-3490.

———. 1995. *Voices of Native America*. Q UP ART, QUA-20450.

———. 1999. *Champion Round Dance Songs, Volume 1*. Arbor Records AR-11082.

———. 1999. *Schemitzun '93–'99: The Best of the Best*. SGS-91899.

———. 1999. *Gathering of Nations Powwow 1999*. SOAR S-200.

———. 2000. *Hinckley Northern Style*. Arbor Records AR-11162.

———. 2000. *Hinckley Southern Style*. Arbor Records AR-11152.

———. 2001. *Hinckley Northern Style*. Arbor Records AR-11412.

———. 2001. *Hinckley Southern Style*. Arbor Records AR-11422.

———. 2001. *Jingle Dress Songs, Volume 1*. Arbor Records AR-11482.

———. 2002. *Chicken Dance Songs, Volume 1*. Arbor Records AR-11712.

———. 2002. *49er Songs, Volume 1*. Arbor Records AR-11832.

———. 2002. *Jingle Dress Songs, Volume 2*. Arbor Records AR-11722.

———. 2002. *Men's Grass Dance Songs, Volume 1*. Arbor Records AR-11702.

———. 2002. *Men's Traditional Songs, Volume 1*. Arbor Records AR-11732.

———. 2002. *Round Dance Songs, Volume 2*. Arbor Records AR-11792.

———. 2002. *Stick Game Songs, Volume 1*. Arbor Records AR-11742.

Whitefish Bay. 1999. *Ndoo Te Mag*. Arbor Records AR-11022.

———. 2000. *Pow Wow 2K*. Arbor Records AR-11172.

———. 2002. *Anishinaabe Meenigoziwin*. Sunshine Records SSCD-4439.

Young Grey Horse. 2001. *TP-Creepin.'* Arbor Records AR-11302.

Interviews Cited

Curtis Assiniboine, July 7, 1998

Stewart Astleford, July 5, 1999

Gabe Desrosiers, October 9, 1999

Gabe Desrosiers, May 31, 2000

Gabe Desrosiers, January 13, 2002

Gabe Desrosiers, September 15, 2007

Mike Esquash, September 5, 1999
Mike Esquash, July 27, 2006
Brandon Friesen, October 14, 1999
Brandon Friesen, July 30, 2006
John Marlow, February 8, 2000
Ness Michaels, July 14, 1998
John Morris, October 9, 1999
Red Tail Singers, March 5, 2000
Andy White, September 6, 1999

Page numbers followed by "n" indicate endnotes; *fig.* refers to the photo gallery following page 140.

Aboriginal Peoples Music Program (Canada Council), 165
adoption of Native children, 305n29
advertising, 304n24
aesthetic allegiances, 256–58
aesthetic values: ethics and aesthetics of singing, 110–11; genre and assumptions about, 209–10; grain of the recording and, 235–40; high fidelity, 237–38; intertribal ideology and, 63, 110, 257; judging criteria for singing, 71–77; presentational and participatory values, tension between, 77–78, 245, 309n6; standardization and, 63, 110, 257; standardization vs. regionalism, 78–79. *See also* liveness and studio mediation; recording culture and live vs. mediated performance; singing and singing competitions
affective alliances, 256–58
age: sound systems and, 119; vocal style and, 80; youth and aesthetics, 110–11
Aglukark, Susan, 277
Akipadryan, Brian, 253–54
Albers, Patricia C., 294n1
alcohol and drugs, 128, 289–90n3
amplification and sound systems, 36, 118–19, 300n4
Anishinaabe Meenigoziwin (Whitefish Bay Singers), 299–300n13
Appadurai, Arjun, 170, 171

Appreciation (Thank-you) songs, 43
Arbor Records, *figs.*; author's apprenticeship at, 293nn10–11; catalog greeting, 208; competition with other labels, 162; contract negotiations and relationships, 164, 174–80; distribution circuits, 172–74; ethnography and, 14–15, 262–63; formation of, 13, 158–59, 293n9; funding and grant proposals, 164–65; *Hinckley Pow Wow Northern Style*, *fig.*, 190, 231; *Hinckley Pow Wow Southern Style*, 190; industry changes and, 271–79; licensing negotiations and market construction, 166–72; *Native American Heritage Series*, 168–69; offices and staff, 158, 270–71, 304n16; racial difference, cultural misunderstandings, and, 180–85; signing artists, 159–64; *Stick Game Songs, Volume 1*, 169–70; vendor connections, 163–64. *See also* recording studios and recording process; Studio 11
arena directors, 35
articulation: critiques of traditional-modern articulation, 260–62; Hall's concept of, 8–9, 292n7; powwow music, relevance to, 9–10
art mode of collaboration, 237
Assiniboine, Curtis, 162, 183, 200, 276, 302n6

Assiniboines, 295n4. *See also* Carry the Kettle (CTK) powwow

Astleford, Stewart, 159, 173, 304n16, 305n25

Auslander, Phillip, 306n1

Australian Aboriginal dance troupes, 296n12

authenticity: academic authority, assumption of, 309n8; aesthetic allegiances, affective alliances, and, 256–57; articulation theory and, 10; documentary realism, 224, 237, 238; ethnomusicology and, 264–67; genre worlds and, 211; invention of tradition and, 295n3; liveness, studio mediation, and, 216–17, 222–24, 236, 255–56, 307n9; marketing and, 170–71; modern technology and, 260; phonographs and, 309n9; traditional vs. competition powwows and, 32, 57, 252–53. *See also* liveness and studio mediation

authorial voice, 18

award institutions, 1990s boom in, 5–6

Badel, James, 237

band manager role, 127–28

Barthes, Roland, 234–35

Battle River, 90, 160, 214

Bayaka (Sarno and Krause), 266

Bear Creek: Arbor Records and, 163; Jingle Dress songs and, 69; listening posts and, 274–75; recording of first CD, 67; at Schemitzun Annual Green Corn Festival and Powwow, 2

bed tracks, 191–93

Bee, Tom, 166, 190, 292n5, 308n2

bells, overdubbing of, 215–16

Benjamin, Walter, 170

Big Wind Singers, 302n15

Blackfeet, 97, 98

Blacklodge Singers, 176, 304n22, 305n26

Blanket dance songs, 101

Blum, Stephen, 70, 195–96

booths at powwows. *See* vendors at powwows

border, international (U.S.-Canada), 292n8

bounce, 103–5

Bourdieu, Pierre, 187–88, 306n1

Boyz, The, 251

Brady, Erika, 309n9

Brokenhead Ojibway Reserve powwow, 45–52

Browner, Tara, 28, 66, 68, 250, 291n4

Buchanan, Donna A., 304n21

Bullers, Susan, 291n4

Burke, Heather, 110

Canada Council for the Arts, 164–65

capture, metaphor of, 204–5, 236–39, 241–42

Carry the Kettle (CTK) powwow: children at, 33–34; Grand Entry, 33, 35–39; history of, 295n4; location of, 32–33; physical and temporal organization of, 34–35

cassette technology, 156–58, 207–8

CD Plus, 173

cheating, 54–55

check beats (honor beats or hard beats), 83, 100, 198, 299n9

"Cher" effect, the (vocoder effect), 217, 218, 223, 224, 227

Chicken dance, 300n14

Chicken dance songs, 84–85, 97, 108, 284–85

children: adoption by non-Natives, 305n29; learning to sing, 132; at remote recording session, 263–64; reservation powwows and, 33–34

click tracks, 192

Clifford, James, 18, 27, 114

collaboration, modes of, 236–37

colonial power relations, 259, 260

Color Guard, 37

color procession, 36–37

competition powwows: Carry the Kettle powwow, 32–45; cheating, 54–55; culture, tradition, and the "problem" of competition, 52–60, 70; drum hopping restricted at, 72, 78; drum whistling restricted at, 50; incentives for singing, 130–31; as intertribal space, 61; intertribal values, standardization, and, 257; order of events at, 35; physical organization of, 34; sacred-secular continuum and, 60–62; traditional powwows vs., 29–32, 47–52, 61–62, 252–53, 258; tradition discourse and, 57. *See also* economics of powwows; judging

composition of songs, 101–3

compression, 198, 226–28, 233–34, 306n6, 307n6

conjectural vs. organic historical forces, 292n6

Contemporary Native music: Arbor and, 203; distributors for, 166; Donovan's *Journey Home* as, 206, 207; gender and, 206; as genre, 208–11, 259, 302n4; Grammies and, 6; growth of, 276–77. *See also* singing and singing competitions; world music and world beat

contemporary powwows. *See* competition powwows

Contemporary (Word) songs, 87–91, 282–83

contracts, 164, 174–80, 183

copyright, 250

Cornelius, Richard, 291n4

corporate culture, 186

couples dances. *See* social and couples dances

Cozad, 300n15

craft union mode of collaboration, 236–37

Cree: Chicken dance and, 300n14; Round dance songs and, 93, 96; singing style, 80, 81

Cree drums, style of, 69

cries and shouts, 83

Crow Hop songs, 84, 86, 93–94, 96, 284

Crow nation, 93, 98

cultural authority, 205. *See also* power relations

cultural capital, 202

culture: articulation theory on, 9; corporate organization and production and, 186; cultural identities and articulation, 10; Geertz on social relationships and, 112; invented tradition and, 294n3; marketing and exoticization of, 171; preservation of, 245; racial and cultural difference, equated, 182–84; recording culture and, 3; traditional powwows and, 58–60; traveling culture and the culture of travel, 114–17. *See also* recording culture and live vs. mediated performance

Cuwkencaayu, Chief, 295n4

Dakota, 92, 96

Dakota Travels, 242

dance competitions: Australian Aboriginal groups, 296n12; at Carry the Kettle powwow, 41–42; categories, 41; history of, 53–54

dance specials: at Carry the Kettle powwow, 40–41, 42–44; history of, 54; host drums and, 120, 300n6; payment for singing, 121

dance splits, 48

dancing: at Brokenhead powwow, 47; at Carry the Kettle powwow, 38–45; dancing out, 41, 296n10; exhibition dances, 42; footwork patterns, 296n11; intertribal rounds, 38, 47; melody and danceability, 81; participation and reaction to musicians, 75–76; practicing, 247–48; singer commitment to dancers, 106–10; social memory and, 61; song appropriateness for, 76–77, 108; song types and dance categories, 84–86;

dancing (*continued*)
specials, 40–41, 42–44; traditional vs.
contemporary, 258–59, 294n2
day pay (drum splits), 48, 120, 268
Densmore, Frances, 1–2, 297n16
Deschambeau, Phil, 270–71
Desrosiers, Dianne, 115, 268
Desrosiers, Gabe, *fig.*; about, 16–17; on
alcohol and drugs, 128; on being a
singer, 109–10; on dance categories,
294n2; on family tradition, 131–32;
grain of the recording and, 236; on
pickup singers, 134–35; on reputation, 244–45; roles in Northern Wind
Singers, 122–23, 127–28; at Schemitzun
powwow, 115; at Sisseton Wahpeton
Oyate Wacipi, 268; on song composition, 102; on song ownership, 248–49;
on song types, 92, 95–97, 98; sound
effects and, 253–54; on supratribal
world, 258; on tails, 84; on traditional
vs. competition powwows, 30–31, 58,
59; *21st Century* recording session and
studio mediation, 217–24. *See also*
Northern Wind Singers
Diamond, Beverly, 206, 264
digital audio workstation (DAW) systems,
227
discursive productions of Nativeness, 196
displaced syncopation, 81, 104
distribution and distributors, 172–74, 207,
303n11
documentary realism, 224, 237, 238, 265,
267
Donovan, Mishi: background, 191; *Journey Home*, *fig.*, 189–97; listening posts
and, 274; recording control and trust
relationships, 206–7; social power and,
197; *The Spirit Within*, 203
Double Beat songs, 86, 94–95
double leads, 102–3
Doyle, Peter, 232
Drawmer compressor, 227–28

dreams as song sources, 102, 300n17
drugs and alcohol, 128, 289–90n3
drum carriers, 123–24, 301n8
drum groups ("drums"): at Brokenhead powwow, 46; at Carry the Kettle
powwow, 42; economics of, 117–22;
equal participation in, 72–73; family
groups, 122; gender roles and, 135–
40; host drums and invited drums,
35–39, 119–20, 300n6; learning new
songs, 129–30; Northern style and,
79; prestige structure, 112–13, 244–45,
300n1–301n2; recording, control of,
202; regional styles, 68–69; rehearsal of
songs, 129–30; relationships, regional
and intertribal, 133–34; repertoires and
song exchange, 125–26, 248–49; singing
ability, learning, and group membership, 130–35; social discourse, musical, within, 130; social roles in, 122–28;
stacked, 73; technical perfection and,
251–52; traveling culture, 114–17. *See
also* singing and singing competitions;
specific groups
Drumgroups.com, 269
drum hopping, 48–49, 72, 78, 133–34
Drumhop Productions, 269, 279, 280
drumkeepers for traditional drums, 48,
49–50, 301n8
drumming and drum beats: bounce and,
103–5; Cree style, 93; Crow Hop, drum
patterns for, 93–94; digital effects
never applied to, 224–25; song types
and drum beats, 84–86; straight drumbeat, 89; unity of drumbeat, 71–72. *See
also* singing and singing competitions
drum order, 38
drum roll calls, 36
drums (instruments): contemporary, 49;
costs of, 117; respect for, 49–50, 75,
123–24, 224–25; of Spirit Sand Singers,
117–18; traditional, 48–50
drum splits (day pay), 48, 120, 268

drum tracks, 192
drum whistling, 50–52, 109, 297n16
dual production, 234–36
Duck-and-dive songs, 86, 97–98

Eagle Feather Pickup song, 38
Eagle Ridge, 215–16
Eagle Staffs, 36–37, 42, 98
Eagle (or eagle-bone) whistles, 50–52
economic capital, 200
economics of powwows: drums and PA
    systems, 117–19; drum splits, 48, 120,
    268; host drums and invited drums,
    119–20; as incentive to record, 244; new
    songs and, 248; payment in traditional
    powwows, 48; prize money, 115–16, 269,
    303n13; profits, 121–22; selling tapes
    and CDs, 121; singing without pay, 119;
    vendor booths, 34, 45–46, 295n6
economics of record companies. See
    record labels and powwow music
    industry
effects, digital: liveness and, 217–18, 220–
    21, 223–25; postproduction and, 227
Elk's Whistle, 35–39, 42
Ellis, Clyde, 61
emcees, 35, 37–38, 108
engineering. See recording studios and
    recording process; recording tech-
    nology
entrance tropes, 225
entrepreneurial mode of collaboration,
    237
enunciation and phrasing, 106
equalization, 229, 233, 307n7
Esquash, Gerald, 123
Esquash, Kevin, fig.
Esquash, Michael, figs.; about, 12–13; on
    clarity, 106; on drumming styles, 69;
    on judging criteria, 71–77; as leader/
    manager, 127–28; Little Ron and, 139;
    new songs and, 129–30; Powwows.com
    podcast, 279; on repertoire, 125–26;

on respect for drums, 123–24; as ritual
    specialist, 301n7; on sacred-secular con-
    tinuum, 60; on singing quality, 64; on
    song composition, 101, 102; on sound
    gear, 118; on starting the group, 125; on
    travel, 112
ethics: ability and the social ethic of par-
    ticipation, 77–78; aesthetic allegiance
    and, 257; ceremonial singing, 119; com-
    petition circuit and, 113–14; drums,
    respect for, 49–50, 75, 123–24, 224–25;
    host-guest relationship and obliga-
    tions, 48, 61; legitimacy of competi-
    tion powwows and, 60–61; participa-
    tory vs. presentational, 77–78, 309n6;
    self-policing, 59; singing, ethics and
    aesthetics of, 110–11; song aesthetics
    and, 109; traditional vs. competition
    powwows and, 57–58. See also power
    relations; social relationships; tradition
    discourses
ethnomusicology: entrance tropes and,
    225; liveness and, 232, 264–65; moder-
    nity and tradition discourses and, 258–
    62; politics of pleasure and, 257–58;
    recording culture and, 262–67; techno-
    logical hurdles and, 226; world music
    and, 187
European market, 166–67
exhibition dances at Carry the Kettle
    powwow, 42
Eyabay: compliments to, 107; Contempo-
    rary style of, 90; contracts and, 174–75,
    177–79; double leads and, 102–3; lead
    singers in, 123; listening posts and, 275;
    singing style, 70; song naming and,
    250–51
Eya-Hey Nakoda, 35–39

FACTOR (the Foundation to Assist Cana-
    dian Talent on Records) grants, 165
faders, 307n7
family drum groups, 122, 137

family tradition of singing, 131–32

Fancy dancing: at Carry the Kettle powwow, 43–44; modernity discourse and,
295n3; Southern Straight songs and,
100

Fancy dancing, Men's: at Carry the Kettle
powwow, 44; Crow Hop and, 93; Shake
songs and, 91; song types, 86; trick
songs and, 99

Fancy dancing, Women's: Crow Hop and,
93; Fancy shawl dancing at Carry the
Kettle powwow, 43–44; song types for
shawl dancing, 86

feasting, 47, 54–55

feather pickup, 39

Feld, Steven, 70, 266

Fe, Pura, 276–77

Festival Records, 207

Fewkes, Jesse Walter, 1–2

fidelity, perfection in, 253

field analysis: genre worlds and, 210–11;
recording process and, 187–89, 202,
203; sub-fields, 306n1; Turino and,
306n1

finances. See economics of powwows

fire, ceremonial, 46

Fisher, Mike, 200, 201, 202

flags, 36–37, 42

Flag songs, 38, 42, 84, 98–99

food vendors, 34

Foot Slide songs. See Crow Hop songs

Fort Berthold Reservation, fig.

forty-nine dances, 289n3

Foundation to Assist Canadian Talent on
Records (FACTOR) grants, 165

441 Studios, 270, 276

Fourstar, Robert, 35

Fourth World pan-Aboriginalist discourse, 296n12

free agents, 134

Friesen, Brandon, fig.; Arbor Records and,
158–60, 163, 171, 174–80, 304n16; artist relationships and power dynamics,

203–7; career of, 13–14, 293nn9–10;
grain of the recording and, 236; on industry changes, 270–79; live vs. studio
recording and, 213–24; Naxos negotiations, 166–67; postproduction and, 228;
production and engineering, 190–95,
198–99; racial politics and, 180–82

Friesen, Jamie, 158, 190, 304n16

Frith, Simon, 209, 210, 212, 303n9, 307–
8n9

Furlong, Helen, 302n16

gating the amplifier, 307n5

Geertz, Clifford, 27–28, 225

gender: drum groups and, 135–40;
ethnography and, 302n14; power dynamics in recording and, 206; singing,
gendered nature of, 65; tribalism, intertribalism, and, 139

geno-recording, 235–36

genre: contemporary vs. traditional Native music, 209, 259, 302n4; fields, mediation, and, 208–11; gender and, 206;
process and, 189; Studio 11 and genre
knowledge, 188–89

genre worlds, 210–11, 237–38

Gerbrand, Derek (Purple), 181–82, 197–
200, 305nn28–29

Gillette, Rusty, 269, 280

giveaways, 43, 297n13, 301n6

Goldstein, Kenneth, 307–8n9

Gould, Glenn, 238

GQ Smooth, 190

grain of the recording, 234–40

Grammy Awards, 6, 13, 154, 292n5

Gramsci, Antonio, 292n6

Grand Entry: Brokenhead powwow, 46;
Carry the Kettle powwow, 33, 35–39;
Flag songs and, 98; Hinckley Grand
Celebration Powwow, fig.; standard
components of, 296n8

grants and funding, 164–65, 305n30

Grass dance songs, 84, 242

Grass dancing: Chicken dance songs and, 85, 97; Crow Hop and, 93; drum whistling and, 297n16; old-style vs. contemporary, 294n2; song types, 86; tradition discourse and, 295n3; women and, 137

Gray, Herman, 172

Groove Town, 191, 193

Grossberg, Lawrence, 257

Hall, Stuart, 8–9, 292n7

Handler, Richard, 295n3

hard beats (honor beats or check beats), 83, 100, 198, 299n9

harmonizers, 136–37, 138

Hart, Mickey, 266

Hartlooper, Justin "Dutch," 158, 190, 193, 206, 305n28

Hatoum, Rainer, 92

Hatton, O. Thomas, 130–31, 137, 138, 299n9

Heartbeat of Nations powwow, 117

Heluska song form, 298n6

Hennion, Antoine, 267

Herzfeld, Michael, 297n20

Heywahe, John, 38

high-context communication, 293n12

high fidelity, ideology of, 237–38, 307n9

High Noon, 44, 90, 91, 105

Hinckley Grand Celebration Powwow, figs.

Hinckley Pow Wow Northern Style (Arbor Records), fig., 190, 231

Hinckley Pow Wow Southern Style (Arbor Records), 190

Hobsbawm, Eric, 294n3

honor beats (check beats or hard beats), 83, 100, 198, 299n9

Honor songs, 43, 84, 120, 285–86

Honouring Our Elders (Lake of the Woods), 197–202, 205, 207–8

Horsetail, 200

host drums, 35–39, 119–20, 300n6

host-guest relationship and obligations, 48, 61

hot-five method, 299n9

Howard, James H., 290–91n4

iconicity, 297–98n20

identity, "Native" or "Indian": articulation theory on, 9; discursive and processual productions of Nativeness, 196–97; gender roles and, 139; genre worlds and, 211; intertribal social relationships and, 117; recording and mediation of, 195–97; sacredness and, 60; Samuels on, 260; traditional vs. competition powwows and, 57, 62

identity construction, 289n4

Ikwe Nagamonan (Northern Wind Singers), 95–97, 129

imagined audience, 258, 267

imagined markets, 168, 170, 209–10, 265–66

Indian Country Today "Reflections" articles, 53–57

Indian House, 6

Indian identity. See identity, "Native" or "Indian"

innovation, formal, 102–3

intertribal events. See competition powwows

intertribal genres. See dance competitions; dancing; songs

intertribalism: aesthetic values and, 63, 110, 257; competition and risk of division, 59; competition powwows as intertribal space, 61–62; gender and, 136, 139; identity and, 3; imagined audience and, 258; indigenous modernity and, 7–8; Pan-Indianism, 290–92n4; powwow music as genre and, 258; powwows and, 4; sacred practice and, 60–61; web of social relationships, 117, 133. See also identity, "Native" or "Indian"

interviews, ethnographic, 18–19

invited drums, 120

invocations, 38
Iron Swing, 40
Issacs, Tony, 308n2

Jackson, Jason Baird, 291n4
Jingle dress dancing: Crow Hop and, 93; drumbeats for, 84; Maggie White and, 299n13; regalia, non-Ojibwa elaborations of, 114; Side-step songs and, 95; song types, 86; traditional vs. contemporary, 294n2; Whitefish Bay Singers CD, 299–300n13
Jingle Dress DVD project, 164–65
Jingle Dress songs, 69, 284
Journey Home (Donovan), *fig.*, 189–97
judging: at Carry the Kettle powwow, 40, 296n9; criteria, 71–77; head judges, 79; perceptions of, 52–53; practices and scoring, 71; presentational and participatory values, tension between, 77–78
Juno awards, 6, 13, 203

Kealy, Edward, 236–37
Kisliuk, Michelle, 266
Krause, Bernie, 266

Lake of the Woods: Arbor, choice of, 161–62; *Honouring Our Elders* distribution, 207–8; *Honouring Our Elders* recording session, 197–202, 205
Lake Vermillion Singers, 229
Lakota, 92, 96
LaRocque, Emma, 259
lawsuit over gender rules, 135–36
lead and seconds, 82–83
leaders of drum groups, 127–28
lead singers, 72–73, 122–23
Learch, Patricia Barker, 291n4
Levine, Victoria Lindsay, 291n4
licensing negotiations and deals, 166–68, 207, 274
limiters, 230
liner notes, 169, 265–66

Linnekin, Jocelyn, 295n3
listening posts, 274–75
Little Ron, 139
Little Spirit Singers, 137–38
liveness and studio mediation: aesthetic ideal and discursive trope, 215–16, 253–54; authenticity and, 216–17, 222–24, 236, 255–56; cultural authority and, 205; difference between studio and live, 219–22; digital effects and, 217–18, 220–21, 223–25; Eagle Ridge live recording, 215–16; ethnomusicology and, 232, 264–65; grain of the recording and ideological discourse, 234–40; Kealy's three modes of collaboration, 236–37; live, studio, and remote recording, 213; middle ground and, 255–57; multi-tracking and, 217–18, 223–24; Northern Wind Singers' *21st Century* and, 217–25; postproduction and mastering, 225–34; preference for live recording, 213–15, 222–23; Red Tail Singers' *Red Tail, Volume 1* and, 227–31; scholarship on, 306n1; social power and, 239–40; spaciality, placemaking, and, 232–33, 238. *See also* recording culture and live vs. mediated performance
Longclaws, Carolyne, 52–53
Longhouse, 274
Long Lodge, Chief, 295n4
low pass filters, 228

male gender roles, drum groups' role in shaping, 138–39
Mandan Midwinter powwow, 215
Mandaree powwow, 107–8
Mandaree Singers, 90, 91, 119, 300n1
Manuel, Peter, 252
markets, construction of, 166–72, 207–10, 265–66
Marlow, John, *fig.*; Arbor and, 159, 304n16; on competition, 162–64; licensing negotiations and, 166–67; royalties dispute, 184–85

mastering and post-production, 225–34. *See also* liveness and studio mediation

McAllester, David, 241

McKennitt, Loreena, 194

mediation: genres, fields, and, 208–11; intercultural contact, studio as place of, 211; meanings of, 22, 189; musical style and, 70–71; politics and, 2; recording methods, power distribution, and, 205–7; recording studio as site of, 189; as term, 189; theory and, 66. *See also* liveness and studio mediation; recording culture and live vs. mediated performance; recording studios and recording process

Medicine, Beatrice, 294n1

Meintjes, Louise, 189, 224, 306n1

melody, 80–81

memorial dance competitions, 40

Menenick, D. J.: on drumming aesthetics, 63; on performance aesthetics, 103–5; on singing aesthetics, 73–74; on song types, 84–85; on traditional powwows, 58–59

Menenick, John, 58–59

Men's Fancy dancing. *See* Fancy dancing, Men's

Men's Grass Dance. *See* Grass dancing

Men's Traditional dancing, 86, 91, 98

Michaels, Linda, 149

Michaels, Ness, 149, 175, 177

microphone configurations, 198, 233

middle ground, 255–57, 308n5

Midnite Express, 90, 91

Miller, Derek, 276, 277

mistake-free performances, 251–52

mixed beat, 91

mixing and mixdowns, 194–95, 197, 202

modernity, indigenous: affective alliances and, 257–58; alternative modernities and modernist-reformism, 309n7; aspects of, 7–8; critiques of traditional-modern articulation, 260–62; ethnomusicology and, 258–62; Hall on social

formation and, 292n7; traditional vs. competition powwows and, 60–61, 62; "tradition and change" narrative and, 261–62; tradition as resource strategy and, 259–60

money. *See* economics of powwows

Moore, Everett, 269

Moosomin, Art, 126

Morris, John, 64, 106–7, 244

Motown Records, 278

MP3 file format, 272

multitracking, 217–18, 223–24

music industry. *See* record labels and powwow music industry

Mystic River, 99, 300n15

naming of songs, 250–51, 308n2

National Academy of Recording Arts and Sciences (NARAS), 6, 292n5

Native American Heritage (NAH) series (Arbor Records), 168–69

Native American Tube, 272

Nativeness. *See* identity, "Native" or "Indian"

Naxos International, 166–68

Ndoo Te Mag (Whitefish Bay Singers), 160, 184

Negus, Keith, 10, 169, 186, 210, 304n18, 304n20

Neskahai, Arlie, 92

Nettle, Bruno, 300n17

Nez Perce, 98

noise gate sound processors, 307n5

Northern-style singing. *See* singing and singing competitions; song categories

Northern Wind Singers, *figs.*; CD tracks, 282–86; Desrosiers and, 16; drums, 118; Fisher and, 200; *Ikwe Nagamonan*, 95–97, 129; Jingle Dress songs and, 69; learning new songs, 129; members of, 286–87; *Northern Wind Vol. 10*, 221, 253–54; Side-step songs and, 95; social roles in, 127–28; traditional powwows and, 58; *21st Century*, *fig.*, 217–25, 229–

Northern Wind Singers (*continued*)
30, 250; at University of Oregon pow-
wow, 116. *See also* Desrosiers, Gabe
Northern Wind Vol. 10 (Northern Wind
Singers), 221, 253–54
Northwest Angle, 133
Norway House Powwow, *fig.*

Oglala Sioux, 298n5
O'Grady, Terence, 291n4
Ojibway: Brokenhead powwow, 45–52;
cultural elaborations and transformations of style of, 114; drum groups,
style of, 69; gender roles, 139; Side-step
songs and, 95–96; Waywayseecappo,
52, 297n17
one-stops, 174
Onion Lake powwow, 78–79, 121–22, 124,
126
order of events at competition powwows,
35
organic vs. conjuctural historical forces,
292n6
originality, importance of, 102, 124–25,
247–48
outboard effects processors, 227
overstepping, 172, 248, 304n23
O'Watch, Chief James, 38, 41, 43
Owl dancing, 84
ownership, cultural, 280–81
ownership of songs, 49, 248–50

packaging strategies, 167, 169, 265–66,
309n8
Pan-Indianism, 290–92n4
Parker, George, 233, 269
participatory dances, 40
participatory values, 245
participatory vs. presentational values,
77–78, 309n6
PA systems and amplification, 36, 118–19,
300n4
payment. *See* economics of powwows

P&D (pressing and distribution) deals,
273–74
"Pearl Jam" effect, the (reverse reverb),
217, 218, 220, 307n3
Pearson, Arthur, *fig.*
Peasley, Robert, 179–80, 183, 276
perfection, technical and performative,
251–53
Pete, Shonto, 63, 73–74, 84–85, 103–5
Peterson, Richard, 209
pheno-recording, 235–36
phrasing and enunciation, 106
pickup singers, 134–35
pipes and smoking, 48, 297n15
piracy, online, 272
pleasure, politics of, 257–58
Porcello, Tom, 224, 306n1
"postindian survivance," 260–61
post-production and mastering, 225–34.
See also liveness and studio mediation
power relations: colonial, 259, 260; Fourth
World, 211; grain of the recording and,
239–40; producer-artist relationships
and, 197, 203–7. *See also* gender
Powers, William K., 68, 88, 291n4, 298n5,
299n7, 300n17
powwow circuits: defined, 11; history of,
29–30; longevity on, 172. *See also* travel
powwow culture, 11, 289n3
powwows: Brokenhead Ojibway, 45–52;
Carry the Kettle, 32–45; culture, tradition, and the "problem" of competition,
52–60; drugs and alcohol at, 289–90n3;
Heartbeat of Nations, 117; Hinckley
Grand Celebration, *figs.*; Mandan Mid-
winter, 215; Mandaree, 107–8; "mega,"
29, 54; as modern phenomena, 8; Norway House, *fig.*; Onion Lake, 78–79,
121–22, 124, 126; physical organization
of, 34; sacred-secular continuum and,
60–62; scheduling of, 295n5; Schemitzun, 2, 115–16, 160, 300n15, 303n13;
scholarship on, 4; Shakopee Mdewa-

kanton, 67, 242, 299n10; Shoal Lake, *figs.*; similarities and variations, 291n4; St. Thomas University, 135–36; Swan Lake, *figs.*; tribal affiliation and, 28; University of Oregon, 116; Waywaysee-cappo competition, 52. *See also* competition powwows; traditional powwows; *specific topics*

Powwows.com, 161, 272, 279

powwow trail, 11, 57, 292n8

Pow Wow TV, 272

Prairie Chicken, Trevor, 196–97

presentation dance styles, 40

presentation vs. participatory values, 77–78, 245, 309n6

pressing and distribution (P&D) deals, 273–74

prestige structure for drum groups, 112–13, 300n1–301n2

processual productions of Nativeness, 196–97

production: "dual," 234–36; field analysis and, 188; Kealy's three modes of collaboration, 236–37; on Mishi Donovan's *Journey Home*, 189–94; post-production and mastering, 225–34; producer-artist relationships and power dynamics, 203–7. *See also* liveness and studio mediation; recording studios and recording process

Pro Tools, 226–30

public access to powwows, 61

Purple (Derek Gerbrand), 181–82, 197–200, 305nn28–29

push-ups, 82–83, 100, 299n7

race: cultural and racial difference equated, 182–84; cultural misunderstandings and, 183–86; record labels and Native American staff, 180–82

Race Day Promotions, 270–71

Ranger, Terence, 294n3

rap artists, 182, 190, 206

rattles, 253–54, 308n4

recording culture and live vs. mediated performance: aesthetic allegiances and affective alliances, 256–58; aesthetics of the powwow grounds, the studio, and liveness, 254–55; capture and, 241–42; ethnomusicology and recording culture, 262–67; meanings of recording culture, 3; middle ground and, 255–57; naming of songs and, 250–51, 308n2; new labels and, 279; originality, new songs, and, 247–48; reasons for recording, 243–46; song ownership and exchange and, 248–50; sound effects and, 253–54; taping vs. commercial recordings, 247; technical perfection, aesthetic of, 251–53; tradition and modernism discourses and, 258–62

recording studios and recording process: ethnomusicology and, 187; field analysis and, 187–89, 202, 203, 210–11; genre classification and mediation, 208–11; Lake of the Woods recording session, 197–202; live, studio, and remote recording, 213; market differences and, 207–8; mixing on Mishi Donovan's *Journey Home*, 194–95; native identity, mediation of, 195–97; as place of intercultural contact, 211; producer-artist relationships and power dynamics, 197, 203–7; production and engineering on Mishi Donovan's *Journey Home*, 189–94; symbolic and cultural capital and, 200, 202. *See also* liveness and studio mediation; Studio 11; *specific studios*

recording technology: challenges of, 226; the "Cher" effect (vocoder effect), 217, 218, 223, 224, 227; compression, 198, 226–28, 233–34, 306n6, 307n6; equalization, 229, 233, 307n7; historical role of, 1–2; and liveness, production of, 216–17; microphone configurations, 198, 233; microphone setup, 198; mix-

recording technology (*continued*)
ing, 194–95, 197, 202; "Pearl Jam" effect
(reverse reverb), 217, 218, 220, 307n3;
reverb, 199, 228–29, 230, 232–33, 306n7;
sequencers, 192, 306n2

record labels and powwow music industry: aesthetic transformations and, 254–55; Bill C-31 and, 154–56; cassette technology, impact of, 156–58; categories of independent labels, 6–7; changes in industry, 271–79; contract negotiations and relationships, 164, 174–80; distribution, 172–74; family relationships and, 304n16; grant proposals and funding, 164–65; Indian casinos and, 151–54; licensing negotiations and market construction, 166–72; majors and independents and, 146–48, 172, 273–74, 303n9; new labels, 269–70, 279–81; 1990s boom in, 5–6, 144–45; race, culture, and, 180–86; reputation of, 160–63; signing artists, 159–64; social and economic factors in development of, 151; Sunshine Records, 148–50; world music and, 150–51. *See also* Arbor Records; Studio 11

Red Cap, 1–2

Red Tail Singers: Blacklodge and, 304n22; *Red Tail, Volume 1*, 227–31, 250; remote recording session in Idaho, 263–64; song naming and, 250; traditional powwows and, 58. *See also* Menenick, D. J.; Pete, Shonto

regionalism: singing styles and, 68–69; Southern-style songs, 300n15; standardization vs., 78–79

rehearsal, 129–30

remote recording, 213

reputation of recording companies, 160–63

respect for drums, 49–50, 75, 123–24

retail sales, 173–74, 272, 275–76

reverb, 199, 228–29, 230, 232–33, 306n7

reverb, reverse ("Pearl Jam" effect), 217, 218, 220, 307n3

reviews of powwow music, 160–61

Rez Cue Records, 179–80, 279

ritual specialists, 301n7

rock music: Arbor and, 208; authenticity and, 170–71; echo and reverb in, 232; Friesen on growth of, 154; liveness and, 216, 306n1; Sunshine Records and, 13, 145; voice as documentary in, 224

romance. *See* snagging (courtship)

Roseau River Ramblers, 40, 176

Round dance songs, 86, 283; Side-step and, 96; as song type, 92–93

royalties, 161, 177, 179, 184

royalty (Powwow Princesses and Braves), 38

Ruffle (Shake) songs, 86, 91–92

sacred vs. secular, 60–62, 102, 300n17

Sahlins, Marshall, 145, 260

Samuels, David, 8, 260

Sandstorm (Spirit Sand Singers), *fig.*

Sarno, Louis, 266

scheduling of powwows, 295n5

Schemitzun Annual Green Corn Festival and Powwow: Battle River at, 160; Bear Creek at, 2; prize money at, 115–16, 303n13; "Switch songs," 300n15

Schibler, Shawn, 270

Scinocca, Paul: Arbor and, 270–71, 309n1; engineering and production, 192, 193; Nativeness question and, 195; Purple and, 181–82; on race, 185; recording courses, 305n28; Studio 11 and, 13, 158; studio work, 190

scratch tracks, 191–92, 306n2

Sells, Cato, 1

sequencers, 192, 306n2

Shake (Ruffle) songs, 86, 91–92

Shakopee Mdewakanton powwow, 67, 242, 299n10

Shallcross, Rob, 190, 293n11

Shoal Lake Powwow, *figs.*

Shoshone, 139

shouts and cries, 83

Shoyo, Leonore, 301n10

Side-step songs, 67, 86, 95–97

singing and singing competitions: ability and learning, 131–33; at Carry the Kettle powwow, 39–40; at ceremonial or other functions, 119, 301n7; clarity, quality, power, and blend, 73–75; critical evaluation by singers, 64–65; ethical self-policing and, 59; gendered nature of, 65; incentives for, 130–31; judging criteria and aesthetic preferences, 71–77; lead singers, 72–73, 122–23; performance aesthetics, 103–10; presentational and participatory values, tension between, 77–78; social memory and, 61; standardization and regionalism, 78–79; style distinctions, 67–70; symbolic discourse and musical practices, dialectic of, 70–71; Traditional and Contemporary contests, separation of, 89–90; unconscious theory and, 66–67; youth and, 110–11. *See also* competition powwows; recording culture and live vs. mediated performance; song categories; songs

singing groups. *See* drum groups ("drums"); *specific groups*

Sisseton Wahpeton Oyate Wacipi, 268–70

Sizzortail, 159, 164, 190

Skinner, Alanson, 300n14

slang, 250–51

slide step songs (slides). *See* Side-step songs

Smith, Claire, 110

smoking and pipes, 48, 297n15

snagging (courtship), 56, 57, 131

Sneak-up songs, 86, 91–92, 283

SOAR (Sound of America) Records, 153–54, 166, 190, 207

social and couples dances, 92–93

social formation, Hall on, 292n7

social life of recordings. *See* recording culture and live vs. mediated performance

social memory, 61–62

social relationships: contract relationships, 164, 174–80; culture of travel and, 116–17; between drum groups and recording companies, 185–86; Geertz on culture and, 112; masculine socialization in drum groups, 138–39; new labels and, 279–80; record labels and, 163–64; snagging (courtship), 56, 57, 131; social roles in a drum group, 122–28; studio mediation and, 223–24; travel and regional/intertribal relationships, 133–34; and tribal styles, blurring of, 135. *See also* gender

Somerset Entertainment, 274

song categories: about, 84–87; Chicken dance, 97; Crow Hop, 93–94; distinguished by use, 100–101; Double Beat, 94–95; Duck-and-dive, 97–98; Flag, 98–99; Round dance, 92–93; Side-step, 95–97; Sneak-up and Shake (Ruffle), 91–92; Southern Straight, 99–100; trick, 99; War dance complex (Contemporary and Straight songs), 87–91

songmaker as social role, 124–25

songs: appropriateness of, 76–77, 108; community ownership of, 49; composition and sources of, 101–3, 300n17; exchange of, 126, 248–49; form and structure, 82–84; learning new songs, 129–30; naming of, 250–51, 308n2; new, importance of, 247–48; Northern style, 79–81; traditional drums, attachment to, 48. *See also* singing and singing competitions

sound effects, 215–16, 253–54

sound systems, 36, 118–19, 300n4

Southern drum groups, 79, 159

Southern powwows, 68

Southern Straight songs, 86, 99–100, 300n15

Southern-style songs, 300n15

spaciality, 232–33

spatial organization at competition pow-wows, 34

Spears, Kim, 193

specials. *See* dance specials

Spirit Sand Singers, *figs.*; drums, 117–18; enunciation and, 106; Esquash and, 12; evaluation of taped music by, 253; formation of, 125; at Onion Lake powwow, 78–79, 121–22, 124, 126; repertoire, 125–26; *Sandstorm*, *fig.*; social roles in, 123, 127–28; Southern Straight songs and, 100. *See also* Esquash, Michael

Spirit Within, The (Donovan), 203

spot checks, 54, 297n18

Spotted Eagle, Douglas, 292n5

stacked drum groups, 73, 134

standardization: aesthetic values and, 63, 110, 257; of evaluation, 65; folk genres and, 252; liveness and, 240; mass media and, 252; Nativeness and, 196; of Northern-style competition powwows, 30, 32, 34; regionalism vs., in singing, 78–79; terminology and, 88; traditional powwows and, 47

Stick Game Songs, Volume 1 (Arbor), 169–70

Stoney Park, 178

straight drumbeat, 86, 89

Straight songs: as song type, 87–91; Southern, 86, 99–100, 300n15; vibrato and, 106

Straw, Will, 187

Strongfront productions, 270–71

St. Thomas University powwow, 135–36

Studio 11, *figs.*; author's apprenticeship at, 293n11; ethnography and, 14–15; facilities, 158; formation of, 13, 158; genre knowledge and, 188–89; personnel changes, 304n16; recording courses, 181–82, 305n28. *See also* Arbor Records;

liveness and studio mediation; recording studios and recording process

Sunshine Records: contracts, 174–75, 176–77; Friesen and, 13; new labels and, 279; position in powwow recording industry, 148–50; recording method, 213

Swan Lake Powwow, *figs.*

Sweet Grass Records, 162, 178

Sweetgrass Road, 135–36

Switch songs, 300n15

symbolic capital, 200

symbolic discourse and musical practices, dialectic of, 70–71

syncopation, displaced, 81, 104

tails, 83–84, 96

Tankel, Johnathan David, 235

taping: aesthetic discourse of commercial recordings vs., 247; at Carry the Kettle powwow, 42; singer-dancer interactions and, 76; song dissemination through, 250; song ownership and, 249

tempo, 84–85

tessitura, 69, 80

Thank-you (Appreciation) songs, 43

theoretical knowledge, 66–67

throat grabbing, 80

time, "Indian," 295n7

TKO, 182, 305n30

Traditional dancing, Men's, 86, 91, 98

Traditional dancing, Women's, 92–93

traditional method of honor beats, 299n9

Traditional Native music: Arbor and, 159, 271; genre worlds and, 208–11; *Native American Heritage* (NAH) series (Arbor Records), 168–69; song styles, traditional, 90–91. *See also* singing and singing competitions

traditional powwows: album sales and, 160; Brokenhead Ojibway traditional powwow, 45–52; competition powwows vs., 29–32, 47–52, 61–62, 252–53, 258; drum hopping and traditional drums at, 48–50, 78; drum whistling at, 50–52; non-Native spectators at, 52; payment in, 48; public access and, 61; sacred-secular continuum and, 60–62; tradition discourses and, 32, 57, 59–60, 62; variability of, 47

tradition discourses: affective alliances and, 256; articulation theory and, 9–10; authenticity and, 171, 213, 295n3; Clifford on, 27; critiques of traditional-modern articulation, 260–62; culture, tradition, and competition as problem, 52–60; ethnomusicology and, 258–62; family tradition, 131–32; gender relations and, 136; invention of tradition, 260, 294n3; invocation of, 32; liveness and, 215, 255–56; mediation and, 256–57; new songs and, 248; pan-tribal and intertribal, 32; postcoloniality and, 309n7; recording culture, Native culture, and, 3; recording practices and, 222; traditional powwows and, 32, 57, 59–60, 62; tradition as resource strategy, 259–60, 261. See also modernity, indigenous

travel: with drums and equipment, 117–18; Esquash on, 112; regional/intertribal relationships and, 133–34; traveling culture and the culture of travel, 114–17. See also powwow circuits

tremolo beat, 91
tribal affiliation, 28, 169, 171–72
Trick songs, 86, 99, 285
trust, 185–86, 206–7
Turino, Thomas, 306n1, 307n1, 309n6
Turtle Island Music, 144, 269, 276, 279
21st Century (Northern Wind Singers), fig., 217–25, 229–30, 250

unconscious theory, 66–67
understepping, 172, 248, 304n23
unison singing, 80, 105
University of Oregon powwow, 116
Utes, Northern, 1

Valaskakis, Gail, 27
Vander, Judith, 139, 301n10, 302nn15–16
vendors at powwows: at Brokenhead traditional powwow, 45–46; at competition powwows, 34; connections with record labels, 163–64; as distributors, 173; fees for, 295n6
Vennum, Thomas, Jr., 139, 297n16
Veteran's songs. See Victory songs
vibrato, 68, 69, 105–6
Victory songs (or Veteran's songs), 38, 46, 101
visions, songs received through, 102, 300n17
Vizenor, Gerald, 260–61
vocal lines, manipulation of. See effects, digital; liveness and studio mediation
vocoder effect (the "Cher" effect), 217, 218, 223, 224, 227
Voices of Native America sample bank, 197
Voices of the Rainforest (Feld and Hart), 266
volume, 80

Wacipi Records, 162, 276, 279
Ward, Graeme, 110
War dance at Southern powwows, 299n11
War dance songs, 87–91
War Pony Records, 269, 279
Waterman, Christopher, 109
Watson, Morely, 38
Waves Audio plugins, 228–30
Waywayseecappo competition powwow, 52
Waywayseecappo Ojibwa First Nation Reserve, 297n17
Web 2.0 technologies, 272–73
webs of significance, 27–28
White, Andy: on culture and tradition, 58–60; Jingle Dress DVD project and, 164–65; royalties advance incident, 184–86; on singing competitions, 70; on singing quality, 64; on traditional drums, 49–50

White, Maggie, 165, 299–300n13

White, Richard, 308n5

Whitecalf, Darlene, 167, 178

Whitecalf, Ted, 178, 204, 214

White family, 164–65

Whitefish Bay Reserve, 51, 133

Whitefish Bay Singers: *Anishinaabe Meeni-goziwin*, 299–300n13; contract nego-tiations, 177; Desrosiers and, 16; Jingle Dress songs and, 69; *Ndoo Te Mag*, 160, 184; Side-step songs and, 95

White Lodge Singers, *fig.*

White Turtle Women Singers, 135

Winnipeg, 143–44

Wityshyn, Waylon, 229, 293n11

women: all-female drum groups, 137–38, 139; as harmonizers, 136–37, 138; sec-onds and, 83. *See also* gender; *specific dances*

Women's Traditional Dancing, 92–93

Wonksheek Records, 269–70

Woodlands Indians, gender policy of, 135–36

Word (Contemporary) songs, 87–91, 282–83

world music and world beat: Arbor Records and, 146; ethnomusicology and, 187, 263; indices of Nativeness and, 197; marketing and, 167, 304n19; powwow music industry and, 150–51

Wutunee, Winston, 176

Christopher A. Scales is an associate professor of ethnomusicology in the Residential College in the Arts and Humanities at Michigan State University. He has engineered, produced, and performed on several powwow and contemporary Native music CDs for Arbor Records and War Pony Records, independent record labels specializing in North American Aboriginal music.

....

Library of Congress Cataloging-in-Publication Data
Scales, Christopher A. (Christopher Alton), 1966–
Recording culture : Powwow music and the Aboriginal recording industry
on the Northern Plains / Christopher A. Scales.
p. cm. — (Refiguring American music)
Includes bibliographical references and index.
ISBN 978-0-8223-5323-2 (cloth : alk. paper)
ISBN 978-0-8223-5338-6 (pbk. : alk. paper)
1. Indians of North America—Music. 2. Sound recording industry—
United States. 3. Sound recording industry—Canada. 4. Music and
technology. 5. Powwows. I. Title. II. Series: Refiguring American music.
ML3557.S23 2012
781.62'97071—dc23
2012011590